Memoirs

SAVE BIG!

OTHERS PAY
$5.99
NEWSSTAND
COVER PRICE

YOU PAY
$1.99
AN ISSUE
We'll pay the tax!

HELLO! CANADA

hellomagazine.ca/deal1

Check one:
- ☐ **53 ISSUES** (1 year) for $1.99 an issue – **Save 67%***
  – **we'll pay the tax!**
- ☐ **26 ISSUES** for $2.29 an issue – **Save 62%***
  – plus taxes.

NAME _____

ADDRESS _____

CITY _____ PROVINCE _____ POSTAL CODE _____

EMAIL _____

☐ Bill me later in full   ☐ Bill me later in 4 easy instalments

Exclusive to Rogers customers: you save when you add *HELLO!* Canada to your monthly Rogers bill. Go to **hellomagazine.ca/easy**

P71B02010

CANADA POST / POSTES CANADA

Postage paid
if mailed in Canada

Port payé si posté
au Canada

Business Reply Mail

Correspondance-
réponse d'affaires

7242830

01

1000066639-L3P0B4-BR01

HELLO! Canada
PO BOX 919 STN MAIN
MARKHAM ON L3P 9Z9

Memoirs

NANA MOUSKOURI
with Lionel Duroy

Translated by Jeremy Leggatt

Weidenfeld & Nicolson
LONDON

First published in Great Britain in 2007
by Weidenfeld & Nicolson

First published in France in 2007
as *La Fille de la Chauve Souris*
by XO Editions

1 3 5 7 9 10 8 6 4 2

© 2007 XO editions
Translation © 2007 Jeremy Leggatt

A Reed in the Wind, lyrics by E. Marnay, music by E. Stern
Retour a Napoli, lyrics by P. Delanoë, music by H. Giraud
By Praying Aloud, lyrics by R. Bernard and P. Delanoë, orchestration by R. Chauvigny
Quand on s'aime, duo with Michael Legrand, lyrics by E. Marnay, music by M. Legrand
Le Jour où la colombe, lyrics by E. Marnay, music by N. Heiman
Pame mia volte sto – lyrics by Perialis, music by M. Hadjidakis
A Hard Rain's A-Gonna Fall, lyrics and music by Bob Dylan
Daughter of the Sun, lyrics by J.C. Brialy, music by N. Mouskouri, arrangement by L. di Napoli
I'll Remember You, lyrics and music by Bob Dylan
Unless otherwise credited, all pictures © Nana Mouskouri Archives

A CIP catalogue record for this book
is available from the British Library.

ISBN-13 978 0 297 84469 3

Typeset by Input Data Services Ltd, Frome

Printed in Great Britain by Clays Ltd, St Ives plc

Weidenfeld & Nicolson

The Orion Publishing Group Ltd
Orion House
5 Upper Saint Martin's Lane
London, WC2H 9EA
An Hachette Livre UK Company

The Orion Publishing Group's Policy is to use papers that
are natural, renewable and recyclable products and made
from wood grown in sustainable forests. The logging and
manufacturing processes are expected to conform to the
environmental regulations of the country of origin.

www.orionbooks.co.uk

To Jean-Claude Brialy, my very best friend.
To my dear children, Lénou and Nicolas,
To André, the love of my life.
Thanks to him, I've always been 'the singer'.

Contents

Introduction

'Quincy, do you know a French singer who wears big, horrible glasses but who sings very well?'

The man calling the legendary musician-producer Quincy Jones was Harry Belafonte. He happened to be in London on the night of the 1963 Eurovision Song Contest. Doubtless having nothing better to do, he had switched on the television and had seen and heard me sing.

Quincy Jones' answer wasn't very satisfying.

'French . . . glasses . . . no, doesn't ring a bell.'

'Come on, think, man! If you ever heard this girl you'd never forget her!'

'I know only one girl who sings in glasses, Harry, and she sings very well, but she isn't French.'

'What's her name?'

'Nana Mouskouri.'

'Good God, that's her, Quincy! That's her! I remember now, that was the name they said! Nana! Nana who again?'

'Mous-kou-ri. But she's not French, knucklehead, she's Greek! And I know her very well, as it happens. Very, very well! We even made a record together.'

'No! I don't believe you.'

'She was here in New York with me last summer. The record just came out.'

'Well, that beats everything! So what do you say – is she the genuine article?'

'Do you think I would have made a record with her if she wasn't?'

'Send me a copy, please. Send me everything you've got on her.'

Harry Belafonte had just parted from Myriam Makeba, with whom he had made several tours across the United States, and he was on the

I

lookout for a new partner. He mentioned this to Quincy, asking him to keep quiet about it for the moment. Before committing himself to anything, he wanted to hear everything I had done so far, to find out everything about me.

One person he called was my French producer Louis Hazan, who respected his request for secrecy. Another was the head of Mercury, Irving Green, whom I had met earlier in New York when recording with Quincy.

After some time had passed, Belafonte asked Quincy and Irving Green to bring me over to New York, whereupon Quincy told me for the first time what was afoot. 'Harry's interested in you,' he said. 'He saw you on Eurovision and wants to meet you. Come spend a few days in New York and we'll talk, and while you're here we can make another record.'

He said no more, but those few words were enough to make my head whirl. How on earth could Harry Belafonte (I used to listen to him ten years earlier in our tiny Athens apartment) *be interested in me*? Belafonte, whose albums were among my most treasured possessions ... was it really possible that I would be sitting face-to-face with this legendary figure tomorrow?

Quincy Jones and Irving Green were waiting for me at the airport. It was already dark in New York, and we were scheduled to have dinner with Harry Belafonte and his wife Julie at Trader Vic's, the Polynesian restaurant in the Plaza Hotel. Approaching the city, I found it hard to keep calm and listen to what the two men were saying. Lord above, would I even find the strength to look Belafonte in the eye?

Harry was a man of breathtaking good looks, very tall and elegant, and he and his wife made a magnificent pair. My shyness was probably obvious to them from the first second, because they greeted me with great warmth, chatting to me as though we had always known one another. Gradually, our talk turned toward music, and more specifically toward Greek music. Harry wanted to know where I had grown up and who had taught me to sing. I described my early years at the Athens Conservatory, my love of jazz, of Ella Fitzgerald, and my early struggles as a singer in various nightclubs in the Greek capital. When we said goodnight (we had arranged to meet again mid-morning at his head-quarters on Sixty-Seventh Street), I had the happy feeling that I was among friends I could trust.

When I got there, I found myself in a vast room where about sixty people, all men, were sitting talking around little tables. The noise was deafening. At the very back was a podium where two men with bouzoukis sat waiting. Clearly these musicians were here for me, and I was expected to sing.

Then a man came over to greet me with a broad smile, introducing himself as Harry Belafonte's orchestra leader.

'Harry's very sorry,' he said. 'He can't be here – a last-minute problem. But let me introduce you around and we can talk for a while.'

I discovered that all these people worked for Belafonte – his musicians, assistants, sound engineers, technicians, press officers, and manager. Most were black; only a handful were white.

Then my cordial host asked who I was, and I told my story again.

'I knew you were Greek,' he broke in, 'which is why I had a couple of bouzouki players come along. Would you like to sing something for us?'

'Oh, absolutely not! I didn't come here to sing.'

'Oh! But Harry said you . . .'

'No. That wasn't our understanding at all!'

'What a pity. These guys will play whatever you want, you know. Surely you can sing us one or two?'

'No, I don't like singing until I've had time to rehearse.'

But then I realized I was putting him in an embarrassing position. Perhaps all these people were here just to listen to me. Perhaps I had misunderstood Harry's words last night. I had no idea, but I felt that by sticking to my guns I was going to hurt his feelings.

'Very well,' I said, 'I'll sing, but without the bouzoukis, without anyone. I prefer it that way.'

'Great! Thank you so very much.'

He raised a hand, the entire throng fell silent, and all eyes focused on me.

My eyes closed as I stood on the edge of that little podium, unaccompanied, and sang a cappella a half-dozen of the Greek songs that had always moved me most. I followed them with a couple of my favorite French songs. When I opened my eyes every man in the room rose to his feet and applauded. I took a deep breath and raised my eyes – and there was Harry Belafonte, standing tall and handsome at the other end of the room. He wore a cap and a leather jacket, utterly different from the man in a three-piece suit I had met the night before. Our eyes met, and he smiled. How long had he been there? At what point had he come in?

Later, someone told me that Harry's 'last-minute problem' was just a stratagem to avoid having to get rid of me in person if I disappointed him. He had posted himself in the room next door with all the equipment he needed to listen to me. Once convinced of my ability, he came back into the big room on the opening bars of my last song.

He came over, took me in his arms, and said:

'Now, do you think you're up to a few numbers with my musicians?'

'I haven't prepared anything.'

'I realize that, but Quincy says you know all the standards.'

'Okay, we can give it a try.'

In less than fifteen minutes the musicians and I were in sync. I don't know who suggested 'Sometimes I Feel Like a Motherless Child', but after a few seconds' hesitation we were into the rhythm, as though we had rehearsed it the day before. Then I launched into the first lines of 'I Get a Kick Out of You', the musicians caught up with me in mid-flight, and it was suddenly such a delight to see their smiles that I closed my eyes to keep the intoxication alive.

Then we were in Harry's office, and I listened as he told me in calm, serious tones that he would like to have me alongside him on his next tour. The suggestion that I might step into the shoes of Myriam Makeba, Africa's leading singer, seemed so unbelievable that I listened in total silence. For a moment I simply floated between dream and reality. Was I really in Harry Belafonte's office in New York? Was he truly proposing that I be his partner for the next two or three years? The whole thing seemed so implausible, so improbable, that I finally interrupted him in a voice I barely recognized.

'Excuse me . . . You really want me to sing with you?'

'That's what I'm proposing, yes.'

'But . . . I mean . . . are you sure? You're not going to . . .'

'Change my mind? No. Why else would I have asked you here?'

And then, as though he himself were suddenly struck by doubt:

'But you haven't told me yet whether you'd agree . . .'

'It's the most wonderful proposal anyone ever made to me, sir.'

And I meant it. I was thirty-three, and the road I had traveled had been long and very hard . . .

I

'What is War'

A spring night. The movie theater was empty, the film had been over for some time, but we put off going home to bed. Bathed in sweat, my father scrambled down from his projection box and came to join us in front of the open-air screen. I don't recall the movie he had just shown, but it must have been a good one; otherwise he would never have let us see it. Mama seemed far away. From time to time, in a familiar gesture, she patted her hair back into place whenever the breeze blew it into disarray. My big sister Eugenia gazed at the stars. Then she suddenly started talking about the movie, telling us how much she had enjoyed this or that scene. Come to think of it, maybe it was *The Wizard of Oz* with Judy Garland. Possibly . . . In any case, we had seen and loved *The Wizard* so many times. Eugenia was in ecstasy, and Mama was smiling at her absentmindedly, as if her thoughts were elsewhere. What could she be thinking of? Perhaps of Papa, who was now sitting on the stage a few feet away from us. He had just lit a cigarette and was looking out over the seats of his little open-air cinema as though he needed to count them over and over again. How many of them were there? Forty? Fifty? On rainy nights we helped him fold them and put them under cover.

There we were, all four of us seated at the foot of the screen, our legs dangling off the platform, when a dull roar suddenly filled the sky. It sounded like an impending storm, the distant roll of thunder, and I remember my mother's surprise.

'Do you hear that, Costa?' she called out. 'What is it?'

Eugenia stopped talking and Papa raised his eyes to the mountains,

6

for the sound came from there. He said twice, '*I don't know . . . I don't know*' and suddenly fell silent. He knew, we all knew: the sky had filled with black cross-shaped shadows. Very soon there were so many that they blocked out the stars.

'My God,' said Mama, 'airplanes!'

The sound of the planes pierced our souls and made the earth shudder. Throughout the time it took them to fly over Athens, my father sat in dead silence, as if turned to stone. Recalling it today, in light of the sorrows to come, it was an appalling, terrifying sight. But at the time I was unafraid. We had already caught a glimpse of aircraft: in fact, sighting one was a major event that had Eugenia and me running and jumping for joy. But so many planes, and in the middle of the night – that was something we could never have believed possible. Where had they come from? Where were they going? What were they doing? I simply remember my father's few barely audible words once the roaring had faded into the distance:

'So it's war.'

War? I had never heard the word.

'What is war?'

My father wasn't listening. He had already dropped down from the little stage.

'Aliki,' he said to Mama. 'Let's go home. We mustn't stay here.'

That night the first bombs fell. They marked the start of the German attack on Greece, so that I can put a precise date to that evening on which our lives were turned upside down. It was 6 April 1941, and I was six and a half.

For years I believed that my first childhood memory was that wave of aircraft flying over the little cinema where my father worked. That before it, my memory had retained nothing. But I was wrong. Now I recall our excitement on evenings *before* the war when Papa's friends came to our house to play cards. Even before they handed their hats to Mama, three or four men, cigarettes dangling from their lips, would take from their pockets the small gifts they had brought for us, the daughters of Constantine Mouskouri. A chocolate bar, a ball, a pencil . . . On card-playing nights, we gave up our bedroom to them and slept together in the big bed in our parents' room. As we spluttered with mirth, Eugenia mimicked the voices reaching us through the adjoining wall: 'I fold . . . I raise you . . . I call.' This was big business and the players took it very seriously.

Of course it was fun for us to be in the same bed, but what I believe comforted us most was the reassuring feeling that those deep manly voices protected us from the whole world. All night long a slit of light shone below the closed door, and we fell asleep to the smell of tobacco that little by little wafted into our room.

They were no longer there at daybreak, and now it was Mama's voice that awakened us from slumber. On some mornings she paced frenetically up and down the room where the men had played, and her agitation froze our hearts. What could have happened to put our mother into such a state between yesterday evening, which had begun with such warmth and friendship, and this anxiety-laden dawn? Eugenia went on sleeping, or else pretended to be asleep in order to avoid explaining things to me. I curled up under the covers, a knot in my stomach, listening to every word.

'You knew this was going to happen, Costa, you knew!'

Papa, his voice almost inaudible, replied:

'No, you never know that kind of thing . . .'

'Why didn't you stop? Why did you let it go on so long?'

'When you're hosting the game, Aliki, you can't just quit whenever it suits you . . .'

'No, the truth is you *can't* stop! It's in your blood!'

'Be quiet! Stop talking, Aliki, I beg you!'

'No, I won't stop! I don't have a penny for food or for our girls, and you don't give a damn, all you want is for me to let you go on sleeping . . .'

A chair hit the floor, then another. Papa started to yell in his turn, and I covered my ears to shut out their yells, particularly Mama's, which soon trailed off into sobs.

I have relived that scene so often, at ten, at twelve, and even now as I reconstruct it in my memory, that I am doubtless minimizing the particular terror it inspired in me at the age of six, when I understood neither the reason for their quarrels nor what was at stake.

Strangely enough, it was the German invasion that allowed me to give a name to the frightening darkness that came over my parents on certain mornings and drove them apart, a darkness that neither of them ever mentioned to us.

A few days after the bombers roared overhead on that April night in 1941, I happened to witness a dramatic exchange between my father and mother. Mama had been crying, and she turned away to hide her tears from me, while my father stood pale and silent by the window.

As I screwed up my courage to ask – just this once – what was going on, Mama must have noticed my bewilderment.

'Papa's going to war,' she said.

I looked first at her and then at my father, and for the second time I asked:

'What is war?'

Papa turned around.

'It's when people don't like each other, Nanaki,' he said very calmly. 'They fight, they *make war*. Do you understand?'

I understood that the airplanes of a few nights earlier did not like us, and that my father was going off to fight them. More confusedly, though, I sensed something else – that my parents too must dislike each other because they fought. Yes, that's it: I think that as soon as that word *war* was explained to me I at once connected it to the noisy squabbling that awakened us on those sad mornings. And the information brought me a kind of relief: my parents' behavior was not so extraordinary after all. It had a name. They were simply *making war*.

After Papa left for the front, Mama shut herself in their bedroom to hide her sorrow from us. Eugenia and I didn't cry. I believe we had no awareness of danger. Thinking back today, I believe our conception of war was rather more comforting than otherwise, since our parents, often so antagonistic, seemed inconsolable when they had to separate . . . So it seemed you could sometimes make war and sometimes love one another.

How did we survive through the seven months Papa was away fighting the Germans? The open-air cinema was closed, but its owner, Mr

Yiannopoulos, did not move us out of the adjacent house. It was a tiny dwelling, located just behind the screen, originally built for a caretaker. That was why it had only two small rooms and a kitchen. Mr Yiannopoulos was fond of my father, doubtless believed the war would not last too long, and counted on reopening his cinema in the near future.

We no longer saw much of Mama, who left me in Eugenia's keeping (my sister was the older by two years). She left to look for work, and I think she found a job as an usherette in one of the few movie houses still open, probably through my father's contacts in the business. An usherette, or else a cleaning lady. Eugenia and I, along with our dog and our birds, waited in the house all day for her to return. I don't remember how many chickens we had at that time, but there were a lot, and they often escaped from the henhouse to peck about under the kitchen table. And their chicks as well: they would feed from our hands and follow us about, pecking at our shins as if seeking to play. Every morning we had fresh eggs. There was also a bird-coop my father built when one of his friends gave him a pair of doves. They multiplied, and soon the dovecote was full of birds. And of course there was our little female dog . . .

Very surprisingly, I even remember when she was born, although I believe that took place a long time before the war. In any case, it was in the morning. I was playing on the little stage below the screen when I heard faint whimperings below. The stage was flanked by two bushes planted in small flowerbeds bursting with daisies. The sounds came from one of them. I must have been scared, because I went to get Eugenia before investigating. We listened together as we leaned over the flowers, and Eugenia saw her first, curled up among the daisies: Mr Yiannopoulos' large bitch had just brought a puppy into the world . . .

She was so pretty that we gasped.

Then we had a debate over which one of us would pick up the puppy.

'You go ahead,' said Eugenia.

'No, I'm scared. Its mother will bite me.'

'But she knows us, and Mr Yiannopoulos said she never bites children.'

'Well then, you pick it up if you're not scared.'

'No, you're the one who heard them, so you pick it up.'

And Eugenia pushed me in among the daisies. I took the puppy in my arms. Its mother growled but didn't bite me.

*

Our puppy was no longer a puppy when the war began, and perhaps Mama drew a little comfort from knowing that her daughters had a pet to guard them. In fact, when the air-raid sirens began to howl, the dog went with us to the shelters. I can still see the three of us racing madly through the deserted streets to the basement of the Fix brewery, about a hundred yards from our house. Eugenia dragged me along by my hand, urging me to greater speed. 'Faster, Ioanna, faster, or the planes will see us.' And our little dog kept her speed down to ours, as though she had no intention of abandoning us to the bombs.

How tough Eugenia was! Once we were inside those dingy cellars, sometimes lit by a solitary candle, sometimes pitch-dark, and full of the sound of women praying, Eugenia refused to join their litany. Instead, she did exactly what Mama had told us to do – she sang. She was only nine, but she had the courage to sing out in her clear voice while above us we heard the droning of the first bombers and sometimes the crash of explosions that made the ground shake. I timidly accompanied her, and sometimes one or two women's voices would join ours.

It never even occurred to us that Mama might be somewhere out there under the bombs. She told us that she too sang during the raids, and I think it seemed to us that she was somehow protecting us from harm. Maybe we thought no German plane would ever kill anyone who was only singing.

And then one day Papa was back. He seemed to have returned from the land of the dead: his eyes were huge and set in deep shadow, he was unshaven, his hair was dirty, his uniform was dirty, but we didn't care. We were so glad to see him again that we burst into tears. But why didn't he come in? Why was he standing beside the hen house instead of coming to us, taking us in his arms, bouncing us on his knees? It was as if he didn't see us, as if he no longer saw us. Then Mama took a few steps toward him and gently held his face in her hands, kissing him, whispering into his ear. He raised his head and opened his mouth as if telling us to come to him, and at last we hurled ourselves against his legs. He wrapped his arms around us, hugging all three of us together, and in the same moment something impossible happened, something terribly sad: Papa began to sob. It was the first time. We had never seen him weep, or rather break into such sobbing, and his tears at once lent an unbearable weight to his return. I think in fact that we drew away from him as though we understood that unlike us, Papa was not weeping for joy but out of a sorrow beyond our comprehension, a sorrow that submerged him. A sorrow so deep we knew there was nothing we could do at that moment to comfort him.

Papa was weeping for losing the war, for the dark days this catastrophe held in store for us, for his wife and daughters, and for Greece. It would take me years to understand him and to share his tears in secret. I would become a mother myself in 1968, under untroubled Swiss skies, at almost the very moment when an authoritarian regime seized power in Greece, and I would think back at that moment to the terrors our parents must have endured, knowing that their children now lived in a Europe plunged into fire and blood. In 1968, what we called the 'Greece of the Colonels' (the military junta which had seized power in a coup) was our badge of shame, and Europe was still cut in two. But Western Europe was in the process of building and we could dream of peace for our children. What kind of future could people have dreamed of in the fall of 1941, when Hitler's victorious legions entered Greece?

Papa was back from the front but the movie theater didn't reopen. Mr Yiannopoulos called to see us and shut himself in to talk with our father, but nobody told us why we could no longer show films. Meanwhile, Papa built himself a small radio set with valves and spools of wire he got from friends. He spent hours in his bedroom listening to that radio, the volume turned low, but whenever he went into the city, Eugenia and I glued ourselves to that radio. We picked up voices from all over the world, and sometimes American singers whose vibrant notes recalled the good old days of our movie theater.

We were no longer allowed to go out because Mama said we ran the risk of being picked up by the Germans. She said that they were everywhere, that they went into buildings and arrested men.

'I know,' said Papa.

'You know, but still you go out.'

'I have things to do.'

'What will become of us if you're caught?'

'Don't worry.'

He said nothing about what he was up to, but sometimes he was away for two or three days in a row. I don't remember how Eugenia and I discovered that he was still making war. Perhaps he told Eugenia in private, and she relayed his secret to me in a whisper. So when he went away, Papa was meeting other men, friends, like the men who used to come around for all-night card games. At least that is what we thought, and it comforted us.

Mama continued to work at various jobs, returning exhausted and with an empty shopping basket. She said there was no food in the stores. Luckily we had eggs, she said, and I believe she sometimes waited until we were asleep to pluck a chicken or two for the pot.

The Germans must have been hungry as well, because one day three soldiers broke into the hen house and took our chickens. We watched them through the bedroom curtain. It was the first time we had seen German soldiers so close up. I don't think Mama was there, but I remember her tears later when we inspected the empty hen house.

They left the doves, but we no longer had anything to eat. Papa said the doves would have to look out for themselves from now on, and he opened the dovecote. They left, but hesitantly, flying around above our heads before settling on the branch of a big acacia tree, as if they sought to be considerate and not leave us so quickly after all these years, and their polite behavior helped soften the separation.

Besides, almost all of them had returned by nightfall. Papa smiled: it was obvious he wanted to say something, perhaps to thank them, but he couldn't find the words. We felt the same. We watched them, counting them over and over again, and Eugenia kept saying:

'Look at that! They've all come back! I can't believe it ... I can't believe it.'

Little by little, though, their numbers diminished, and one day none of them returned.

Mama no longer sat down to eat with us. She cooked chickpeas, just a handful brought home wrapped in a scrap of newspaper which she produced as triumphantly as if she had brought home a treasure. Eugenia and I shared them, Mama claiming that she wasn't hungry. It would take us the duration of the war to realize that she was lying. Rainy days became occasions for feasting because we collected snails and frogs. Mama had nothing with which to flavor the snails. They tasted like salted rubber, but there were enough of them to fill our stomachs, which was all that mattered. The little dog (she too was hungry) shared the snails and frogs with us.

Mama occasionally took us into the city. She must certainly have had good reasons for doing so, because nobody strolled in the streets of Athens as winter approached in 1942. The emptiness of the streets was the first thing that struck me. Where had everyone gone? In the old days it was difficult to negotiate the crowds on the sidewalks of beautiful Leoforos Syngrou Avenue, which passed close to our house and went all the way to Piraeus. Now the stores were closed, and the few passers-by were women in black headscarves, hurrying along and hugging the fronts of the buildings. And there, suddenly, was a man's body lying across our path. He wasn't moving, he seemed to be asleep.

'What's wrong with him, Mama?'

'Hush, don't say a word, not one word! I'll explain later.'

As we went by the man, we could see something was amiss. His clothes were too small for him, or rather his skin looked too tight, as though his body had swollen.

Further along there were others like him, blown up like balloons and prostrate on the sidewalk. But as we hurried along, a truck drew up. German soldiers grabbed the bodies roughly by their arms and legs and swung them into the back. Eugenia and I had to stifle our screams of horror.

'Be quiet, I beg you!' Mama hissed. 'Don't say a word!'

We said nothing. But when we got home Mama didn't deliver the promised explanation, and we didn't dare refer again to that horrifying sight – men and women being tossed like logs into the back of a truck.

I think the realization that they were dead entered our minds only gradually. And we guessed the rest from our parents' conversation or from remarks made by the few friends who called on us. All grown-up talk in those days was about the disappearance of this or that acquaintance. So-and-so had 'gone' last week. Another, 'unfortunately,' was unlikely to last much longer, 'considering his present condition.' Where could all these hungry people, hounded by starvation, be 'going'? For some time Eugenia and I pondered the question. Finally we made the connection between the corpses on the sidewalks and those mysterious 'journeys' undertaken to escape destitution. They were indeed 'going' somewhere – but toward death, just like those bloated bodies on the sidewalks whose souls had flown away. Their 'journeys' were merely an adult euphemism for the horror of the situation.

During that first winter under German occupation, two thousand Greeks starved to death every day. We would know it only later, once peace had returned.

Our house was gradually emptying, but we were unaware of it. We only realized that we no longer had anything when winter ended and we had to move. Mama had been selling all our possessions in order to buy handfuls of white beans or chickpeas at unheard-of prices. She sold her wedding ring, her few dresses, her watch, our dishes, sheets, our big wardrobe (how could we have failed to notice that it had disappeared?), and finally the kitchen table, chairs, lamps, and our clothes.

She waged a secret war to ensure our survival, to triumph one day at a time. Curiously, I have no recollection of my own hunger but clearly recall my distress at seeing how thin our little dog had become, how sadly her deeply-shadowed eyes gazed at us. I recall too how determinedly I scratched the floor of the former hen house in search of moldering grains of corn which I fed to her with encouraging noises. I know today that Mama must have looked at us with the same eyes: we must indeed have been so pitiful-looking that she forgot her own suffering in order to turn everything that came her way into food.

But there must have come a time when she had nothing left to sell. And a time when she told my father, with a distress I can only imagine, that she no longer saw any way of saving us, of ensuring that we too did not join those who 'went'. Because otherwise I cannot imagine my father envisaging the slightest alteration to his movie theater, to the little cinema that was his whole life.

*

Not saying a word to anyone, Papa removed a few chairs from his cinema and came home with a small sum of money.

'There you go,' he said, 'this should get us through a few days.'

She didn't ask him where those few notes came from. Perhaps she told herself she would know soon enough.

What happened next was terrible – much worse than death in the eyes of our parents who were so acutely alive to honor, dishonor, and what others might think of them.

Mr Yiannopoulos, the theater owner, very soon saw that the chairs had disappeared. My father must have confessed that he had sold them to feed his family. I know nothing of what followed between them (Papa never told us), but I can imagine that it was a scene of high drama. At a time when people everywhere were starving, Mr Yiannopolous was not particularly concerned about our suffering. Did my father think he could liquidate a business's assets on the pretext that his family had nothing to eat? A business that did not belong to him, of which he was only a minor employee? Papa had always considered Mr Yiannopolous his friend, and had often told us so with a pride that wholly convinced us. It was obvious, after all, that Mr Yiannopolous was much more important to us than the men who usually came to visit. Not so. Mr Yiannopolous was not his friend, and it must have been a terrible shock to Papa to realize this and admit to Mama that he had been wrong. Mr Yiannopolous no longer wished to know him, or any of us. He gave us a week to get out, to leave the little house behind the screen in the condition it was in when we moved in. He told us to go away, saying he never wanted to hear from us again.

I can never forget the day we left, with all that remained of our possessions heaped on a little cart harnessed to a donkey. Were the neighbors watching? Were people already talking about what was happening to us? I burned with shame for Papa and Mama. They no longer had the strength to exchange a word. They moved around like shadows. They seemed crushed. I was ashamed for myself as well. In truth, I believe I was encountering shame and humiliation for the first time and trying vainly to defend myself against them. I was seven, but because of the war I had never been to school and knew nothing about life. How do you fight back against finger-pointing neighbors, against failure, retribution, destitution? It made me sick to my stomach.

We went on foot to the Gouva district in the suburbs. The parents of a young man my father had trained to be a projectionist had agreed to rent us a room in their house. Just one room for the four of us, but we had so few possessions that we fitted in without difficulty. Our own beds had been sold and all we had was our parents' bed. We divided it at night: Eugenia and I slept on the mattress, which we put on the floor, while our parents slept on the base. We kept our few clothes in a chest.

It was also in this chest that Mama hid the little money she earned. After that winter and the first months of German occupation she found work again, perhaps in a movie theater that reopened in the city center, or else in a music hall. She walked all the way to work. She came home weary, and all day long my sister and I waited for her. We were not allowed to go out. Gouva was a poor neighborhood, full of dark corners and vacant lots. There was no asphalt on its twisting streets, and Communist resistance fighters had turned it into one of their strongholds. There were often skirmishes with the Germans; gunfire was heard, and Mama was afraid we might get ourselves killed.

Was Papa still working with the anti-German Resistance? I don't know. At all events, he now committed an act of folly that drove Mama into a state of despair bordering on madness. It took us back to the worst moments of their quarrels.

One evening, Mama opened the chest to put her day's (or perhaps week's) wages inside. We heard her cry out:

'Eugenia, Nana, who took the money I left here?'

Naturally, neither of us could say. The only one who could have touched it was Papa, whom we hadn't seen for two days.

He came home at midnight, and the sparks immediately flew. He had been gambling and had lost all the money Mama had scraped together. She did not utter a single word of reproach when she learned that he had sold the theater seats. She knew it was for us. But this – how could he do this? Couldn't he see that she was draining the last of her energy just to bring home enough to feed us? He did not react to her shouts. It was true, he said, but now he wanted to be allowed to sleep: it was too late at night for an argument. At that, she threw herself upon him as though she wanted to kill him. Papa had to defend himself, and Eugenia and I threw ourselves screaming between them, begging them to stop. But Mama was crazed with anger, exhaustion and loneliness, and I don't believe she even heard us. Before the war she tried to spare us such scenes, probably from shame. Now she was beyond shame. We had lost everything, everything, right down to the respect of our former neighbors. And now the man who was supposed to be standing by her was robbing her. With hindsight, it seems to me that Mama would have liked to die that night, to have done with the darkness of her existence. Life outside was already so hard: how then could she go on, how could she continue to hope, if she was lied to, robbed and humiliated in her own home, or rather in this tiny room that we had been reduced to calling our home?

Papa shouted that she was insane. His face was bleeding, but even blood no longer affected Mama.

Eugenia screamed:

'No! No! Stop, Mama! Stop! Please!'

And suddenly the door slammed. For a second Mama seemed completely stunned. Papa was gone. Papa had run away. She took a few steps between the bed and the door and then collapsed on the bed. All the fear and anger that had made us scream and race around was transformed into sobs. Eugenia went to sleep next to Mama, and I lay down beside our little dog.

Papa had disappeared, and Mama acted as though he had never existed. She no longer mentioned him, and we didn't dare say his name in her presence. I do not know how long this separation and Mama's silence lasted. Maybe two or three weeks.

But I remember my relief the day she finally expressed her concern for him.

'Has Papa been in touch with you?' she asked one morning.

And before we could even reply:

'At least I have to know where he went.'

For a few days, she looked for him. Finally, some friends told her where to find him, and one night she brought him back to the house.

He had lost weight, he was unshaven. It was as if he had returned again from the war.

Did Mama decide that the loss of his movie theater had filled him with such despair that he had returned to gambling? Or was I the one who decided that later on, in order to find an excuse for him? I don't know, but even today that explanation sticks in my mind: in mourning for that theater which had been his passion, Papa lost his head.

He was home again, and we slipped back into the strange routine that was our life in those days. Eugenia and I were still forbidden to leave the house. We were immured in that small room and we spent most of our days lying side by side on our parents' bed. We slept; when we woke up, we chatted a little, sometimes we sang, sometimes played a little game or simply wandered about the room. Then we went back to sleep, and when we opened our eyes again it was already evening. I know for a fact that there were days when we ate almost nothing. In truth, we were slowly being extinguished – like two candles gradually guttering down for lack of oxygen. But we were not aware of it.

Sometimes we leaned on the windowsill and stayed there, staring out, until weariness overcame us. Our room looked out on a small unpaved square with a well in the middle. It was there that we drew water for drinking and bathing. The Germans also came there for water, and sometimes they loitered beside their truck talking among themselves as one of them filled their jerry cans.

It was on one of these occasions that we witnessed a drama which still haunts me, as though on that day I crossed the invisible frontier that is supposed to offer lifetime protection from the abyss.

Eugenia and I were watching the soldiers around the well. It was a little bit like a game in which we tried to make sure we weren't seen. But suddenly an enormous explosion splintered our windowpanes. I don't know now whether it was the blast or fear that threw us to the ground. When we rose to look out, the square was a scene of horror. One of the Germans lay on the ground. He had lost a leg, and blood was gushing from the wound. The others were racing for cover, and I think we heard shots and the wailing of sirens.

Then two or three trucks full of soldiers roared to a halt in the square, and soon we heard a violent knocking at the front door. 'If ever the Germans come here, hurry down and open the door,' Mama had warned us. 'The most important thing of all is not to let them think you were hiding.' We opened the door, and they immediately shoved us aside and ran from room to room. Swinging around suddenly, one of the soldiers hit us both hard with his rifle-butt. Eugenia fell, and I struck my head against the wall. But he had not done it deliberately. I have a clear memory, the kind that often sticks with us in such moments of madness, of the seconds that followed. Our eyes met, and I saw in the soldier's face a kind of surprise, of bafflement to see us lying there barely conscious at his feet.

We didn't interest them: they were looking for men. We realized this after they left, as we saw them hauling into the square everyone they had found in the neighboring houses – even young boys who seemed barely older than Eugenia.

They lined them up at gunpoint, shouting and hitting some of them in the back, others in their legs. My heart pounded, and Eugenia was pale as a ghost. She whispered that they must be seeking the man who had thrown the grenade.

'What will they do if they find him?'

'I don't know,' she said.

It seemed to me that the yelling and the thud of rifle-butts went on for a long time. We were too scared to breathe, yet it was impossible to avert our eyes, to stop looking. It was exactly as though the boys in the square were our brothers and the men our fathers. We couldn't turn away, couldn't think of something else.

And suddenly they killed one of them, in front of the others, before our eyes, and I believe they killed another as we stifled a scream that turned into a sob. And we ducked beneath the window ledge and saw no more. Witnessing that murder was so horrifying that we wanted to batter our heads against the wall to forget what we had seen, to erase it, to forget it. My God – just to have been somewhere else when it happened! When we recovered our senses, we were in one another's arms, weeping. The soldiers were shoving the other men into trucks.

That night, we told Mama that the Germans had been attacked, that a soldier had lost a leg, that they had arrested all the men in the neighborhood, but we did not mention the man who was executed before our eyes, nor the other one who was probably shot while Eugenia and I, traumatized by terror and anguish, ducked out of sight under the windowsill. Perhaps it would have helped us to tell her, but we couldn't; there were no words. It was as if the pain had instantly acquired a hard shell in the bottom of our hearts, had become stone, unreachable, impossible to dislodge.

Neither Eugenia nor I would ever speak of that episode again. Not to each other, not to our mother. This is the first time, as I write these memoirs, that I have attempted to recall the scene and to describe it in simple terms. I believe I am doing it in order to understand a terrible recurrent dream that I've had ever since. In it I am a child running across the muddy ground around the well in that square. The longer the dream lasts, the more exhausted, more terrified and more frantic I become. What has happened to the path I was on? Am I losing my reason? My terror increases, my stomach contracts. And I keep on running, gasping for breath, my heart thudding as if about to break. Dear God, what will happen to me if I can't get away from here? Then the nearby well begins to draw me in. I try to keep away from it, terrified of falling into it. I hate its cold, black mouth, but at the same time it continues to exert its pull. I realize, with a growing sense of horror, that it must be my only way of escape from this place, this nightmare.

Mama's conclusion from our account of the drama was that if my father had been there he too would have been arrested and perhaps shot. Perhaps it was to flee this accursed spot that we moved house yet again. Our new home was closer to our former neighborhood. It was near Filopapou Hill, in the house of friends of Papa, much warmer-hearted people than our former hosts, if my memory is correct. This family had two teenage sons whose different fates would strike us forcibly a few years later, during the civil war. All by themselves the two of them embodied the whole tragedy of Greece: the elder boy was an officer, loyal to the king; the younger a Communist. Eventually they hated each other so bitterly that the younger son rejoiced when his brother died in the fighting.

But in 1941, when we first met them, they took us in with warmth and generosity. The older son devoted all his energies to finding food for everyone. He sometimes brought back from his trips to the mountains a kind of wild salad (I remember it as delicious). You carefully washed the roots and then cooked the leaves, like spinach. His young wife was full of kindness toward us, and I recall that it was our contact with her that gave me my first inkling of physical love, of desire. I even began to wonder how babies were made, and she explained it to me with a delicacy that left me full of dreams. Observing the way she looked at her husband, and certain tender gestures she reserved for him, I was soon astounded to realize that I had never seen my parents kiss or even hold hands.

Doubtless the German occupation became less harsh in 1943, for that autumn, just before my ninth birthday, I found myself at school for the first time. Eugenia was two classes ahead of me, because unlike me she had begun her schooling before the war.

I remember my curiosity, my excitement. We sat three to a desk, and for the first time there was someone looking after us – a pleasant but demanding lady. We no longer had time to sleep or dream, to wonder if Papa would return home at night: suddenly we found ourselves with a considerable number of things to learn. I had the feeling that I was emerging from a protracted lethargy, and I hung on our teacher's words with single-mindedness and intense eagerness.

We couldn't afford notebooks, so I scrawled my first letters on the back of my father's old movie scripts. Back then, every movie scheduled for projection came with dialogue notes or screening notes, and luckily Papa had kept them all.

How did Mr Yiannopolous find us again? Surprisingly enough, after behaving so harshly, he had come to apologize, Papa told us. He proposed that Papa take over the movie house again and return to our little house behind the screen. On hearing the news, I realized how much I loved the place and how sorely I had missed it. The little stage below the screen! Movies! And everything the movies taught us about the greatness and beauty of the world, life's mysteries, people's love for one another, how people dressed, walked, danced, sang ... That tiny stage where I secretly mimicked Judy Garland in *Everybody's Singing* and *The Wizard of Oz*, or Marlene Dietrich in *Shanghai Express*, in *The Blue*

Angel ... Oh, Marlene Dietrich! Her inimitable way of moving about, of flaunting her long lashes and her cigarette-holder ...

We found it hard to believe that Mr Yiannopoulos would really restore this little Garden of Eden to us, but he did. A few weeks earlier, we had watched the British tanks roll into Athens. Mama wept, we applauded, and the soldiers blew kisses and tossed us chocolate bars and even a can of corned beef from their turrets.

Very soon there was a rumor that soup kitchens would be opened, and Mama took along the only container she could find, a cracked enamel bowl we had once used to feed the chickens. Was the bowl too small? Or were the rations strictly portioned out? I have no idea. But I remember that blessed day when the war ended and the four of us once again sat around a table, just like before. But only Eugenia and I ate. Papa and Mama had divided the soup in two. They said they were not going to eat, and Eugenia and I made no protest. Yet we knew it was unjust, unthinkable. And even if we hadn't known, all we had to do was look into their faces. Their enormous eyes, deep-set in hollows, told us that the smell of the soup was driving them crazy.

'Don't eat too quickly,' was all Mama said. 'You'll make yourselves sick.'

How could we have been so selfish?

Later on, I was angry at myself. Very angry! And it occurs to me that my lifelong determination to repair the injustices, the countless wounds inflicted on my parents, originated in this innocent, childish debt I owed them.

2

Papa Had Hoped to Have a Boy

I wish I could remember the name of the movie with which Papa reopened the theater doors early in 1945. Was it David Butler's *The Littlest Rebel*, with Shirley Temple? No, I believe we saw that one just before the war. (Just like every other film starring Shirley Temple, who shared pride of place in my heart with Judy Garland.) Besides, it must have been a British movie, because the British had just liberated us and were provisionally running the country. So I lean toward Anthony Asquith's *Fanny by Gaslight*, with Stewart Granger.

With Papa locked away in his projection booth, lining up his reels and making the final adjustments, I stood on the stage looking out over the rows of empty seats with a lump in my throat, midway between laughter and tears. Could life really begin again as though nothing had happened? The last time the family had gathered here, helping Papa count the seats, was that April evening in 1941 when hundreds of aircraft suddenly filled the sky. Then I was six and a half; now I was ten. I believe I was waiting for the surge of emotion that used to fill me as dusk made its swift appearance and we waited for the first spectators to trickle in. Would I be overcome by the same curiosity, the same excitement? As if we had not lived through what we had endured since then? Yes, the old feelings seemed to be there, unchanged. Oh, the thrill when the first couple came in, the wife seeming to hesitate over which would be the best seat, with me dropping behind the bush in the same instant, determined not to be seen!

My heart beating fast, I spied on them from behind the daisies. There

were couples and whole families, and every one of them had that moment
of hesitation before choosing a seat. Sometimes they recognized friends
and made a detour to greet them and exchange a few words. Did my
ten-year-old eyes tell me how much they had changed in the last four
years? Remembering the scene today, I can't help thinking of what they
had gone through. All of them had been hungry, and many had lost loved
ones, a child, a mother, a father. Sometimes their whole families and all
their possessions as well. When I think of the Greeks of 1945, all I see is
sad, emaciated faces. But it probably didn't shock me back then. What
did strike me was their look of expectation, the hunger they all shared for
a film that would transport them far from where they were to a world
utterly unlike their own. You saw it from the way they took their seats and
their satisfied eyes as they looked at the screen. Well, that's something
that hasn't changed, I said to myself, just as impatient as they were for the
show to begin – something the war hadn't managed to destroy.

Fanny by Gaslight was a drama about a minister of the British crown
who hires his illegitimate daughter as a lady's maid in order to help and
protect her. But his wife, unaware of the existence of this illegitimate
child (conceived many years earlier), suspects her husband of deceiving
her and threatens to divorce him. Driven to distraction, the man kills
himself. Stewart Granger did not play the lead role, but thanks to him I
discovered that night that a young man could turn my head. It was a
disturbing feeling, which I mastered only little by little, but it meant
that I would wait with growing excitement for each of the handsome
Stewart's new films.

When the show was over I returned to my hiding place at the foot of
the screen. There I watched the spectators slowly come back down to
earth and stand up as if from a good night's sleep, and I recognized
something that would never have occurred to me before the war but
which now sprang to mind: they were no longer the same people, the
movie had transformed them. The tension had gone from their faces,
and they seemed to float between sleepiness and a sense of liberation, as
though they had been separated from themselves, from their suffering,
and now saw the world through a child's eyes.

When he joined us, my father too was transformed. I could have
sworn he was younger.

'Papa, did you see how people are no longer the same at the beginning and the end of the movie?'

'Well, what do you think happens? That they change halfway through the show? Of course they're the same!'

Neither my mother nor my father understood what I was trying to say, and they never tried to understand. So this transformation people undergo at the movies assumed a considerable importance in my child's mind, like a unique discovery that no one else shared but which never ceased to fascinate me. Why? What did my wonder at the secret power of movies reveal about my buried desires, my dreams?

I found the beginnings of an answer a few months later, at a variety show to which my father had managed to get us tickets. It was the first time I ever entered a real theater and viewed a live performance. The show was a kind of revue, a blend of sketches, acrobatic numbers, ballet, and song. Very soon I began to weep. Not from boredom or fear: I wept because I was not on the stage, or rather because of the distance that separated the little girl I was from the performers I was watching.

Fifty years and more have gone by, and today I can describe very simply what I experienced that night. But at the time I was ashamed of those stupid tears and the distress they caused my mother.

'Why did you cry the whole time, Nana? Didn't you like it?'

'I don't know.'

'Your father was so glad to get those tickets.'

'Don't tell him I cried. I'll just turn my head the other way.'

Eugenia was in seventh heaven, and when we got home she did all the talking while I concealed my sorrowful longings in our bedroom.

Several times in the days that followed, Mama talked to me. She wanted to understand – and so did I. It was very strange at the age of ten to weep throughout a show created expressly to dazzle, charm and amuse. Very strange!

And suddenly as I sat there, drawn in on myself like a snail, eyes swollen, my mother probing me again, I felt my anger rise, a truly hate-filled anger.

'I don't like my life!' I exploded. 'I don't want to go on like this!'

'You don't like your life, Nana? But what do you know about life?

The war has only just ended. Soon everything will be much better.'

'You don't understand. I don't want to be in the audience while they're up on stage.'

'Well, where do you want to be?'

'Up on the stage!'

'On the stage? Doing what?'

'I don't know. Anything. But I don't want to be in the audience any more. It's horrible being down there with them.'

'How can you say that? Everyone was laughing and clapping.'

'Yes, and I was so unhappy!'

'I could see that.'

'I would rather have left the theater.'

In fact, though, I didn't utter those last words out loud. I was suddenly ashamed to realize that I was jealous. So I had wept from bitterness and jealousy throughout the show. How could I admit that my heart was full of such hateful, contemptible feelings? Nowadays I deplore envious people, yet it was envy that first set me on the path I already yearned (however confusedly) to embark on. I did not yet know it, but I wanted to be on the performers' side of the frontier, side by side with the people who lifted us out of ourselves, transforming us for a few brief hours.

What did my parents say to one another about it? No doubt they were concerned over my fascination with the movies, with performers. I worked well at school, but I spent almost more time on our little stage imitating Shirley Temple in *Poor Little Rich Girl*, or singing 'Over the Rainbow', the song from *The Wizard of Oz* which I knew by heart. I believe Mama finally told Papa that I had wept in the theater. Because soon after that episode (quite incomprehensible to him), he sought the advice of our kindly next-door neighbors, and the word *conservatory* was heard in the house for the first time.

These neighbors weren't simple folk like us. They lived in a stately, beautiful house whose majestic railings rose a few steps away from our little backyard. They often came to the cinema, always taking the trouble to greet Papa and to ask Mama how we were doing in school. Sometimes they would chat with us or tease us.

Papa told me that he spoke to our neighbor of my astonishing passion for the movies, mentioning to him that I imitated Hollywood's younger stars and danced all on my own on our stage.

'I see. Well, perhaps she wants to go into the movies,' our neighbor apparently said. 'But that's a road full of pitfalls and unknowns . . . better not to think along those lines. What else does your daughter like?'

'As I said, she likes dancing . . . And singing too, like her mother.'

'That's true; your wife has a nice voice. We sometimes hear her singing.'

'Well, it's the same with Nana. She sings all day long.'

'Then why don't you enroll her at the Conservatory?'

I was only ten, but I remember Mama's excitement when my father reported this conversation. So there was a school whose sole aim was to turn you into a singer! It was obviously the first she had ever heard of it, and she was immediately in favor. She said that Eugenia and I, who sang so beautifully, would surely be accepted by this school. She was happy and seemed full of excitement, and I no longer recall whether it was that day or a little later that I heard her say: 'I too would have loved to study music!'

In any event, that remark made me look at my mother with new eyes, as though suddenly aware that she had lived a life of her own before bringing us into the world and even before she met Papa. Why did she talk about herself so seldom? Perhaps it was the war or the many disappointments of her life with my father. All we knew in those days was that she was a native of Corfu and came from a big family. Eugenia remembered that we had gone to Corfu in 1939 to see her village and meet our uncles and aunts, but I was too young to remember . . .

Mama would have liked to study singing. If she had known about it, she might have entered the Conservatory and become a singer . . . By slowly developing this slender thread while I took my first steps at the Conservatory, I gradually learned where I came from, where Eugenia and I both came from.

Mama spent only two or three years at school, in her mountain village about an hour's walk from the city of Corfu. Just long enough for her to learn how to read and write. She was one of nine children, and I never knew exactly where she stood in the sibling hierarchy. The boys worked the land and handled the olive presses, while the girls worked as house-maids in homes in and around Corfu. So at the age of nine or ten Aliki entered the service of her aunt and uncle – a couple who had themselves found work in the home of the Kapodistrias family, a name illustrious throughout Greece. Count Ioannis Kapodistrias (John Capodistria) became the very first ruler of independent Greece in 1827, but he was assassinated four years later. Aliki would remain with this couple until she was eighteen, helping to run the household and cook their meals.

She told me that she sang well, and that others noticed it, but in those days you wouldn't dream of becoming a performer, of earning a living with your voice. What future did she dream of, then? She wanted to leave, to say goodbye to the tiny island of Corfu and travel to the mainland, and I believe she once came close to eloping with a sailor. At eighteen, she was a pretty girl, and there must have been many sailors around. She probably saw him again and gave him – and herself – some hope, but then she pulled back. At the last moment she decided not to go with him, and his ship left port without her.

It was after this disappointment that she went to see Maria Kapo-distrias, the family's unmarried daughter. Maria was not much older than Mama, and the family knew Mama well, for her aunt often brought her to the house to help with cooking or ironing. Maria was about to leave for Athens, and Aliki, who also wanted to leave and see Athens, asked her if she might have need of a *cameriera*, a housemaid.

'Let me think about it,' said Maria.

And a few days later:

'Fine. I'll take you with me since you're so anxious to go.'

It was 1924 when she first saw Athens. One year earlier, Kemal Atatürk's Turkey had insisted on a population exchange with Greece. Four hundred thousand Turkish Muslims left Greece for their country of origin, while one and a half million Greeks were expelled from Turkey. These refugees converged on Athens and its large port of Piraeus, seeking work. Destitute families slept in the streets or in the communal barracks that sprouted in the suburbs. Mama was astonished by all this poverty, by the violence of relations between different groups, by the hardships of which she had had no inkling. Life in Corfu was not easy but everyone managed to find work there. Here, men and women who had recently arrived were begging the people of Athens not to let their children starve ... Was Mama sorry she had left her family? It is very likely. But she steeled herself and learned to look out for herself.

When she had to leave Maria Kapodistrias' service she struggled hard to find work, eventually landing a job as usherette at the Ideal, one of the big movie theaters in central Athens. There, in 1929, she met my father for the first time. He was the Ideal's projectionist. She remembered that he was highly respected; in those days, good projectionists were hard to find.

Constantine Mouskouri was twenty-two in 1929, one year younger than Mama. His parents came from the Peloponnese, but he was born in Athens. Why had his family come to Athens? My father didn't tell us, and perhaps he never knew, because the family very soon came to grief. He was fourteen when his mother died, leaving behind three boys and a little girl, whose father put her in an orphanage. The boys took care of themselves. Constantine could read and write. He had left school and picked up occasional jobs in workshops repairing the electrical appliances which were then all the rage – ventilators, radios, illuminated signs.

It was there that he encountered his destiny in the person of a customer who took a liking to him. Papa was lively, intelligent, curious, smiling. As this man watched him work on a disassembled radio, perhaps he was impressed by Papa's skill. In any case, the two of them struck up a conversation.

'Everything electrical fascinates me,' said Constantine.

'So I see. What do you want to do later on?'

'I don't know.'

'If you like, I can teach you a trade. Have you ever seen a movie?'

'Gosh, no! I don't have enough money.'

'How would you like to go tonight? I can get you in for free: I work in the projection booth.'

Next day Papa became this providential man's assistant. He remained in the job for two or three years, learning the trade and becoming a projectionist in his turn. And a good one, beyond any doubt. He was soon noticed by the two leading theater owners of the day, Damaskinos and Michaelidis. They owned most of the movie houses in the center of the capital, in particular the Palace and the Ideal. He was put in charge of the projection booth at the prestigious Ideal.

Mama's looks went straight to his head. But he was shy, and let a few days go by before plucking up his courage to invite her to the terrace of the café across the avenue from the Ideal. That is all he ever told me. In Greece, parents are reluctant to discuss their love for their spouses with their children. Mama secretly dreamed of a man who would protect her and with whom she could build a family. But she was on her guard. Back then, all young women shared a fear of the kind of man who might destroy their honor. So she forced the issue: if he loved her as he said he did, then he must marry her! He agreed. A few months later, in the spring of 1930, without really knowing each other, they tied their lifelong knot.

Their first child was born in 1932, and they gave her the pretty name of her late grandmother, Constantine's mother Eugenia.

At this time Damaskinos and Michaelidis sent Papa to Khania, the second largest city of Crete, where an open-air cinema was about to begin operation. He would not be required to stay there for long: he was simply to help the manager with the technical installations and with the theater's official opening.

My parents later told me they were warmly received by the manager and his family. He offered them a room in a tall, narrow little house which also included the projectionist's cabin. My father had only to walk down a few steps to be at work behind his projector.

It was in that room that I was conceived. And it was in the streets of Khania, walking with Eugenia, feeling me grow inside her, that Mama's illusions were first shattered. Papa was with her yet he wasn't. He would go out to meet a friend and not return until the small hours. He had a good job and they should have had enough money to live on, but the money disappeared, and Papa often had to sign away the following month's pay. Mama was aware that many Greek men gambled, but with him it was an obsession that devoured everything, that made him lose his head. I believe that their first quarrels erupted in Khania, a place far from the rumors of impending war, where they might instead have drawn closer to one another. It was a little city with a slightly Venetian feel to it, slumbering elegantly between the White Mountains – always snow-capped in winter – and the deep blue of the Sea of Crete. Papa was an affectionate, generous man, and if Mama's reproaches drove him to violence it was because he was angry with himself. He was ashamed, but he lacked the words to tell her so and very quickly resorted to anger. Later on, I so often saw them hurt each other that I can readily imagine what went on before I was born.

Mama had already given him a daughter, and now Papa wanted a son. That was what he said, over and over again, on evenings when he didn't go out to play cards but stayed at home, dandling Eugenia on his knees or gently placing his ear against Mama's stomach with that sudden impulsiveness typical of men. Mama would gladly have given him the gift he hoped for, and although she didn't really care what my gender would be, she sometimes caught herself wishing for a boy.

The night her labor pains began Papa was nearby, playing cards with a few men inside the theater, just three floors beneath our room. Mama was alone with Eugenia, and sent her to get help. The manager and his wife came running.

'I'm going to tell Costa,' said the man, at once turning to go downstairs. Papa left the card game and came up to gauge the situation for himself.

'Right,' he said, meeting Mama's imploring gaze, 'I'm off to get the midwife.' He hurried back downstairs, but couldn't help looking in to see how the game was going. After a while he sat down and picked up his cards again.

It appears that the other players kept reminding him that his wife was in labor and that the midwife would certainly not come if he didn't go fetch her.

So he left, but nobody could say after how many hands. Nor whether he was winning or losing.

By the time he picked up the midwife it was too late. Mama had brought me into the world as best she could with the help of the manager's wife and eldest daughter, Ioanna, who would be my godmother and whose name I was given as a mark of gratitude. It was Ioanna who changed my sister's name from Eugenia to Jenny, and she has been 'Jenny' ever since. All that was left for the midwife was to register the birth and administer post-natal care. It was 13 October 1934.

I can picture my mother's resentment and humiliation when she heard about my father's behavior that night. I can also imagine my father's disappointment at Heaven's refusal to give him the hoped-for boy. 'What a shame you're not a boy!' he told me as soon as I was old enough to hear.

Did my parents' love life end there in Khania as a result of that episode, so disappointing for both of them? That is what I believe today as I remember Mama's melancholia when we were little, the sadness that overwhelmed her on certain days, and those few words (also heard very early, but whose implication was lost on me at the time): '*As soon as you're grown up, I'm leaving.*' She was probably afraid to pronounce the word 'divorce', which to her implied shame. But she needed to utter out loud her hope for another kind of life. Perhaps she also needed to convince herself that she would have the courage to leave.

On our return from Khania, Mr Yiannopoulos offered my father the projectionist's job at our little open-air theater. Our parents had not saved a penny, and although the adjoining house was really too small for the four of us, it seemed a gift of providence. We moved into it in 1936, a year when Greece was deep in social and economic crisis. With the approval of King George II, General Metaxas had just assumed dictatorial powers in order 'to save the country from the abyss of Communism,' as he put it. In other words, life in Athens was not easy. For once, our parents must have felt they were enjoying the protection of Heaven.

Jenny remembers that our respective roles were portioned out to us most curiously before the war: she was the girl of the house, talented and industrious. Mama taught her embroidery, knitting and darning. I was the boy Papa had hoped for in vain; he took me to soccer games every Sunday. No sooner was the war over than the whole system reasserted itself in exactly the same way, and by now I was old enough for it to stick in my memory. Jenny helped Mama, while I worked hard to interest myself in soccer and retain what my father taught me of sports. I was entirely aware of his disappointment at my failure to be male, and I did all I could to act as though I were a boy and thus to be worthy of his affection.

But that didn't stop him saying, Sunday after Sunday, 'What a pity, Nana, that you're not a boy!' And I also remember how this enduring regret of his eroded my sense of self-worth and, little by little, *destroyed* me. Perhaps 'destroyed' is too strong – an adult term – but I can find no other to convey the hopelessness that sometimes overwhelmed me. I felt rejected, useless, a failure. I longed to disappear. I never again wanted to meet that disappointed look in my father's eyes, a look that appeared whenever he recalled the boy denied to him.

I was not even allowed to play soccer with the boys to console my father (in those days, there was no such thing as a girls' soccer team). Compounding my deficiencies, I turned out to be horribly inept in sewing class at school. It was Jenny, skilled and swift, who invariably took over my work and saved my skin. As a result I felt good for nothing – neither for standing in as a boy nor for handling the tasks expected of a girl.

'That child,' my parents would tell their friends, 'either weeps or else she laughs, but she weeps a lot more than she laughs. The rest of the time she doesn't say a word, she just sits in her corner.'

It's true that I didn't say much, but I laughed all on my own, and I was even swept away with happiness on evenings when we were allowed to watch the scheduled movie. I tested the salutary power of actors and performers on myself: they lifted me out of my sorrow and transported me into the world of dreams.

Which was precisely the story of little Dorothy, played by Judy Garland in *The Wizard of Oz*. Dorothy lives in Kansas. She isn't very happy in the midst of a family in which nobody pays her any attention. When a spiteful woman tries to steal her dog, she appeals to her family for help, but not one of them lifts a finger. So Dorothy decides to escape. As she flees through the chaos of a tornado she is knocked unconscious by a window blown out of its frame and enters the land of dreams. This land is cheerful, and it is in color, whereas the real world was black and white. Eager to meet the wizard of Oz, she asks the Munchkins, the inhabitants of this sun-filled land, to show her the way. She is joined by a scarecrow, who is full of ideas despite his claim to have no brain. Then a man made of tin, who contends that he has no heart, tags along. Finally a lion, insisting he is a coward, completes the little group. Along the road they meet a witch who tries to block their way. Pooling their talents, they manage to kill her and find the wizard.

Later on, once I was in my teens, I developed a deeper appreciation of the moral of Victor Fleming's movie, and it inspired me in shaping my own life. In the end, the wizard is revealed to be a charlatan. It is true that he advises Dorothy to return home. But the important lessons come from the Scarecrow, the Tin Man and the Cowardly Lion. They show her that we must use our intelligence, our heart and our courage in order to surmount problems rather than put our trust in some magician who doesn't really exist. Like Dorothy, I remembered that lesson.

Papa's realization that I was a good singer, good enough to consider applying for the Conservatory, pierced the leaden skies of my childhood like a bright shaft of light. It didn't matter that I was still too young for the Conservatory: the notion was now firmly in place. And singing offered me what soccer denied – I could exploit it to the hilt and at last win Papa's heart. I saw him relax before my eyes, I saw him put on a broad smile, and I whispered to myself that for now, at least, his disappointment at my gender was diminishing.

I remember the lady who interviewed us (Mama, Jenny and me) at the Conservatory. She was a German, smiling but with an underlying severity. She heard me first, followed by Jenny and then delivered her judgment: 'The young one has true feeling for melody, but her voice is a little hoarse. Her sister's voice is magnificent, and she has a fine pair of lungs.' I thought to myself (but without a trace of jealousy) that even in singing Jenny was more talented than I was. But Jenny didn't identify herself with Judy Garland, she was not dying to perform on stage, and she hadn't wept throughout that variety show. I was the problem, not Jenny, so Mama talked about me. The German lady understood at once, and she was looking at me when she said that we would have to wait a year or two, that I was still too young to enter the Conservatory. I later realized that Jenny would have been accepted there and then, but neither she nor Mama pressed the point, and the German music teacher (who may well have suggested it) said nothing further.

Meanwhile, I had to content myself with school, where I was an attentive pupil (although the teachers reported that I was 'perhaps too well behaved'). Because we had not attended school during the war, Jenny and I were both two years older than our classmates. How had other girls of our generation managed? All of a sudden it seemed that we were the only ones to have missed out on school. I believe this situation inhibited me somewhat. What's more, I didn't want to attract attention to myself. I wanted no one to know my background – a father who failed to come home every second night, Mama's shrieks and tears when he reappeared, their terrible quarrels, our poverty, our lack of basic necessities . . . It seemed to me that I was the only one to have such parents, and that the best way of deflecting attention from them was to be a model student.

Our compulsory school uniforms were helpful in that endeavor: everyone had to wear a little black dress with a white collar, effectively concealing the black sheep in the flock. Otherwise, on non-school days, we had only one kind of garment, a pretty flower-pattern dress with white shoes, which Mama gave us for Easter. It was spring clothing – perfectly appropriate for a season in which the acacia bloomed and the scent of flowers wafted a festive atmosphere through the streets of Athens. When school reopened in the fall we dyed the shoes black and Mama bought us dark sweaters that transformed our summer dresses into winter clothing.

For Greek Orthodox Christians like us, Easter was much more important than Christmas. We are more concerned with celebrating Christ's resurrection than his birth. For instance, we don't exchange gifts at Christmas, but at Easter we receive an egg adorned with red candies (and new clothes in the Mouskouri household). And the religious celebrations throughout Easter Week are sumptuous, awe-inspiring, magnificent. For children like me, dying to escape the world of black-and-white, that miraculous week seemed truly to embody the land of dreams, the luminous land of dreams.

We spent the week at church or in processions – every evening, prostrating ourselves, praying, singing in chorus. Easter celebrations were my first encounter with the performing arts, well before I discovered the movies. And it was very early on, in church, that I encountered the joy of shared emotion, of hearts uplifted, of the power of song over the human spirit. And the power of words and images, for each year we listened with the same fervor to the story of Christ's Passion as though we were hearing it for the first time. It was in church that I first glimpsed the possibility of another world, a world attainable on condition that you wanted it enough and strove to acquire the means to create it.

Mama had been raised in this religious and moral environment, and she rather than Papa was the one who made us go to church. She was the one who spoke to us of the patron saint of Corfu, Agios Spyridon, whose mummified body we bore through the city streets. It was a deeply moving procession, with people throwing themselves flat on their faces, praying, weeping, swooning ... According to legend, the saint's body failed to rot away because God protected it. But one had to be worthy of God's protection, and Mama showed us the way: never cheat or lie; take a stand against injustice ...

I concurred. I loved everything Mama said, I was utterly convinced that she was right, and I worked hard to keep from sinning. In fact, it was in this frame of mind that one day I found myself judging my father.

That morning I was leaving for church for confession. Mama stopped me on the threshold.

'Your father is home, Nana,' she said to me. 'He came home late last night. Before you leave you should wake him and ask his forgiveness.'

Right then I didn't hesitate for a second, and my father, still half-asleep, forgave me. But immediately afterward, all the way to church, I felt a mounting anger of an intensity I had never before experienced: 'Why did I go and ask his forgiveness?' I asked myself. 'To give someone your forgiveness you have to be a saint yourself, and I don't believe Papa is any kind of saint. He's been playing cards again all night long, he's making Mama unhappy, he's making all three of us unhappy. He knows it, and he makes no attempt to change.'

I was more than angry: I was disgusted. Perhaps this was the first time in my life I was fully conscious of injustice, and ready to rebel.

I had another new experience that year: I discovered myself, my face, my body. This had not interested me at all during the war, when we probably didn't even possess a mirror. But now we had a small mirror above the sink, and I didn't like the girl I saw. My face seemed an expressionless blank, my eyes were set too far apart, my cheeks were too full. In short, nothing of what I saw pleased me, unlike Jenny who was so beautiful. Until then, it had never occurred to me to compare the two of us, but now that I had this picture of myself I couldn't help thinking of Jenny's face. She was full of light, alive, luminous, while I seemed to be the personification of grayness.

I was about to write that I found my face gloomy and misty, just like my life as a substitute boy, when suddenly the word *misty* takes me back to my twelfth year, which I spent in the classroom. Everything that winter seemed bathed in gray. Since I was taller than my classmates, I was always seated at the back of the class, and although I was a diligent pupil I had trouble following the teacher's discourse when she explained it on the blackboard. One day she asked me to answer the question she had written there, and I couldn't even see the question.

'Could you read it out to me, Miss? I can't read it.'

'What do you mean, you can't read it? Can't you see the letters?'

'Yes, but it's as if they were in a fog.'

'Come closer and tell me whether you see better.'

I moved to the front row and was able to see the letters. I went home that night with a short note saying I should consult an eye doctor as soon as possible.

How angry my father was! He wasn't unkind; he was much angrier with himself than with me. But he was genuinely angry.

'You saw perfectly well when you were small, Nanaki.'

'So why can't I see the blackboard properly any more?'

'Why? You want to know why?'

'Yes please.'

'Because you watch movies the wrong way round – from behind the screen!'

'Well, that's sometimes true, but not all the time . . . I often watch them from in front.'

'Yes, but when I tell you that you aren't to watch a film, you watch it anyway from behind the screen. Do you think I haven't noticed?'

'I'm sorry. I didn't think it was serious.'

'Yes it is – very serious! Because that's what has damaged your eyesight. Let's hear what the doctor has to say. I should have put a stop to it, punished you, it's all my fault.'

No. It was nobody's fault – not his, not mine. The doctor told me I could go on watching films from behind if I wanted to. The fact was: I was shortsighted.

Mama had never had much formal education, but she knew many sayings and she taught them to us. One of her favorite expressions involved the story of a vine growing over a bower. The bower was unsightly because it leaned sideways under the weight of the vine, and one day a donkey knocked it to the ground with a good solid kick. After that, the bower was not salvageable. Thus, when nothing can be done about a situation, we speak of 'the donkey's kick'.

And that saying was on my mind when I came home with my first pair of glasses.

'This time it's hopeless,' I said to myself as I examined my face in our little mirror.

The world had miraculously emerged from the mist, but what I saw of myself didn't encourage me to seek a place in that world.

3

The Big Screen, the Stage and the Song

J enny and I went to the Conservatory together. The German woman who had given us our audition accepted both of us into her class, which was on Thursdays. Maybe it was Mama, with her profound sense of fairness and impartiality, who had requested this: at home, whenever one of us received a present, the other was automatically given the same gift.

Yet Jenny and I were different. I believe everyone (and especially our father and mother) was made immediately aware of it at the first little show we put on for the Conservatory parents.

The show consisted of each student in turn performing the same piece. It was a musical re-enactment of an old Greek folk tale, the story of a young man who repents during confession for having made love to a girl and then abandoned her. He sings of her beauty, of their love, their sin, and his subsequent flight. But against his expectations, the priest refuses to absolve him. The priest's words had a tremendous impact on the fourteen-year-old girl I then was. Perhaps I was hypersensitive simply because I was unhappy and lacked all confidence in myself. In any case, I was the only girl that night who breathed a dramatic intensity into the priest's words. It left the grownup spectators speechless – and utterly transformed Frau Kempers' view of me.

Jenny sang first, and I still remember how fully her voice rang out in that small theater. She played the young man, then the priest; and her voice took wings as she sang condemnation of the youth's conduct. I believe the audience was dazzled by her stage presence, by the musical

40

perfection of her voice, and by her self-assurance at the tender age of sixteen. When the parents rose to applaud her I felt the same pride I had experienced in the playground at school when I was pointed out as Jenny's younger sister. Her beauty and her aura temporarily relieved me of the pain and darkness that weighed down on me. Just as she did during the war, Jenny was now protecting me again, clearing the way for me with her spontaneity and energy.

Now it was my turn to sing, and I had to fight the stage-fright paralyzing my vocal chords. I knew that my first notes were pathetic, but the emotional power of the story soon came to my rescue: I felt I truly *was* the repentant youth who abandoned the girl after having his way with her and who now implores Heaven's forgiveness. Deep within, I believed he did not deserve forgiveness: my heart was with the girl whose life was now ruined – which is why I sang the priest's terrible words with such passion:

'If you loved her and abandoned her, then may God curse you!'

What power I put into proclaiming that doom-laden judgment: '*May God curse you!*' It was a cry of anger. I was no longer myself but the voice of outraged justice.

An immense silence followed my performance. I stood there alone in the center of the stage, and the audience made no move to applaud. They just stared as though stunned. My parents appeared to be weeping. Frau Kempers was unsmiling, her features seemingly turned to stone. Then suddenly she stood up and began to clap, and the entire audience followed suit.

I didn't yet know that this was the first public appearance of the singer I was to become a few years later, but I will never forget that first 'recital'. I realized that on the stage I could conquer my fears, forget them, in order to express the feelings that swirled within me. I found that my voice (although far from perfect) conveyed emotions that, just like in the movies or theater, had the mysterious power to carry people away from the real world. Three or four years earlier I had wept with jealousy as I watched those performers onstage. I instinctively felt that I belonged with them, not with the audience. Now I was sure of it, despite my glasses, despite everything...

*

A year or so before the modest little show that influenced my vision of the world so powerfully, I left elementary school to enter high school, which we called the gymnasium. That too was good news. Whereas there were just two streets to cross to reach my old school, I now took the train with Jenny, who already attended the gymnasium. There were only two stations, but it was still a journey that took us into another neighborhood and gave me the impression I had suddenly grown up.

As was to be expected, Jenny had already paved my way. Even before I opened my mouth or handed in my first homework, friendly smiles and encouraging words greeted me: 'Ah, Mouskouri's sister! I'm sure you and I will get along just fine ... ' For Jenny was not only the top student in her class but generous, full of fun, and always ready to organize group games or expeditions.

Without meaning to, my sister represented a challenge. How could I live up to her example? She was like a math problem to me, but unlike Jenny I was no good at math. I had to apply myself, mustering all my powers of concentration. During this period, I became aware of a character trait of mine which, all my life, would motivate me to forge ahead: a dread of disappointing those who took me under their wing and had faith in me. I did not want to disappoint our teachers, who were so anxious to help. I wanted them to be as proud of me as they were of Jenny, but she was a tough act to follow. Once again, it was Jenny who kept me from falling down by re-doing my embroidery or sewing assignments at home in the evenings, just as she had done in elementary school.

That year we took our first steps at the Conservatory. As if by a miracle, the singing opened my classmates' hearts to me. Whereas I had always been alone in elementary school, I made my first friends at the gymnasium during music classes. The teacher noticed me, she had me sing, and soon we organized a little choir in which I was the star. Whenever there was a festive occasion, Jenny and I were always the ones chosen to sing in front of the whole school.

For me, the gymnasium soon became like church, a place where life's colors pleased me. School was a place of apprenticeship and friendly interaction where I felt confident, supported, respected. In short, I fitted in.

Ironically, my years at the gymnasium – the happiest and most ful-filling of my life to date – were the very years, 1947-1949, that saw Greece collapse into full-fledged civil war. Royalists and Communists were slaughtering each other in the mountains, at a time when the scars left by German occupation had not even begun to heal. But whereas enemy occupation had had a direct impact on my family, the civil war seemed far removed from us. We heard news of it, of course – sometimes appalling news. For the most part, however, the conflict did not disturb our teenage lives, supervised as we were by teachers anxious to let us grow up free of hatred and violence.

When did we leave the open-air cinema of our childhood and the little house behind the screen? I believe it was in 1946. Papa was offered an indoor movie theater which operated all year round, and after he accepted, we had to seek new lodgings.

We moved into the basement of a rather dilapidated house in the Neos Kosmos district, which at that time was just a rundown suburb with streets full of potholes. The apartment was small: two rooms and a kitchen with a bare mud floor. Our new place, like the house we had just left, had no bathroom. The washing and toilet facilities were in the courtyard, and we shared them with all the other families in the building. We referred to our new home as a ground-floor apartment, but it was really a basement. The windows of the two bedrooms opened at sidewalk level, and we had to climb two or three steps to reach the courtyard from the kitchen.

At first I was not too shocked by the physical condition of the old building. After all, it was not so different from our previous house, except that we no longer had the acacia and our little garden. But as I entered my teens, and became aware of the home environments of my classmates, I soon learned how different we were from other people. It wasn't that they were wealthy, but it was evident that their parents strove constantly to improve their lot, enlarge and embellish their houses, and take advantage of the progress Greece was beginning to enjoy in spite of the civil war. With us, there was nothing of that kind. We seemed grateful simply to survive. Mama sank into depression, and Papa con-tinued to return at dawn two nights out of three – that is, when he didn't

43

stay away for a whole week. Slowly, the truth began to sink in: if we were living like cave-dwellers, half-buried beneath street level, too poor to enjoy the sunshine, it was because Papa gambled away all the money he should have been spending on his family.

I compared us to cave-dwellers, but drowning victims would be more accurate. That subterranean apartment in Neos Kosmos is forever associated in my memory with the water that continually leaked into our house. I had nightmares that the water rushing into our kitchen and bedrooms would one day engulf us all in a dark liquid shroud.

It was during the first heavy autumn rains that the problem first caught us unawares. Mama was making soup for our evening meal, and we were preparing vegetables. Suddenly there was water on our mud floor. A puddle that spread across the kitchen, under the table, under the Propane bottle, and beneath the sink. At first it seemed like an evil conjurer's trick, for none of us could see where the water was coming from. We immediately attacked it with buckets and mops, but the water kept coming, and soon it was lapping at our ankles. Only then did we connect the phenomenon with the torrential rain outside. It was nighttime, so we couldn't see it, but we could hear it in the courtyard, which was flooded from all the rainwater streaming off the small hill projecting above our building. But it was not entering through the kitchen door. So how was it getting into the house? My God, through the walls! It was seeping through the walls! Jenny, who saw it first, let out a scream of fear. At first it made little blisters on the plaster, then it began to flow in earnest, but so hard to see on that rough plaster wall that you had to touch it with your finger to realize how fast it was pouring in.

That evening we gave up on our soup. We spent the whole dinner hour mopping. But even the concerted efforts of the three of us were not enough to prevent the water from invading our bedrooms and insinuating itself beneath the beds and chests of drawers. It was terrifying. As we waged our silent battle, we couldn't believe that this was happening, that it was even possible. We felt like hunted animals, dazed and out of breath. When the rain stopped and we could finally go to bed, within our saturated walls, we no longer possessed the strength to say a word. We felt dirty, humiliated, utterly destroyed, as though we had been locked in hand-to-hand combat with an inhuman enemy who had trampled and half-drowned us before suddenly deciding it had done enough for the time being.

From that night on, we knew that every heavy rainfall would bring another flood. We knew it, yet our parents did not even think of leaving, and Jenny and I did not protest. In some strange manner, we accepted what was happening to us. As though we considered it a just retribution from Heaven for our father's irresponsibility. Day by day he was leading us toward disaster, and we accepted the situation as if it were ordained by fate. Mama, as we dimly realized, had resigned herself. Now Heaven had sent us another calamity, as if to jolt us from our apathy, as if to see whether, this time, we would rebel. But no, we made not the slightest effort.

Why did I make the connection between the catastrophe of a father addicted to gambling and that of seeing our house flooded whenever it rained hard? Naturally enough, I suppose, because any other father would have got us out of there. But this thought did not occur to me until later. At the time it was far from my mind. The connection lay elsewhere, and has remained intact in my childhood memories: I had always feared that people would learn that my father gambled, and now I also feared they would learn that I lived in a house that was waterlogged whenever fate pleased. Both circumstances pervaded me with the same sense of shame and humiliation.

On my saint's day (Saint Ioanna), 7 January, Mama agreed to let me invite my closest friends to the house for tea. I must have been in my second year at the gymnasium because our little dog was still there (she would die soon afterward). This tea was an event, for we weren't in the habit of entertaining. To prepare for the occasion, we spent all the early-morning hours cleaning our bedroom (which would serve as the living room) from top to bottom. By arranging our beds to form an L and covering it with cushions, we contrived a handsome couch. Mama brought out some little doilies, as well as candles to be lit when darkness fell.

And then, with the housework done, we baked cakes.

Soon there was a knock at the kitchen door and I rushed to open it. It was Helena. We kissed on the threshold – and I automatically glanced up at the sky. Dear God, huge clouds were forming! While Helena shed her coat I prayed, silently but with all my might: 'Lord, if you absolutely have to make it rain, I beg you to wait until my tea-party is over. I am willing to bale and mop all night long, but please grant me this afternoon.'

My other friends arrived, we ate the cakes and I organized games, but I was so horrified by the color of the sky that I was only half-present at my own party. I couldn't help watching the clouds out of the corner of my eye, either through the bedroom window, set high in the wall, or else through the kitchen door whenever I popped out to get more candies or fruit juice. What would my friends think if the heavens opened and the water rose in the kitchen and then raced across the bedroom floor where we were reclining around a board game? Just imagining it made my blood run cold. They would have to get up, they would see Mama and Jenny on their knees, I would have to ask them to leave ... The shame of it! How could I possibly return to the gymnasium after that? And what if the very worst happened ... I mean, what if the septic tank beneath the communal toilets were to overflow (as had happened before), its hideous stench filling our apartment ... I couldn't bear it. All day long, I shuddered to think of it.

But God heard my prayer and had mercy on me. By the time my last guest left, not a single drop had fallen.

Did Mama and Jenny pray as well? I believe they did, judging by their relief and sudden gaiety when the three of us were finally alone. That evening we sang as we collected the dirty plates and glasses, and we were still full of gratitude when we went to bed.

I had just fallen asleep when the deluge began. It was the swishing noise of running water that awakened me.

'Water! Water! Mama! Jenny! Wake up!'

Both bedrooms were awash, and I remember bursting into tears as I scrambled about in my nightgown.

Mama said a few consoling words. Kind as always, Jenny told me to go back to bed: 'The two of us can handle it.' Neither realized that I was crying for joy. I was beside myself with gratitude to God, and as promised I spent the rest of the night toiling with bucket and mop.

*

Two or three years later, while sopping up water in the middle of the night as we had done so many times before, I suddenly became aware of the ordeal our parents were inflicting on us. I can still see myself abruptly throwing my mop aside and telling Jenny in solemn tones:

'If I get married one day and have children, I swear I'll do anything to spare them this kind of thing.'

I was fifteen or sixteen, and those were my exact words: sensible, uncomplaining, devoid of anger. Just a whiff of bitterness, which had taken a long time to surface, triggered this determined declaration from a teenager sensing that she would soon be a woman.

Yes, I was obedient, well-behaved, and introverted. This finally began to irritate Jenny, who was discovering boys, laughter and a hunger for life. All of a sudden she was suffocating at home, what with Mama's melancholy and all the annoyances of our daily life: Papa's absences, our unpaid bills, the periodic flooding which we had to conceal from friends and neighbors in order to hold our heads up. She didn't rebel: all she wanted was to test her wings, like those doves we had once released from their cage. She wanted to be able to come home when she pleased without having to explain herself. Mama simply couldn't believe this was happening.

'And you think I'm going to let you go off just like that and come home in the middle of the night?'

'I'm seventeen. I'm not a child any more.'

'You'll do as I say, and that's all there is to it!'

'So I can't go out?'

'When you're married you can do what you like. Until then you'll stay at home.'

And to keep her in the nest, Mama tied Jenny up. Not with handcuffs, just a string wound around her wrist and attached to her bedstead or the back of her chair. But it was just as effective as handcuffs: neither Jenny nor I dared to untie a knot made by our mother.

Meanwhile, though, I was free to come and go. That was what infuriated Jenny.

'You're a sly one, Nana,' she told me. 'You never say what you think, so Mama leaves you alone.'

'But I don't *want* to go out at night.'

'You could at least take my side. If both of us were screaming at her, Mama would give in.'

'All right, next time I'll try, I promise.'

But when the opportunity presented itself, I was unable to utter a word. Their yelling traumatized me. It brought back the worst of our parents' brawls, when they punched each other, their faces bleeding. And we had thrown ourselves between them, crying because we thought they were going to kill each other. Jenny had lived through that horror. How could she even think of repeating it?

I was literally unable to do so.

'Jenny,' I said to her one day. 'I can't do it, I can't yell, I can't fight.'

'Everyone can fight. Just do as I do.'

'No, I can't. My throat closes up when I start to shout.'

I hated quarrels, I hated violence and war, but I couldn't explain why.

There was no more money in the house, not even to buy food. Papa had lost it all.

'I can no longer pay for the Conservatory,' Mama told us one day.

I don't think either of us replied. It was like the flooding – basically, we accepted the fact that Papa was dragging us down with him. No doubt any other outcome would have surprised us.

I was with Mama when she had to tell Frau Kempers the news. Only today, as I recall how proud Mama was and how sensitive to other people's opinion of her, do I realize how hard it must have been for her to request that interview.

Frau Kempers was as inscrutable as ever when she invited us into her office. She was not a demonstrative woman: the only sign of emotion she permitted herself was a small characteristic nod when you sang well.

Mama began to speak, and our teacher's face imperceptibly darkened. She listened, never interrupting. Of course Mama did not mention that our poverty was the result of Papa's gambling. She merely said that her husband was a humble projectionist and, due to the rising cost of living, they could no longer pay the Conservatory fees.

Frau Kempers understood. She acquiesced wordlessly. At that juncture I assumed that we would get up and leave. In fact, Mama was getting ready to do so; she had already risen from her chair and was pretending to check that her handbag was securely closed.

'If I may speak frankly,' began the great lady with the gaunt face.

Mama froze. I shared her consternation. So this wasn't over: we hadn't been sufficiently humiliated. Now we would have to discuss it, convince her that we were the poorest of the poor.

'If I may speak frankly,' Frau Kempers continued, 'I think it's a pity for the older sister to drop out. She has a superb voice and excellent prospects. But I believe that it's even worse for the younger one, because if you don't let her go on singing I don't know what will become of her.'

She paused. She didn't look at me. Her pale blue eyes focused on Mama. But Mama seemed paralyzed, and my own heart had stopped beating. What did she mean? What would she say next?

'The older girl is more talented,' she went on as Mama remained mute, 'but I'm not sure she really wants to sing. It's different for the little one. She doesn't have her sister's voice, but she has the desire to sing; she burns for it. Do you understand what I am saying, Mrs Mouskouri?'

Mama nodded. Of course she understood: at my age, she too had dreamed of singing. As for me, my head was spinning: I had never been paid such a compliment in my life. It didn't matter that Jenny was the better singer. I already knew that – I had known it from the start. But for Frau Kempers to appreciate my passion, and to advocate for it, was something I could never have dared hope for. What better way of telling me that I was important in her eyes? That I had a place in the world?

'I understand,' said Mama softly. 'I understand. But unfortunately we can't . . .'

'I know. I heard you loud and clear. May I suggest a solution? If Jenny agrees, she can leave the Conservatory. But I will keep the little one, and you may pay me later if you ever have the means.'

'That's not possible!'

'Mrs Mouskouri, it *is* possible, since I'm the one suggesting it. Don't be embarrassed, and don't thank me. I am doing it for Nana because she deserves it.'

The meeting was over. I felt overjoyed, flattered and, at the same time, terribly worried for Jenny. It was unfair, and Mama, so obsessed with fairness and equal treatment, could not deny it.

That night we had a long talk with Jenny. I wanted to be sure that she did not share my burning desire to sing, as Frau Kempers had so accurately expressed it. Jenny tossed my question back at me:

'What about you, Nana? If you had to stop, how would it affect you?'

'I don't know, it would be terrible, I love singing so much . . . In fact, it's the only thing that makes me want to go on living.'

'Then the teacher is right. You have to stay, Nana.'

'Because you don't feel that way about singing?'

'That's right. The idea of leaving doesn't bother me. I'm not sure I want to be a singer later on.'

'Really? You're not just saying that, are you?'

'I like going out, I have other interests . . . Haven't you noticed?'

What did Jenny really think? Many years later she admitted to making a sacrifice for me that night when she realized that singing was of colossal importance to me. If I had known at the time, I would not have agreed. But perhaps, deep down, I didn't *want* to know. Subconsciously, I sensed that my whole life turned on Jenny's decision.

From then on I took lessons from Frau Kempers, without Jenny's beautiful voice to accompany me. Although we didn't wish it to be so, our paths – parallel for so many years – began to diverge. I concentrated more and more on singing and music while Jenny, determined to win her freedom, met a man some twenty years her senior who would open life's doors for her and become her husband.

His name was Demostanis, and he was in the restaurant business. He knew all the tavernas where one dined while listening to the folk groups of the day. He and my sister were very soon engaged, and his arrival in our family was like a spring day after an endless winter. He was cheerful, congenial, enterprising, and he enjoyed going out in the evening and being entertained. Athens had many pleasures to offer, now that the civil war was over and King Paul I, brother and successor to George II, had gained the upper hand over the Communists. But it was not thought proper for Jenny and Demostanis to go out alone while they were not yet married ('what would the neighbors say?' Mama fretted), so we all went out together as a family. Jenny's fiancé was happy to invite his future parents-in-law, and I was included, too, as he was quite fond of me.

Sometimes I went along just for the pleasure of listening with Jenny to the old Greek songs whose words we knew by heart. But increasingly, I preferred to stay at home alone and listen to Radio Tangiers. For several years now, this station had been bringing us all the songs popular in America, and jazz in particular. I spoke no English, but I wrote down the lyrics phonetically. Then, when Ella Fitzgerald, Billie Holiday or Mahalia Jackson came on the radio, I sang along with them. Frau Kempers was unaware of my passion for jazz and popular music from England and America. Something told me that if she found out, she would not be very happy about my spending time on modern compositions rather than on Liszt, Schubert, and Schumann. So I kept it a secret. Radio Tangiers was my clandestine Conservatory. But it did not detract from my commitment to the lyric art. When I worked on the music of Franz Schubert in particular, I experienced an intensity of emotion that sometimes brought me close to tears.

All the other girls attending the Conservatory had pianos in their homes. Clearly this was a luxury we couldn't contemplate. But Mama found a solution. One of Papa's uncles, a nationally renowned mathematician, lived in a beautiful apartment in the center of Athens. Knowing that he and his wife had a piano they hardly ever played, Mama called them. She made no mention of the straits we were in, merely saying that we temporarily needed a piano. In the end, my great-aunt agreed to let me go to her home once or twice a week to practice. To avoid paying for train tickets, I went on foot, arriving hot and out of breath in their hushed apartment. Regrettably for me, the old lady asked me to use the soft pedal in order not to disturb her husband, who was working. I hated the soft pedal; I wanted to hear the notes soar. Since it was springtime, I wanted to throw the windows open and sing my heart out. But I reminded myself that this was better than nothing. Then, after two hours of piano playing cooped up in the gloom of that music room, I returned to Neos Kosmos humming Schubert.

I learned to sing in English the same way I had picked up piano playing, by sounding out the notes. I sang Ella Fitzgerald from my phonetically spelled texts, without understanding the words. (At the gymnasium we studied French, not English.) Papa liked to hear me sing 'Lullaby of Birdland' and other classics made famous by my great American idol. It pleased me no end to perform mini-recitals for him on the clay floor of our kitchen.

'How is it you speak English so well?' he asked one day.

'I listen to the song on the radio and repeat it exactly. Just like the old days when I sang "Over the Rainbow". Do you remember?'

'Yes, I used to say to your mother: "Look at her. She's like a little performing monkey. Put her on a stage and she turns into Judy Garland."'

After one of these home performances, I must have mentioned how much I would like to learn English, because one evening my parents told me about friends who knew of an unusual teacher, an old blind man who apparently gave English lessons for free.

'We spoke to our friends about you,' said Papa, 'and they promised to find out more and get back to us.'

For several days I secretly dreamed of a miracle, imagining this unknown teacher to be like the wizard of Oz. I would set out to find him, and as a reward, he would convey the language to me with a wave of his wand: 'Away with you, my child: the world now belongs to you!'

In a way, that miracle came to pass. Soon I was told that this man had agreed to meet, and he was expecting me. When I went to his home, a very charming old lady opened the door. She was his sister, with whom he shared a comfortable apartment. I learned that the old gentleman, a former naval officer, had spent many years ashore in the major English ports, returning to Greece only when forced to by age and failing eyesight.

We hit it off at once. I liked his manners, his willingness to take time to explain things, his refusal to move too fast, and his expectant way of tilting his head to listen, as though everything I said was of interest to him. My curiosity about English amused him, especially the fact that I wanted to learn the language in order to sing Ella Fitzgerald – and my latest discovery, Elvis Presley! I remember returning home after three or four of his lessons, thrilled that things were going so well, when a thought suddenly dawned on me: since my teacher clearly liked me but couldn't see me ... that must mean that I was beautiful on the inside! Obviously, it would never have occurred to me had he not been blind. But the idea was very welcome in those difficult years of adolescence when, to make matters worse, I was putting on weight. I didn't like my looks and avoided looking at my face and figure in mirrors or reflected in store windows. But thanks to this man, I discovered that in spite of everything I was likeable.

It was a monumental revelation, and I would go on to build my whole life as a performer around it. Through music and song, I was going to express the beauty that I assumed was inside me. Because of my inner beauty, people would accept me and love me in spite of my glasses and my extra pounds. They would love me in every country in the world, a thought that never ceases to amaze me.

Now, back to my English lessons. Initially, we had no books, and I learned solely through conversation. Later on, I had the good fortune to possess an American dictionary. It was sent to me from the United States, and I long regarded it as a quasi-sacred object. Were there no English-language dictionaries for sale in Athens in the early 1950s? Evidently not, since my parents had to turn to my godmother (daughter of the theater manager in Khania, Crete), who now lived with her husband in America. Ioanna, her name now anglicized to Joanna, the woman who helped Mama bring me into the world, had not forgotten us, and one day this wonderful dictionary arrived in the mail. From then on, whenever I found a word or a grammatical form difficult to grasp, my teacher would ask me to read aloud what the dictionary had to say. Then he would nod his agreement:

'You see? That explains it perfectly. Do you understand now?'

Even if I didn't understand right away, I pretended I did because I knew I could re-read the dictionary's definitions at my leisure when I got home. After a year, the lessons came to an end. But with the dictionary's help, I continued to study English by myself. The day finally came when I was able to transcribe 'Jailhouse Rock', the great Elvis's latest hit, without a single spelling mistake.

Although I was crazy about jazz and rock and roll, my future path seemed set in concrete: I would be a concert singer. Or perhaps an opera singer like my fellow Greek, the great Maria Kalogeropoulos, better known to the rest of the world as Maria Callas. This was the dream of my parents, who shared a religious reverence for opera. They could not afford the best tickets, but thanks to my father's connections with show-business technicians, he always managed to get us a folding seat at the end of a row. We saw *La Traviata, Carmen, Norma*, and others. Twice we saw Verdi's *Nabucco (Nebuchadnezzar)*, my father's favorite opera. In 1951 Maria Callas swept the Italians off their feet at La Scala in Milan and, ever since, her name was on everyone's lips. She performed in New York, London and Paris . . . Would I walk in her footsteps one day? My parents, afraid of getting carried away by impossible dreams, tried not to set their hopes too high. When they discussed my prospects, they often rebutted each other:

'If she doesn't manage to become a soloist, at least she'll sing in the chorus,' said my father. 'Our daughter, a member of the chorus ! That alone would be terrific, don't you think?'

'Of course, but you know as well as I do that she can do better than that!'

'It's up to Frau Kempers to decide.'

'True, but if Nana sets her mind on being a soloist, I believe she can do it.'

Had I really 'set my mind' to it? In truth, I had no plans beyond the next several months. I was entering my junior year in the gymnasium and had other concerns. Besides, I didn't want to have to choose between jazz, rock and roll, and classical music. I was working on the first two in secret. Officially, I was studying classical music. The arrangement suited me just fine!

Perhaps Frau Kempers shared my parents' wildest hopes, but she was not the kind of woman to indulge herself or to dream aloud. What would my destiny have been if Frau Kempers had taken me all the way at the

Conservatory? God did not wish it. He called her to Heaven that year, leaving me cruelly bereft of an honest and generous lady without whom I would probably never have become a singer of any kind.

My grief over her death was so unbearable that I struggled to drive it out of my memory. I have an image of myself teetering on the edge of an abyss, feverishly listening to Radio Tangiers to keep myself from getting dizzy and falling into the void. I sang everything that entered my head, from Bessie Smith and Billie Holiday to the 'Voi che Sapete' aria from the *Marriage of Figaro* – the piece we were working on the day before Frau Kempers died. Music took up my days. The nights, however, brought back my old nightmare. I was haunted once again by the little girl running frantically around the square, terrified by the dark gullet of the well where the Germans had executed the young man, and unable to find the way out.

4

Try an Audition on the Radio

*H*ow long did I keep going in circles, trying to run away from an anguish that caught up with me at night? I no longer contemplated returning to the Conservatory. Frau Kempers had graciously waived the tuition, and that kind of thing doesn't generally happen twice. But as so often in such situations, my father found a solution. One of his projectionist friends mentioned a former sound technician whose musical talent had earned him, early on, a place in the operatic chorus and, eventually, a professorship at the Conservatory. Perhaps he would accept me as one of his students. For one thing, he might be prompted to do so out of a sense of solidarity among people in the movie business. Papa went to see him. I don't know what he said, but the man agreed to meet me.

'Now it's up to you to convince him,' my father told me.

'I'm scared ... I won't be able to say a word. You know how shy I am.'

'So don't speak, Nana. Just sing! I only asked him to listen. Once he hears you sing, he'll be a changed man. You'll see.'

Papa was right. The austere, busy man who greeted me was a different person after listening to me. He not only became talkative: he suggested on the spot that we prolong the audition with a first lesson.

My new teacher was very different from my old one. Frau Kempers had realized that singing was, for me, a matter of survival and she devoted herself to me with a selflessness that I appreciated more and more the longer I observed her successor. Giorgios Djouaneas was exclusive and controlling; very soon, I became his possession. Since he

56

felt that I was making progress, he began to envisage a future as a soloist for me, concurring with my parents in that regard. I often sensed that he wanted it more than I did, as though it were his own future at stake.

But Mr Djouaneas was less austere and more open to life than the subdued and circumspect Frau Kempers. In particular, he sang in a choir that performed musical programs on the radio. One day, he invited me to go to one of his broadcasting sessions. That was my entry into the legendary station that I had been listening to for the last ten years. Originally, it featured primarily Greek folk music and pop, but now it was gradually overtaking Radio Tangiers and the BBC as a source of rock and roll, jazz, and the music of European performers. That day, I not only attended a live broadcast of my new teacher singing with his choir: I took a decisive step toward my future destiny. A step that would rapidly lead to conflict and then to an open break with this same Mr Djouaneas.

For months, my ear had been glued to the radio as the hosts of various music shows invited listeners to be a contestant in their musical quizzes, which were broadcast live. I longed to participate, especially since I could answer any question they might ask. For instance, they might play a song, and you had to name the artist; or else they gave you a title, and you yourself had to sing the song. Yes, I was keen to take part, but if Mr Djouaneas had not invited me to the station, I would probably never have pursued it.

Now that I was familiar with the station, I screwed up the nerve to return there several times. I was by myself and intoxicated by the feeling that little Nana, always so well-behaved and sensible, was deviating from the straight path. My musical knowledge got me noticed by the people who ran the station. No doubt they were also impressed by the way I sang because, after one of these broadcasts, a gentleman took me politely to one side. The national radio orchestra, he said, was looking for soloists and regularly held auditions for that purpose.

'You should enter your name,' he said.

I was so confused and shaken that I could not reply. For a minute or two, the man must have taken me for an idiot.

'You should turn up for these auditions,' he repeated. 'I think you have a good chance of being selected. Do you understand? Do you know what an audition is?'

This time I nodded, but I was itching to leave.

'Do you want to know the date of the next one?'

'Uh, I guess so,' I managed to murmur, with fear rising in my stomach as though I were committing an unforgivable sin and could already hear the priest thundering: 'Get you gone, and may God curse you!'

I finally got out of there and raced home. Only when I was back in my bedroom, my face scarlet, my heart pounding, did I find that I still held the crumpled piece of paper on which he had scrawled the day and hour of the next audition. But I could not see myself as the winner . . .

Did I even tell my parents about this audition? No, it seems to me that I rehearsed in secret. I was then in my final year at the gymnasium, preparing for my baccalaureate, which in Greece is awarded on the basis of final written and oral exams at the end of the year. I was worried that my parents would not be happy to learn about this distraction from my academic studies. I said nothing to Mr Djouaneas either, but for different reasons. The very idea that I was flying with my own wings, or rather *trying to fly*, would make him furious. And if he did find out, he would discover that I wasn't singing classical arias but Greek folk tunes or contemporary numbers from the variety stage – songs that come to us now from all over the world – and I had a feeling that Mr Djouaneas would not approve.

I was trembling from head to toe when I introduced myself to the panel. And I could tell right away that the audition wasn't going to go well. I knew far more foreign songs than Greek ones, whereas they wanted to hear me perform numbers from the national repertoire. Finally, we settled on a handful of titles, and I launched into them. But my voice, so full when I sang for my father in our little kitchen, now sounded weak, hesitant, pitiful. And the more anxious I became, the more my voice let me down.

Even before hearing the result, I knew I had blown this first professional opportunity. I trudged home, kicking myself all the way.

*

At least I passed my baccalaureate! It was out of the question for me to pursue my studies any further, and the immediate problem I faced was how to make a living. In this same year – 1954 – Jenny got married. This brought our parents a bit of financial relief, as they only had me to support now. Still, they were eager for me to shoulder some of the household expenses.

Through my brother-in-law, I learned that the United States embassy was looking for secretaries of Greek origin. None of us knew what was expected of a secretary, but I spoke English (a source of great pride to my parents), which in their opinion easily qualified me for an interview.

The lady I met was very kind. We had a brief conversation in English, and when I realized that she was screening me, I was sure I had the job.

'Very good,' she said. 'Now I'll introduce you to the person who will be supervising your work.'

This was another woman, and again we chatted a while. I felt I was handling things well. She was relaxed and smiling. Finally, she said:

'Now let's see what you can do.'

Then she took me into another room and sat me down at a typewriter.

'Insert a sheet of paper and I'll dictate a short letter to you.'

Good Lord above, I had never laid hands on such a device!

'I'm afraid I can't . . . '

'You can't insert the paper?'

'No, I can't do anything. I don't know how a typewriter works . . . '

I realized at once how ridiculous I was. What was the use of a secretary who couldn't type?

The lady too seemed astonished:

'You can't type?'

'No, I'm so sorry.'

'Then we can't hire you. It's out of the question . . . '

I felt crushed by shame as I got up. Why hadn't I checked in advance to find out what they needed? Why had I wasted the time of these nice women?

'Forgive me, forgive me,' I kept murmuring.

I fled the embassy in a sweat, my face as red as though I had been caught ransacking the office drawers.

In the following days, I bought two instruction books in order to teach myself typing and shorthand. I was so angry with myself! I secretly hoped that learning those skills would give me a second chance; that is, an opportunity to redeem myself in the eyes of those two women at the Embassy who had been so well disposed toward me.

Would I have become a singer if the embassy had hired me as a secretary? Life at twenty is still so vulnerable, so uncertain. A girl could easily take the first path that opens and commit herself to a direction that has nothing to do with her deepest aspirations. In my case, my lack of qualifications, so devastating to me after that job interview, proved to be providential.

As it turned out, it was the radio that offered me a second chance. A few weeks after the fiasco at the embassy, I was asked to another audition with the national radio orchestra, conducted by various popular composers. For a young woman in need, the reward if selected was substantial: to sing once a month on a live broadcast in return for a small fee. This time, I did notify my parents, and they were solidly behind me.

Necessity may have helped me overcome my stage-fright that afternoon. In any case, I sang almost as well as when I was alone with Papa. However, I wasn't the only candidate, and they told me they would give me an answer in a few days.

At that time, we still lived in Neos Kosmos, in our little two-bedroom, flood-prone apartment. Since we had no telephone, we used the phone in the neighborhood grocery, as did most of our neighbors. We also gave the grocery's phone number to people who needed to call us. That was the number I gave to the panel members at the radio station – never imagining such a call would have on the neighborhood.

The grocer sent over his youngest son with the message: a gentleman from the radio had called, and I was scheduled to take part in the broadcast! Thank you, Lord, oh thank you! Mama burst into tears. I just stood there stunned, which was not the reaction that the little messenger expected. His glee melted away like snow in the sunshine.

'Aren't you happy?' the boy asked. 'My Papa said—'

'Oh yes, I certainly am happy! Thank you. And please thank your father.'

'He told me to run as fast as I could. He said it was wonderful news and you would be so happy.'

'It *is* wonderful news!'

For the grocer – and before long the whole neighborhood – it was the event of the week. The little Mouskouri girl was to sing on the radio! That very evening I heard people talking about it. People hailed me and pointed me out in the street, children ran after me, and I was a bit uncertain of what I should say. No, I didn't know the gentleman from the radio, I didn't know when the broadcast would be aired, I didn't know if my picture would be in the papers or if the newspapers would even mention me.

But the news spread, finally reaching the ears of our landlord, who informed us the following week that he was raising our rent. He no longer had to be compassionate, he wrote in his notification letter, since I was now 'a celebrity who sings on the radio ...'

My paycheck was tiny, but the first broadcast went off remarkably well. I sang a few old Greek songs, followed by Ella Fitzgerald. And then – since the Greek public was just discovering another world – I was asked to sing jazz and rock. The audience shouted song titles at me, and since I knew them I sang them all. Suddenly, I was impervious to stage-fright, carried away by feeling, just like the night of the recital at the Conservatory, when my voice was a conduit for the emotions of the young man and the priest ...

Apparently I impressed some people because after the show the pianist who had accompanied me, Kostas Yanidis, came over to talk. Would I be interested in performing with his band when they had a booking? Or appearing with them on other radio programs? He said that, like me, they could play folk, popular music, and also the jazz standards from America.

'Why not? Yes, I'd like to ... but I'm not sure ...' I was still caught up in the intoxication of this first broadcast, overwhelmed by emotion, unable to think ahead, unable to set my feet back on the ground so quickly ...

Whether it was through this band, or simply by word of mouth, I seem to remember receiving offers for other radio shows the very next day. I rehearsed dutifully, presented myself at the station in my only going-out dress, a dark blue taffeta, and wearing my ever-present glasses. Each time, the same small miracle occurred: emotion swept me away, and during the broadcast I watched a transformation come over the faces of the few people in the studio audience. I was reminded of the moviegoers at my father's little cinema whose faces were transformed as they watched the show. Could my voice possess the mysterious power to lift people out of themselves, to open the secret doors of the imagination?

I hadn't seen it coming, but little by little a kind of whirlwind was brewing around me. At first, musicians would seek me out after a broadcast and ask if I knew such-and-such jazz club, where they performed in the evenings. No, I would reply, I don't go out, I don't know any jazz clubs or any other kind of club, just a few tavernas thanks to my brother-in-law. They gave me a strange look, as if wondering: where did she learn to sing like that if she doesn't go to clubs? I never mentioned Radio Tangiers or Frau Kempers or my blind English teacher. But they would not be put off. They handed me a note with their names and the club's address and made me promise to drop by some night. I was twenty years old, but Mama didn't allow me to go out alone, so I had to sneak out in order to go listen to them. Once I got there, I had no money and dared not sit down, but they would see me and insist that I join them. Stage-fright made me short of breath, made my legs wobbly, made me feel like I was about to faint. But from the very first note, I was another person. Transported by emotion to a different place. When I walked on stage, the spectators kept talking among themselves. But when I started singing, they went quiet, and I could tell by the expression on their faces that they felt what I felt.

It wasn't always jazz; it might be a club featuring Greek folk songs or popular contemporary ballads in a variety of different languages. In either case, I usually ended up singing one or two songs that brought me prolonged applause. Sometimes the club owner, as if to apologize for having showcased a relative unknown, reminded the audience that I regularly sang on this or that radio program.

It wasn't long before the club owners themselves asked if I would sing on their stages on a routine basis. Yes! Of course I would! I was beginning to realize that I could earn my living this way. Enough, at least, to help out my parents and pay for my lessons at the Conservatory with Mr Djouaneas.

Little by little, my life – so empty a few weeks earlier when I thought of becoming a secretary – was filling up. Several afternoons per week I spent at the radio, and every night I sang in clubs and tavernas. I had no particular preference for one venue over another. I would drop in at one place, sing for a half-hour in return for a small fee, and then speed off to another destination. Almost every night I spotted familiar faces, and I soon realized that the world of nightclub musicians is quite small. After you finish your own set, you go somewhere else to listen to others. You see what they do, you discuss this or that artist, and you offer tips and borrow ideas. After just two or three months I knew virtually all of them, and I'm fairly certain that they had all checked me out, too.

It may have been Mimis Plessas in person, or one of his musicians, who suggested that I drop by the Rex cinema to take part in his Sunday morning jam sessions. At that time, Mimis was the foremost pianist in Greece, and he sponsored these gatherings at the Rex. All the young performers and groups seeking to make a name for themselves congregated there. In my eyes, Mimis was a superstar, but whenever I ran into him at the radio station he had a few words of praise or encouragement for me. In any case, encouraging enough that one day I found the nerve to cross the threshold of the Rex. The atmosphere was extraordinary! All categories and all styles of music were welcome. Soon I was up on the stage myself, still in my taffeta dress, singing rock and roll. They cheered me and asked me back for the following Sunday. At my second appearance, I sang Greek songs.

It was during one of those mad mornings at the Rex that I first encountered the Trio Canzone, a group made up of three young guys originally from Thessaloniki. This group had a most unusual repertoire of Mexican and Spanish songs laced with typically Greek sounds. I was a little tense as I listened to them because I was to go on right after them. This time I would sing jazz and perhaps, just to be provocative, two Schubert *Lieder*. Why not? After all, the three boys had just sung us some Mexican folk songs.

I quietly returned to my seat upon leaving the stage, but then something bizarre happened. During a break between performers, as people were getting up to stretch their legs, one of the boys from Trio Canzone came up to me and touched my throat with his finger. With a delightful smile, he said:

'I've just been listening to you, Miss, and I think there's gold in there.'

'What?'

Despite myself, I jumped.

'I'm sorry, I didn't mean to scare you,' he went on. 'I was very impressed by your voice.'

'Oh, thank you. Thank you so much!'

He walked away, no doubt shaking his head. As for me, I wished I could just disappear. The more I forgot about the real world when I was onstage, the more inept I felt once I returned to earth.

It would take me several months to learn that this boy's name was George Petsilas. Over the next few years he entered my life little by little, until one day he became my husband . . .

Mama had kept Jenny on a very short leash. How did she feel about my spending half the night in the clubs? I usually found her, tired and worried, waiting just inside the door when I came home. But there was no man in my life, not yet, and as I recall, no particular desire to find one. Thinking back to my early days as a budding pop singer, all I remember is the intoxication of singing and the gratitude I felt toward my listeners. As I took my final bows, I looked out into the audience and saw that they were deeply moved. For that, I was thankful.

Perhaps Mama sensed that singing was the only thing that interested me, and therefore I was in little danger of frequenting the dens of iniquity she had declared out of bounds for Jenny. Of course it didn't hurt that I came back with money. I handed my earnings over to her without keeping any for myself, and we needed money so badly!

But Mr Djouaneas couldn't care less about these considerations. He saw me make my debut at the radio: little did he know that it was thanks to him! That was bad enough. Then he found out that I worked at tavernas and clubs, performing the kind of music he didn't respect. He said nothing at first, but his anger built up over time.

'All that jazz singing is ruining your voice. Besides that, you don't get enough sleep, and your performance suffers for it.'

'I really need to work.'

'Do you want to be an opera singer or not? It's up to you.'

As time went on, his tone hardened. Finally, he delivered an ultimatum:

'We can't go on like this, Nana. If you want to stay at the Conservatory you'll have to give up the night clubs. The radio and the Rex, fine, but no more clubs!'

'I can't. I wouldn't even have enough to pay for your lessons.'

'Don't bring that up again. I'm tired of arguing about it. You have one week to make up your mind.'

In a panic, I ran to ask another Conservatory teacher if she would take me on. She left me no hope, and for a whole week I went through mental torture.

My final meeting with Mr Djouaneas was stormy and dramatic. A half-hour later I left the Conservatory for good, expelled with no hope of appeal.

Was this the end of my career as a lyric soprano? I told myself it wasn't, but knowing how disappointed they would be, I couldn't muster the strength to tell my parents the news. They dreamed of hearing me perform Verdi or Puccini. They had little regard for performers who played in tavernas ('Those singers who display their legs,' as Mama would say with a touch of scorn). Now, nightclubs were all I had left.

But fate sent me a sign that same week. As I searched for the right words to tell my parents the bad tidings, a well-known Athens nightclub, the Mocabo Lido, offered me a contract. As their band's lead singer, I was guaranteed a modest but regular paycheck. It was the first such offer I had ever received.

Telling myself that this good news would partly allay my parents' disappointment, I decided at last to bring them up to date. Papa simply collapsed. He suspected that none of this would have happened if we had had enough money to pay the Conservatory tuition without forcing me to get a job. As always when he felt guilty, he took refuge in anger. But his rages no longer frightened me. I knew he was yelling at me because he was angry with himself and didn't know how to handle it, and in response, I felt like taking him in my arms. Which is exactly what

I did fifteen years later when he came to hear me sing at the Théâtre des Champs-Élysées in Paris, and I found him sobbing in the wings. I might have been thrown out of the Conservatory, but now I was being honored at the Champs Élysées, the renowned theater for live classical music and jazz. It seemed to Papa that at last I was getting what I deserved. His sin was wiped out, forgiven. He could finally weep.

My mother's heartache when I had to leave the Conservatory was of a different nature. She was deeply disappointed, of course, but her chief concern was that I might be led astray in the nightclub world. However, the prospect of a second income for our family gave her some hope, especially since she was going to hide the money. Papa would not be able to lose it at the card table.

5

I'm Twenty-three and I'm a Disaster...

*A*h, Miss Mouskouri, I was afraid I'd never reach you. This phone is a nightmare. Are you available for a concert on the night of July Fourth?'

'A concert? On July the Fourth? But that's tomorrow, isn't it?'

'Yes, I'm so sorry about the lack of notice. Our singer just cancelled, and you would take her place. I've been told that you sing perfectly in English.'

'I don't know who you are.'

'Sorry, I forgot to introduce myself. My name is Takis Kambas. I'm the coordinator of the concert. God, this is such a disaster . . . '

'Yes, I can sing in English.'

'Oh, what a relief! So, are you free tomorrow evening?'

'Not really. I would have to find someone to replace me. But Mr Kambas, you haven't told me anything about this concert.'

'My apologies. I'm so upset I'm forgetting everything. Here's the deal: you'll be singing on an American aircraft carrier for four thousand sailors and a group of distinguished guests. You're used to such things, aren't you? I don't know you personally, but I've heard about you, and . . .'

'I've never sung for four thousand people.'

'Don't tell me you're backing out! I have absolutely no one else to turn to!'

'No, no, don't worry, I'll be there.'

'You must be on board by mid afternoon. The ship's name is the

Forrestal. You can't miss her; she dwarfs everything else in the bay ...
Go to the port in Piraeus. A launch will pick you up at the US Navy
wharf to take you out to the carrier. I'll be on board myself to greet you.
You'll have just two hours to rehearse with the band before the concert
begins.'

'What do you want me to sing?'

'They say you do wonderful imitations of Ella Fitzgerald, Billie
Holiday, Judy Garland ...'

'Oh yes, I adore them.'

'You've saved me from a nightmare. I can't thank you enough ... '

'I promise I'll do my best.'

'You're the greatest! Okay then, I'm counting on you for tomorrow
afternoon, around four ... '

The next day, 4 July 1957, was of course the US national holiday.
Americans celebrate Independence Day wherever they find themselves – in this case aboard USS *Forrestal*, flagship of the Sixth Fleet,
currently in port of call at Piraeus.

I felt so dizzy I had to sit down as soon as I hung up the phone. Tomorrow I would be singing in front of four thousand pairs of eyes ! I was
twenty-two and I had never performed anywhere but in nightclubs in
front of no more than one hundred spectators. My excitement at singing
for such a huge crowd was at odds with the panic rising within me. The
very thought of it was terrifying! On the other hand: what luck! If I could
come through this ordeal, I thought, my life would be changed forever. If
four thousand people liked me and clapped for me, it would be as though
the entire world were applauding me. Furthermore, the fact that my name
came up when someone like Takis Kambas was looking for a jazz singer
was an indication that I was now fairly well known among Athens' young
artists. I wonder who suggested me to him. While making the rounds of
the clubs at night, I crossed paths with many musicians – it could have
been any one of them. Or even the great Mimis Plessas ...

I had to move fast. First, I had to tell the Mocabo Lido I would be
absent tomorrow night. They would ask why, and I'm a bad liar. Never
mind, I would tell them the truth, and if they were unhappy about it, too
bad. It was the owner himself who picked up the phone.

'I've been invited to sing on the American carrier.'

'Tomorrow? For Independence Day?'

'That's right.'

'That's wonderful, Nana! We'll tell our customers the Americans picked you, and once word gets around, they'll be packing the club every night!'

'Oh, good, I'm so relieved. I was afraid you would be angry.'

'Angry to hear news like this? Not on your life, sweetheart. The Mocabo's lead singer on the *Forrestal*? The best publicity in the world!'

Good, now to decide what to sing. And which dress to wear – maybe the black, which made me look slimmer ... Then round to the shoe-maker's to pick up my shoes, the ones that brought me good luck ... ask Mama to do my hair.

I didn't sleep much that night, but I wasn't tired next day when I got off the train at Piraeus. Under a burning July sun, I walked along the quay looking for the American wharf. I found three sailors waiting for me, and we immediately sped off by motorboat out to the carrier. Access to the deck was via a ladder that looked minuscule welded onto the ship's massive wall of steel.

I will never forget the look on Takis Kambas' face when he first set eyes on me. Apparently he was expecting a long-legged Hollywood blonde with a wasp waist; instead, fate sent him a rather plump brunette wearing big black-framed glasses.

'What a disaster!' he mumbled, without even bothering to hide his disappointment.

He didn't utter a word of welcome. The more he examined me, the more dejected he looked. Consequently, I did not feel obliged to reassure him. I stood there in stony silence, watching him mop his cheeks and forehead.

'What a disaster!' he said again. 'Why did she have to get sick today of all days?'

His referring to the other singer provoked me into speaking up:

'I'm not a bad singer, you know. There's no reason for you to work yourself up into a state.'

'I know, I know, everyone says you sing well. But that's not enough. Would you at least take off your glasses?'

'Don't worry about my glasses. Once I start singing, people forget all about them.'

'Oh Lord, I don't know how we're going to get through this . . . '

'Well, Mr Kampas, I'd like to start rehearsing now. Will you please take me to the band?'

'Yes, yes, of course. But this is really a tough break. Could things get any worse?'

He led the way, and he never stopped mopping his face as we negotiated the passageways. He was a short, plump man, awfully high-strung, I thought, for someone whose job was organizing concerts.

'The ambassador and his wife will be here, as well as the admiral,' he moaned from the depths of his despair.

Fortunately, the musicians were more welcoming, and by the time we got through the first song, there was a marked increase in their friendliness and interest in me. But Mr Takis Kambas didn't wait to hear the first notes. I saw him hurrying away, still mopping his forehead with his moist handkerchief.

The stage was set up on the bridge. On the deck below, dignitaries would occupy the first rows, seated in red-velvet chairs. The four thousand sailors would be packed into a huge square marked off by a rope and a string of lights that illuminated the gathering dusk.

I was scheduled to perform last, after a whole range of attractions, in particular the Athens Ballet and its beautiful girls.

The carrier's band opened the proceedings, followed by a fine, deep male voice reading out the program. When I heard my name I thought my heart would stop. Those of us waiting to go on were also on the bridge, but backstage. Night was falling, and the Bay of Piraeus formed a luminous backdrop, as though the whole city had eyes only for us aboard this gigantic aircraft carrier whose searchlights ascended toward the stars.

The closer the time came for my act, the closer Mr Kambas came to a nervous breakdown. He looked over at me with the eyes of a drowning man, unable to imagine my entrance as anything but a disaster. At one point, I offered to try to do without my glasses, but he didn't seem to think it would make any difference. Although I was the one whose life was on the line, it was Mr Kambas who trembled as though his last hour was at hand. Eventually, I felt sorry for him, which helped me forget my own stage-fright.

'Mr Kambas, it's obvious that I'm a disappointment to you, but try to have a little faith.'

'Have you seen Marilyn Monroe? That's the kind of woman Americans go for ...'

'Well yes, but they also like Ella Fitzgerald, and she's neither blonde nor slim, is she?'

For a moment, his face brightened. Then he collapsed once again into anguished hand-wringing. I turned away from him, determined to pull myself together and not to allow his disbelief and doubts to affect my performance.

At last my turn came. I remember closing my eyes as I made my entrance. I could hear the crowd breathe, and the sight of them would have made me stumble. Somehow I made it to the microphone and, without waiting for the music, launched a cappella into the first words of 'Pete Kelly's Blues', Ella Fitzgerald's wonderful song: 'There are sad things, there are bad things, the blues ...'

Right then and there – even before the orchestra could play a note – there was deafening applause! I opened my eyes in time to see hundreds of men fling their sailor hats into the sky. Their pleasure was a gift, thrilling to receive. Then the orchestra chimed in, and my stage-fright evaporated. I was alone with the music, transported far away from the ugliness in the world, as if only my soul were singing.

At the last notes of 'Pete Kelly's Blues', the sailors rose to their feet, and now it was not just applause but a roar. Next I sang 'Lullaby of Birdland', and they snapped their fingers in time with the music. All these men were so enthusiastic and rapt that they reminded me of the throngs of faithful on Easter Sunday. When I glanced at the dignitaries sitting at the foot of the stage, I caught a look of delighted amazement on their faces.

I had given the orchestra a list of my entire repertoire; of course, it was understood that I would be singing only a small part of it, plus a bit more if there were calls for an encore. It was up to Mr Takis Kambas to decide how long my act would last. After four songs, I took a break. Meeting him backstage, I no longer recognized the man. His handkerchief was nowhere in sight. He was beaming and couldn't have been more excited if Marilyn Monroe herself had appeared.

'You were phenomenal!' he yelled in my ear as four thousand men stamped in rhythm on the deck. 'Go back out there and sing anything you want. Just keep it up!'

I was on stage for more than an hour, and I never sang better in my life. The songs were by artists who had accompanied me since adolescence: Billie Holiday, Nat King Cole, Judy Garland, Mahalia Jackson, and of course the incomparable Ella Fitzgerald.

When the final curtain fell, I too was no longer the same. I felt that I had discovered my true inner self and was able to offer it up to the audience, to make it known and loved. When I climbed aboard, I didn't like myself very much; now here I was loving myself through the eyes of others. And this miracle I owed to my voice. It had drawn these men to my soul. My voice made them forget my less-than-perfect figure and my sad face, which the glasses did nothing to improve.

The show over, I wanted to disappear the same way I arrived. But the admiral wanted to congratulate me. So did the ambassador and the rest of the illustrious guests, who were all smiling at me, engaging me in conversation, kissing my hand. It was so overwhelming that I was at a loss for words. I simply staggered off on Mr Takis Kambas' arm like a young woman who has had too much to drink.

For the next few days, Greek Radio re-broadcast excerpts from that concert, including several of the songs I had sung. I was unaware that we had been recorded, and only learned of it later from other people. They talked of nothing else at the Mocabo Lido, and as the owner had hoped, my budding prominence attracted new customers. Our neighbors also viewed me with new eyes. One day I was at the corner grocery talking with the owner, whom I'd known since I was twelve. When he mentioned hearing me on the radio, other shoppers overheard, and a small crowd gathered. They were mostly housewives, some of whom had snubbed me in the past. Now these same women seemed awestruck.

But I was much too shy to say anything at all. Stammering a few barely audible words, I fled the grocery.

My parents were secretly ashamed that I worked in a nightclub, and they never dreamed that my appearance on the *Forrestal* would have such an impact. Suddenly, overnight, they were as proud as could be. I wasn't an opera singer, but for the first time the radio described me as 'a young Greek singer' whose talent had aroused 'the Americans' enthusiasm and curiosity.'

And not just the Americans, it turned out. A few weeks later a small music publisher, Odeon, approached me with an offer to make my first record. They knew of me and had heard me sing, 'Fascination' (an American hit) on the radio. Their idea was to record that same song in English on one side and Greek on the other. Why not? I knew nothing about legal matters, so without even reading it I signed a contract with Odeon. The record was released shortly after we recorded it; there was no photo of me on the cover, just my name and the song title. I would never receive a penny for that recording, which came and went unnoticed. But years later, when I wished to make another record for another company, Odeon stirred up all kinds of trouble, claiming that they had an exclusive contract with me. Unfortunately, that experience taught me nothing, and when the time came to sign the next contract, I again neglected to read a word of it.

Mama went over and over our accounts and finally concluded that we could afford to move. No doubt my increased earnings made it feasible. In any case, we left that ghastly apartment in Neos Kosmos for the more residential district of Ilianou. My parents picked out a little two-room apartment there, on the ground floor of a four-storey building. In one respect, the new place was the same as the old one: I had no bedroom of my own and slept on a foldaway bed in the living room. The great innovation was that at last we had a bathroom!

When I saw that bathroom with its lavatory bowl and bathtub, I felt we were getting a taste of the opulence I associated with the high society of Athens. I was twenty-three years old, and up until now I had bathed at the kitchen sink, in water we heated in our zinc laundry pail. My head was spinning at the prospect of luxuriating in steaming hot water in that spotless enamel tub. It was a claw-foot tub supported on four mighty lion paws, and I couldn't wait to stretch out in it!

Good fortune breeds more good fortune. Next, one of Athens' most exclusive clubs, the Astir, asked me to audition for them. The man who made contact was their orchestra leader and pianist, a man named Spartacus. He was a musician very highly regarded by the Athenian elite.

'You're the talk of the town,' he said to me. 'I would love for you to try out.'

'I'd be glad to!'

The Astir hired me, and soon I was singing every night, stationed a few steps away from Mr Spartacus' piano, accompanied by a real orchestra. I sometimes felt that this highly cultivated man, the darling of high society, looked askance at my chubby body and plain dresses, but as soon as I started to sing he forgot about my appearance. No doubt our affluent customers thought us an odd pair: Spartacus elegant as a prince, table-hopping at the intermission, with a smile for everyone; and me, my usual self, shy and awkward as soon as I left the stage.

One evening I recognized Maria Callas sitting at a table with her then-lover, Aristotle Onassis. Dear God, how could I sing in front of Callas? I had idolized her since my first days at the Conservatory. In my family, she was revered as the greatest of sopranos. Maria Callas! Mr Spartacus naturally went over to greet her, and as I watched them chatting I worried that I didn't have the nerve to perform in front of her. How I wished I had come onstage with my eyes closed! Then the orchestra struck the first chords, and I took refuge in the music. I forgot her; I forgot myself, becoming nothing but a disembodied voice.

After a short break, I was returning to the stage when the club's maître d'hôtel approached me with a slip of paper in his hand:

'Do you know this song? Madame Callas would like you to sing it for her, and says to tell you that she will be most grateful.'

He handed me the card. On it, the diva had written the title of an old Greek song my mother sang when we were little, 'I amygdalie' ('The Almond Tree'). I wasn't sure I remembered the words, but I quickly went over them in my mind. Then I raised my head, and the great prima donna smiled at me.

I blushed out of self-consciousness and nodded, 'Yes.'

In the following days, she came back several more times, and luckily I was able to remember the lyrics of all the old songs she requested.

One night I noticed that she was there by herself, and this time the little note she sent did not bear the title of a song. It merely said: 'Would you like to join me for a moment at the intermission?'

'Please sit down,' she said. 'I wanted to thank you for all those songs. They were my childhood lullabies. Yours too, I imagine.'

'Yes, my mother used to sing them to my sister and me.'

'I've heard good things about you. For instance, I've been told that you're very versatile: that you can do every kind of music there is. Where did you learn to sing?'

'I taught myself, at first. Then I attended the Conservatory for a while.'

'Really! So you wanted to sing opera?'

'That was my goal at one time, yes. But my teacher refused to allow me to earn my living by singing in nightclubs, and he expelled me.'

'I see.'

She sat silent, studying me with a serious expression. Then, with great warmth, she took my hand and spoke to me in the familiar 'thou' form, which in Greek is reserved for friends, family and intimates:

'You know, life may have given you a gift that day. There are so many of us who want to sing *Norma*, *Tosca*, and *Traviata*, but ours is a very cruel art, and in the end very few make it . . .'

She paused. Then she said:

'It's better to be a great popular entertainer than an unknown opera singer. The important thing is not what you do but *how well* you do it.'

I suppose I simply nodded, too intimidated to make any kind of reply. But long afterward, when I thought back on those two short sentences I realized how true they were. And how prophetic.

But apparently the passion I put into my singing was not enough for the Astir.

After a month or so at the club, Mr Spartacus sent for me. I arrived confident and smiling, because I felt I was appreciated. It made my fall all the harder.

'I have to let you go,' he began. 'I'm very sorry, but we're not taking in as much as we hoped. I'm going to make do with the young man who substitutes for you on your nights off.'

It was such a shock that my wits almost deserted me.

'But how can that be? The club is full every night, and I always get encores ... I don't get it.'

'You would understand if you were the one in charge of the books.'

'If it's only a matter of money, I'd be willing to take a pay cut. I've been so happy singing at the Astir.'

'No, I'm sorry. It's out of the question.'

I had a feeling that Mr Spartacus was hiding something from me, and I began to get angry.

'Listen, you may as well tell me the truth, because I'll find out sooner or later. I know I sing better than that young man, but you're keeping him and letting me go. That makes no sense. I don't believe it's the money. Be honest. Why are you firing me?'

'Please, Nana, just drop it.'

'Mr Spartacus, I want you to tell me the *real* reason. I will not leave until you do!'

I had no idea I was capable of such anger. But I didn't deserve to be fired, and now I was truly incensed. Mr Spartacus realized that I meant what I said: I had no intention of leaving that room until he told me everything. Certainly, he was taken aback that this shy, quiet girl, whom he thought of as docile, was standing up to him.

He began to pace up and down. 'I was trying to spare your feelings, Nana. But since you insist on the truth, I'll be blunt. And too bad for you if it's hard to take!' he exclaimed. 'The fact is, a number of the ladies have complained that you are not ... not attractive enough. I mean for the Astir, of course, where our clientele is ... very elegant, very sophisticated ... '

'What? They complained that I'm too ugly? This is outrageous!'

I hate screaming, but I do believe that at this point I raised my voice. I was shouting to keep from bursting into tears and running away.

'Yes, they have nothing against your voice. In fact, they think you sing rather well. But an entertainer needs more than a voice. They object to your figure, your clothes, your hair, your glasses ... Please don't make me go on ...'

How did I manage to get out of there? I don't know. I remember running along the seaside, choked with tears, to catch the bus home.

Papa and Mama were appalled by the news. By a curious coincidence, the dressmaker who made my clothes, a good friend of Jenny's, happened to be at our house that day. She began to cry, and I reassured her that it was I – and not her dresses – who wasn't pretty enough for the Astir. Racism, sexism, ageism, and now discrimination on the basis of aesthetics – Good Lord in Heaven, what next? Years later, when my wonderful guitar player Yussi Allies, a South African black, spoke to me of apartheid, my empathy was due in part to that episode at the Astir.

Several of the musicians in the Astir orchestra were as shocked as I was; they urged me to appeal to the club manager. My parents endorsed that idea, and Papa promised to come with me.

The manager received us. But Papa, who had talked of nothing else but our grievances all the way to the club, was scarcely inside the door when he was struck dumb. So I did the talking ... I told the manager it was unfair to fire a performer just because of her looks or her unfashionable clothes. If the ladies in question had come to me instead of complaining to Mr Spartacus, I would have made an effort to be more elegant. When someone like me is unsophisticated due to her upbringing, she should be helped rather than crushed. Right? I was a singer, everyone said I sang well, and it was not fair for me to lose my livelihood just because my appearance didn't appeal to certain people.

The club manager agreed, but declared that the matter was out of his hands. Mr Spartacus was solely responsible for the artistic side of the business, and this was his decision. All my fervent pleading was to no avail. Rejected and humiliated, we took our leave.

Afterwards, I learned that it was the wives of the Astir's board of directors – and in particular, this manager's spouse – who had insisted that Mr Spartacus fire me. I also heard that Spartacus, perhaps fearing for his own position, did not say a word in my defense. But two years later, after my triumph at the first Festival of Greek Song, Mr Spartacus offered to give me back my old job at the Astir, claiming that he was 'devastated' by what had happened. I turned him down flat.

The *Forrestal* concert and my stint at the Astir enhanced my reputation in the little circle of Athens musicians, and I easily found steady work in the city's tavernas and nightclubs. Among others, I crossed paths again with the Trio Canzone, a group I had always liked. George Petsilas, the man with the laughing eyes who told me during that matinee at the Rex that I had gold in my throat, always had a friendly word for me. At the radio station one day, I harmonized with George and his two friends, Kostas and Philippos, and we improvised a piece together. The studio audience applauded enthusiastically and called for encores, so we teamed up together for the rest of the program.

Would we have continued our collaboration if Mimis Plessas had not happened to be passing by and pricked up his ears? It seems unlikely, given the confusion in which we all worked at that time, each one grabbing whatever opportunity presented itself.

But Mimis Plessas was listening, and it was Mimis who first came up with that wild idea:

'Not bad, what you do together ... Why not form a quartet?'

Had it come from anybody else, we would have dismissed the suggestion as far-fetched. But coming from him – a well-known pianist and composer – it sounded like sound, helpful advice. After all, why not pool our talents, rather than every man for himself?

At this point in time, when my career as an artist was still in its infancy, Fate suddenly smiled upon me. A certain man entered my life. He was the man who would open the world's doors for me: Manos Hadjidakis.

6

A Composer Named
Manos Hadjidakis

*I*t was a radio musician who told me one day that Manos Hadjidakis was looking for me.

'He wants to meet you.'

'Manos Hadjidakis! Are you sure?'

'Yes. I told him I was bound to run into you.'

'Are you kidding?'

'No, really, it's true.'

'But why would he want to see me? He has all the singers he wants. I'm a nobody . . .'

'He told me he had heard you sing.'

'No way!'

'If you're free tomorrow, I'll take you to see him.'

'Really? But what does he want?'

'I think he wants someone for a song in a movie.'

When I told the Trio Canzone that evening that I might be working with Hadjidakis on a movie soundtrack, there was a clamor of protests. Hadjidakis represented commercial success and glamour. He appeared in magazines alongside movie stars like Katina Paxinou, Melina Mercouri and Alexis Minotis. He lunched with the prime minister, Constantine Karamanlis, maybe even with King Paul I . . . Hadjidakis was another world. He was rich and famous, which meant that he had 'sold out'. As for us, we might be poor, but we were true artists.

'Come on! You're not really going to see that guy?'

'Why not?'

'Because you're an artist, and he's a pillar of the bourgeoisie.'

'You don't know him any more than I do. Before he got rich, he was a musician, just like us.'

That *just like us* did not go over very well, and when we parted that night, it was clear that in their eyes I was preparing to betray them.

The radio musician took me, not to Hadjidakis' home, but to the studios of Finos Films, a major movie company. The musician didn't go in; he left me at the door.

Timidly, I asked for Mr Manos Hadjidakis.

'Do you have an appointment?'

'I believe he asked to see me. I'm a singer.'

'Oh, good. Right this way.'

The young woman pushed a door open and I found myself in a big smoke-filled room where several men were chatting.

'He's the one sitting at the piano,' she whispered to me before leaving the room.

Curiosity gave me the courage to take a few steps in his direction. He was a round-faced man with a cigarette in the corner of his mouth. He had swiveled his piano stool around so that his back was to the keyboard, and he seemed to be having an intense discussion with his companions.

Suddenly he noticed me and cut short his conversation.

'Ah, here she is! You're about to hear the most wonderful voice in all Athens.'

Right away, even before Hadjidakis finished his sentence, I recognized Mr Finos, the producer, among the other men. And he recognized me, too.

'That's your singer? But I know her very well: she's the night owl's daughter!'

With a burst of laughter, Mr Finos spread his arms wide in greeting.

I was mortified, unable to move. When I was little this man had held me on his lap. How could he speak of my father in such insulting terms? I knew very well that people called Papa 'the night owl' because he spent his nights gambling, but Mr Finos was also in a position to know that Papa was one of the city's top projectionists. Why hadn't he said 'I know her very well; she's the daughter of Costa the projectionist'? Everything would have been different: I would have glowed with pride. As it was, his words stopped me in my tracks. I had never felt so hurt, humiliated, demeaned.

Fortunately, Mr Finos attributed my paralysis to shyness, and after a few seconds I cooled down and recovered some of my composure.

'Come closer,' he said. 'Don't be bashful. Manos has talked of nothing else but you for the last three days.'

Manos stood up to shake my hand, then immediately sat back down at the piano.

'Listen to this,' he said, and he began playing a melody completely new to me.

'Do you think you could sing to that?' he asked when he had finished.

'Yes, I think so.'

'I don't have the words yet. Just sing *la-la-la* to give us an idea.'

'OK.'

'Are you ready? Let's go!'

I sang it once, twice, three times, while Manos Hadjidakis accompanied me on the piano. During several of the passages, I heard him softly humming along with me.

After the last note of my third rendering, he turned to me, his face beaming. It was like a signal: every man there began to applaud. Mr Finos hugged me. 'There!' said Manos, 'isn't she amazing?'

Then to me he said:

'Rehearsals begin tomorrow at my house. Are you available for this project?'

'Yes. But what is the song we're going to do?'

'I'm composing the score for a movie Finos is producing. I'd like you to sing this song in the film.'

'That sounds great.'

'See you tomorrow then? Early afternoon, right after lunch.'

It was Manos' mother who opened the door. A smiling, bustling little woman.

'Come in. He's expecting you.'

He was already at the piano. Even in the entrance hall, I could hear the notes soaring through the air, filling the whole apartment.

As before, Manos was wreathed in cigarette smoke. He abruptly stopped playing the piano as soon as he saw his mother and me in the doorway.

'Ah, there you are! Come on over here. Hurry! ... Mama, please excuse us; Nana and I need to get started. Don't forget to close the door behind you. Thanks, Mama.'

He handed me a sheet of paper covered with his handwriting.

'Here, read this; it's the first few lines of the lyrics.'

And then, without further ado, we got down to work. He was tense and feverish. It was obvious that he could have no peace until we produced a finished creation.

We created the song in a single whirlwind session, and it was a wild ride. We took the words, interwove them with the music, bent them, stretched them, wore them out. We polished them and tossed them around like a juggler throwing balls in the air. From time to time, we stumbled, went backwards, changed a rhyme here and there. Halfway through, Manos would tear out his hair, shouting 'No! This is all wrong!' Then he lit yet another cigarette, went back to the first verse and started all over again.

I had never before been present at the birth of a song. It was fascinating to witness the near-madness that took hold of Manos, consumed as he was by the creative process. And I was gratified from the start by the man's confidence in me. He trusted my instincts absolutely! Just yesterday, we had never met; today, he acted as though his life depended on me ... He seemed ready to smash his head against the wall if we didn't succeed. Was this what a true artist is like? Someone so focused on the object in his path that he cannot see past it to conceive of any future beyond the problem at hand? Observing Manos led me to speculate that when an artist is working, he forgets his fame and everything great and beautiful he has ever created – so much so that each new project finds him once again teetering like a tightrope walker above the abyss. I was in absolutely unknown territory. Nevertheless, it wasn't long before I too was ready to sacrifice everything in order for this work to see the light of day. For Manos and me, this little scrap of music was our salvation: it would shed its light upon us and give us grace.

Little by little, the song blossomed. At last, the moment arrived when I gave my voice free rein, and simultaneously, Manos played with a new fluidity. The song was perfect! We were like horses suddenly turned loose, galloping in the wind. We had no notion of what sustained us, whether it was the words or the music, since the two were now forever bonded.

That song was entitled 'Pisso apo tis triandafilies', 'Behind the Rose Bushes', and I would appear briefly on-screen as I sang it. In addition, on that same evening, after our afternoon of songwriting, Manos got the bright idea to include the song on a record we would make together.

Yes, the very same evening. And there's another reason I'll never forget that day. It was the occasion of my first meeting with the poet Nikos Gatsos. If Manos Hadjidakis opened the doors of the world for me, Nikos Gatsos opened the doors to my soul. He helped me to learn to know myself, and in the process to accept myself the way I am and correct my failings.

When Manos Hadjidakis asked me to go with him to the Café Floka that night, I was thrilled. In fact, I was so awestruck by his genius that I forgot I was supposed to be singing elsewhere.

'Come along,' he said, 'I want to introduce you to my friends.'

I nodded happily, eager to follow him anywhere, as though I were his puppy dog. His smile was back. Now that his burden was lifted, he was keen to return to the noisy tumult of the world.

The Floka was somewhat like the Café de Flore on Boulevard Saint-Germain in Paris: a meeting-place for well-known artists, writers, musicians and painters. I would never have dared set foot in it alone. In fact, when Manos first mentioned it I shrank back for a second. What would people think of me, a lowly cabaret singer, in that illustrious place? But then I thought how funny it would be to see the expression on Mama's face when she learned where I spent the evening.

Mr Hadjidakis was about fifteen years my senior, and I obviously had no idea who his friends were. Imagine my surprise when I recognized the aqualine features of the man who stood up as Manos and I went over to embrace him. On being introduced to the great man, I was briefly struck dumb. Nikos Gatsos was one of the most admired poets in Greece. He was also well-known abroad, as I later found out. He first caught the public's attention with a collection of poems entitled *Amorgos*. This book, initially published in the middle of the war, was rediscovered a few years later and now, in the late 1950s, it graced the windows of every bookstore in Athens. 'Conceived and written during the German occupation, in the nation's darkest hours,' said Jacques Lacarrière in his introduction to a French-Greek edition, '*Amorgos* was – and still is – a song of resistance, a rejection of destructive nationalistic tendencies, and at the same time a radiant hymn to the vitality of the language. It was – and still is – one of the most glorious springtimes Greek poetry has ever known.'[1]

What did Nikos Gatsos think of me that night? I remember that he watched me closely, as was his custom (I realized later that he preferred to get to know people in silence, by pure observation). The author of *Amorgos* had a refined, slightly aloof manner. Half-hidden behind a cloud of cigarette smoke, he studied me a while, then asked how I had become a singer and what kind of music inspired me. Dying inside from shyness, all I could do was stammer incoherently. But Manos Hadjidakis finished all my sentences for me; then he went on to rave about me. His friend listened attentively, occasionally nodding solemnly.

What was the great poet's reaction when Manos Hadjidakis, carried away by his enthusiasm, suddenly threw out the idea of making an album with me as the singer? With hindsight, I think the poet only liked his friend the more for his mad impulse. For my part, I was in a daze. And I worried that Gatsos would judge me (something he never did with anyone).

Fine. Now what were we going to include on this album besides 'Behind the Rose Bushes'? I don't recall exactly when Manos Hadjidakis suggested 'Paper Moon' ('Hartino to fegaraki'), whether it was that night or subsequently. In any case I did record 'Paper Moon'. That beautiful, poetic song was the beginning of my friendship with Nikos Gatsos – and of a rivalry with Melina Mercouri that poisoned our relations for several years, until Melina in turn became my friend.

*

---

[1] *Amorgos* by Nikos Gatsos, Desmos Editions, 2001.

'Paper Moon'! Its magnificent lyrics were by Nikos Gatsos, the music was by Manos Hadjidakis. The two men originally wrote the song for their mutual friend Melina Mercouri, who was scheduled to sing it on stage in a Greek version of Tennessee Williams' *A Streetcar Named Desire*. When Manos first suggested that I sing it, Melina Mercouri had not yet performed the song in public. (I believe the play was still in rehearsal.) Whatever the case, I was still too new to the game to guess that she might take it badly. I therefore naively agreed to record the song.

Looking back on it today, I think this episode perfectly illustrates how wrapped up Manos was in his new protégée, the little unknown singer I was back then. How could he ask me to record a song written specifically for someone else? It was an affront to Melina Mercouri, who was already a star. Manos appeared oblivious to his own lack of tact. But Nikos Gatsos was well aware of this breach of good manners, which may explain his initial lack of enthusiasm for my interpretation of the song. He was in the studio when I recorded 'Paper Moon', and I could see that he was irritated – unlike Manos, who seemed to be floating on a little cloud. During a break, Nikos finally told us what was on his mind:

'Your interpretation is all wrong,' he told me.

Before I could answer, Manos broke in:

'You couldn't be more mistaken, Nikos. Nana's interpretation is right on the mark.'

'You think so? I listened carefully, you know, and the words don't have the same power the way she sings them . . . '

I understood from this exchange that they were comparing the ways Melina and I sang 'Paper Moon'. Melina was an actress, a renowned performer, and when I heard her sing it later I knew immediately what Nikos meant. On Melina's lips, the words possessed a dramatic force that my interpretation lacked. Nikos missed that dramatic quality, whereas Manos preferred the stark simplicity of my version.

It took almost a year before Nikos Gatsos revised his judgment and gradually leaned in my favor. He finally admitted it to me one evening, an unforgettable evening because it marked the beginning of a friendship that would last until his death thirty years later, in 1992.

That evening I was singing at a taverna called the Dzaki. Gatsos was often there with his friend, an English poet who lived in Athens. I was in the habit of sitting at their table for a moment during intermissions. By now, 'Paper Moon' was part of my repertoire, and I sang it nearly every night, always with the same feeling. Nikos Gatsos no longer talked about my interpretation: it was a silent sore point between us – until that particular night when I came over to the two friends' table right after singing 'Paper Moon'.

'I've been thinking,' Nikos suddenly said. 'I've come here many times to hear you sing. And now I know that you and Manos were right: the way you sing this 'little moon' is exactly what's called for. The singer should take a back seat and let the music and words find their way to our souls. I can't understand why it took me so long to realize it.'

Nikos briefly took my hand as though asking forgiveness. I was so moved that I wasn't even able to enunciate clearly the only two words that sprang to my lips. In a strangled voice, I whispered: 'Thank you!'

'In a nightclub on the beach near Athens she sang the American hits of the day to the accompaniment of a small band,' he wrote shortly before his death as he recalled our first shared memories. 'But her voice and the endearing warmth of her expression evoked in me the image of a small boat in the middle of the ocean, an image that stayed with me for many years.'

Meanwhile, my record came out. My second record if you count 'Fascination', the single I made for Odeon. That first effort had no success at all. This one, however, elicited interest and curiosity: how could it be otherwise with the names Hadjidakis and Gatsos attached to it? Manos was attempting to invent a style that mingled bouzouki (a rustic, ancestral instrument), Byzantine music, folk music, jazz riffs and classical bits. Regardless of what the Trio Canzone said about him, Manos was a remarkable artist, a composer of genius setting out to revolutionize Greek music. Nikos was an acclaimed poet, and it wasn't often that a poet lent his pen to a composer. My own name on the album jacket didn't count for much, as very few people knew me, but making that record meant a great deal to me. It reassured me that I had not studied at the Conservatory in vain because, just as he utilized a wide variety of instruments both ancient and modern, so Manos Hadjidakis made use of the whole range of my voice's potential. First I was a pop singer; a moment later an opera singer, and then, passing from one phrase to the next, I became a daughter of Ella Fitzgerald. Today, as I recall Manos' wholly original way of *inventing* music, I realize how happy he must have been to find me, a singer who had never wanted to settle on one style over another, a singer who loved it all – everything that could be sung.

From then on, I went to the Café Floka every night after work. Around midnight I would leave the stage at the Dzaki taverna and hurry to meet these two men. Both had profoundly affected me, one through his creative fury, the other by his approach to life. Nikos had a quiet way of observing the world without judging it – then he would suddenly withdraw from the world to immerse himself in gloomy romanticism and calm the ill wind by tossing up three or four magical words:

It takes but a single flower
Or stalk of wheat to bring good cheer, a sip of wine for memory
And a drop of water to transform the dust.[2]

They welcomed me like a younger sister, or like their muse if I may say so (or rather, if I *dare* say so, remembering how the ladies at the Astir had rejected me for not being sufficiently *attractive*.) I had not changed. I wore the same dresses, the same glasses, yet Nikos saw in me 'a small boat braving the high seas,' while Manos claimed I was the only one who knew how to sing what he wrote, the only one who could give a soul to his music.

One night I found them at the Floka with Jules Dassin, the American director of *The Naked City*, among other films. He had just finished making *The Law* with his great love Melina Mercouri (they would get married in 1966). Intimidated, I said nothing and just listened to their talk. I gathered that Dassin was in the middle of shooting yet another movie with Melina Mercouri, and they were getting impatient with Manos Hadjidakis who was writing the score. As usual, Manos was behind schedule. He said he had too many commitments, and it's true, but I think the main reason was that he liked to compose under pressure.

---

[2] *Amorgos*, ibid.

At last Jules Dassin went home to bed, and a little later Nikos suggested, as he often did, that we share a taxi. We hugged Manos and left. I liked riding with Nikos because he never told the taxi driver where we were going: he just said turn right, straight ahead, take the next left, and so forth ... And when the driver – who generally recognized him – asked 'Why not just tell me where you want to go, Mr Gatsos? That would be so much easier,' Nikos would retort: 'Because I want to take certain streets that I like, and you can't guess what they are.' The driver clearly thought Nikos was slightly crazy, which made us laugh.

It was close to four a.m. when I pushed open the door of our little apartment. I was just getting into bed when the phone (we had finally acquired one a few months earlier) roused the whole household. Mama leapt out of bed.

'It's for you Nana, Mr Hadjidakis.'

'Really?'

Yes, it was Manos' voice.

'Come over right away, I need you badly.'

'But what's up, Manos? I just left you! You're not sick, are you?'

'How soon can you be here?'

'I don't know, I was about to go to bed, I'm in my nightgown.'

'Well, get dressed again quick and take a taxi to my house. I'll be waiting.'

Mama was astonished to see me getting dressed.

'My goodness, Nana, you just got home, surely you're not leaving again?'

'Yes, I am! Manos is in a panic. Something's wrong, but I don't know what.'

'He's a grown man, he can look after himself. Do you realize what people will think if they see you leave at this hour?'

'Mama, I'm twenty-four, I don't have to explain myself to the neighbors.'

I left her wringing her hands and ran to the taxi stand.

Manos' mother opened the door, ready for anything at any hour of the day or night.

'Ah, Nana, come in quick. I don't know what's the matter with him.

'That child either weeps or laughs,' my parents would tell their friends, 'but she weeps a lot more than she laughs. The rest of the time she doesn't say a word, she just sits in her corner.' It's true that I didn't say much, but every time I watched a movie, the performers lifted me out of my private woes and launched me into the world of dream.

CHILDHOOD

My parents

Constantine Mouskouri was twenty-two when he met my
mother Aliki. Mama's good looks went straight to his
head, but women intimidated him, and he waited several
days before he dared invite her for a drink on a café terrace. That was all he ever disclosed to me about their
courtship. Without really knowing one another, they were
married a few months later in the spring of 1930.

Papa was offered the projectionist's job in
the little Cretan town of Canea (left),
where an open-air movie theatre was about
to begin operations. It was there that I was
conceived and born on October 13, 1934.

Their first child was born in 1932. She was
given the pretty name of her late grandmother, Constantine's mother Eugenia, but
we always called her Jenny.

One of nine children, Mama was born in Corfu. Jenny remembers the visit we paid in 1938 to her native village, where we met our uncles and aunts, but I was too young to retain any memory of the trip.

With Jenny and Mama at the monument to the Unknown Soldier in Athens, where we paid tribute to our fallen troops.

Jenny

My sister Jenny, talented and hard-working, was a mainstay of the household. Mama taught her to embroider, knit, and mend clothes.

In 1946, we moved to the ground floor of a somewhat dilapidated house in the Neos Kosmos neighborhood. The little two-room apartment is linked in my memory to a persistent nightmare: at every heavy rainfall, water seeped in through the walls and swirled over the floor, threatening to cover us over like a dark shroud. Here, Jenny and I pose with the landlady's three children.

My father wanted a boy, but I was a girl. And what a girl! Not the kind of girl that boys would stare at, the way I saw them stare at Jenny. And, with her glasses and superfluous pounds, not a very sexy girl either . . .

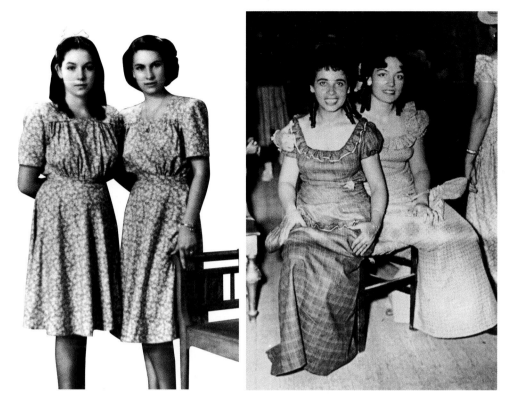

Jenny and I (left) entered the Conservatory together. I remember the professor who interviewed Mama, Jenny and me at the Conservatory, a German woman, smiling but reserved. After she heard us sing in turn, she delivered her verdict: 'The younger girl has a good voice, but it's a little hoarse. The elder girl has a magnificent voice and excellent lungs.' But I'll never forget my first 'recital' (above, with another student). That was when I realized that once onstage, I could master and forget my fears and give expression to the emotions I felt.

With our primary education finished, we entered high school (known in Greece as 'gymnasium'). At the end of every year we marched in a parade held in the Kalimarmaro National Stadium.

Singing was the miraculous key that opened my classmates' hearts to me – I had always been alone in primary school, but in gymnasium I made my first friends during music lessons.

Right: a reunion with relatives at Canea in Crete, where I was born. My godmother is standing at upper left. I was then twelve, and I'm in the middle of the front row, with Jenny on my right.

FIRST STEPS IN GREECE

I was twenty-two and had performed only in night clubs in front of a hundred or so spectators. Yet on the Fourth of July 1957, American Independence Day, I was invited to Piareus to sing aboard the carrier *Forrestal* before four thousand pairs of eyes!

George

Manos Hadjidakis

In the taverns and night clubs of Athens, I met the Trio Canzone and made friends with them. I would sometimes sing with George (center) and his two friends, Kostas (left) and Philippos (right). It was at this time, as I took my first baby steps as a performance artist, that I met the man who would open the world's doors for me: Manos Hadjidakis. I made a fleeting on-screen appearance singing our first song, 'Behind the Rose Bushes', which Manos wrote for a movie. In July 1960, Manos personally escorted me onstage (left) at the second Festival of Greek Song, where we presented two numbers.

We created the song in a single whirlwind session. We took the words, interwove them with the music, bent them, stretched them, wrung them out. We polished them and tossed them around like a juggler throwing balls in the air. From time to time, we stumbled, went backwards, changed a rhyme here and there. I had never before been present at the birth of a song, and it was fascinating to witness the near-madness that took hold of Manos. I was in absolutely unknown territory. But little by little, the song blossomed. I'm not particularly proud, however, of my first caricature as an artist (inset), or of its unflattering caption – 'the Roly-Polys'.

Nikos Gatsos

Nikos Gatsos, a great poet whose words have moved me my whole adult life, explained my soul to me. He taught me to know myself and to accept myself as I am. In 1943, in the middle of the Second World War, he wrote:

'How much I have loved you only I can know,
I who sometimes brushed you with the eyes of the stars
Locked in the moon's embrace and dancing with you
In summer fields amid crumbling houses of stone . . .'

The results of the first Athens Festival left me speechless: I won both first prizes! My photo appeared in every paper, and the press decided that I had become 'the voice of young Greek song'.

George decided to declare his love for me, bringing an abrupt change to our relationship, which had hitherto been one of simple friendship. We became secretly engaged at the Athens Festival. Later, George claimed he had been forced to threaten to break off the engagement unless I agreed to leave my parents' home and marry him. The ceremony took place on December 19 1960.

I've never seen him like this, I can't even talk to him . . . '

I heard him shouting from the music room:

'Don't keep her standing around, Mama, I need her! You can talk later. For now, bring us some coffee!'

I found him at the piano smoking a cigarette.

'Listen to this and then sing it. Okay?'

At that moment, I heard the first notes of a song that would race around the world a few months later and take its place as one of the most recognized melodies of the twentieth century. Entitled 'Ta pedia tou Pirea' ('The Children of Piraeus'), it was the theme song of the movie *Never on Sunday*.

'Now go ahead. Try to apply your voice to the notes. We'll see about the lyrics later.'

I sang, and at once saw Manos' features relax and gradually light up.

'Yes,' he said softly, 'Yes. That's it, that's exactly right . . . '

And then:

'Let's go over it again, do you mind? Would you like a cup of coffee? A glass of water?'

'No, Manos, I'm fine. What a lovely melody! When did it come to you?'

'A couple of hours ago, while I was walking back from the Floka. Okay, let's not waste any time. Are you ready?'

I sang it again and slowly put words on it. The song was perfect: catchy and heartrendingly beautiful. I think Manos' eyes were wet when I saw him grab the phone.

'They have to hear this,' he muttered as he dialed a number. 'They have to hear it *right now*!'

'Manos, I don't know who you're calling, but it's six in the morning!'

He ignored me, and I heard him say:

'Jules! Come over right away! Great news . . . I've got it!'

Half an hour later, Melina Mercouri and Jules Dassin joined us in the little music room. They had jumped straight out of bed and hadn't even bothered to dress. They were in bathrobes and slippers when they arrived, hair disheveled, eyelids heavy.

'Don't say anything; just listen!' said Manos. 'Are you ready, Nana?'

As I sang I looked only at Manos. Not until it was over did I turn towards our two visitors. Their faces took me back to the little theater of my childhood, because they no longer looked the same. Melina Mercouri's eyes were glowing; one might say she was entranced. Jules Dassin no longer looked sleepy; he was wide-awake, sitting up and taking notice. And his handsome face was lit up.

'It's magnificent!' he exclaimed. 'Magnificent!'

'You are the greatest, Manos my love! You're the greatest!' cried Melina, utterly overcome.

Manos beamed. As he got up, she threw her arms around him, buried her face in his chest, and tried to stifle her sobs.

Many years later, Manos revealed that in his youth he was passionately in love with Melina. Half-seriously, half in jest, he added: 'After her, I couldn't look at another woman. That's why I became interested in young men.'

The following day, when we were still in a state of euphoria, I don't know how Manos Hadjidakis had the nerve to propose that I be the one to sing 'Ta pedia tou Pirea' in Dassin's film. Melina couldn't believe her ears. She was the star of the movie, and it was understood from the start that she would be singing it . . .

'Manos, are you suggesting that I lip-sync over Nana's voice?'

'Yes, that's exactly what I'm saying.'

'Are you out of your mind? Have you forgotten that I'm a singer myself?'

'I know perfectly well that you sing, and you do it beautifully. But for this particular song I prefer Nana's voice.'

A few months earlier, I had stolen 'Paper Moon' from her (albeit unwittingly), and here we were again, proposing to repeat the crime with 'Ta pedia tou Pirea'. It was too much! But luckily things were swiftly smoothed over. Manos agreed that Melina would sing his song in the film, and Jules Dassin, who couldn't stand for anyone to upset Melina, was certainly grateful to him. This didn't prevent me from singing it myself, but only on vinyl.

Introduced at the Cannes Film Festival in 1960, *Never on Sunday* earned Melina Mercouri the best actress award, which she shared with Jeanne Moreau. At Hollywood's Academy Awards ceremony in 1961, 'Ta pedia tou Pirea' (under the title 'Never on Sunday') won the Oscar for best original song.

Everyone should know that I owe my first big success to Manos Hadjidakis. A few months before the premiere of *Never on Sunday*, I won first prize at the Festival of Greek Song with 'My Love is Somewhere', ('Kapou iparhi agapi mou') a song Manos Hadjidakis wrote specially for me.

7

'The Voice of Young Greek Song'

The idea for a Festival of Greek Song originated with the director of Greek National Radio, Mr Spiromilios. All the young artists in those heady postwar years knew him and valued him. He was always happy to see us in his studios, and he was interested in every genre of music. No doubt he dreamed of making us known outside Greece while attracting European singers to Greece (for instance the British rock groups just then starting to flourish).

He soon announced the date of the first Festival: 3 September 1959, to be held at the Athinea, a luxurious nightclub on the seashore.

Manos Hadjidakis, a musician greatly admired by Mr Spiromilios, was probably asked to take part in order to lend star-appeal to this first Festival. In any case, Manos dashed off this song for me, 'My Love is Somewhere', and we rehearsed it together. Manos knew very well that I could work with anyone, but he absolutely refused to let anyone else accompany me when I sang one of his works. Mimis Plessas also wanted to participate in the Festival, and he proposed that I sing a very beautiful song he wrote called 'Asteri asteraki'. Obviously, I was to sing this number with the Trio Canzone, since it was Mimis himself who suggested that we team up. Thus, I entered the Festival with two songs.

In the space of a few months, and without being fully aware of it, my life had become rigidly compartmentalized. On the one hand, I was the disciple of Manos and Nikos. On the other, I occasionally sang with the Trio Canzone, turning them into a quartet. I suppose it was the Trio's negative opinion of Manos that first brought about this division, and the clashing personalities of the two sides only reinforced it.

It was clear that my three friends from the Trio and my other jazz-musician friends would be out of place at the Floka, where I joined Manos and Nikos every evening after singing in various nightclubs. The Floka was frequented by famous artists, men and women whose pictures appeared in newspapers and magazines, whose names were household words, who led luxurious lifestyles. The Trio – above all George Petsilas (to whom I was already particularly close) – did not consider the Floka's clientele to be true artists but pillars of the establishment, spoiled by money, easy living, and their connections in high society, big business, and government.

For his part, Manos rarely mentioned the portion of my life spent with the Trio Canzone. When he did, it was to inform me that I was not allowed to record his songs as a member of any such group – his subtle way of letting me know that he didn't think much of my friends. In any case, he didn't know them. They, on the other hand, knew all about him. They seized every opportunity to disparage his pervasive presence, his egotism, his smugness. All I could say was, 'If you knew him you'd see that what you take for egotism is simply the high demands he makes of himself. All great artists protect and defend their work.'

But neither side knew the other. They were two worlds with their backs turned on one another, and if it weren't for me, there would have been no link between them. I linked them in spite of themselves, imparting a bit of one side's point of view to the other party and vice-versa.

Very often I spent the evening singing with George and his two fellow musicians, Philippos and Kostas, and then abruptly left them at midnight to rush off to the Floka. Philippos and Kostas were both newlyweds, so they had their wives to go home to. But George was alone, and when I dashed off he had a wistful look in his eyes. It was easy to see that he would like to prolong the evening in my company. But he never offered to go with me to the Floka, nor did it ever enter my mind to suggest it, as though we both knew it would be unthinkable for George to cross over into that other world.

In the summer of 1959, we began preparing for our appearance at the Festival of Greek Song. I was not yet in love with George; he was becoming part of my life, but only gradually, and for a long time our friendship was platonic. I liked talking to him and listening to him play the guitar, but I forgot him as soon as I got together with Manos and Nikos. What I learned about life from those two men, so much older than I, kept me in thrall and made everything else secondary – including my budding feelings for George and my life at home with my parents. Manos and Nikos fulfilled all my expectations, all my curiosity. Manos brought me to the summit of artistic creation, while Nikos imbued me with the philosophy of the soul, teaching me to know myself, opening my eyes to life's beauty and complexity. Each of them, in short, gave me something neither parents nor school nor Conservatory ever could: knowledge of the world, and the keys to its doors.

I wish I could say that I was simply too busy back then to have a love life. But that would be the easy way out, and besides, it would be a half-lie. The truth is that I had been alienated from myself for so long and felt so unlovable that I couldn't imagine a man falling in love with me. My father had wanted a boy, but I was a girl. And what a poor excuse for a girl! A girl who failed to turn the boys' heads, as I saw them turn to look at Jenny. A girl with glasses and extra pounds who would never qualify as sexy. You can't dream about boys and romance until you love yourself. In 1959 I was twenty-five years old and had never kissed a boy. But Manos and Nikos were about to bring me into the world; they were preparing me for my rebirth. They taught me to love myself a little, so that by and by I came to welcome George's attentions. The song Manos wrote for me to perform at the Festival was entitled 'My Love is Somewhere' . . . and all this time, faithful George was patiently waiting. It seemed an extraordinary coincidence! As though Manos, having brought me out of the darkness, was showing me the way ahead . . .

It was raining in Athens on 3 September 1959, and the whole Festival was disrupted. We had to abandon the Athinea's superb beach and flee to the reception rooms and gilded decorations of the King George Hotel. The rain brought me luck, or maybe the last-minute scramble to the hotel wiped out my stage-fright. I don't really know. We were greeted with high-spirited interest when we came on stage, with Manos holding my hand. He sat down at the piano, and the first notes swept me away. When it was over, we took our bow to sustained applause. Was it a good sign? Or did all the performers enjoy similar ovations?

In any event, I felt full of confidence when the Trio Canzone and I took the stage a bit later to sing Mimis Plessas' song 'Asteri asteraki'. Same applause, same enthusiasm. It gave me no clue as to what to expect. I sat quietly in the wings to listen to the other young artists, whom I encountered in the clubs almost every evening as well as at the radio station.

The announcement of the awards left me speechless. I won first prize for Manos' song, and second prize for 'Asteri asteraki'! How could that be? Did my voice move the judges so much that they forgot my glasses? I was too overwhelmed to say the things I wanted to say. But who cares? Mr Spiromilios heaped me with flowers and praise! I went home to bed in our little apartment without really understanding what had just happened.

Next morning my picture was in all the papers. My celebrity gave Mama a new lease of life. She said the radio talked of no one but me. My parents were not present at the King George and, like me, they hadn't appreciated the full import of the event until now. The three of us slowly took stock of the implications. At first there was nothing but talk and bustle. Reporters cited me as 'the voice of young Greek song'. Station managers pursued me; on broadcasts, I was invariably asked for live renderings of my two prizewinning songs . . . After that, I quickly realized that people saw me differently. Henceforth, the Dzaki was crowded to capacity whenever I was scheduled to appear. The owner spoke to me with noticeably greater warmth than before, and he asked me to perform there every evening. Mr Spartacus, the man who found me so *unattractive*, proposed that he and I team up to form a duo and offered to double my original salary at the Astir. I declined even to think about it. All the other nightclubs wanted me as well. And I, who so recently had to go around from club to club just to eke out a meager living, now found myself with an overabundance of choices – and fees that at long last put some light in my mother's eyes.

All well and good. But apart from all that, my life didn't radically change. I continued to be a nightclub singer, to live with my parents, and to proceed with my education by Manos and Nikos at the Café Floka as well as in Manos' music room.

But I'm forgetting. During this period, I met a man whom I will never cease to like and admire and whose high opinion of me moves me deeply: Constantine Karamanlis. He was head of the Greek government, having been appointed by King Paul I. I first met Prime Minister Karamanlis several months prior to the Festival of Greek Song. I was invited to sing at a press ball that he was hosting in Thessaloniki. After my performance, the prime minister asked me to sit at his table, and we had a long talk. His questions demonstrated his interest in what the country's youth was thinking, how we lived, what hopes we had for the future. I answered him as sincerely and as fully as I could.

One evening, he and his wife came to hear me sing at the Dzaki. At the intermission, he called me over to his table, and we had our second chat. He well remembered our meeting in Thessaloniki and con-gratulated me on my double triumph at the Festival. Then he paid me an unforgettable compliment.

'I must confess that no song has ever moved me so much as "My Love is Somewhere". Manos Hadjidakis is enormously talented, but he's lucky to have you. You are an outstanding singer.'

A few weeks later I received a dinner invitation from Prime Minister and Mrs Karamanlis. That occasion was the beginning of a true friend-ship, one that tied me to both of them. During the conversation, I made reference to my early childhood – and the Greece that I glimpsed from my father's little movie theater. After that, the three of us exchanged our most cherished memories. Constantine Karamanlis, aware that singing and the stage were of the utmost importance in my life, gave me some advice I have never forgotten: 'Now it's up to you to better yourself all on your own. Don't worry about what others are doing; don't be afraid of anyone. Build your own destiny. The only person you need fear is yourself. Be strong; rely on your own inner resources; trust your instincts; have faith in yourself.' Fifteen years later, in 1974, this man would return to Greece to restore democracy after seven years of dic-tatorship. As I watched the coverage on television, I remembered his words. The same advice he gave me must have helped him get through his ordeal: his long exile had surely forced him to rely only on his own inner strength.

Thanks to Constantine Karamanlis, I was privileged to witness two historic events. The Prime Minister loved artists, believing that a society devoid of art was a body without a soul. He therefore included artists on all occasions when history was being made.

For several months, the newspapers regaled us with articles on the engagement of Princess Sophia, daughter of King Paul I and Queen Frederika of Greece, to Prince Juan Carlos of Spain. Then I learned that Prime Minister and Mrs Karamanlis wanted me to sing at a reception they were planning for the young couple. Not wanting to disappoint them, I immediately answered yes without even thinking about it. But when it dawned on me that I, 'the night owl's daughter', would be performing alone in front of such illustrious company, my heart froze.

I have no idea whether I sang well or not that evening. Most likely I came onstage with my eyes shut the way I did on the aircraft carrier *Forrestal*, knowing I had to conserve my energy. Thus, I have no picture at all in my mind of the future Spanish sovereigns. All I remember is Constantine Karamanlis' handsome face as he rose to applaud me at the end.

About a year later another invitation reached me. This time, the Karamanlises were entertaining Jackie Kennedy, wife of the newly-elected American president, and her brother-in-law, Attorney-General Robert Kennedy. I remember that there was some controversy surrounding this visit. The press argued that the king, not the prime minister, should receive the first lady of the United States. Then, too, there was a certain amount of resentment that the youthful American president had not deigned to honor Greece with his own presence ...

This time I was less intimidated. Besides, Jackie Kennedy was very charming and outgoing. She put people at ease and exhibited enthusiasm and appreciation. A few days later I was delighted to accept an invitation to sing for her again aboard a yacht in an Aegean port.

But to return to that fall of 1959. As 'the voice of young Greek song', I was suddenly in much greater demand. Yet I had no manager and no artistic adviser, and I saw no better way for me to get ahead and to make a name for myself than to rehearse for the second Festival of Greek Song. In 1960, the Festival would be held in July in order to avoid the heavy September rains.

Once again, I intended to sing two songs, both by Manos Hadjidakis: 'To kiparissaki' ('The Young Cypress') and 'I timoria' ('The Penalty'). The lyrics of 'I timoria' were by Nikos. And Nikos attended our rehearsals with a critical ear. During January and February of 1960, Nikos also wrote me several very beautiful songs set to music by Manos, particularly, 'Yia ena tin agapi mou' ('For You, My Love').

Meanwhile, Greece's musical awakening was beginning to intrigue Europe, and France in particular. The accolades lavished on *Never on Sunday* at the Cannes Film Festival, followed by the monumental success of the movie's theme song 'Ta pedia tou Pirea', suddenly sparked the interest of recording companies. In Paris, the young director of Fontana, Louis Hazan – who had barely taken notice of the First Festival of Greek Song – now decided to attend the Second. He sent for the songs that garnered the two top prizes for me, as well as the recording I made with Manos Hadjidakis, released on the Greek label Fidelity. Even though Hazan had never seen me, he had heard me, so when he called from Paris to make an appointment with Mr Patsifas, Fidelity's CEO, it was primarily because he wanted to meet me.

Twelve years later, Louis Hazan described his introduction to Greek music for the Belgian monthly *Pleins Feux:* 'It was in 1960. A gentle breeze out of Greece had been stirring the Parisian air ever since the film *Never on Sunday*. People were humming "Ta pedia tou Pirea", learning to like the bouzouki and the sirtaki, and I was convinced that there was a lot more to come out of Greece. So I ordered a sampling of Greek song – and was dismayed to be confronted with a mountain of 45s. To think that I would have to listen to all those! The appeal of certain melodies did not outweigh the monotony of the whole, and I was starting to lapse into a deep boredom when the opening notes of one record suddenly yanked me away from my contemplation of the ceiling. Pure and ethereal, an extraordinary, indefinable voice emanated from the loudspeaker. Who was it? Who could sing like that? My wife Odile knew a little Greek and read the jacket for me: Nana Mouskouri. She was completely unknown to us. I canceled our summer vacation on the spot, and we departed for Athens to attend the festival of Hellenic song.'[3]

The weather was splendid in mid July 1960, and this time the festival took place as planned: at the Athinea, on the edge of one of Athens' most beautiful beaches. For our two songs, Manos Hadjidakis would personally accompany me on the piano. This year, then, the Trio Canzone was not competing with me but *against* me! We didn't plan it that way, but what could we do? The Trio had its own songs, and I already had an accompanist for mine. Maybe this unfortunate state of affairs was the reason George got sick. A few weeks before the festival he declared his love for me, upsetting a relationship which had thus far been merely companionable. When I regarded him differently, I realized that he touched my heart and I was attracted to him. We became secretly engaged at the time of the festival, and maybe George was reluctant to compete with me. In any case, he fell ill, and the Trio had to withdraw from the contest.

My own experience was quite different. The festival brought me public acclaim. To wild applause, my two songs tied for first prize! So for the second year in a row I came out on top at the festival.

Here is what Louis Hazan recalled in that same interview with *Pleins Feux*: 'I waited with feverish impatience for the entrance of the woman whose voice had blown me away! Every time a singer appeared (and they were often quite beautiful and made a fine impression), I'd say to myself "This is the one!" ... only to realize I was mistaken as soon as they opened their mouths. Then a young woman came on, squeezed into a tight black dress, her hair pulled straight back, wearing no makeup, with glasses on her nose, and overweight by as much as seventy pounds! That could not be her! I was crushed. Then, standing absolutely still, eyes closed, hands clasped behind her back, she began to sing in that incomparable voice. Then I recognized her, and I swore to myself that I would make her famous throughout the world.'

In that interview, Louis Hazan didn't mention how tenaciously Mr Patsifas, director of Fidelity, tried to deflect him away from me and

---

[3] Louis Hazan, interview in *Pleins Feux*, Belgium, May 1972.

point him in the direction of prettier singers. Mr Patsifas apparently introduced him to the sexiest performers in his stable, remarking that France would surely be impressed by their beauty. Monsieur Hazan had a hard time getting Patsifas to come back to me. He wanted me and no one else.

That night, or perhaps the next evening, I met Odile and Louis Hazan over a drink for the first time. They were young, elegant, and likable. Odile was ravishing in a Chinese dress slit up the side to expose a great deal of leg. We spoke in English, and the gist of our conversation was that Monsieur Hazan believed strongly in my future and wanted me to go see him in Paris. He didn't know exactly when; he had some complicated problems with contracts to work out; but as soon as he was free, he would let me know.

We parted on that understanding. Odile kissed me on the cheek in the French manner and said once again how moved she and her husband had been by my songs.

A short while before the festival, I was surprised to find a man waiting outside my dressing room at the Dzaki. His face seemed awfully familiar . . .

'Remember me? My name is Takis Kambas.'

'You do look familiar. But I can't quite place you.'

'I was the one who invited you to sing on the aircraft carrier *Forrestal*.'

'Oh, of course! You were so worried . . . You kept mopping your forehead with your handkerchief . . .'

'Well, it was hot that evening . . . Anyway, the *Forrestal* gig brought you luck. You're everywhere now.'

'You think so? I don't know about that . . .'

'I have a proposition for you. Do you know Kostas Yanidis?'

'The pianist? Yes, of course.'

'He composed a song that he'd like you to sing at the Barcelona Festival.'

'That sounds good. How can I get hold of him?'

I liked the song Kostas Yanidis had written, so we made a tape and sent it to Barcelona. (To participate in the festival, you had to be pre-selected on the basis of a demo tape.)

We didn't have to wait long. No sooner was the Athens festival over and the Hazans back in Paris than we received an answer from the Spanish judges: our song was accepted and I was expected in Barcelona in August to sing it in public.

But they expected more than just me. The festival organizers made a rule that each song entered in the contest must be sung twice, once by a man and once by a woman. Kostas Yanidis and Takis Kambas chose a handsome young singer named Alekos Pandas to sing the song, too. Alekos and I made the trip to Spain together, chaperoned by the promoter Takis Kambas. I had never had a chaperone before. By force of circumstance, this funny little anxiety-prone man, the one I was unable to calm down aboard the *Forrestal*, became my first agent.

Oh, that trip to Barcelona at the end of August 1960! My first time abroad! I was nearly twenty-six years old and had never left Greece. I had flown in air force propeller planes in order to go entertain the troops, notably on the island of Rhodes, but I had never set foot in one of those airliners favored by the jet set. I was excited, curious, and terribly scared all at the same time. Hoping it would bring me luck, I packed the black lace dress that Jenny had made for me, the one I wore at the Athens festival. Apart from that dress I didn't know what else I should bring, so I crammed in a whole bunch of useless clothes and other items.

We were scheduled to stop over in Rome and take another plane the next day to Barcelona. The prospect of spending the night in Rome, a foreign city that was strange to me, gave me a panic attack. We'd have to deal with a taxi driver who wouldn't understand us, sleep in a hotel, and the next day we'd have to go through the same thing again to get back to the airport.

It was more than I could take, so catching the merest glimpse of Rome through the aircraft porthole made me want to go home! Terrifying forked lightning ripped the dark sky, heavy rain battered the fuselage, and the Italian capital seemed ready to swallow us whole ...

But for once, Takis Kambas was utterly unperturbed. In the raging storm, he found us a taxi and had it take us to our hotel as if long accustomed to this sort of thing. At this point, he went up a notch in my estimation. Later that night, I went to him for protection, which I would never have done if he hadn't seemed dependable and solid – or at least more so than aboard the *Forrestal*.

That night promised to be awful. Our reservations were in a hotel that bore an uncanny resemblance to Count Dracula's castle in Tod Browning's film. Complete with gloomy tapestries hanging on the walls, candelabras, dark wood paneling, four-poster beds. No sooner was I locked in my room than I thought I was going crazy. The furniture frightened me, from the wine-colored velvet armchair to the monstrous bed, draped as if for a sacrifice. The walls and ceiling were extremely dark, with shadows everywhere. I could have sworn I saw troll-like figures flitting in the corners. In a panic, I ran to the window, but only a faint, dirty yellow light filtered through the small glass panes.

Never had I missed Mama so badly. If I knew how to make a long-distance call, I would have called her for help. But I couldn't use the telephone and lacked the courage to flee into the street. So, with my last ounce of willpower, I got into bed fully dressed. Too scared to breathe, I huddled there with the eiderdown pulled over my head and waited for sleep.

I must have dozed off, because I was jerked awake by a horrendous boom. The crackling, rumbling, booming noise went on and on as though the earth were cracking up and splitting in two. The violent wind and bolts of lightning threatened to knock down the doors and smash the windows. The sky's fury – or Nosferatu's wrath – was going to kill us all.

So I did something that, with hindsight, seems inconceivable: I leapt out of bed and ran barefoot to Takis Kambis' door. He answered my knock so quickly, I knew he hadn't been asleep.

'What are you doing here at this hour?' he asked as he let me in.

He was holding a book in one hand, a candlestick in the other, and his round belly protruded under a long dressing gown the color of a monk's robe. Why the candlestick? And why his strange appearance? The scene was straight out of *Dracula*, and for a second I thought I was having a nightmare. I noticed the title of the book in his hand, and I shivered: *he was actually reading* Dracula! I had a moment of fear. But a split second later, it all added up . . . this particular hotel, the candlestick. Takis Kambas was a connoisseur of Gothic horror tales, and nothing pleased him more than to savor them in an appropriate setting.

'What in the world is the matter with you?'

'I'm scared, I can't sleep.'

'Did anyone see you knock at my door?'

'I don't think so. But what if they did? I'm not doing anything wrong.'

'How can I help you?'

'I want to sleep in here. I'm too scared to stay by myself.'

'Sleep with me? You should be ashamed! You're crazy! Get back to your room right now! What if somebody saw you?'

'Nobody saw me. Let me sleep in that armchair, I beg you! I can't go back to my room.'

'Out of the question! Can you imagine the scandal if reporters found out that you spent the night in my room?'

'I'll tell them I stayed in the chair.'

'Oh, great!' he said sarcastically. 'I'm sure they'd buy that!'

'Who cares what they would buy? I don't give a hoot what people think. I'm never going back to that room! Never! Just give me a blanket; I promise not to budge from this chair.'

He sighed and tossed me a blanket. Then he installed himself under the canopy of his four-poster bed. With his back propped up on pillows and the candle on his night table, he plunged into his book, while outside the elements continued to rage.

I found him in exactly the same position next morning. He had stayed awake all night, while I tossed and turned in fitful sleep.

Arriving in Barcelona gave me a new lease of life. The skies were clear again. The Catalans, like the Greeks, love strolling in the open air, chatting on café terraces, reading the paper on a bench while children play ball games in the park. In the public square, there are people to shine your shoes and people to bring you an espresso. Just seeing the city from our taxi filled me with enthusiasm and confidence. Phew! This glorious world wiped out all last night's memories of Dracula's lair . . .

Barcelona's *Festival Mediterraneo* was scheduled to last all weekend. Since there were two singers for each song, one would sing on Saturday, the other on Sunday. Takis Kambas decided that Alekos should go first, so I spent that Saturday listening to the other competitors while waiting for Alekos to make his appearance. There were Israelis, Italians, French, Spanish, of course, and some of these artists moved me and impressed me greatly. Were Alekos and I even in their league? All of them seemed more at ease on stage than I was, and to make matters worse, most of them were good-looking and beautifully dressed.

At last it was Alekos' turn. It seemed to me that the auditorium held its breath the whole time he was singing. Was the emotion he stirred in me contagious or did it just appear that way? In any case, he sang remarkably well, and the applause he received left me hoping for a very high score. The results were announced shortly: we weren't in the lead, but we were well up in the ranking. What counted was the average of our two scores. If we were to climb to first place next day, everything depended on me.

On Sunday, my stage-fright was intense – even though I should have felt at home, since the setting was reminiscent of my father's little outdoor theater. The festival was taking place in the open air, and the stage, although bigger than the one of my childhood, resembled it by virtue of its simple design. The secret dreams of my childhood had come true! Now they were winking at me and saying: *Well, well, this time it's not play-acting, now it's the real thing!*

It was the real thing, sure enough, but I had never felt more alone. At the two Athens festivals, Manos was onstage with me and I had drawn on his strength. Or else George and his group had been there. In night-clubs, I was no longer apprehensive about performing alone, but to do it in front of a thousand people was a different story.

Standing in the middle of the stage, I closed my eyes and imagined myself in our little cinema with all its seats empty and Papa smiling at me from his projection box. Then I sang as if Papa and I were the only two people present. Of course I heard the orchestra, the same one that accompanied all the contestants, but I was elsewhere, alone with my emotions.

As the last notes faded, I was wrenched from my reverie by applause, and for the first time I opened my eyes. All those faces (that I had pictured with icy stares) were now friendly. Everyone was smiling, some shouted 'Bravo! Bravo!' and the clapping went on forever.

'You sang well,' said Takis Kambas, who was waiting in the wings.
'Oh, thank you, thank you!'

And now, what would the judges say?

I was about to go find Alekos so we could wait for the verdict together, when I saw that Takis Kambas was mopping his brow again.

'You sang very well, but did you notice that little French girl?'
'No, she came on right after me and I didn't really pay attention.'
'You should have seen her; she was terrific.'
'Your loyalty is touching, Takis,' I said dryly.

He hurried off, eyes slightly bloodshot, and I saw him disappear among the technicians and the other agents and managers who were milling around backstage. What was he after? Probably nothing, because he was back a second later, sweating, flushed, collar unbuttoned.

'You should have sung first and let Alekos finish,' he said.
'Why do you say that? It was fine the way it was.'
'Alekos is a knockout. He would have left a stronger impression.'
'Everyone seemed to think I sang well.'
'That's true, but he has a better stage presence. You stand there like a stick! You don't even gesture with your arms! You've got to learn to move around a little.'

And off he went again, leaving me to reflect on his criticism. How could I 'move around' with my eyes shut? I closed my eyes to shut out distractions, so I could concentrate on the music and give sway to my emotional response to the song. But what if he was right? Perhaps there was no place for singers like me who weren't the type to prance around on stage, using movement and lighting effects to enhance their performance.

I didn't see Takis coming, but suddenly he was there, popping up again like a bad penny.

'I can't stand it . . . I just can't stand the waiting . . . I can't take another ten minutes of it. The stakes are so high . . . Can you imagine what it would mean if we win?'

'Have you heard something?'

'No, well, not exactly . . . The word is that you're miles ahead of the rest.'

'We can't count on a rumor. Let's just sit tight and wait.'

'This is a very big deal. I don't know how you can sit there so calmly!'

Off he went. Suddenly I saw him running back toward me:

'We did it! We did it! We won!'

At that same moment, the loudspeaker announced Alekos Pandas' name and then mine. I assumed we were being called onto the stage and glanced around for Alekos. He had been looking for me everywhere; when he found me, we jubilantly embraced. Then together we walked into the spotlight.

The evening of our triumph was simply extraordinary. All the singers who had lived through those two days of anxiety and excitement felt a connection with each other. The shared experience erased the spirit of competition and all the past rivalries, and now we could laugh and sing together.

The party was in full swing when someone told me I was wanted on the phone. He led me to a little booth in the wings.

'That you, Nana? Louis Hazan here. A pleasure to hear your voice.'

'Monsieur Hazan! Are you calling from Paris?'

'Where else? We followed the festival on the radio. You were magnificent. Congratulations on your third great success!'

'Oh, thank you. How kind of you—'

'Just a second, Nana. I have two friends here who also heard you and who'd like to congratulate you. Here they are.'

Another voice reached me:

'Hello, Nana, I'm not sure my name will mean anything to you. I'm Michel Legrand . . .'

Michel Legrand! But of course I knew his name. I owned at least three or four of his recordings, including *Michel Legrand Plays Cole Porter* and *I Love Paris*. He was a great pianist, a musician of extraordinarily wide-ranging gifts, a lover of jazz . . . I felt my heart begin to pound as I struggled for words.

'Yes . . . I know who you are . . . I have your records . . .'

'I just wanted to say . . . You have a superb voice! Louis tells me you'll be in Paris soon and I'm dying to meet you. Bravo! A thousand bravos! But don't hang up. Here's someone else who wants to talk to you . . .'

I didn't hang up. I wondered whose voice I would hear next, and I felt my cheeks turn red.

'Hi, baby, Quincy Jones here!'

For a second I thought they were playing a joke on me.

'Quincy Jones? For real?'

'Yeah, it's me. I just heard you sing, you were fantastic. I think we can do great things together!'

'Oh, I'm not sure I'm good enough to . . .'

'Well, I *am* sure, baby. We have to get together, in Paris or New York. One way or another, we'll fix it up. But here's your boss again.'

A few more encouraging words from Louis Hazan and we hung up. In that little makeshift phone booth, ankle-deep in the cables strung across the floor, I stood there alone, just letting it all sink in. Quincy, that supreme trumpeter, the darling of Duke Ellington, Ray Charles, Sarah Vaughan! Could that really have been him?

Rejoining the other singers, I couldn't hide my excitement. When I told them I had just talked to Quincy Jones and Michel Legrand, there was a moment of stunned silence; then amazement spread across their faces and everyone started talking at once.

'Why me?' I wondered that night after I got back to my hotel room. 'Why me and not some other singer? They're all much more at ease on stage than I am. So much more *attractive*, as Spartacus would put it . . .'

Next morning our two names were printed on the front page of all the newspapers. But when I turned to the section covering the festival, I had a shock. There were photos of every competitor, shown on stage during his act. Every competitor . . . except me! The photographer had shot me from behind, and all you could see of me were my hands behind my back, one on top of the other, as if in handcuffs.

8

White Roses in Berlin

irst Athens, then Barcelona, and now Berlin! The year 1960 was decidedly full of surprises. In the autumn of that year, I ended up in Berlin, thanks to Manos Hadjidakis.

It was an exceptionally busy year. In addition to evenings at the Dzaki, nights at the Floka, and afternoons spent preparing for song festivals, I rehearsed and recorded five songs for the score of a German film entitled *Greece, Land of Dreams*. The director, Wolfgang Mühlersehn, asked Manos to compose the music, and Manos naturally turned to Nikos Gatsos for the lyrics and to me for the singing.

As he was so fond of doing, Manos composed those five songs with every imaginable sound, mixing all the instruments available to him, from bouzouki to violin, from classical guitar to barrel-organ, not to mention the xylophone. But this time, he wanted a chorus as well, and while he was at it, why not the most prestigious one of all – the chorus of our national opera?

Without knowing all the details of the project, the chorus agreed to participate, just for the chance to work with Manos. The chorus didn't rehearse with us; they rehearsed on their own over at the opera house. At last, the date scheduled for recording arrived. All of us crowded into the same studio for the final take (at that time, the technology was not advanced enough for each participant to be recorded separately, with sounds mixed later). The chorus was already in place next to all the other musicians when I entered the studio. Manos introduced me, and only then did the opera singers realize that they were expected to accompany me. I quickly detected that something was wrong, for the chorus leader took Manos aside, and their little talk was clearly not making him very happy.

Then Manos came over to me:

'Nana, would you mind leaving for a second? I have a problem with these people. You can come back as soon as I've sorted it out.'

Somewhat intrigued, I joined the technicians in the recording booth. With the sound cut off, I could hear nothing. But I could see into the studio, and it was an incongruous sight. Manos seemed to be under lively attack by these men and women of the opera, who looked so well-mannered and restrained in their formal attire and whose decorum was beyond reproach just a few minutes earlier. Manos talked to them, but the more he spoke the more vehement they became. What on earth was going on? What last-minute snag could have made them so angry? It was utterly inexplicable, and the technicians were puzzled, too, knowing that a silent studio was not normal.

Finally, Manos beckoned me back into the room.

'Here's the problem, Nana,' he began as the chorus singers stood in a silent group. 'These ladies and gentlemen of the opera find it beneath their dignity to sing with you. They are accustomed to opera soloists – lyric sopranos and tenors and the like. So they consider it a demotion to lend their voices to a popular singer. I told them that I make no distinction between artists, but apparently they do. They refuse to sing with you.'

Manos paused. He looked at me, then at them. He was close enough to me that I could hear him panting.

'Did I state your position accurately?' he suddenly resumed, addressing the leader of the chorus.

'Perfectly, sir.'

'Then let me tell you something. Miss Mouskouri will not be leaving the studio, as you demand. If you're unwilling to sing with her, I don't wish to retain your services. I made my decision a long time ago: she will sing. If the opera chorus doesn't accompany her, some other chorus will. I'll give you ten minutes or so to make up your minds.'

So saying, he nodded curtly to them and led me outside.

Surprisingly, we didn't exchange a single word during those ten minutes. Manos seemed to be nursing an enormous rage as he paced the room, puffing on a cigarette. It took me a while to realize that he was embarrassed for me, and talking about it would make it worse. He felt that even a word or two of consolation in reference to that insult would only add to my mortification and his. As for me, I was on the verge of tears. They were the same kind of tears that drove me to confront the manager of the Astir after Mr Spartacus' humiliating remarks. I resolved never to live through such a scene again, forced to defend myself while choking back the tears. Never again. That meant that my future was in Manos' hands. I was still in the game because he stood up for me and supported me. If he had dropped me, I would be lost.

When we returned, the chorus of opera singers had not stormed off. There they all were in a straight line, their faces inscrutable. The musicians, who had witnessed the whole scene, were astounded. Manos beckoned me to the mike and took his place as orchestra leader, as though nothing had happened.

I don't know where I found the strength to throw myself into the music and forget the rest, but I did, and our second take was a wrap. Considering the atmosphere of distrust, it was miraculous that our voices were able to generate that unblemished emotion. I often think back to that recording session, and it reinforces my faith in music. I must never forget that art alone is capable of transcending our ugliness and inhumanity.

A few months later we heard that *Greece, Land of Dreams* was to be shown at the Berlin Film Festival. I believe the news reached me just after my return from Barcelona. We soon received invitations. The Germans wanted Manos Hadjidakis and his singer – me – to attend. Manos did not hesitate for a second: he refused to go! He had a number of reasons, but they were all jumbled together. Apparently, the prizes he received at Cannes six months earlier for the score of *Never on Sunday* and the unforgettable melody of 'Ta pedia tou Pirea' were enough for him. Furthermore, Berlin did not interest him. He hated travel, he told me; he hated leaving his piano, his apartment, and his city. Above all, he had no intention of setting foot in Germany! It was only fifteen years since the war ended, and he remembered the German occupation, whole families dying of starvation, men shot at random in order to intimidate the Resistance, the destruction, the humiliations . . .

I hadn't forgotten either; in fact, the very name of Berlin sent shivers through me. But Louis Hazan called me from Paris: the Germans, he said, were so enthusiastic over the film's soundtrack that one or two producers had already shown an interest in cutting records. Monsieur Hazan was in touch with them. In light of this, he and Odile were thinking of attending the festival.

'In which case we'll see you there, Nana, right? This event is going to be sensational!'

'Oh, yes . . . I wouldn't miss it.'

I didn't dare tell Louis that Manos Hadjidakis not only refused to go in person, he had forbidden me to attend as well. Two or three nights before at the Floka, the subject had suddenly cropped up:

'And you're not going either, Nana!'

'Why do you say that, Manos? We can talk about it, at least.'

'No discussion! We're not going to grovel for awards from the Germans. What an idea!'

Fortunately, Nikos encouraged me to go.

After Monsieur Hazan's phone call, I raised the subject again, and the conversation immediately became heated.

By now, Manos thought I belonged to him; he couldn't conceive of my disobeying him. Especially since he had made me the ambassador of his music.

'If you go, I'll never speak to you again!'

'Manos,' Nikos said gently, 'you have to allow Nana to fly with her own wings.'

'No, I don't. Nana interprets my music. She will do as I see fit.'

'Well, old friend, I'm afraid I disagree with you on this. I'm urging Nana to go to Berlin. She needs to make herself known outside Greece.'

That night, Manos went home without a goodnight kiss.

And next day, I decided to go to Germany alone.

How I wished Manos were going with me to Berlin! The prospect of that journey filled me with apprehension. I dreaded facing the men responsible for the nightmare that still haunted me. Those giants in olive drab, brutal, cruel, murderous, who shot that young man right before our eyes. I didn't want to think about it. I took comfort from knowing that Odile and Louis Hazan promised to be there. I thought about Nikos; he had looked deep into my eyes and encouraged me: 'Go to Berlin, Nana. Go for it! Don't reject the hand that is offering you a life.'

And off I went to Berlin.

In those days, there was a stopover in Frankfurt, and I remember my delight as we touched down in a sea of greenery, so unlike my own country where the earth is arid and trees die of thirst.

Finally we were over Berlin, and the pilot announced that we were about to land. Germany was still cut in two. The Western half of the former Reich capital was surrounded on all sides by Communist territory, limiting the available space for an airport. That meant that the West Berlin airport, Tempelhof, was hemmed in by tall buildings, and I had a horrible feeling that we were going to smash into them. But we didn't. The plane dived; tilted to one side, edging past the TV antennas; then rolled along the runway at breakneck speed before braking to a final halt in a deafening roar of jet engines. We were safe, and I silently thanked God, as I do every time Heaven is merciful.

God might have watched over me and the other passengers, but not over my luggage. It was not on the plane, and it didn't reach me until next day, so my first purchase in Berlin was a toothbrush. I was driven to the Hotel Berlin, very close to the festival site. I scarcely remember that first day, tired as I was by the journey and quelled by fear at the sound of the German language, which plunged me into the darkest days of my childhood.

At last, Odile and Louis Hazan arrived, and I began to relax. In their company, I slowly regained the impulse to laugh, look and listen. And what we heard that night exceeded all our hopes: *Greece, Land of Dreams* won the award for Best Documentary!

Because it won first prize, record producers counted on our film having commercial success. In consequence, they besieged Louis Hazan with offers. They insisted that I return to Berlin as soon as possible to record the songs. At the gala following the Festival, I was seated some distance apart from Louis Hazan. While he and the record companies planned out my future, I sat at the winners' table receiving compliments in German, unable to comprehend a fraction of what was said. In the middle of the celebration dinner, I was asked to sing one or two songs from the film. I did it with pleasure, only too happy to get away briefly from my hosts, charming though they were.

Three months later I was back in Berlin – but in the meantime I got married ... As George tells it, he had to threaten to break our engagement in order to make me leave my parents and marry him. That may be so, but I wasn't the only one with cold feet. Before committing to me, George suffered anxieties of his own. Some time before the wedding, he was hospitalized for a strange illness that turned out to be a severe allergy. It bloated his whole body, leaving him unrecognizable. So much so that he had his friends tell me not to visit him; apparently he didn't want me to see him like that. At the time, I made no connection between this allergy and our upcoming marriage. That only occurred to me later when I recalled George's description of his first great love affair. The woman was an actress and evidently very demanding and difficult to live with, since he had nothing but horrible memories of their relationship. Was he afraid that I would hurt him the way she did? Did he think I would force him to do my bidding and make him satisfy my every whim?

In a way, I was already making George suffer. I wasn't exactly his 'ideal woman'. He was hurt by my exclusive relationship with Manos and Nikos. Indeed, he was hurt by everything I built that didn't include him. Like a lot of men (especially in Greece), he longed for a self-sacrificing wife, devoted to him, whose world revolved around family life. It was a little early to predict how my life would turn out, but there were already indications: men didn't turn around to stare at me in the streets, but musicians pricked up their ears and wanted to get to know me ... Already, international borders were starting to open up to me. All that must have secretly worried George. He was losing me even before he slipped the ring on my finger. What part would he play in the tumult that we sensed lay ahead? None whatsoever in the opinion of Manos, who behaved as though George didn't exist. Nikos was more considerate of George; nevertheless, he and I continued to meet without him. And now Michel Legrand and Quincy Jones were expecting me in Paris . . . Where would it end?

Yet I was infinitely touched by George's desire to have me all to himself. It was proof of his love, his loyalty, and the dreams of domestic bliss that he harbored. To my twenty-five-year-old eyes, all those things were turning him into the man of my life. At times, my heart burned with love for him, but when I was singing, my passion for music was so all-encompassing that I forgot all about him.

Did I truly love him? As much as he loved me? Today, I realize how innocent I was, how ignorant of what love is and what a successful relationship entails. I learned nothing from my parents. I retained nothing except an incurable aversion to quarrels and shouting. I never saw them look fondly at each other, hold hands, or show the slightest happiness at being together. Nevertheless, I believe they loved each other: they just didn't know how to express it by words and gestures. They had never been taught anything either. They had to make do with what they had . . . just as I had to make do with what little I knew in trying to sort out the jumble of emotions at work inside me.

It's true that it was painful for me to leave my parents. George thought I was afraid of leaving the family cocoon, but the real reason is that I felt terribly guilty about abandoning them. Jenny had blessed them with a granddaughter, Aliki. But they lived vicariously through me. I was the incarnation of their dreams, no less! In a way, I represented the fulfillment of their personal ambitions. I was on track to become the singer that my mother had wanted to be. And to a small degree I made up for my father's failed potential by having a career and conducting my life as a man would. In post-war Greece where women, far from being liberated, were still docile and submissive, I was one of the rare few who earned their living, wore trousers, traveled unaccompanied, etc . . .

My father was so proud of me! Years later, after Mama died, he went to live with Jenny. Every afternoon, when he went to the cafe to play bridge, Jenny gave him a little spending money.

'You know,' he said to her one day, 'the money you give me isn't enough.'

'But Papa, I think it's plenty! What do you do with it?'

'What do I do with it? I buy everyone a round of drinks, if you must know.'

'You pay for people's drinks every day?'

'Sure I do! After all, I'm not just anyone – I'm Nana Mouskouri's father!'

Even after my marriage, I kept my father's name. Like a son . . .

In the weeks before the wedding, as I got ready to leave home to go live with George, I felt I was betraying my parents. It was a double betrayal because Mama didn't like George. She did not consider singing and playing the guitar a fitting profession for a man. In any case, no matter what he did for a living, he had committed the unpardonable crime of snatching me away from them.

Mama wept, and I didn't know what to say to console her. So I was almost happy the day she asked me to buy her an apartment. It was a crazy request – inordinate, considering how little money I made – but at least Mama was offering me a way to purchase her forgiveness.

'If you have to marry, then marry,' she said, 'but you can't just go off like that, leaving us in this apartment. In a few years we won't be able to pay the rent.'

'Fine, Mama, I'll get a loan and buy you an apartment.'

That was it, then. Our wedding was set for 19 December 1960. At the Floka, the news was received coolly. Nikos had nothing to say in the way of congratulations. Manos, who found it hard to forgive my trip to Berlin, spoke brusquely:

'If you've made up your mind, so be it. It's your own business.'

But an hour later, I was astonished to hear him return to the subject. By then, the whole gang was there: I think I remember the poet Elytis being present that evening, as well as the painters Moralis and Tsarouchis.

'You've heard the news, friends?'

All heads turned towards him.

'No. What news?'

'Nana has decided to get married.'

A forced smile here and there was the group's response to this announcement.

'. . . to a man!' Manos added, cutting short the perfunctory congratulations.

Everyone burst out laughing, and I wished I could just disappear. Lighting his umpteenth cigarette, Manos sat back and relished his little joke.

Perhaps it was to make amends that he offered next day to be a witness at the ceremony. More likely, it was a stratagem to make himself the hero of the festivities – and retain his hold over me.

Circumstances proved me right. Publicity hound that he was, he announced my wedding on the radio and alerted all the newspapers. Then, he was the last to arrive at the church, forcing everyone to wait for him before we could walk down the aisle.

The church was crowded. George felt out of place surrounded by all the curious onlookers, and I was rattled. Next morning, the papers ran a cartoon drawing of me, escorted by Manos. The caption was unflattering: they called us 'Xondros' (the 'Roly-Polys'). It was the first time I had ever been caricatured. It wouldn't be the last, either; there would be hundreds more over the years. But this one did nothing for my pride.

The wedding reception was held at the Dzaki, where I still worked. I'd been singing there for some time, but that winter was a little different: Manos (always in need of money despite his growing fame) accompanied me every night on the piano. Thanks to us, the Dzaki was making good money, and it took good care of us. For my wedding dinner, the club set out a splendid table for family and friends. That evening remains a golden memory. After the reception, Manos and I went back onstage the way we did every night, but with hearts more joyful.

We couldn't afford a honeymoon trip. In the days following the wedding, my parents moved into the new apartment I bought for them, whereas George and I kept my parents' old one – that little ground-floor apartment with the bathroom that so dazzled me a few years earlier.

We were no sooner settled in than I had to leave for Berlin. The documentary *Greece, Land of Dreams* featured five songs. The Germans chose two of them for me to record in their language: 'Athina' and 'White Roses of Athens'. There was just one problem: I didn't know any German. But I didn't let a little thing like that hold me back! I was so excited and flattered to be flying off to cut my first record outside Greece. Louis Hazan told me over the phone that the record would be released by a German label that, like Fontana, was an affiliate of Philips. So I wasn't straying far from my adoptive family.

This time I was booked at the Park Hotel. Crossing Berlin by taxi, I was struck by the immensity of the destruction caused by war. Entire blocks of buildings were in ruins, their charred carcasses sticking up into the low January skies. The streets had a look of desolation that wrung my heart. Contemplating these vestiges of war, I slowly became aware of the suffering endured by the German people. Like so many Europeans who were harmed by Nazism, I had never thought about the pain that the Nazi leaders inflicted on the German population. Now that the evidence was right before my eyes, I realized that the Germans were victims, too. And for the first time, I felt compassion for the families annihilated here, helpless prisoners of this apocalypse.

Speaking of ruins, the recording studio itself was housed in the ruins of the former Grand Hotel Esplanade. All that remained of its palatial structure were the cellars and part of the ground floor, where the lobby, the hotel lounge, and a few smaller rooms had been spared. Enormous red velvet curtains had been hung to keep out drafts and hide holes in the masonry. That surreal setting, which might have been dreamed up by Fellini, also included an improvised stage. That's where I would be singing after a few days of preparation. My German producer Ernst Ferch had very pale blue eyes, a chiseled profile, and the tall frame of the officers I passed in the streets of Athens as a child. With elaborate courtesy, he apologized for being unable to offer me a studio with more amenities, and then he proceeded to boast about the excellent acoustics of the place.

While waiting for the recording session, I confined myself to my hotel room with a tape recorder and the German lyrics to my songs. I learned to pronounce the words as I was taught and sang them over and over again in playback. I spent countless hours rehearsing this way, interrupted only by visits from Herr Ferch and his artistic director. The latter occasionally needed to correct my pronunciation, but both of them were surprised by my rapid progress. By the second or third day, we were ready to inaugurate the studio.

This time the musicians were there, along with the whole technical team. This devastated section of street was cut off by the barbed wire of Checkpoint Charlie a hundred yards away. Outside, rain was falling. However, the atmosphere in the ruins of the Hotel Esplanade was warm and friendly. I was greeted with smiles and encouraging words, and in the space of just one afternoon we recorded both songs, re-titled in German 'Weisse Rosen aus Athen' and 'Addio'.

It was an 'historic' day for a little Greek singer like me. I was so thrilled that I had to tell someone, so I called Louis Hazan in Paris. He had me describe in great detail how things had gone, and what I told him seemed to make him very happy. I got the impression that he'd been waiting for the results of my trip to Berlin before casting his nets wider. Just before we hung up, he spoke to me again about coming to Paris.

'Excellent. And now, Nana, we have to record in France.'

'I know, Monsieur Hazan. But the trouble is, I just got married.'

'Then bring George with you!'

'No, that won't work. He has his own commitments. Anyway, I'm just not sure . . .'

'So come alone! What do you say to a first visit one month from now? That would give me time to make arrangements with young composers who are dying to meet you and work with you.'

'In a month? Paris – in a month?'

'Just go back home to Athens, take your time to think about it, and I'll call you in a couple of days.'

9

A Terrified Peasant
Girl at Orly

I still have a photo taken at the Athens airport on the day I left for Paris, in February 1961. As fate would have it, Charles Aznavour flew in from France just when I was about to board a plane to go there. Photographers rushed to take his picture. Someone must have told Aznavour's manager that I was in the airport because he insisted on introducing me to the French singer. That's how the photo came about.

An astonishing photo! Although Charles was ten years older, I almost looked like his mother. My hair piled on top of my head in an enormous bun made me look like an old lady who devoted her time to public charity, my tinted glasses further testimony to a long life of piety – or bitterness. My fat cheeks and fat body betrayed the indifference to sex appeal that one finds in women that no man has looked at in a very long time. I was taller than Charles Aznavour, which only added to the impression that I was older. He wore a shirt buttoned at the collar and a cloak flung back from his shoulders, which made him resemble a schoolboy in a playground.

That said, I should mention that the few words we exchanged (in English) were full of warmth and possibilities. Charles did not know me, whereas I was already familiar with most of his songs. Any time an Armenian meets a Greek, there is generally an immediate sense of kinship and collaboration, as though the bonds between our two cultures, forged during the centuries of Ottoman domination, automatically threw us into each other's arms.

'What a pity I'm leaving,' I said to him. 'I would have loved to hear you sing here in my country.'

'Promise you'll call when I get back to Paris,' he replied. 'By then, I'll have listened to your first records.'

Charles didn't forget me, we did meet again in Paris, and he wrote a song for me, one of the first I ever recorded in France: 'Salvame Dios'.

The Athens I left was dappled by our winter sunlight, warm and tender. Paris lay under the gray sky of a February afternoon. The plane seemed totally lost among dark storm clouds, which occasionally opened to reveal tiny headlights speeding between dark plowed fields, a few spare, huddled villages, blocks of buildings, sudden streaks of glaring sunlight. Then the plane dipped a wing and began its descent, creaking and shuddering as if struck by lightning, and finally the first landing lights of Orly sprang into view below us. We were met by sheets of rain, and when we finally touched down, dirty water splashed up onto the windows. My God! Wasn't I anxious enough already? Who could I turn to? I hoped someone would lend me a helping hand in this country in the midst of a cyclone. I spoke only a few words of French, what little I retained from school. I knew no one in Paris except for the Hazans. I prayed they would be there.

Orly's brightly lit interior was reassuring, and as I lined up to go through customs, my confidence gradually returned. Once past the barrier, I was officially in France, in Paris, and I feverishly scanned the waiting crowd for Odile's lovely face and Louis Hazan's slim frame.

'Odile and I will be there,' he had promised me the day before. 'Don't you worry, Nana, we won't let you down.'

And there they were!

Odile threw her arms around my neck. More reserved, Louis looked at me with a small smile, as though relishing his victory: he'd finally got me to come to Paris!

'You should have seen her arriving at Orly,' he said later. 'Like a frightened peasant woman. She couldn't imagine leaving Greece for more than a few days. The prospect terrified her. But I prevailed.'[4]

---

[4] *Pleins Feux*, ibid.

There was a big difference between the trip to Germany and this one to France. I went to Berlin just long enough to cut one record. Whereas Paris, according to Monsieur Hazan, was where I must progressively put down roots. 'You'll never build a career if you stay in Athens,' he told me. 'If you want to become a great singer, an international singer, you absolutely must be based in Paris.' I wasn't sure about aspiring to greatness, but I did want to sing for the rest of my life. That was certain, and it made me very aware of the stakes involved in this first visit. What sticks in my mind more than anything is what Monsieur Hazan said next: 'I wouldn't ask you to come to Paris, Nana, if I didn't believe you capable of making an international career.' I could not disappoint Louis Hazan. To be worthy of his confidence in me was even more important than my career. Or rather, the two things were inextricably linked. In order to succeed, I needed the guidance of people I looked up to, and it was my determination not to disappoint them that caused me to persevere. Even back in school I tried my hardest not to disappoint Jenny's former teachers. As a little girl, I sang to win my father's affection and make amends for the disappointment my birth had been to him. Then Manos Hadjidakis entered my life, and his expectations, his faith, were what spurred me on to triumph at the two Athens festivals.

We left Orly under a driving rain. As I sat in the back seat of the Hazans' car I resolved to live up to this man's faith in me, no matter what it took. Louis had not replaced Manos Hadjidakis in my heart, nor Nikos Gatsos, who had turned me toward contemplative thought. But Louis Hazan now stood at their side, like the third architect of the artistic life I was building by trial and error.

I was glad that the Hazans did not talk much in the car, leaving me to my silence. I needed all my energy, all my vigilance in order to keep my footing, come to terms with all the upheaval in my life, and take in as best I could the multitude of images filing past my eyes. We drove into Paris, and I was thunderstruck by the blackness of the buildings, no doubt intensified by the rain. This city's very name had dazzled me, but Good Lord, how gloomy and gray it was! However, perhaps I should reserve judgment. The streets were busy, people hurrying past one another in every direction, skillfully maneuvering their umbrellas to avoid knocking off men's hats or stripping off women's veils. The café terraces were packed. Over there, a Métro entrance was swallowing down passengers; and over here, moviegoers were lining up in front of a theater whose enormous marquee cast pools of yellow light on the sidewalk. And so much sidewalk! We hadn't seen a single dirt road since leaving the airport, nor had we crossed one of those little camel-humped bridges that allow passage to only one car at a time. Compared to Paris, Athens seemed to belong to another century. The closer we came to the city center, the more I was struck by the symmetry of the facades. True, they were black, but all those balconies were charming! The tall, curtained windows hinting at the luxury of the interior; the high porches; the lamp posts with the occasional couple embracing underneath – how elegant and romantic it all seemed!

'This is Boulevard Raspail,' said Monsieur Hazan. 'Your hotel is a little farther down.'

He double-parked. I scarcely had time to read 'Hôtel Lutetia' on the façade before someone took my bag and hotel personnel were smiling, urging me to come in out of the rain, bidding me welcome.

'Why don't you take a rest?' Odile murmured to me. 'We'll come and collect you for dinner around eight-thirty.'

I caught my breath when I saw my room. Soft lighting, red drapery, the bed with covers turned down and a little welcome card on the pillow, brightly lit bathroom, fragrant soap, flowers ... Quite honestly, I had never dreamed such luxury was possible. But instead of running a hot bath or jumping into bed, I went straight to the window. Parting the curtains, I sought out the wet night as if running away from the comfort of the room behind me, as if I didn't belong here.

Suddenly, I realized that I was weeping. Leaning against the window, my forehead pressed on the cold glass pane, I found myself gently weeping. I had no idea how long I'd been there like that. My eyes absently followed the comings and goings of cars on the glistening surface of the boulevard, but I was far away. I was thinking of Mama and how frantic she was on discovering that Papa stole the meager sum she had hidden in that chest during the war ... I thought of her perpetual sadness. My mother had been sad as long as I'd known her, ever since she brought me into the world and Papa arrived too late with the midwife ... What was I doing here? How could the daughter of Aliki and Constantine have come so far? It didn't seem fitting for someone like me to be in Paris, in this sumptuous hotel, this palace. Did Fate make a mistake and accidentally choose the wrong person?

Suddenly the phone rang, and I jumped. It was the reception desk informing me that Odile was downstairs. How could the time have gone by so quickly? I hadn't unpacked, hadn't even taken off the coat I was wearing that very morning at the Athens airport when I posed for that photo with Charles Aznavour. Walking past the mirror I noticed my swollen eyelids behind my glasses. Never mind: if they asked, I would tell them I'd been crying. The fact is, I'm such a bad liar I might as well tell the truth.

But they didn't ask. Odile was elegantly dressed, in high spirits, and very excited. We were going to spend the evening at the Blue Note, she told me, a famous nightclub in the Saint-Germain des Prés area. Ray Charles recently performed there, she said. And before his death two or three years ago, Boris Vian used to be a regular.

'You've heard of Boris Vian, haven't you, Nana?'

As a matter of fact, I hadn't. So Louis told me about Vian, the wild, inspired trumpet player and author of *L'Arrache-Cœur* and *L'Herbe Rouge*.

'I know you're going to love this place,' he went on, as we arrived at the Blue Note.

I liked the atmosphere the moment I entered, and the jazz they were playing was very familiar. It was almost like being back in an Athens taverna with George.

All similarity ceased when a stranger came over to our table and asked Odile to dance – right in front of Louis. I had already noticed that all the men turned to look at Odile. She combined the delicate beauty of a Japanese print with splendid fiery red hair, long eyelashes, and an irresistible allure.

Odile promptly took the man's hand – and a moment later they were dancing in one another's arms. How could this be? Why had Louis Hazan let it happen?

'Aren't you jealous?' I timidly inquired.

'No. Why should I be jealous?'

'Because he's dancing with your wife.'

'I don't like to dance. Odile loves it. I'm glad she's having a good time.'

'Honestly? Because George wouldn't be happy at all.'

'Odile is free to do whatever she wants, Nana. We trust each other, you know.'

When Odile came back to the table, her cheeks were a little red.

'How was it?' asked her husband.

'He held me so tight I could hardly breathe! I don't like to be squeezed like that . . .'

'Nana doesn't understand why I let you dance with another man. She says her husband wouldn't stand for it. Did that guy try anything?'

'Let's just say he was very pushy!'

She burst out laughing, and instead of getting angry, her husband smiled at her with great fondness. Was that how people loved each other in France?

I didn't get much sleep that night. I was eager for day to come so I could discover Paris for myself. At present, I knew it only from the movies. I had constructed the city in my mind through the adventures of Gerard Philippe and Gina Lollobrigida in Christian-Jaque's movie *Fanfan la Tulipe*. I followed in Jean Gabin's footsteps in Marcel Carné's *L'Air de Paris*. In another Carné film, *Hôtel du Nord*, I saw Paris through Arletty's eyes. Was that little bridge over the canal still there? Were dancing bears still to be seen around Notre Dame de Paris? Did they still serve onion soup in Les Halles?

That first morning, I had an eleven o'clock appointment with Louis at his office. I took a taxi and, with the help of my pocket dictionary, gave the driver the address in a dreadful accent that must have been incomprehensible. I drank in the scenery all along the way. Monsieur Hazan had told me his office was only ten minutes from my hotel, but that detail had slipped my mind. In any case, I enjoyed the outing very much.

All of a sudden the ride was over.

'This is it,' said the driver.

'What's the name of that church there?'

'That's the Sacré Cœur, Mademoiselle.'

'Thank you so much.'

I was on the famous hill known as Montmartre. After roaming in every direction looking for his office, I went into a café to call Louis Hazan. His tone was harsh, almost unrecognizable.

'Where are you, Nana? I expected you ten minutes ago.'

'At Sacré Cœur.'

'What in God's name are you doing at Sacré Cœur? My office is nowhere near there! It's on the other side of the city!'

'Oh, Mr Hazan, I'm so sorry.'

'No more so than I am. Find a taxi and get here as quickly as you can.' Fontana Records was a subsidiary of Philips Records, the label founded by Dutch electronics giant Philips. Fontana had its own two-storey building in the thirteenth *arrondissement*. I was an hour late. Monsieur Hazan was waiting for me in the doorway of his office.

'Ah, Nana, I see you finally made it. Listen: because of you, the entire morning was wasted. This is the first and last time. If it happens again I'm putting you on the next plane to Athens.'

'I'm truly sorry, Monsieur Hazan. I got lost because my French is so bad.'

'I don't doubt it. That's why, as of today, we're going to speak nothing but French. Come on in.'

Paralyzed by shame, I remember nothing of our conversation that first day – except that Louis started off in French but gradually reverted to English once he realized that I didn't understand a word he was saying. By the end, he was smiling again as he said:

'Good! Now I'm going to introduce you to your artistic director.'

He picked up the phone, and seconds later, Philippe Weil came in.

It didn't take long to perceive that Philippe and I were opposites: he was very much the cocky, wisecracking Parisian, whereas I was shy, introverted, and full of complexes. Funnily enough, we hit it off immediately, mainly because of our mutual love of jazz.

Philippe Weil had worked hard in the month preceding my arrival. That very afternoon he'd arranged a meeting with two writers who had a song for me. In the meantime, he took me to lunch. He couldn't get over the fact that I knew all the jazz standards, and I had to tell him all about Radio Tangiers, the jam sessions at the Rex, and the anger of my teacher at the Conservatory.

Eddie Marnay and Emile Stern were already waiting when we got back to the Fontana offices. Eddie was the lyricist, Emile the composer. Emile immediately sat down at the piano and played the melody of the song they had written for me – the first song I ever recorded in French. It was called 'Un roseau dans le vent' ('A Reed in the Wind'):

Un roseau dans le vent qui se couche
Il embrasse l'étang sur la bouche
Et dans un million
De tourbillons
Tout bleus
J'aperçois tes yeux
Penchés sur noire amour . . .

A reed bends in the breeze
To kiss the pond's lips,
And in a million ripples
Shimmering so blue,
I glimpse your eyes
Brimming with our love . . .

'Does it suit you?' asked Philippe Weil.

'It's very nice,' I said.

In reality, I was completely out of my element. The music had nothing in common with Greek melodies, and I didn't understand one word of the lyrics Eddie and Emile intoned for me. I had doubts that I could ever learn to sing in a language so alien to me.

It was raining and night was falling as I returned to the Hôtel Lutetia. Once in my room, I found it difficult not to burst into tears. What would Louis Hazan think if he saw me in this state after he had pinned such hopes on me? I felt guilty about the people rushing to show me their work, willing to offer me airfare, taxis, this luxury hotel. All that for a little nightclub singer who wanted to hide under the covers and weep. And tomorrow I had meetings with other songwriters . . . I only hoped I would have the strength to keep going. Fortunately, Odile had promised to stop by and take me to dinner. Unlike her husband, Odile didn't intimidate me: she was protective, spontaneous and affectionate.

We must have talked that night of my despair at ever mastering French, for early next morning I was awakened by a call from reception. A package addressed to me had just been delivered. It was marked urgent; could the bellboy bring it up?

The package contained a big tape recorder with a charming little note in French from Monsieur Hazan: 'Dear Nana, here's something to help you get used to our language. Don't worry, just keep repeating what you hear on this tape and you'll see: French will soon become second nature to you.'

He used the familiar 'tu' form. I knew enough French to be touched by this sign of friendship. However, knowing the distinction between the two forms of 'you', I couldn't bring myself to do the same. It didn't matter if he called me 'tu'; I would still address him by the more formal 'vous'.

The tape consisted only of pronunciation exercises. I had to learn to stop rolling my r's by reciting words like *roulette, roi, reine, rare, Rouen* into the mic, then listening to myself and correcting my mistakes. I also had to learn nasalized vowel sounds that don't exist in Greek, such as *on, an* or *in*.

It was amazing how much progress I made and how much self-confidence I derived from these exercises after just an hour or two. And my enthusiasm was still undimmed when I met my artistic director, Philippe Weil, in company with Hubert Giraud and Pierre Delanoë. The three of them greeted me warmly, and I was immediately won over by the song Giraud and Delanoë brought with them. The melody of 'Retour à Napoli' was sun-filled, sensual and joyful, and I didn't need to understand the words to feel that I was back under my own sky.

'I love it!' I cried. I spoke a bit too soon, considering the ordeal that learning to pronounce Pierre Delanoë's lyrics was about to put me through.

In the course of the day, we selected the other two songs for this first 45 rpm record, scheduled to come out that spring: one was a Greek song by Manos Hadjidakis, 'O imitos' ('The Mountain of Love'); the other was 'Le petit tramway', by Georges Magenta and Jacques Larue.

*

Now we could begin work, and in mid-February 1961 we all gathered in the Blanqui Studios.

As I recall, recording 'Roseau dans le vent' took us just one afternoon. I had worked so hard on that first song with the tape recorder in my hotel room, taking the time to understand the words, that I was able to forget the technical difficulties and let my emotions take over.

But with 'Retour à Napoli' there was a snag. I connected with the music, but I had problems with the pronunciation.

> *Jambes nues, elle a couru*
> *Dans les rues, dans les rues*
> *De Napoli, Napoli,*
> *Du soleil dans les cheveux*
> *Et les yeux, et les yeux*
> *Remplis de ciel bleu.*

> She ran barelegged
> In the streets, in the streets
> Of Naples, Naples,
> The sun in her hair,
> And her eyes, her eyes
> Filled with blue sky.

I had practiced all night long, but I still couldn't manage *jambes nues* or all those r's in the first two lines! Had Pierre Delanoë done it on purpose? I was unable to maintain the right tempo, my voice struggled like a person thrashing about in a bramble bush, and the result was deplorable. It was enough to make you cry. Pierre Delanoë didn't cry, but he did tear his hair out, raise his arms to heaven, and explode in anger. He ended up berating me and insulting me. I understood how disappointed he must be – he was a man with an exquisite ear for the music of language. But the more discouraged and angry I felt, the more my abilities deserted me. How would it end?

Luckily, Philippe Weil remained cool. After six hours of frustration, sequestered in the studio, the whole team was on the verge of a nervous breakdown. Weil called a halt and told everyone to take a break. However, he told Delanoë to go home.

'Leave it to us. Come back tomorrow morning; I promise you won't be disappointed.'

To me, he said:

'Take your time, Nana. Everyone here knows how tough this is for you. Don't think about anything but yourself. We're here to help you, not hassle you.'

His confidence in me renewed my determination and gave me the heart to keep trying. Two hours later, we had a wrap.

After a week in France I returned to Greece, feeling disoriented and dazed by what I had gone through. Recording that first disk was such an ordeal that I had no time to think about George or to miss him. Now that I was flying back to him, I looked forward to seeing him again, but at the same time, I was filled with a vague apprehension. While I was traveling and recording, he and his friends were still performing in the nightclubs of Athens. I was conscious of a gap insidiously widening between us, and it worried me. I knew that my absence hurt George, that he preferred me to stay home, close to him. I also sensed that the success I was having must wound his pride.

It was on that return flight that I first realized how different George and I were in how we felt about music. George was a law student in Thessaloniki until one summer he decided to form a group and head for Athens. It wasn't supposed to be a permanent change; he thought of music as just a way to earn a little money before returning to his law studies and taking up a *real* profession. Yet he never returned to Thessaloniki, and in the end he made music his sole career. But music wasn't his first choice, I reflected; he merely took the path of least resistance and settled for second best. Whereas for me, music was my passion, my only passion . . . Much more than a profession, even the most prestigious of professions: it was my vital force, my soul's expression, my *true calling*. I would fade away and die if I were not allowed to sing. It was my acute awareness of this that drove me to accept every challenge – such as the two recordings I'd just made in languages I could not speak. Would George die if he were forbidden to sing? No, I did not think so.

How could I break it to George that I was scheduled to return to Paris in two months to make a new recording? It was sure to hurt him if I spoke of Monsieur Hazan's enthusiasm, my budding friendship with Odile, and my collaboration with Philippe Weil. How could I tell him that all these important people believed in me?

The life I returned to was not easy. After paying the rent and making the mortgage payment on my parents' apartment, we barely had enough money for food. George didn't complain, but I could tell from his eyes that he had hoped for something different. Every night he played the guitar and sang in the same tavernas where he and I had met three years earlier. He made only a modest living, and I was already bringing in more money than he did – a fact I wished I could hide from him. Greece was only just beginning to be open to new ideas and other cultures. It was very unusual, even shocking, for a woman to earn more money and be more successful than her husband. Granted. Nevertheless, he would get over it if he were happy with his life and if he saw a future for himself in music. But I had the feeling that he had second thoughts, that he was looking elsewhere, and there were times when he gave me the impression that he regretted abandoning his studies.

Out of consideration for George, I went to the Floka less often, and I refrained from talking about my delight at the prospects Monsieur Hazan dangled before me. Louis would have me singing on all the world's stages! Thinking of where it all might lead one day made me giddy and warmed my heart. And I was angry with myself for this pleasure, which I was unable to share with my husband.

10

New York with Quincy Jones

I n May 1961 I was back in Paris. This time, the Hazans put me up in a small hotel on the same street where they lived – Rue Montalembert, a stone's throw from Boulevard Saint-Germain. In the meantime, I had learned a few French expressions by heart, plus a few hundred words, and now I could ask my way. Paris was now more familiar, and with the arrival of spring this city, which had once seemed so gray, looked almost festive.

In quick succession, I heard my first French recording (it had just come on the market) and my German record, 'Weisse Rosen aus Athen'. Oddly, neither of the records had my picture on the cover. I tried to convince myself that I didn't care. But this decision to erase me, to hide me from the public gaze, was hurtful. I experienced again the sadness of my childhood. Still now, as in the past, I was not the hoped-for person. The Germans elected to illustrate my record with a pretty girl posing in front of the Parthenon with a rose in her hand. The French went about it a bit more discreetly; they adorned the jacket with a bouquet of microphones. Naturally, I kept my disappointment to myself.

It was too early to know how the French recording would be received, but Louis Hazan had very good news from Germany. Shortly after its release, 'Weisse Rosen aus Athen' made it onto the chart of top-selling records. The song was on everyone's lips and was being played on all the radio stations.

'Really?'

'Absolutely, Nana. Since your record is off to such a fast start, I can even advance you a little money if you need it.'

That news somewhat made up for my photo's absence from the record jacket. I consoled myself, just as I had done on the carrier *Forrestal*, with the thought that I could be loved despite everything, since Heaven had blessed me with a voice.

Philippe Weil had four new songs for me to record. Two of them would soon be finalists in the Coq d'Or de la Chanson Française 'Ton adieu' ('Your Goodbye') by Pierre Delanoë and Hubert Giraud, an 'Je reviendrai dans mon village' ('I'll Return to My Village'), by Eddie Marnay and Emile Stern.

After that, it was back to Athens. But according to Louis Hazan, things were on the move. He told me that because of my success in Germany, the Netherlands had already requested me to travel to Amsterdam to record 'White Roses'. Italy and Spain (aware that I'd won first prize in Barcelona) were lining up as well.

The plan was for me to return to Paris in the fall to cut a third disk, which we hoped would reach even more European countries.

In midsummer 1962, as I continued to perform at the Astir and Dzaki, I received two pieces of encouraging news in quick succession. My record went gold in Germany, meaning that it had sold a million copies. One million! Louis Hazan had to tell me three times before I believed it. It was staggering to think that a million German households had welcomed me into their homes. At about the same time, an invitation arrived from the Elysée Palace – the French president's official residence. I was invited to sing at the Palais de Chaillot on the occasion of the visit to France by the Shah of Iran and his wife, Empress Farah (whom the French persisted in calling by her maiden name, Farah Diba).

So the Elysée had heard of me! I wondered if it was due to my success in Germany. Going by what Monsieur Hazan told me, I didn't think I could give the credit to my two French releases: although favorably received by the critics, my records had not sold well in France. Perhaps I should attribute the Elysée's invitation to the infatuation with Greece that continued unabated since *Never on Sunday*.

Meanwhile my German producer, Ernst Ferch, asked me to consider a tour in Germany as soon as possible. A tour ... I had only a vague notion of what that would entail, and I wavered between excitement and anxiety. What a joy to sing every night! But how could I get by in a country whose language I couldn't speak?

Louis Hazan favored the idea, just as he favored everything that distanced me from Greece and launched me into the outside world.

It was pleasant autumn weather when I returned to Paris in early October 1962. The leaves on Boulevard Saint-Germain were beginning to change color, and I was humming the classic collaborative success of Yves Montand and Jacques Prévert, 'Les feuilles mortes' ('Autumn Leaves'), whose lyrics I could at last understand. Not in a million years could I have foreseen that forty years later I myself would record that song in homage to Prevert, Montand, and Mouloudji – and that it would become one of my best songs in English. Upon my arrival at Orly the previous evening, I was honored by my very first reception committee – reporters and photographers who were there to document the moment I received a pearl necklace from the Elysée as a welcoming gift. The next morning, as I passed a newspaper stand, I spied a photograph of myself on the front page of a newspaper. I didn't venture to buy it, but I did walk over to get a better look. The photo showed me biting a pearl, as the journalists had requested. The caption took me a few minutes to decipher: 'Nana Mouskouri, la perle des voix, chantera à Paris pour Farah Diba' (Nana Mouskouri, that pearl of a voice, will be singing in Paris for Farah Diba.)

That night I celebrated my twenty-seventh birthday. Next day Farah Diba was twenty-three. My birthday was 13 October, hers was 14 October. I thought it was a good omen.

I decided to wear the black lace dress Jenny made for me, which had brought me luck at the Athens and Barcelona festivals. This night in Paris was the last time I ever wore it. Roland Ribet, of whom more later, was about to become my manager, and he declared war against black.

'All dressed in black, you look like a Sicilian widow,' he grumbled. 'You'd be so much prettier in white or red!'

'I'm not a cover girl,' I replied. 'As long as they like my songs they can take me as I am.'

But Ribet was not yet part of my life, and I appeared on the stage of the Palais de Chaillot sheathed in black lace, sporting the 'cat eye' glasses I wore at the time.

To think that the sovereigns of Iran, along with General de Gaulle and his wife, were just on the other side of the footlights! The thought was so intimidating that, as usual, I kept my eyes closed. I sang only Greek songs that evening, transported by Nikos' verses, which never ceased to move me, and by Manos' unique style of buoyant, swinging music.

Other singers preceded me, one of them being Charles Aznavour. I was delighted to meet him again after the show, when General de Gaulle introduced us to his guests. I was struck by Farah's lack of affectation. I appreciated her fond words about Greece, as well as the supportive comments by General de Gaulle and his wife. I remember the astonishing youthfulness of the Shah, who held my hand in his while he said in perfect French, 'Bravo, Mademoiselle, you are a woman of great talent.'

A few days after that gala evening, I was confined in the Blanqui Studios to record my third French disk. This time, three of the four numbers were the songs by Manos Hadjidakis that had brought me fame in Greece. The first was 'Roses blanches de Corfou', the French version of my gold record 'Weisse Rosen aus Athen', which Manos originally composed for the documentary *Greece, Land of Dreams*. The other two were 'La procession' ('I Timoria') and 'Adieu mon cœur' ('Addio'). The fourth song, 'Sonata', was French. Romantic and nostalgic, it was written for me by Eddie Marnay and Emile Stern.

It was during this stay in Paris that I encountered Edith Piaf. Of course I had heard her sing, but I had never seen her. She was appearing at the Olympia, and Monsieur Hazan decided to take me there. I wish I could find the right words to express the feelings that swept over me the second she stepped on that bare stage, dressed all in black, her frail body and white mask of a face in the spotlight. With the faintest of smiles, she approached the mic, and suddenly the audience held its breath. One could hear her soft footsteps on the boards. As for me, my heart stopped beating. And suddenly she was singing. Whereupon, as though it could hold back no longer, the auditorium erupted in a brief spasm of wild applause ... And then there was only the voice of Piaf ... and us, her listeners, weeping. At least I, for one, couldn't hold back my tears. How was it possible for simple words and notes to evoke so much emotion, regret, and nostalgia? Piaf stripped us down to our core and wrenched our hearts, leaving us quivering with empathy for her loneliness, her mass of sorrows, and her despair ... Why do I even speak of words when most of the lyrics were unintelligible to me? Unless I understood them without knowing them. Unless Piaf's voice uttered them so clearly that the whole world understood.

'I noticed that you were crying,' Louis Hazan said as we left.

In fact I was still crying, but now I was angry as well.

'I should be ashamed to call myself a singer,' I said. 'After hearing her, I don't think I'll ever again have the audacity to appear on a stage.'

I still remember Hazan's reply as we stood on the steps of the Olympia Theater among the milling spectators:

'Now listen to me, Nana. Not only will you have that "audacity", but one day it'll be your name displayed in big red letters on this very marquee.'

Next night, Odile came to get me for dinner. All day long I'd thought of nothing but Piaf. I was in a highly emotional state, on the brink of tears, my nerves raw and exposed. An entire day spent wondering how I could dare sing after this woman ... And why even bother, since I could never rise even to the level of her ankle? It was Odile who found the words that got me back on my feet again and set me on the right path. She restored my desire to sing, the thing that had always been my mainstay and without which I would surely fall apart.

'You know,' she said, 'there aren't two Piafs in this world, just as there are not two Callases or two Judy Garlands. Your goal is not to be equal to them but to find your own place. Each artist is unique and so is what he or she has to say. Once you've discovered yourself, you won't be a copy of Piaf or Judy Garland – you'll be Nana Mouskouri, and you too will be unique.'

I had been drowning, and with those few words Odile saved me.

As the winter of 1962 began, I flew to Germany. This time I would be away for a whole long month, and I felt a little bit as though I were leaping into the abyss. I was scheduled to make this first tour in the company of two German singers, Heidi Brühl and Gerhard Wendtland, both of whom had gold records of their own. Louis Hazan told me that the German press was already calling us 'the three golden voices'. I was the only foreigner in our trio, and the only one never to have gone on tour. The same band would accompany us throughout. I wondered how well the German musicians and I would get along and worried about my ability to communicate with them. In spite of having a lot to be concerned about, I would have been perfectly happy with the way my life was going – except that I felt guilty for being happy! I had just spent Christmas with George and reproached myself for leaving him again so soon. And for abandoning my parents, who didn't understand the need for all this traveling. Wasn't success in Greece enough for me? Why change horses in midstream and leave Athens just when I was starting to make a name for myself here? Wouldn't I end up forgotten in my own country?

Our itinerary was to carry us right across West Germany: Hamburg, West Berlin, Hanover, Munich, Stuttgart. As soon as I arrived, I met my traveling companions. The two singers, Heidi and Gerhard, would make the trip in their personal car along with their respective assistants or managers, I didn't know which. The band would travel by bus. And what about me? Did I have a car, a personal manager, a secretary, a dresser? No, I had none of that. In that case, it might be best for me to travel with the musicians; there should still be some empty seats on the bus. Sure enough, it wasn't much trouble to find a seat for me, along with space in the baggage hold for my suitcase – and we were off.

From the very first rehearsal, the musicians and I saw eye to eye. I don't know what secret language we used, but the minute they heard me sing our mutual understanding was established. And from the start I felt that they enjoyed playing for me. You could hear it and see it on their faces. I think they realized that, living for music as I did, I liked them right away and appreciated their contribution. I sang Manos Hadjidakis' most beautiful songs, and I felt sure the players sensed the beauty of Nikos Gatsos' lyrics. Of course we performed 'Weisse Rosen aus Athen', and in addition 'Les enfants du Pirée', 'Addio' and 'La procession'.

I had to battle stage-fright every night before going on stage, but from the first notes I ceased to be me and became something light, disembodied – as though all that remained of my body, racked by doubt and anxiety moments earlier, was a soul and a voice to express gratitude for the gift of living, loving, and sharing. During this tour, I felt for the first time that I existed independently of Manos. I was being applauded and acknowledged for myself, not as the voice of Manos Hadjidakis and not as his creation. Perhaps Odile's prophecy was coming true and I was on my way toward 'finding my place'. Flying solo, far removed from my two mentors, gave me an opportunity for introspection; the time had finally come for self-discovery.

Looking ahead to the singer I would become and the life in store for me kept me in a state of excitement and anticipation. A little nervous energy of that sort was the least of what I needed in order to put up with the daily difficulties of touring – nights too short for adequate sleep, the monotony of driving mile after endless mile, physical discomfort, and above all the anxiety that seized me every afternoon when dusk fell and I began to count the hours till I had to go on stage. Focusing on my goal helped me endure the solitude of our days off, when all the musicians returned to their homes and I was left alone to wander the suburbs of a city obscured by fog. I no longer asked myself why I was doing this; I knew why. As Nikos suggested, I had reached for the hand that promised me a future, and now I was following the path of my personal destiny.

Unexpected news awaited me on my return to Paris. Quincy Jones wanted me to fly to New York to make a jazz recording. When Monsieur Hazan told me, I couldn't believe it. Quincy and I had not spoken since that brief phone call between Barcelona and Paris. Why this sudden wish to work with me?

'Come on,' I said laughingly to Louis. 'He doesn't know me. He doesn't even know I like jazz.'

'There you're wrong. He thinks you do marvelous Ella Fitzgerald standards.'

'You're kidding; he's never heard me sing jazz!'

'Oh yes, he has! Do you really believe he'd bring you all the way to New York if he hadn't heard you?'

'But how? When?'

Then Monsieur Hazan reminded me of an incident I'd forgotten about. One year earlier, on that terrible day when I had such trouble recording 'Retour à Napoli', something happened to cheer me up; at the time, I considered it absolutely spontaneous and unmotivated. As soon as 'Napoli' was in the can, Philippe Weil brought three great jazz musicians into the studio: the pianist Georges Arvanitas, the bass player Pierre Michelot, and Christian Garros, the drummer.

'Here you go, Nana,' said Philippe. 'Now you can relax. These guys are here just for you. It's a token of my appreciation!'

Despite my weariness the idea of singing a few standards delighted me, and for the space of an hour the four of us had a great time jamming together.

What Philippe didn't tell me was that he recorded the whole session and sent the tape to Quincy Jones.

A composer, trumpeter and arranger of genius, Quincy was at that time the artistic director of Mercury, an American label soon to merge with Philips. His plan was to have me record a jazz album for worldwide distribution. Monsieur Hazan was all for it, and lectured me at length on the opportunity this invitation offered me.

Opportunity? Well, of course, but I was so disturbed by the prospect of going to the United States that I scarcely heard what Monsieur Hazan was saying. Back then, America was still the last-ditch destination for Greeks forced to emmigrate to another country. For years destitute families had exiled themselves there, praying that Providence would come to their aid. Some of them we never heard from again, which only intensified the fear we felt at the thought of that vast, uncivilized country. Even the ones who made a success of it reported to us how hard they had struggled in order to survive. It was no good telling myself that my situation was different – the idea of going to America stirred up old nightmares . . .

But at the same time, it was so exciting! America was the land of James Dean in Elia Kazan's *East of Eden*, James Dean again in Nicholas Ray's *Rebel Without a Cause*, the land of John Wayne in John Ford's *Fort Apache*, of the unforgettable Marlon Brando in *On the Waterfront*, of Marilyn Monroe and Judy Garland. All my buried childhood dreams came back to the surface: I remembered longing to be a character on the screen. How I'd love to see Busby Berkeley's *Babes on Broadway* again, or George Cukor's *A Star is Born!* For an instant, I wondered if life was performing a magic trick by thrusting me into a movie!

I felt a little drunk after I left Hazan's office. Returning to my hotel that clear February afternoon, I got some odd looks from people on the Boulevard Raspail as I walked along, talking to myself.

Louis' parting words had been:

'Now go home to Athens and get some rest. I'll expect you back here in spring to make a new record. And this summer: New York!'

What would George think of all these plans? I was returning from a tour in Germany only to announce that I wouldn't be with him this summer. We'd been married now for almost eighteen months, and so far all my exciting projects had been abroad: in Germany (where I was probably as well known now as in Greece) and particularly in Paris, home of everyone working to build my future.

He protested for the first time:

'It's as if we don't even live together,' he said sadly. 'You and I are each doing our own thing . . . We can't go on like this . . .'

He was right, but what was the solution? I felt guilty about causing him unhappiness. But for things to change, I would have to give up everything being offered to me – all these invitations to sing – and that would be like giving up breathing. If I sacrificed my singing for the sake of our marriage, what kind of couple would we make: me, a wife unable to hide her bitterness and regret, and George, a husband whose career was on hold, always hoping for recognition that might never come?

Toward the end of our last meeting, Monsieur Hazan slipped in a remark that I pretended not to catch:

'If things go on this way, Nana, you'll have to think about permanent residence in Paris. All these hotels and airplane tickets cost a fortune, and anyway it would be so much better to have you right here, on the spot.'

I didn't want to think about it, even though it often kept me awake at night. With me in Paris and George in Athens, what would be left of us?

I don't know what possessed me to pick Takis Kambas to go with me to New York. To his credit, that funny little man, so tortured by doubt and anxiety, had booked two of my earliest successes: the *Forrestal* concert and the Barcelona festival. On the other hand, his presence at those events hadn't been that helpful; in fact, his lack of faith in me could have been disastrous. Never mind, I needed a companion for my trip. Also, I was afraid my English wasn't adequate, whereas Takis spoke it fluently.

The closer the departure date came, the more nervous I got. What if I disappointed Quincy Jones? Odile Hazan, the only person I dared confide in, didn't think it possible. She had heard a preliminary version of my latest record (featuring in particular 'Savoir aimer' and 'Ce soir à Luna Park') and like her husband she believed that, as I gained confidence, my voice was gradually reaching its full potential.

Our trip was only days away when a disaster occurred that filled Paris with horror: an Air France Boeing crashed on takeoff at Orly, killing 130 people. The tragedy was on every front page and, since it had happened so recently, it was difficult not to think of it in the car taking us to Orly. Takis Kambas, who joined me in Paris, was white-knuckled and positively mute. Luckily, Odile insisted on coming to the airport with us, and she tried to distract us by describing the latest skits by Fernand Raynaud at the Théâtre des Variétés. But she too was worried sick, and suddenly she whispered in my ear:

'In any case, plane crashes don't happen every day. There won't be another one for a very long time – it's the law of statistics – so you don't have a thing to worry about.'

Should I have communicated her soothing words to Takis, feverishly mopping his brow as we took off? I didn't have the energy to talk. Instead, I spent the whole flight making a mental list of songs I might sing if Quincy stuck a mic in my face the second we disembarked.

But Quincy wasn't at the airport; he sent us his car, which left us nothing to do but enjoy the scenery. As we crossed the bridge into Manhattan, I gasped in amazement at the untold number of immensely tall skyscrapers. These massive steel towers, many of them with glass facades, glittered like mirrors under the noonday sun. So this was New York! I didn't think such a city could exist anywhere in the world, and Takis Kambas (his smile restored) was amused by my astonishment.

'Take a good look at the sky, because in a few minutes you'll have to crane your neck to see it.' Indeed, as the traffic inched its way into

Manhattan we gradually had the impression that we were moving along the floor of a gorge. The light seemed to be funneled down the steep walls of the buildings, on which the sun from time to time etched huge incandescent triangles. If I dared, I would have told Takis that it recalled my first visit, as a child, to the Temple of Zeus in Greece. At one point, I stood transfixed between two columns, awed by the grandeur of the site. Tilting my head back, I looked up at the sky, and suddenly the sight of the sun so far away and so high caused me to have a dizzy spell.

Likewise, when I stuck my head out of the window and looked up at the tall buildings, I experienced an attack of vertigo and had to hold on to my armrest and the back of the driver's seat to steady myself. Now we were definitely in Manhattan. When we stopped at a traffic light, the city's hot breath came in at us through the open windows: it was lunchtime, and the sidewalks exuded the smell of hotdogs and hamburgers, mixed with the somewhat nauseating odor of coffee, followed suddenly by the stench of trashcans – and of tar, because when the sun gets hot enough, it melts the asphalt in places. Numbers of diverse, colorful individuals weaved in and out of shops, restaurants, residential brownstones, office buildings, in an inextricable tangle. Good Lord, everyone certainly was tall! Much taller than people back home in Greece. Women walked alone, spine straight, shoulders back, head held high, their blonde hair blown about by the warm breeze. The men wore elegant white shirts with their jackets slung casually over one shoulder – exactly like Humphrey Bogart in Howard Hawks' *The Big Sleep*. Were all Americans so tall and good-looking? I turned my head and saw a policeman on horseback crossing the street at the next intersection ... Now, Takis told me, we were in an upscale area – driving west on Fifty-Ninth Street, headed for Fifth Avenue, the city's most fashionable thoroughfare. Our taxi turned south on Fifth, made an immediate right into Grand Army Plaza, and sailed up to the main entrance of the Plaza Hotel. Central Park was right across Fifty-Ninth Street.

So this was the fabled Plaza. It occurred to me that this hotel must be the New York equivalent of the Lutetia in Paris. I was immediately struck by the Edwardian elegance of the sumptuous lobby with its bronze statues bearing luminous globes; the dark, gleaming furniture and luxurious carpets. Everywhere, enormous fans circulated fresh air.

As soon as I was inside my room, I had the same impulse to do what I did on my first night at the Lutetia: I ran to the window. But this was so different! My room faced Fifty-Eighth Street, but it was impossible to see the street, the cars, the people moving below. My room was too high off the ground, I supposed. In proof of this, the windows had been adjusted to make it impossible to lean out of them. On the other hand, I couldn't see even a sliver of blue sky. Therefore, my room must be halfway up the building . . . So instead, I looked into the windows of the office building across the street. Men were talking on the telephone; others were writing, bent over their papers, cigarettes dangling from their lips. A young woman crossed the room without giving them a single glance; a second later, she passed by again with a pile of folders in her arms.

The phone jolted me out of my absentminded musings. Quincy Jones! 'Hi, baby. Good trip?'

'I just got here. The hotel is fabulous!'

'Did you find the music?'

'What music?'

'Look around your room. I sent over a bunch of stuff. Just to give you something to do. I'll come by to pick you up tonight. Till then, have a good time!'

I wanted to ask what time he was coming, but he had already hung up. So I searched my room and discovered a treasure. There, on top of a chest of drawers, were all the recordings arranged by Quincy, his personal records, a record player, and a pile of books on jazz.

For lunch, Takis and I went downstairs and had a hamburger. Then I let Takis take off to roam the New York streets, which he knew well, while I went back upstairs to immerse myself in jazz. In a few hours I was going to be face to face with a man who worked with Duke Ellington, Sarah Vaughan, Ray Charles and Count Basie. The thought of it was both exciting and chilling. As always, I dreaded disappointing anyone who had singled me out. And as usual, the best way to calm myself was to play records of the greats and superimpose my voice over theirs.

Quincy finally arrived, and when I got downstairs he opened his arms wide to give me a hug. Perhaps he sensed my anxiety because the first things he said were meant to reassure me. He told me he was very impressed by the recording Philippe Weil had sent him, and he sensed that my voice had a wide range of possibilities. That night, he took me to listen to some young singers at the Apollo Theater. Our dinner afterward was very pleasant and companionable.

He wasn't sure when we could begin work. Possibly in three or four days. Right now, he was recording with Dinah Washington and Johnny Mathis . . .

He called me the next evening.

'How was the Big Apple today?' he asked.

I decided I should stop worrying about Quincy, above all stop torturing myself, and start enjoying 'the Big Apple' – New York City.

So the very next day I did just that, setting out with guidebook and subway map in hand. All on my own I explored Brooklyn, Chinatown, Chelsea, Harlem and the Bronx. Every evening, Quincy called with the same question: 'So, how was the Big Apple today?' And I would describe my day.

But one day, he surprised me.

'Take it easy, baby,' he said. 'Tonight I'm taking you to meet the masters of jazz. It's time to introduce you to the best of the best.'

He came to pick me up, and we drove through the summer night to Harlem to hear Louis Armstrong, Chet Baker, Dizzie Gillespie, Miles Davis, and a few nights after that, the idol of my teens – Ella Fitzgerald!

I wept as I listened to her. Luckily, Quincy didn't notice.

Three weeks went by. Takis Kambas was long gone. To spoil my niece Aliki, Jenny's daughter, I ransacked the treasure trove of children's toys at FAO Schwarz, across from the Plaza on the corner of Fifth Avenue and East Fifty-Ninth Street. I had plenty of time on my hands. Then suddenly, Quincy was free! A&R Studio on Forty-Eighth Street was available to us. Its founder Phil Ramone would be our sound engineer. Besides his other accomplishments, Phil Ramone is an innovative record producer who has worked with Frank Sinatra, Bob Dylan, Billy Joel, Luciano Pavarotti, and countless other great artists such as Paul Simon and Barbra Streisand.

The first two or three days were difficult. I had a list of quite a few songs to choose from, but Quincy and I had trouble finding the right fit. We were groping our way and making very little progress. Quincy was tense and demanding.

'Come on, baby,' he urged. 'Convince me!'

Luckily, as in Germany, and as always, the musicians were on my side. They could hardly believe that a singer from so far away, from a tiny country dangling off the edge of Europe, knew so many of the old American jazz standards. When I sang they smiled, and afterwards they applauded and hugged me.

Out of twenty songs, we finally settled on a dozen, including 'What Now My Love', 'No Moon at All', and 'Love Me or Leave Me'. We recorded those songs over three or four days, during which everything miraculously clicked. Thrilled and working at fever pitch, we took advantage of the miracle – not wanting to come down from our high, afraid to stop while we were on a roll, reluctant to lose a second while divine inspiration was upon us . . .

Quincy got what he wanted, the musicians were full of praise, and I could only thank them over and over again. Without them, the music would not have possessed me as it did.

We agreed that, in a few weeks, Quincy would join me in Paris at the Blanqui Studio to do some last-minute fine-tuning.

That night he drove me to the airport after our last day of recording. I was exhausted and at the same time loopy with excitement and happiness over the experience we had just shared.

I was between laughter and tears as we hugged each other on parting. I realized how fond I was of this man and this country that seemed so scary before I arrived. Now I couldn't wait to come back.

I was late and had to run very hard to make it to the gate. Not until I was aboard the plane did I remember what Monsieur Hazan said to me when he phoned the day before.

'I have good news for you, Nana. I'll tell you about it when you get back to Paris.'

'Why not tell me now?'

'Artists must not be disturbed when they're working. Finish what you're doing with Quincy Jones first. Just wait and see: I know you'll be glad.'

II

Outstage in Two Minutes

*I*t was barely daybreak when we landed at Orly. I hadn't slept a wink during the flight. I was too impatient to see the Hazans, tell them about my American adventure, and hear the news Louis Hazan had for me.

It was still too early to rouse them, so I ordered coffee and a croissant at the airport café. All around me, men were smoking Gauloises, cigarettes with black tobacco smoked only in France. Suddenly, the mingled aromas of coffee, cigarettes and my croissant filled me with happiness that was almost painful. France was my adopted country, but I felt as if I'd returned to my native land. 'God, it's good to be home!' I said to myself. I smiled at the waiter, at the smokers, at all of Orly airport which was now so familiar. I thought back to that day when I anxiously searched for the Hazans in the waiting crowd, the first time I arrived here from Athens 'like a terrified peasant'. Was it possible that France had already appropriated so much space in my heart?

Then I was in a taxi rolling along on this August morning with the sun barely above the horizon. I had the driver drop me in front of a bakery on Boulevard Saint-Germain. The trees looked enormous, now that their boughs swelled with foliage. Some of the branches were long enough to brush against the buildings. The sidewalks were still empty at this hour. Out in the street, which was built of paving stones, a car or two drove slowly past every now and then. I planned to wake the Hazans with croissants. I knew Odile would throw her arms around my neck, while her husband would show more restraint. He would stand back with that slight smile of his, not quite sure of his attitude toward me.

145

'She looks sweet enough, but she's proud – and stubborn as a mule,' I heard him tell Philippe Weil one day, and he was only half-joking.

I rang the bell, and everything went the way I expected. Odile, still in her nightgown, welcomed me with a torrent of excited questions and affectionate words. Then Louis, already in shirt and necktie, asked me to sit down while Odile prepared coffee.

'Well, Nana, how did it go with Quincy Jones?'

I launched into a long saga, digressed, lost my thread, and finally wound down.

'Well, that's great!' he said when I was through. 'Now guess what's next. Do you want to know what we have lined up for the fall?'

'Oh yes, please tell me. I can't wait to hear!'

'The Olympia! The headliner is Georges Brassens. You will open for him.'

The Olympia! The first image that leapt into my head was of course the one and only, the incomparable Edith Piaf. I was speechless, stunned. And I probably turned pale, because Louis found it necessary to add:

'I'm counting on you. This is a once-in-a-lifetime opportunity.'

He was right, of course, but I needed time to process it. This was huge . . . overwhelming . . . Me at the Olympia! I couldn't believe it.

'How did this come about? I'm not very well known.'

'Roland Ribet persuaded Bruno Coquatrix.'

'I don't know anyone named Roland Ribet.'

'But he knows you. You'll be meeting him tonight, and if everything works out, you can hire him as your manager.'

By the time I left the Hazans I was exhausted, knocked off my feet. I would see them again that night in order to make the acquaintance of this Monsieur Ribet. I was glad that Philippe Weil with his irreverent, irrepressible sense of humor was going to be there, too. Phew! In the meantime, I only wanted to fall into bed and sleep at last. With a sigh of relief and gratitude, I made it to my room at the Hotel Montalembert.

Roland Ribet had laughing eyes and a pleasant face. But I sensed right away that behind his agreeable façade, the man had a critical eye and a sharp tongue. It was too soon for him to accuse me of dressing like a 'Sicilian widow', but I saw him looking sideways at my clothes and 'cat eye' glasses, and I had a feeling that he was about to put me on trial. A friendly trial – nothing like the harsh judgment rendered by Mr Spartacus and the ladies at the Astir – but strong censure nonetheless. He would mount a vigorous offense, and I would be on the defensive. For it was crystal-clear that Roland Ribet didn't find me very 'attractive' either. On this particular evening, he confined himself to questioning my first name, Nana. Wouldn't this be the right time – before the Olympia and while I was still relatively unknown – to change my name to something . . . well, something more appealing to the popular taste?

I told him I didn't like my real first name, Joanna. My parents only called me that when they were reprimanding me. Nana is the shortened form of Joanna. Since it was my father's pet name for me, I associated it with my father's pleasure in hearing me sing.

'It may not have commercial appeal,' I said, 'but Nana is my name and I'm sticking with it.'

'What if I insist?'

'No, I don't think it would do any good.'

Philippe Weil burst out laughing, Louis Hazan remained impassive, and Odile studied me with a thoughtful frown. Looking back on that evening and keeping in mind the trouble she took throughout that fall of 1962 to help me improve my 'look', I think Odile must have gauged the difficulty of the undertaking and asked Roland Ribet to leave things to her.

Next morning, I flew to Athens, eager to see George again and tormented by the thought that our reunion would not last more than ten days or so. I had to be back in Paris in early September to record some new songs and then get ready for the Olympia, where I was due to perform in December. This time, Louis Hazan insisted that I take up permanent residence in Paris, and I agreed to let him find me a room to be my first pied-à-terre in the French capital. I was gradually withdrawing, already starting to put down roots far from Greece and far from George.

He and his group were performing in Rhodes in August, so that was where I joined them. What bliss to have a little time together after so many long weeks apart! A little time for loving, talking, strolling. George had matured a lot during my absence, and he and his friends had reached some important decisions. They resolved to concentrate on Greek music and give up Mexican folk songs. With that in mind, they added a fourth musician capable of playing the bouzouki and the guitar both equally well. They sought Manos Hadjidakis' advice, and he suggested that they call themselves 'The Athenians'. Under this new, clearly identifiable name, they had just snagged their first engagement outside Greece: in the fall, they would be playing at the Blue Note in Amsterdam.

This development filled us with hope. Suddenly, my spending the fall in Paris seemed less of an obstacle to our relationship. The two capitals were only an hour apart by air. George would join me in Paris on his days off, and I would fly to Amsterdam to spend weekends with him.

I was no longer a total stranger in Paris. I had a garret room in the heart of the Latin Quarter, I was a regular customer at the corner grocery, and I had a concierge who knew me and kept my mail for me. My room was tiny. Scarcely through the door, I bumped into the bed. Being directly under the roof, the ceiling was slanted, and I kept knocking my head on it. But the room was cheap, which was all that mattered. Back in Greece, my family needed money. My parents had trouble making ends meet, and so did George's. In addition, Jenny's husband had suffered business setbacks. According to Greek custom, the one on whom fortune smiles must share his good luck. So I kept only enough for my needs and sent as much money as possible to all of them. This situation did not frustrate me, and I felt no resentment at all. In fact, the very natural act of sharing spared me the guilt I would otherwise feel for being so far from my loved ones, and for not being like all the other wives, concerned solely with their homes and the health and happiness of their husbands. I derived pleasure not from earning money but from singing. I couldn't get over how lucky I was that my records were selling. Hard to believe that people were paying me to do what I loved!

During that month of September, I recorded two new songs, 'Crois-moi ça durera' ('Believe Me It's Going to Last'), by Pierre Delanoë and Gilbert Bécaud, and 'Je reviendrai my love', the adaptation of an English song, 'Roses Are Red'. More important, though, I spent many afternoons in Odile's company. It was the first time we were able to really get to know each other. On leaving the Blanqui Studio, I went to meet her at the Café Flore or Les Deux Magots or the Closerie des Lilas, and little by little I learned how women in Western Europe led their lives – and how different it was where I came from. Odile herself was the embodiment of refinement and elegance. One glance at the two of us would illustrate the gulf that in those days separated our two countries.

Gently, without rushing me and without ever hurting my feelings, she made little suggestions to improve my appearance. One day she mentioned that a few days earlier she passed by the Yves Saint-Laurent boutique and spotted a pair of trousers she wanted me to try on.

'It's funny,' she said, 'but I thought of you the moment I saw them.'

'Who is this Saint-Laurent?'

'He's a fashion designer. Remember the plum-colored outfit I was wearing yesterday? Well, it's one of his. I have to go back there in a little while. Why not come with me?'

It was a pleasure to see Odile at Saint-Laurent. She was at ease, laughing, and tossing her long red hair. Without making a big deal about it, she showed me the trousers and said it was up to me. Of course the salesgirls saw that I was her friend and rushed over to offer their advice. While Odile was trying on a blouse, I tried the trousers. She was right: they were becoming. Little by little, I began to regard myself in a new light and also to examine myself with the discerning eye of those amazing salesgirls, who could have stepped right off the page of a glossy fashion magazine.

One day, I happened to remark how much I admired Maria Callas. Odile seized the opportunity to tell me about the doctor who changed Callas' life.

'She used to be fairly hefty, you know, and this Dr Heschberg worked miracles.'

'I didn't know that. I could stand to lose a few pounds, myself.'

'That's true, you'd be so much prettier. Why don't you go see the man?'

'Do you know him?'

'No, but he lives in Paris.'

'Will you make an appointment for me?'

'Of course!'

Dr Heschberg saw me two days later. He questioned me at length about my eating habits, and quickly picked up on my taste for sweets, particularly pastries. He drew up a list of things I could eat and provided a number of sample menus. Then, on another sheet of paper, he listed all the foods I must avoid. Sugar was one of the banned items, and I objected because I was an avid coffee drinker. The doctor asked if I was capable of consuming sugar in moderation. No, I didn't think so, and from that day on I decided to give it up completely, including in coffee.

'Very good,' said the doctor. 'Now it's all up to you. Come back in three weeks – but only if you've shed eleven or twelve pounds.'

I saw the surprise on his face when I entered his office three weeks later. I had lost twenty-two pounds!

Odile was delighted, heaping me with praise and encouragement.

'Now let's do something about your hair!' she exclaimed happily.

Why not? I generally wore it shoulder-length or in a bun. I wasn't sure there was any way to improve it, but my experience with Dr Heschberg taught me that some people can perform miracles, so I agreed to go with Odile to Alexandre's.

This time, the result was not good. The master stylist gave me bangs, Anna Karina style. They made my face seem heavier and formed an unsightly clump above my glasses. I quickly went back to my old hairstyle, parted down the middle, which at least had the merit of simplicity.

It was still only October. The Olympia lay far ahead, but Odile and I were already thinking of what I would wear. She took me to Dior and Louis Féraud, as well as back to Yves Saint-Laurent. That was how we made the acquaintance of a young Norwegian designer, Per Spook, who had just joined the House of Féraud. He was tall, handsome, very charming, and at the same time, modest to the point of shyness. I liked the simplicity of his creations and the respect he showed his models. He spoke little, knew how to listen, and was attentive and considerate. We soon established a rapport. He said to give him a little time, and he would have some sketches to show me in a few days.

For my birthday, on 13 October, Odile gave me a Hermès bag, a shoulder bag so elegant it took my breath away.

'For me? This is crazy, Odile, it's too beautiful!'

'Put the strap over your shoulder and walk around with it so I can see.'

I did so, and caught a glimpse of 'the new me' in a mirror. I had changed so much in only a few weeks!

'It looks great on you!' Odile exclaimed. 'Now you're a true Parisienne!'

Years later, Odile told me the story behind the Hermès bag. The wife of Jean-Jacques Tilché (then Philippe Weil's assistant artistic director) quietly pointed out to Odile that my handbag was plastic.

'It's sort of embarrassing; people look at her funny,' she said. 'Somebody should tell her.'

'I know,' Odile nodded. 'But everything in its proper time. Nana is very sensitive, and I don't want to hurt her feelings.'

That was why she used my birthday as an excuse to get rid of my old bag, which the salesgirls at Yves Saint-Laurent must have laughed at behind my back.

'Odile and I helped her a lot,' Louis Hazan later recalled, 'but without forcing the issue. She had to see for herself the need to fight that terrible Greek pride of hers. She had to come to the realization on her own that making an effort to be more attractive was nothing to be ashamed of.[5]

Did George find me attractive? Did he notice my metamorphosis the next time we got together for a couple of days? Yes, but he didn't seem very glad about it. Who talked me into going on a diet? Where did this new dress come from? And that handbag? I sensed that all these questions stemmed from his fear of losing me. In truth, it would never even occur to me to look at another man. But whether it made any sense or not, George was jealous.

It was my fault, I decided. George was Greek, deeply imbued with our culture and customs, and little by little he saw me shift allegiance to a different culture. He had never met the Hazans or Philippe Weil or

---

[5] *Pleins Feux*, ibid.

Roland Ribet, and there was no telling what he imagined them to be like. I ought to introduce them. I wanted him to see how generous and selfless these people were, concerned only with initiating me to the ways of the world and providing me with the keys to success. Unfortunately, we never got around to it. George and I had so little time together, and it went by too fast.

With George back in Amsterdam, I went back to spending time with Odile, who took charge of my Parisian education. She brought me to the Louvre, where I saw the Venus de Milo for the first time. The statue was discovered a century and a half earlier on the Greek island of Milos and purchased by the French as a gift for King Louis XVIII. Many Greeks are very bitter about the countless treasures carried off from our country. I didn't feel that way when I saw the Venus de Milo. I was proud that she was here in France, superbly displayed at the Louvre, where millions of people could admire her and marvel at the glory of Greek culture. If she had stayed at home, she might never have become famous at all.

At night, the Hazans often took me with them to the clubs in Saint-Germain des Prés. That's how I met Serge Gainsbourg and Dario Moreno. Gainsbourg was rather reserved but friendly. He was curious about where I came from, and we enjoyed chatting together. At that time, he was unknown and still working for other people. Odile introduced me to his first song, 'La poinçonneuse des Lilas' ('The Lady Ticket Puncher at the Lilas Métro'). Dario Moreno was already a star, and some nights ended with all of us standing around Dario singing Mexican songs.

My French was improving. I noticed it in October when I went back to the Blanqui Studio to record. I no longer rolled my r's, I had almost lost my Greek accent, and I no longer needed a dictionary to decipher lyrics. One year and eight months ago, I was practicing with a tape recorder in my room at the Lutetia. I had come a long way since then. Now, in October 1962, I was about to record 'Salvame Dios'. Charles Aznavour and I had kept in touch, and he had adapted the song for me.

The Olympia engagement was drawing near, and I spent the last two weeks of November rehearsing and preparing myself psychologically. I was to sing only three or four songs, selected from among my first recordings – 'C'est jolie la mer' ('The Beauty of the Sea'), a Greek song by Ianis Ioanidis and Manos Hadjidakis, 'La procession', also by Manos and Nikos, 'Ce soir à Luna Park', and 'Un roseau dans le vent'. I was slimmer than ever, and the dress created for me by Per Spook – black, with a spangled collar – gave me a silhouette I would never have dreamed of two months earlier.

Georges Brassens' name was spread across the music hall's façade in huge red letters. I was scheduled to perform right before the ventriloquist Jacques Courtois. On the marquee, my name appeared just above his in very small letters, which suited me just fine. As did the dressing room assigned to me, the smallest of the three. That lessened the challenge, I told myself: a failure on my part would not shake the foundations of the legendary Olympia Theater. I was well aware that Bruno Coquatrix was of two minds about my appearance on the program. He was interested in young artists who made the cover of the entertainment magazine *Salut les copains*, such as Johnny Halliday, Sylvie Vartan, or Claude François . . . Sylvie had already appeared on the Olympia's stage in the early part of this same year, when she opened for rocker Vince Taylor. She would be back again in the first weeks of 1963, with Claude François, Little Eva, and the electric Tornados, in a show whose title summed up the coming decade in France: *Les idoles des jeunes (Idols of the Young Generation)*. Bruno Coquatrix didn't rank me among those 'idols'. Clearly, he was waiting to see what the public thought of me.

Before going on stage, I had a bout of stage-fright that threatened to choke me. In spite of that, the premiere went wonderfully well. I opened with 'C'est jolie la mer' because I knew how powerfully Manos' music worked on me. At once, I was carried away, and all fear was gone. The polite applause when I made my entrance heartened me. I was aware that many people in the audience were hearing me sing for the very first time, and I longed to communicate with them and have them share my feelings.

Did I succeed? The first feedback came from Brassens himself. After listening to me, he commented in true Brassens style: 'That Greek kid will go far!' He was talking to Bruno Coquatrix. And how did Bruno react? When he passed Brassens' remark along to me, it was with a little smile that said, 'If that's what Brassens thinks, then it must be so.'

My heart went out to Georges Brassens: he suffered from chronic kidney trouble. Some nights he was in such pain from renal colic and kidney stones that he could not go on. Sometimes he had to leave the stage in mid-performance. Bruno Coquatrix was aware of the risk, but instead of canceling the show, he had a lineup of superstars ready to step in, including Colette Renard, Mouloudji, Ferré, Bécaud, and Béart. Whenever Brassens had to be taken to the hospital, one of these other artists would arrive within minutes and perform in his stead. It was a wonderful thing, very moving, and I believe very few people asked to exchange their tickets.

As for me, I spent the evening backstage listening to them. Ardently.

From the start, I was enchanted by the spirit of the venerable music hall. I loved its slightly lopsided stage, its creaking floorboards, its maze of dark backstage passageways, and even the drafts of air that assailed spectators as they exited their boxes. The stage director, musicians, and technicians were all very accommodating, considerate, and helpful, and they always had a word of praise and encouragement. Everyone called the stage director 'Doudou'. One of his jobs was to let us know how much time was left before we had to go on stage. You might suppose he'd be associated in my mind with the fright that seized me five minutes before my entrance. But you would be wrong. Doudou had his own special way of defusing the tension. In my case, for instance, he refrained from yelling 'Nana Mouskouri – two minutes!' Instead he sighed as if about to swoon with rapture, '"C'est jolie la mer" in two minutes,' which made everyone smile. And I would run over and hug him.

The curtain came down for the last time on Christmas Eve. I still didn't know if the public liked me or if any of the influential critics had reviewed me. At any rate, I scarcely had time to savor my experience at the Olympia. The first day of the new year, 1963, I was off to make my first record in London. It was my very first time in the UK, a country very important in my professional and musical life.

The weather was so bad over Orly that January morning that the flight to London was canceled. The passengers were driven to the Gare du

Nord railroad station. We had to take the train and then the cross-Channel ferry. At first I tried to keep a sense of humor about the whole thing, never suspecting the bureaucratic obstacle that lay ahead.

I had never crossed a national frontier aboard ship, so when we reached England I was surprised to find myself in a long queue waiting to go through customs before going ashore. In one line were passengers bearing work-permits, in the other those who did not, and of course I was standing in this second line. I noticed that there were many Greek, Italian and Spanish workers on board, and a man waiting with me explained that these immigrants were returning to Britain from vacations spent at home with their families.

When it was my turn at the gate, the conversation was brief:

'Why are you going to London?'

'To make a recording.'

'Your work-permit, please.'

I felt my legs wobble.

'But . . . I don't have one.'

'Next!'

The next passenger was breathing over my shoulder, and I went and sat down out of the queue, utterly stunned. Why didn't they ask me for a work-permit when I flew to Germany? What would happen now? Would I be put back on the ferry under police escort, while the executives at Philips awaited me vainly in London? Good Lord, how humiliating! I found nothing more intelligent to do than burst into tears.

By good fortune, a kindhearted man came and sat next to me.

'Why are you crying, Miss?'

I told him I couldn't go ashore, and that it was a disaster for me.

'Have you got a return ticket?'

'Yes.'

'Any money?'

'Yes, a little.'

'And what are you supposed to do in London that's so important?'

'I'm a singer, they're expecting me to make a recording.'

'Well then, you have a hotel, an address?'

'Of course.'

'Calm down then, stop crying, and let me explain. It's the customs officers' job to turn you back, because lots of illegal workers try to get into England via the ferry. Don't do what you did before. Get back into the same queue, and when the man asks you what you propose to do in London, tell him you're a tourist and show him your return ticket.'

'I can't. He'll recognize me.'

'No, no. At least give it a try, otherwise you won't be able to disembark.'

The next few minutes were agonizing. I imagined myself being called a liar, being put into handcuffs, being hauled off to prison ... But the customs man barely looked up as he stamped my passport.

It was ordained that my first trip to London would not be all roses. As I left the studio after my third day of recording, I overheard the director of Philips UK discussing me with his artistic director.

'I don't understand why Hazan is spending money on that girl. She sings well, but personally I don't think she has a chance of making it ...'

'You're wrong there,' said the other man, Jack Banerstock. 'I'd be willing to bet that she'll be a success.'

'Oh, really? Well, I'm going to call Hazan and let him know exactly what I think.'

That morning, I had bumped into Rod Stewart and Serge Gainsbourg who were recording in studios close to mine. We agreed to get together that night, but now I had no heart for the meeting. Utterly crushed, I went straight to my hotel. What would Louis Hazan think if that man called him? His faith in me would surely be shaken. My first German record had admittedly sold well, but my French sales were still in the lower brackets. I dreaded to think of a future without Monsieur Hazan's support.

My thoughts were running along these gloomy lines when Serge Gainsbourg called me. He and Rod were waiting for me in the hotel bar.

I remember that we spent the evening discussing our rapport with the public. Serge had been struck by my appearance at the Olympia, singing with my eyes closed and my hands behind my back.

'At the start,' I said, 'I don't have the courage to look at the audience. 'It comes only very gradually.'

'Well, I have no wish at all to look at them,' Serge told me. 'In fact, I often turn my back on them. I prefer the cinema to the stage – at least you're all alone then.'

'You don't want people to like you?'

'No, I don't think so. In any case, I don't like them.'

'I'm like Nana,' said Rod. 'I need applause. That's why I do my best to stir them up.'

Why did Serge sing if he didn't like his audience? I remember being disturbed by his words. For me, singing was intimately linked to my need to communicate my feelings to others. I finally solved this strange contradiction by telling myself that Serge was the purest artist among us, a creator. He had no need of other people's approval to forge ahead.

On my return from this English interlude, I stopped off for a few nights to perform at the Ancienne Belgique in Brussels. The previous week, Sylvie Vartan had raised scandalized eyebrows there. They were still talking about the event, and about the vitriolic article by the entertainment critic of *L'Echo de la Bourse:* 'She is eighteen years old, of Bulgarian origin, and she's being trumpeted as the latest idol offered up to the hysterical adulation of young rockers in black leather jackets. Poor little kid!'

My own reception was quite different. Neither hysterical adulation nor black leather jackets in the auditorium. A religious silence, and polite applause. Was that what it took to conquer the world? 'A great success, an accomplished singer whose shyness contributes to her appeal,' noted the manager of the Ancienne Belgique on a piece of paper that was later leaked to me. 'But badly dressed. Very poor results at the box office!'

12

'Sometimes God Closes a Little Door and Opens a Bigger One'

O n my return from the interlude in London and Brussels, everyone wanted to know about my participation in the upcoming Eurovision Song Contest. Not only had my London worries failed to discourage Monsieur Hazan, but the whole Philips team was now squarely behind me.

My artistic director Philippe Weil, with whom I had enjoyed such good relations, had been asked to step aside for a newcomer, Gérard Côte. He joined us from a rival company where, I was told, he had played an outstanding part in promoting the career of Gloria Lasso, a Latin singer who was very famous in France.

It was obvious at once how different the two men were. Philippe Weil adored music and performers. He could spend hours, never losing patience, in quest of perfection, as he had made clear during that horrible recording of 'Retour à Napoli' ('Come Back to Napoli'). Gérard Côte, on the other hand, seemed more concerned about my hair, glasses, and clothes than the songs I sang. But perhaps Louis Hazan believed it was in those details that my persona was still lacking, rather than my artistic side?

In any case, Gérard was determined to put all his weight behind my bid for the Eurovision 1963 Grand Prix. Candidates were already jostling in the lists. Alain Barrière would be flying French colors; Françoise Hardy would sing for Monaco; Heidi Brühl (with whom I made my first German tour) would represent Germany; and Ester Ofarim, a magnificent Israeli singer, would bear the Swiss flag.

And whose colors would I be flying? RTL (Radio Television

Luxembourg), and in particular Roger Kreicher and Monique Le Marcis, were unanimous in insisting that I represent Luxembourg. Why not, after all? Louis Hazan and Gérard Côte were also in favor. All that remained was finding a song that had a chance of victory.

Raymond Bernard and Pierre Delanoë quickly came forward with one, a song made to measure for this kind of contest: 'A force de prier' ('By Praying Aloud'). It was easy to master, and no doubt skillfully crafted to stir feelings and gather support on the very first hearing. Strangely, though, it failed to speak to me. Tunes by Manos and lines by Nikos set me dreaming, but I was unable to relate to this song's lyrics, which struck me as completely hollow and utterly unlike the person I am:

> A force de prier chaque nuit, chaque jour,
> A force d'implorer tous les dieux de l'amour,
> A force de chanter ton nom comme un poème,
> A force de t'aimer, it faudra que to m'aimes.

> By praying aloud every day, every night,
> By begging the gods for the gift of love's light,
> By singing your name to the heavens above,
> By loving just you, and craving your love.

Gérard Côte was enthusiastic, however, and I believe my hesitation irritated him. I don't know why I finally gave in, rather than refuse to sing it. Perhaps because I was the lone standout, and because once again I couldn't bear the idea of letting down all these people who believed in me.

That year, the Eurovision contest was not shown live before an audience, but filmed in a BBC studio. This was yet another handicap for me. As I told Serge Gainsbourg, I needed to feel the spectators' presence, to sense their breathing and their mood, in order to get in touch with my own emotions. I had to feel something of the order of Communion. How could you melt with feeling in front of a camera? I was not an actress, merely a singer, and it didn't help that this song failed to draw me out of myself.

The result was disastrous. I finished in eighth position, far behind Alain Barrière, who came in fifth with 'Elle était si jolie' ('She Was So Pretty'), and Françoise Hardy who was sixth with 'L'amour s'en va' ('Love Goes Away'). A Danish pair, the Ingmanns, won the Grand Prix with Dansevise (Dancing).

It was a huge disappointment. Jacques Hélian, music critic for *Bonne Soirée*, sank me with a few sentences that took me back all the way to Spartacus and the Astir: 'Nana Mouskouri, representing Luxembourg, is the perfect image of the international performer. What talent ... she sings ... she moves you to tears. But alas – the eternal problem of her appearance just won't go away! Otherwise, Nana Mouskouri might easily have won.'

I was frankly shaken. And not for a second did I foresee that this miserable Eurovision failure had just flung open America's – and even the whole world's – doors for me!

The very next day after the results were announced, I flung myself into my first recording of Greek songs under a French label. I wanted Manos and Nikos to enjoy the fame they deserved, and I chose our most beautiful songs: 'Paper Moon', 'The Young Cypress', 'Les enfants du Pirée', 'Somewhere in the World' ... I was returning to my sources on the heels of a Eurovision contest which had left me feeling that I had somehow lost my soul, and I rejoiced to find that the emotions of my beginnings were still intact.

I sang with all my faith, all my hope, and it helped to heal the wounds I had sustained in the first weeks of the year. Of course, I noticed that there was a new face in the recording booth at the Blanqui Studios, a young, long-haired man with light blue eyes who watched me with a friendly, curious expression. He very quickly emerged from the booth to tell me how much he liked my singing and my voice. We chatted. His name was André Chapelle, he had grown up near Beaune among the great vineyards of Burgundy, but music interested him much more than the vintner's trade. One evening, he came to tell me he thought that the disk we were recording was a safe bet to win the Grand Prix of the Académie du Disque.

'It's sweet of you to be so encouraging, but you know, a lot of people sing better than I do . . . '

'These songs are absolutely overpowering. I'm convinced you'll win the prize.'

André was right. Our recording carried off the prize, and two years later he became my artistic director. The most honest, the most talented, the most demanding, and the most passionate of artistic directors. Many years later, after George and I divorced, Andre came into my life. He is now my husband, and still my most faithful artistic brother-in-arms.

'Sometimes God closes a little door and opens a bigger one,' my mother often told us when we were young. Doubtless that was what He intended when He shut the Eurovision door in my face – first making sure that two highly influential people would be listening to me that night, and that they would immediately seek me out.

The first one had little trouble tracking me down, since she was the producer of the Eurovision show. Yvonne Littlewood, who also directed the program, called me a few days after my failure. She told me she had been impressed by my voice and my artlessness, and she wanted to invite me to her Saturday night musical broadcast.

I was both intimidated and hesitant. It took me several seconds to believe in this stroke of luck, and then of course I accepted.

This time, the skies were kind, the plane took off on schedule, nobody asked for my work permit, and Yvonne Littlewood's welcome reconciled me with London. I sang live, the broadcast seemed to go very well, and that evening, without realizing it, I forged a lasting bond of mutual esteem and trust with Yvonne. Four years later, she invited me back to the BBC for six weeks, and the resulting series of broadcasts over the next ten years (aired in every English-speaking country and even beyond) familiarized a vast stretch of the planet – from Australia to Singapore by way of New Zealand, India, Japan and Thailand – with my voice.

The other influential viewer of my Eurovision performance was of course Harry Belafonte. Forty years after that first encounter of ours, when he asked me if I would join his team, Harry Belafonte wrote:

'When I heard Miss Mouskouri for the first time, I knew at once that she was the one I wanted. What an extraordinary voice she had! So poignant, so unadorned, so fluid . . . '

The night after he made his offer, I was unable to sleep. Naturally, I was terrified by the thought of the challenge ahead. Naturally, I was insanely fearful that I might disappoint this man. But from now on, all questions of this nature – they would arise each time a new door opened for me – were accompanied by another more secret, more intimate concern. How would George accept the prospect of such long separations? Shortly before this trip to New York, we had decided to buy a small apartment in the Boulogne-Billancourt district in Paris. Monsieur Hazan was still urging us to settle there, and had even agreed to advance a large part of the money we would need. So now I was establishing myself more firmly in France, a step all my friends and associates welcomed. All except George! I knew that deep down, he would have preferred to remain in Greece forever. But he had accepted the idea of this apartment; it was his way of showing how important I was to him. I had flown to New York full of gratitude toward him and full of faith in our joint future. How could I inflict this new cause for distress on him?

Around the middle of the night my worries gave birth to a solution. Next morning, once again sitting across from Harry Belafonte, I mustered the strength (or should I call it the nerve?) to propose the arrangement I had dreamed up: 'If I come with you, would you agree to hire a Greek musician?'

'No, I'm afraid that wouldn't be possible. I have my own musicians, and can't afford to take on even one more person. Who is this musician?'

'My husband George. He's a very good guitar player.'

'Ah! I understand . . . Listen, I'll talk to Irving Green about it. Perhaps we can find some kind of compromise.'

I returned to France with the compromise in my pocket. It was agreed: George would play with us on every tour, and we would quite simply split my fee. I was happy for both of us. Once we reached an agreement, Belafonte said he looked forward to the contribution George would bring to his own musicians. I had noticed, in fact, how eager they were to discover new sounds, new voices, and I believed that they would welcome George the way they welcomed me, and with the same eagerness to make music together.

I've just written that 'I was happy,' that 'I believed ... ' But in the end, the only one for whom I couldn't speak was George. No doubt I was sure that he would jump for joy. But of course it was the opposite that happened.

George was outraged. How dared I mention his name to Harry Belafonte? He himself was just an amateur, a minor Greek guitar player, and I wanted him to work in the orchestra of one of the greatest stars in the Western hemisphere! It was madness, he said. He would be the laughing-stock of the whole of America, ridiculed, humiliated. He told me to call Belafonte right away, apologize, and tell him George wouldn't be joining him.

'You're quite wrong, George. I'm not ashamed of you, I love hearing you play ... '

'I'm not qualified to play in a professional orchestra!'

'Just work on your playing, and you'll be up to their standard quicker than you know.'

There is one advantage to avoiding noisy quarrels, to defusing conflicts: you give yourself time to think.

Two or three days later, George was no longer talking about canceling, and I caught him listening to Belafonte's records ...

Then the whirlwind swept me up again. I continued to record *My Favorite Greek Songs* at the Blanqui Studios. I left to make recordings in the Netherlands, in Italy, and then in Germany, where my first album came out. I sang just about everywhere, in clubs and small auditoriums. It was on one such occasion, as I left the stage of the Megève Casino in Switzerland, that I ran into the couturier Guy Laroche. I had already met him in Odile Hazan's circle.

'Nana, come and have a drink. I'm here with Alain Delon. We just heard you sing, and he'd like to meet you.'

'I can't, I'm sorry. I have to get back to Geneva for the first flight out tomorrow morning, and my pianist is waiting for me.'

'Just five minutes!'

I gave in. My head was still full of the voice and eyes of Delon's character, the handsome Tancred, in Luchino Visconti's *The Leopard*. But the Alain Delon I met that night more closely resembled the star of Henri's Verneuil's *The Big Snatch*, which had only just come out.

Delon was inquisitive, cocky, utterly without shame. He was both charming and a charmer, and after just ten minutes he rose and held out his hand.

'Come on, let's go to the poker tables.'

'Absolutely not. I never gamble.'

'Is that so? Why not?'

'My pianist is waiting for me, I have to leave.'

'Forget your pianist. I'll drive you down to Geneva myself.'

'I don't think so. Once you start to play, you forget the time.'

'How do you know that if you never gamble?'

'I'm not going to tell you the story of my life.'

'Oh, come along. Please!'

I don't know why, but I gave in again, and asked my pianist to wait just a little longer. I certainly wasn't going to tell Alain Delon how my father had lost track of the time on the day I was born. No. But I can't deny that I felt the same delicious little thrill Jenny and I shared as we nibbled chocolate in our parents' bed while the men smoked and gambled in the room next door. Perhaps it was the urge to relive those moments, to be a child once again?

Alain Delon played, winning over and over again, and I began to feel that same fever (a fever I knew all too well) rising within me.

'Good,' I said. 'Now I really have to go.'

'No, you're bringing me luck, stay!'

I stayed. I was torn between fear and fascination. Perhaps I had never come as close as this to gambling, perhaps I had never been so like my father. Thanks to this man Delon, half-human, half-tempter! But I did not forget the time, as if the child I had once been lived on inside me.

'Now I must leave,' I said.

'No! Can't you see I'm winning?'

'Yes, but I don't want to miss my plane.'

'Then give me something that's important to you. Quick!'

I hunted feverishly through my bag, and came across the medal awarded me at the Barcelona festival, attached to my key-chain.

'There, I'm sure this will bring you luck.'

'Thank you. If I win I'll send you flowers and I'll take you out one night for dinner. If I lose, I'll disappear from your life. Bye-bye, off you go now!'

A few days later, I was alone in our Boulogne-Billancourt apartment, sitting on the floor (I no longer had the money to buy a couch), when the doorbell rang. It was a superb bunch of flowers. But on the attached card, Alain Delon had written: 'Thank you. In spite of everything I lost.'

That Boulogne apartment! I had been singing for six or seven years, and it was the first space on earth that had ever belonged to me. A thousand square feet on the ground floor of a small modern building behind the Molitor swimming pool. The living room opened on to a tiny garden that also belonged to me. I can still see myself sitting cross-legged in the center of that living room and saying over and over again: 'It's mine! It's mine! Everything here is mine! And I earned it all with my work and my songs!' Even today, recalling that feeling makes my heart beat a little faster, as though that first flush of proprietorial joy had never left me.

My American commitment was coming up, and the possibility of an appearance at the Bobino music hall in Paris was in the air. My manager, Roland Ribet, was apparently on the point of signing. Meanwhile, though, life wasn't all sunshine. When I didn't have to fly six or seven hundred miles for a one-night stand, I found myself sandwiched between two established stars. Or else (briefly) holding up the first half of a program, as I did at La Tête de l'Art, the luxurious restaurant/music hall on Avenue de l'Opéra, where the comedian Fernand Raynaud topped the bill. Fernand was by now a living legend, a creator of unbelievably funny sketches, but he had begun to drink more and more to conquer his terrors. His one goal was to get on and off stage as quickly as possible, before he became too drunk to stay on his feet.

'What's her name, that little Greek chick, the one who doesn't sing all that badly?' he would splutter as he roamed backstage in his trademark knee-length raincoat and bow-tie.

'Nana Mouskouri, Monsieur Fernand? She's probably in her dressing room.'

'Oh, that's right, that's right.'

He knocked at my door and I opened it.

'Who's the nice person who'll let Papa Fernand go on first? Why, the sweet little Greek beauty!'

'Oh no, I can't!'

'And why won't she help him out?'

'I'd love to. I'd love to help you, Monsieur Raynaud. But I can't follow you on the stage! You know very well why not, don't you? People are still talking about your sketches, still laughing at them. Weeping with laughter, even ... What hope do I have with my little songs if everyone is crying with laughter?'

13

From Danish Royals to French Reds

etween my first appearance (in Brassens' long shadow) at the Olympia and my Bobino date, for which I was rehearsing in early 1963, the French press discovered me. I gave a few interviews, in which I haltingly described who I was and where I came from. 'Forced to abandon opera, the little Greek singer has become an international star,' said the magazine *Femmes d'Aujourd'hui*.[6] Everything I said was recorded faithfully enough, yet that wasn't exactly the way things had happened. I felt somewhat ashamed at suggesting that I might have been a great operatic soloist. It was true that my parents were far from rich, but now I was pictured – against my will – as a victim of poverty. Lord, how difficult it is to talk about oneself, to protect oneself from journalistic shorthand, from outright fairytales. It was the first time such things had happened to me.

And the picture of me that began to emerge seemed a million miles from the reality! *TV Moustique*, for example, had this to say: 'She is now an international, multilingual star, the holder of a Gold Record. She's available only in brief interludes between plane flights or recording sessions. Black stockings, flat-heeled shoes, schoolgirl skirt and sweater, and the square glasses she has worn since the age of ten – even onstage ... Despite all this travel, she's never really learned how to pack. Because she knows she's made to live in a house. And all her songs express that longing. Like the beautiful peasant girl in her song, she yearns for the

[6] *Femmes d' Aujourd'hui*, 15 August 1963.

happy day when – having garnered kudos and laurels in the frantic pursuit of success – she will be free to hasten into the shadows to sit at the feet of the one waiting for her.'[7]

An international star? A very overblown judgment, in my opinion. And I was puzzled at being presented as one of those Hollywood-style divas who have to be caught at odd moments – 'between plane flights' – in their busy lives. Could my words have hinted at such fantasies? I recorded a lot, that was true, but I traveled a lot more by subway or in taxis than by plane. As for yearning to return home, like the peasant girl in my song, that gave me a wry smile. If they only knew! Just the day before, George had hesitantly suggested that we go back to Greece one day – to which I responded, perhaps a little too sharply, 'No, I'd die if we went home. Please don't try to hold me back, George, I absolutely have to keep moving, traveling, singing for the rest of my life.'

I was to perform at the Bobino after the leading lights – Juliette Gréco, Serge Reggiani, and Léo Ferré – had displayed their wares. I was fully aware that it was a major event, and the whole Philips staff was on a war footing. To meet the expectations of the Bobino's patrons (more *intellectual*, I was told, than the Olympia's audiences) in the small auditorium, it was decided that I would wear not a full-length dress but a skirt ending just above knee-level, at that time the height of fashion.

'And no glasses!' my artistic director Gérard Côte cut in.

These decisions were conveyed to me with such authority that I dared not protest. Louis Hazan nodded silently, as though Gérard had said out loud what he was himself thinking.

So no glasses. This decision dismayed me. Throughout the afternoon preceding the premiere, I was swept by fits of anxiety, as though I had been asked to appear onstage half-naked. I now realized how comforting those glasses (which in my teens had seemed to complete the total disaster of my appearance) had become for me. As a girl I thought the real problem was that my eyes were too wide-set. I felt that the glasses somehow corrected this hideous deformation, which again became apparent to me the instant I removed my glasses. My widely-spaced eyes

---

7 *TV Moustique*, 23 May 1963.

. . . It was as though I had been yanked back to my fourteenth year. How could I confide these childish secrets, these infantile fancies, to men trying so hard to promote me?

Yet over the years, those glasses had become a mask which I felt shielded me from possible acts of cruelty. Shielded behind them, I felt in a sense untouchable, and they permitted me to sing with my eyes closed.

For two nights I sang without them, feeling fragile, vulnerable, unprotected, almost shameful. Then I told Monsieur Hazan that there would be no third performance without my glasses. It was too hard: either I wore them or I wouldn't get out of bed. On the third evening, the glasses were back.

Did the critics appreciate my efforts to please the public (for it was in those terms that Gérard Côte expressed it)? The fact is, they didn't even mention the glasses: they merely praised my Greek songs and deplored the poverty of my French-language repertoire.

'What a pity that professional lyricists,' wrote one critic, 'feel obliged when adapting a Greek or Italian or Portuguese song to deck it out in characterless couplets instead of rendering its truth and its flavor. For surely Nana's best songs are those which evoke for us the narrow streets of Corfu? Or which bring to life the labor of harvesting under a blazing sun as the weary girl longs for the end of the day and her return to the arms of the one awaiting her? But what does it matter? What lingers with us and fascinates us is Nana Mouskouri's voice and its curious resonance – the harmonious marriage of inspiration and interpretation.'

Despite this faint praise, the critics' remarks about the poverty of my French repertoire struck home. Claude Dejacques became my artistic director, replacing Gérard Côte. Claude was an important figure at Philips. He already managed several performers, all much better-known – such as Yves Montand – and this time I was truly afraid I had been relegated to a back shelf. But almost at once I had good news: André Chapelle, the young man who encouraged me so warmly during the recording of my Greek songs, became Dejacques' assistant. No one actually said whether he would be looking after me or not, but I sensed such mutual artistic understanding between the two of us that his arrival cheered me enormously.

*

It was André who thought of introducing me to Michel Legrand, the man who called with congratulations after my triumph at the Barcelona festival. Michel and Jacques Demy had just finished making *The Umbrellas of Cherbourg*, a musical comedy that some people loved and some loathed – but that was already being talked up for the Cannes Film Festival. A tall young man of flamboyant genius, with mischievous but affectionate eyes, Michel had been wondering for years how we had managed not to come across one another. The problem was, he never stopped working, either playing the piano or composing or performing with songs like 'La valse des lilas' or 'Quand ça balance', or '1964'... Right now, he was in New York, where his album *I Love Paris* had brought him instant celebrity.

He played 'The Umbrellas of Cherbourg', his most recent score, for me. It was performed wonderfully in Demy's film by Danielle Licari. Maybe Michel immediately sensed my wish to sing it myself, for I seem to remember him suggesting just that.

'I would simply love to,' I said.

'Well then, come over, we'll give it a quick try, just to see ... '

So there he was, sitting at his piano with me beside him, libretto in hand. It was exactly like that memorable night when I sang the first phrases of 'Never on Sunday' for Manos Hadjidakis. This time, though, I was very much a latecomer to the music he had scrawled on the sheet I had in my hands. It didn't matter, though. The feeling was there.

We had just started studio rehearsals when Michel asked me to accompany him to Cannes, where the entire cast of the movie was to gather. André Chapelle urged me to go. He would be there, and so would Louis Nucera, my press agent, with whom I was on very close terms. Perhaps it was Nucera's presence that decided me. In any case, I agreed to go, not realizing that those few days in Cannes would mark a turning-point in my relations with France.

We all stayed at the Hotel Martinez. From the very start, I found myself among men whose intelligence, artistic flair and cultural background opened horizons whose existence I had never suspected. Louis Nucera was not yet the writer he would shortly become, but he was a friend of Joseph Kessel, of Georges Brassens, and of Jean Cocteau (who had only just died). He had hilarious exchanges, at once warmhearted and passionate, with André Asseo (like himself a former journalist turned music publisher, and very close as well to Joseph Kessel and Romain Gary). Asseo spoke of those two writers as if they were his intellectual mentors. I listened as he described their world with the same relish, the same benevolence one finds in Kessel's novels, which only sharpened my own craving for travel. Nucera introduced me to another of his friends, the painter Raymond Moretti, who had worked with Cocteau and who now spoke of his master Picasso in terms that resonated deep within me. It was in exactly such terms, I told myself, that I would have liked to tell them about Nikos Gastos. Gérard Davoust was also present. At that time a producer with Philips, he was already an astonishing discoverer of talent. Listening to him talking with Michel Legrand was like journeying from the Bronx to the heart of Africa via Latin America. Rounding off our select little group was André Chapelle himself, never missing a single exchange but never putting himself forward.

Within three or four days, we had woven a web of artistic and intellectual connections, and I couldn't help comparing those encounters in Cannes to my meetings with Manos and Nikos at the Floka five or six years earlier. For the first time since my arrival in France, I felt I was part of a spiritual family. I was no longer the little uprooted Greek peasant girl Louis Hazan first met at Orly. I had been accepted among people I admired, people who had confidence in me. They would all remain my friends, and eventually I would have the honor of introducing to them Manos Hadjidakis, driven from Greece by the colonels' regime, and hungry to meet artists with whom he could work.

In that spring of 1964, *The Umbrellas of Cherbourg* carried off the Palme d' Or at Cannes, and we all floated back to Paris on a little cloud.

I believe it was once again Michel Legrand who suggested that we make a record together, right after we finished recording 'Umbrellas'. The project excited Eddie Marnay, who co-authored the four songs with Michel. One year later, on my return from my first American tour with Harry Belafonte, we made that recording. One of its songs, deliciously jazzy, was 'Quand on s'aime'. It was soon on everybody's lips:

On peut marcher sous la pluie,
Prendre le thé à minuit,
Passer l'été à Paris,
Quand on s'aime.

You can walk in the rain,
Drink small-hours champagne,
Build castles in Spain,
When love's your refrain

In the meantime, however, I was enjoying renewed success in Germany, where I won second prize at the Baden-Baden Song Festival with a pretty, nostalgic song: 'Wo ist das Glück vom vergangenen Jahr?' ('Where is the Happiness of Yesteryear?'). And I won an award at the Song Marathon with 'A force de prier', which had failed to bring me luck at the Eurovision contest. I also recorded *Nana Mouskouri in Italia*, 'Longing', 'My Coloring Book', 'Mamma', 'The Power and the Glory' as well as several singles in Great Britain, including 'The White Rose of Athens', which was exported worldwide and which became a big hit across Europe and Scandinavia. It also made my name known as far away as South Africa, Australia, New Zealand, and Asia.

And then one day, Greece's young King Constantine remembered me. I had sung at the party celebrating the engagement of his elder sister Sophia to Prince Juan Carlos, the future king of Spain. Constantine II, son of Paul I (who had reigned only a few months), was engaged to marry Princess Anna-Maria of Denmark, and Copenhagen's Royal Palace told me it would like me to sing at a reception in the capital to mark Anna-Maria's departure for Athens. I quickly realized that the date would be difficult to reconcile with my other obligations. The day after the Copenhagen reception, in fact, I was due to sing in Paris at the popular annual celebration of the Communist paper *L'Humanité*. The only way of managing it was to charter a private plane, which is what I decided to do. Not for a second did I consider letting the French Communist Party down or saying No to the king of Greece.

The party was held in the Royal Palace and attended by Anna-Maria's parents, King Frederick IX and his wife Queen Ingrid. I was struck by the simplicity of their welcome. I had been forewarned that the royal couple did not follow the same formal routine as the queen of England, that the Danish sovereigns traveled openly about Copenhagen, often on bikes, but even so I was agreeably surprised. Before I climbed on to the little stage where a piano had been installed, the guests listened politely as Anna-Maria's friends read her little poems or stories written in her honor. Meanwhile the Danish king and queen (I had been seated beside them), doubtless realizing that I did not understand what was being said, asked me in undertones about daily life in Greece. Little by little, they moved on to the image of the monarchy in Greece. Did the Greeks like their king? How did the press talk about him? Was the palace properly situated? Wasn't it a little too far from the center of Athens?

I replied as best I could, overcome by shyness but nevertheless determined to describe things the way they were. And I suddenly realized that despite their power, these sovereigns were like every parent in the world: they were worried about their very young daughter (Anna-Maria was only eighteen) and wanted to know whether she would feel loved and protected. Suddenly full of sympathy for them, I surprised myself by saying: 'I think everyone likes our young King Constantine, your majesties, and I'm sure it will be the same for Queen Anna-Maria.' When the Greek sovereigns went into exile three years later (after accusing the colonels of 'leading Greece into disaster'), I thought back to that evening and pictured the sorrow of young Anna-Maria's parents.

Then it was my turn to sing. Greek songs, of course, and then a few of my French and English hits. I was accompanied only by my pianist, and the simplicity of this arrangement proved astonishingly moving. Conversations died away, and soon the elegant, youthful spectators, there to honor the future queen of Greece, were sitting silently on the floor, listening to me religiously.

A very different reception awaited me next afternoon at the 'Fête de L'Humanité.' Two hundred thousand people were crowded onto the lawns of La Courneuve Park in front of a huge red-draped stage equipped with giant amplifiers. I had never sung for such a big crowd, and I had to fight back my trembling as I adjusted the mic and said a few preliminary words while the ocean of spectators seemed suddenly to hold its breath. Did I have any chance at all of reaching them? Only moments before they had been applauding their new General Secretary, Waldeck Rochet, who greeted me with a frosty smile while the crowd, fists raised, sang the *Internationale*.

Yet, after fifteen minutes or so, I felt that emotional contact was establishing itself, and when I opened my eyes, I saw that the people in the front rows were already seated. Very gradually, the guests were surrendering to the music. The gathering lost its regimented look, people stretched and moved around, each spectator sought his own vantage point, and I believe that by the end everyone was seated, in a silence that recalled the attentive silence of the young guests in Copenhagen just the day before. I sent up private thanks to music. People fought over ideas. Sometimes they killed one another – as I remembered from my own adolescence in Greece – but music had the power, at least momentarily, of soothing passions and assuaging hatreds. And in that brief window that opened on time, it was impossible not to see that we are all alike. That everyone deserves understanding and compassion.

I was thus briefly able to summon up understanding and compassion – yet I was blind and deaf to George's distress. Hired against his will as a member of Harry Belafonte's orchestra although he knew neither the singer nor his musicians, although he had never set foot in the United States, George was going through a very difficult period. He had withdrawn from his own group to familiarize himself on his own with Belafonte's rhythms and music. He no longer had the support of his three friends, he no longer played alongside them in the clubs of Amsterdam and Athens: he was cloistered in our Boulogne-Billancourt apartment. No doubt he played the guitar a few hours every day, but the truth is that he was lost, disoriented. And meanwhile, during the fall of 1961 which preceded our departure for America, I was feverishly recording another disk at the Blanqui Studios, or performing in Copenhagen or at the Fête de *L'Humanité* ... With nothing to do, anxious about what lay ahead, and secretly humiliated at finding himself a house-husband, George gradually shut himself away in resentment and depression. How could I possibly have failed to notice? While I sat by his hospital bed after he attempted to kill himself one night in New York, I thought back over the events of the past months and recalled that Louis Hazan himself had warned me. 'Nana,' he said, 'you've brought your husband to Paris, and now you're leaving him alone with nothing to do. Much too alone. Be careful. I don't think it's good either for him or for you.'

14

On the Road with Harry

f I had doubts about my idea of getting George aboard the Harry
Belafonte bandwagon, the welcome awaiting us in New York
would have dispelled them. Harry spread his arms wide and
hugged us both, rolling out the red carpet for George and insisting right
away that he play a guitar melody and some of Manos' old refrains. The
musicians were full of questions and very warmhearted, the way some
Americans can be. They urged him to play, and listened with faces
shining with excitement and delight, so much so that we wanted to
embrace them or burst out laughing. After his months of protracted
anxiety, George seemed to relax. Not only did nobody look down on
him, he was even regarded as a kind of mascot figure with his bouzouki
and his music – at once lighthearted and melancholy – from far away.

Then, almost immediately, rehearsals began. Together, Harry and I
sang the lovely, nostalgic 'Try to Remember', and a traditional Greek
song, 'Erini'. Demanding, a perfectionist, Belafonte never went home
to bed until everyone had given of his best. We had to learn to harmonize
our styles, and the orchestra had to familiarize itself with the Medi-
terranean music Harry was just discovering. In that situation George
appeared on the scene like the answer to our prayers: he played wonderfully and I was secretly very proud that he was with us.

Then it was agreed that I should sing four songs. One was French,
'Les parapluies de Cherbourg', which everyone loved. Two were Greek,
chosen from among the most beautiful works of Manos and Nikos. And
then there was a kind of folk-rock (or perhaps Gospel) song, 'Wayfaring
Stranger', born of the tradition that inspired me at the time and from the

region where we happened to find ourselves. But they all had to be rehearsed with the orchestra, and it took a month of dedicated collaboration.

Harry Belafonte rehearsed his own projects. I knew his show was completely new, quite different from the one he put on with Myriam Makeba. Two veteran New Orleans musicians, an extraordinary duo, were also part of the project. One of them, Brownie McGhee, walked with a limp and sang the blues to the magical strumming of his guitar. The second, Sonny Terry, who was blind, accompanied Brownie on the harmonica. Just the two of them made the transatlantic trip (and after that the whole of America) worthwhile.

The entire troupe was on the move in the bus early each morning. We set out for twelve months, with no clear idea of possible requests for extensions because everything would depend on how successful we were. We went to Phoenix, Chicago, Los Angeles (six weeks!), and took in Canada, stopping off in Victoria, Calgary, Toronto, and Montreal.

I had never given a thought to the racism they said was so rife in America, and it was only after we piled on to the front seats of the bus that I had my first intimation of it. It didn't disturb me that George and I and two other guitar players were the only white performers in the company, but I was made curiously uneasy by the words sung out by one of the orchestra musicians as he climbed aboard the bus and saw our faces among all the black ones: 'I see the Man still gets to sit up front.' It was of course said as a joke, but some jokes quickly turn heavy as lead, particularly when repeated every morning . . .

What did such remarks imply for us? In fact, they masked a powerful sense of injustice, echoed by Belafonte himself. As Harry escorted me back to my hotel after a show, both of us delighted with how well the evening had gone, he said to me out of the blue:

'You and Myriam are both great singers, true nightingales, but you'll go farther than she will.'

'How can you say that? Myriam Makeba is known the whole world over, and I'm a long way from there . . .'

'Yeah, but you're white!'

His words made me so angry that we came close to quarreling. Yet his bitterness was well-founded, although it would take me weeks to understand this. I knew nothing then about heartland America, and it was Harry who described for me the long struggle of the Reverend Martin Luther King Junior, recipient of the Nobel Peace Prize in 1964. Harry was one of his close supporters. The year before, he had backed King's march on Washington to secure equal civil rights for colored people. I was unaware that until then, colored people in the South had been forced to give up their seats to whites on public transport . . .

Our shows were as neatly regulated as a musical score. Harry would of course open, singing a few heartbreakingly beautiful blues phrases without musical backup. Then the orchestra would come in and the audience would begin to stir. After three or four of his songs, Brownie and Sonny came on, majestic, magnificent. Harry then left them alone on the stage, returning to sing with them and bring the first half to an end.

My turn came in the middle of the second part of the show, when I joined Belafonte to hum 'Try to Remember' in unison (it would later become one of my European standards, with the title 'Au cœur de Septembre', 'Era Settembre' in Italian.) Then we sang 'Erini', and after that I was alone on the stage. Harry finished the show on his own, calling us all back onstage to thank the audience and listen to its acclaim.

Harry's stagecraft fascinated me, and I would spend the whole of the first half in the wings, devouring him with my eyes. I had learned from Brassens that you could be yourself onstage, and had envied his simple, natural way of smiling at the audience. Back then, though – trembling and terror-struck – I felt unable to smile.

From Belafonte I learned obsessive concern to maintain the highest standards, ceaseless striving for perfection, mastery of the slightest move. In a way, he was the opposite of Brassens. He rehearsed every-thing, calculated everything, not unlike Yves Montand, for whom he had the highest admiration. Despite this perfectionism, he evoked levels of emotion in the audience that went straight to my heart. How did he do it? During the rehearsals that preceded every show, he and I had a minor falling-out. He wanted me to *act as if* the spectators were present, and I responded a little sharply:

'No, Harry, my feelings depend on the actual moment, on the response the audience transmits back to me. I need that little space, I need a little room for improvisation.'

He wasn't happy with that, telling me that even feeling could not be improvised. So was he then an actor of genius? I don't know. In any case, whenever we sang 'Try to Remember' together, the experience gave me gooseflesh.

We sang in little 3,000-seat places such as campuses or in sports arenas seating thirty thousand. In Pittsburgh we were given the Arena, with a capacity of 45,000, and in Los Angeles the Greek Theater, seating eight thousand. We were light years away from the Olympia's 1,100 seats or the Bobino's 650. During that tour, I learned not to sing with my hands behind my back, to open my eyes . . . and even to smile!

'She returned slimmer, tanned, her hair sporting a central parting, and with an onstage confidence that is now very much her own,' Louis Hazan said later. 'She had found her image! She was ready to conquer France!'[8]

The press sang our praises, and I blush (well, almost) at mentioning here a few examples, so over-the-top do they seem to me now:

'Belafonte never rushes, and that may be the key to his highly persuasive charm,' wrote the *Chicago American*'s music critic. 'If a song rolls along, he'll let it roll on. For this and his ability to pick material literally out of the air around him, he offers a modern minstrelsy of virtuosity in one whale of an evening.

'Nana Mouskouri, a Greek kitten, made her American debut last night with, among other things, as touching a rendition of "Wayfaring Stranger" as can be imagined. One automatically senses the personality of a star to the manner born . . . Mouskouri is in the highest artistic strata of new female vocalists.'[9]

'With horn-rimmed glasses, in a red and white folk-like costume, she looked like a pretty young PhD candidate about to do a thesis on Greek

---

[8] *Pleins feux*, Op.cit.
[9] *Chicago American*, 26 May 1965.

ethnographic song,' wrote *The Gazette*. 'That is, until she sang. She has one of the clearest voices and sincerest styles to turn up in a show in a long time.'[10]

'Every four years,' said Montreal's *Les Nouvelles Illustrées*, 'Harry Belafonte embarks on a major tour. And every four years, he comes onstage with a female singer in whom he believes heart and soul. His choice fashions careers. He is the living dream of United States performers.

'Onstage during his tours, deploying the candor Americans use so well, Harry Belafonte stops singing and says in substance: "I've discovered a new star, a singer whose voice will surpass anything you've heard so far ..." And without further delay, he interrupts his own performance to introduce his new choice and asks her to take his place at the footlights and sing.

'Four years ago, Belafonte "canonized" Myriam Makeba. This time, during a visit by the singer to New York, his choice fell on Nana Mouskouri. Nana accepted this dazzling nomination with the stoic calm of a Greek peasant woman. Now she sings every night in a different American city. She has been a huge success, as attested by the telegram Belafonte sent to Paris: "She's broken the bank!"'[11]

And Montreal's *Le Petit Journal* added: 'Right from the start, she seduces her audience. She is a truly remarkable singer.'[12]

During that whirlwind of a tour which seemed never to end, Quincy Jones called me one night just as I left the stage. He wanted me to meet a young pianist of exceptional talent, Bobby Scott.

'Can't it wait, Quincy?'

'No, it's an urgent matter. Take a plane one day when you're not singing and meet us in New York.'

Irving Green and Quincy picked me up at the airport, just as they had met me to take me to the restaurant where Harry and Julie Belafonte were waiting for me.

---

[10] *The Gazette*, 11 May 1965.
[11] *Les Nouvelles Illustrées*, 1 May 1965.
[12] *Le Petit Journal*, 16 May 1965.

This time, there was no question of a new tour, just cutting a record with Bobby Scott. It would be my second American album (following *Nana Mouskouri in New York*, produced by Quincy and recorded somewhat frenetically during my first New York visit three years before).

Bobby Scott and I hit it off from the very first. You could even have called it love at first sight – except that I didn't fall in love with Bobby. But I did fall under the spell of his enormous talent. He and Quincy had already thought of several songs the two of us could perform together, such as 'I Love my Man' or 'Half a Crown', but we had barely mentioned their titles before Bobby was sitting at the piano and I was singing with him.

The only way I could fit the making of this new album with Bobby Scott into Harry Belafonte's tour schedule was by shuttling back and forth to New York, where Irving Green had arranged a studio for us at Mercury on Fifth Avenue. I hate flying, and the idea alone should have worn me out, but the opposite happened. I was so delighted to be rehearsing with Bobby that it increased tenfold my pleasure at being back onstage with Belafonte. As though instead of tiring me, singing filled me with energy.

And Irving Green waited on me hand and foot. Around fifty years old, built like John Wayne, enterprising and good-humored, Irving clearly looked on me as his own daughter. He met me at the airport, took me back to my hotel after rehearsals, nagged me if I went walking alone through the streets of New York after midnight. When Irving wasn't chaperoning me, Quincy (who couldn't resist coming into the studio while we were working) would take over. He and Irving seemed terribly excited about this record. It was an excitement they transmitted to the entire Mercury staff. One day the great Sarah Vaughan visited us. They had spoken to her about our record, and I was temporarily too awestruck to speak. Another day, Quincy introduced the charming Barbra Streisand to us, and this time it was Bobby Scott who couldn't utter a word. In fact, Irving Green's secret ambition was to keep me in the United States. Both he and Quincy were convinced that a great career awaited me on the North American continent. The success of the Belafonte tour could only have reinforced this feeling – but they never mentioned their dream to me. They probably figured that I would realize it all on my own.

Well, I suppose it just wasn't my style to realize that sort of thing. Only later, when I was back in France and puzzling over Louis Hazan's somber expression, did I realize what they had been planning for me. My reaction was astonishment at the thought that Louis (to whom I owed everything) could seriously have believed that I would betray his friendship and trust by settling in the United States!

But for the moment, I had the feeling that I was living in an enchanted dream, moving between the ovations that greeted the Belafonte shows and the pleasures of musical exploration with Bobby Scott. The son of a Cherokee father and an Irish mother, grandson of a black squaw, of a Catholic grandmother and a Jewish grandfather (unless it was the other way around), Bobby Scott was a tormented soul who sought to express through music the feelings that roiled him. He was the most moving, most erudite pianist I had ever known, and it didn't matter whether he played or talked: he never bored me for a second.

What about George in this frenzy of activity? He was an accepted member of the orchestra, but it was as though events were conspiring to drive us apart. The tour's growing success in city after city meant that I was increasingly monopolized by Harry Belafonte. He wanted me by his side at press conferences, in private meetings with the critics, in his discussions with our orchestra leader, his promoter, or any other member of the numerous general staff under his command. He wanted me with him everywhere. And as the weeks went by, an intimacy grew up between Harry and me that couldn't possibly go unnoticed by the people around us. Harry was attractive and a charmer, always skirting flirtation, as if he wanted to prove to himself that no woman could resist him. He was indeed very handsome, perhaps even irresistible, but oddly enough the game didn't tempt me, and the idea of cheating on George never crossed my mind for a second. But I did let Harry hug me, kiss me on the cheek, and put his arm around my waist in the fever of the final curtain, and this probably hurt George without my knowing it.

I understood later that the sudden irruption of Irving Green, Quincy Jones and Bobby Scott into my life aggravated the distress he already felt. He accompanied me to New York three or four times, but Irving Green took control of me as soon as we arrived and I never had a moment for George alone. What did he think about these men gravitating around me? After the drama I am about to describe, he told me he spent that period afraid that I would abandon him, that one or another of them would replace him in my heart. He didn't like living in Paris with me, he said, because he suffered the same fears there, but America was much worse. He was afraid of all those men; they were friendly enough, but nothing more. He felt that the odds were against him in the struggle; he was convinced he was going to lose me, and it threw him into bottomless despair. George was intelligent, quick on the uptake, and it was obvious to him that Irving Green wanted to keep me in America for good. To George, that represented the ultimate threat.

But he was unable to speak, unable to tell me of his fears. Unless the fault lay in me – unless I was too swept up in my passion for music, too flattered that so many eminent people acknowledged my talent, to be able to listen to him ... Whatever the reason, we didn't exchange one word about what was tormenting him. We shared the same bed, but he was drowning and I saw nothing.

One night when we left the recording studio very late, Irving and Quincy escorted me home. Irving had rented me a small apartment, much more comfortable than a hotel room, on a weekly basis, and that night I was now eager to be back with George. I imagined that he was already asleep.

I went in, took off my shoes, switched on the hall light, and my eyes fell on these words, scrawled on a sheet of white paper: 'Make sure you don't bury me alive.'

It was a terrifying sensation, as though the floor was falling away beneath my feet. But I found the strength to run to the bedroom, turn on the light and jump on the bed. George was unconscious, but he was still breathing. An empty phial of sleeping tablets lay on the floor by the bed. I shook him. I shouted through my tears:

'George! George! No, oh no! Please ...'

I called Irving, who had a phone in his car:

'Irving, quick, George is in a very bad way!'

'Go downstairs to the doorman right away. Tell him to call an ambulance and a doctor. We're on the way, we'll be there in five minutes ...'

Irving and Quincy rushed into the apartment, out of breath. Then came the doctor and the ambulance, which took George to hospital. The police arrived. At one stroke, it was as though all the frenzied activity that had kept these past months so exhilarating had been canceled out. What did it all mean if George died? I felt myself tumbling, tumbling downhill as if dragged down into the depths of the abyss.

At dawn, we were all still at the hospital. George was out of danger, but my heart was in a thousand pieces. What immense sadness he must have felt to reach this point! How had I failed to see? To foresee? Now for the first time the thought flashed across me that *I was incapable of love*, and that plunged me in its turn into unspeakable terror. Any other woman would have seen, would have heard. Another woman would not have let her husband lose himself. I thrashed about all alone, weighed down by a guilt that made me want to smash my head against the walls. To spare Quincy and Irving – both of them speechless with horror – the spectacle of my distress, I shut myself away in the nurses' little office and poured out bitter tears.

Was it plain stupid to think I was incapable of love? Could you learn how to love? What kind of woman was I to trigger such a desperate act by the only man in my life? All these questions hammered at me, and I collapsed. I thought back to my parents' union – two beings who never ceased to clash, to lacerate one another, who never exchanged a single tender gesture – and told myself they had taught me nothing of love. That was true enough – but I was thirty, I was no longer a child. I could have learned all by myself. How disembodied I must have been to remain ignorant of love's communion, of that subtle exchange of gestures and glances that was apparently enough for others to reveal themselves, to see into each other! I had a terrible need to talk, and it was Nikos I wanted to talk to. Nikos, so adept at reading the soul's secrets. I yearned to be with him on this infinitely sad morning. No other man in the world could listen to me better, hear me, comfort me, lead me through the darkness that shrouded my world.

*

The police called the three of us in – Irving, Quincy and me. The commissioner wanted to understand. I believe he suspected first Quincy, then Irving. But how could we explain to a man inured to criminal investigations that nothing of that kind had occurred, no marital infidelity, nothing sordid, and that I was simply ashamed at having loved my husband so poorly? Words were certainly inadequate, clumsily wielded, and sorrow made things worse ...

That first night following the drama, as George slowly recovered in the hospital, I finally called Nikos. What a relief to feel him so near, so present! We chatted almost serenely, despite the vice that seemed clamped around my heart. It was Nikos who revealed how well George had been able to express his despair in those simple words: 'Make sure you don't bury me alive.'

'I believe that in writing those words,' he said to me, 'he wasn't just thinking of the death he sought.'

'What do you mean? What else was he thinking of?'

'Of your life, Nana. Maybe I'm wrong, but I hear the suffering of a man condemned to silence by your determination to live.'

'... Condemned to silence by my determination to live ...'

'Yes. You know, I believe a man would have to love you infinitely in order to follow you. Even to the point of forgetting that he himself exists.'

Nikos said no more. He did not like to explain himself. He believed that one should be able to guess unaided what lay behind such words. And after we hung up that night I finally succeeded in looking at our life through George's eyes. Since we had known one another, I had done nothing but go forward by striving to meet all the challenges that came along. I had never sought his advice before accepting the offers that came my way: Berlin, then Paris, then New York, then all of America. Never, because it seemed obvious to me that everything that was good for me was also good for him, because we loved one another. In the name of our marriage, I had sought constantly to associate him with my own success, even to the point of imposing his presence on Belafonte. And then suddenly this soundless scream – 'Make sure you don't bury me alive'! Yes, of course – what room had I made for George in my triumphal forward march? The higher my passion for singing carried me, the more he lost his footing and gasped for oxygen. I had gradually asphyxiated him. And then I understood what Nikos had said: 'A man would have to love you infinitely in order to follow you. Even to the point of forgetting that he himself exists.' What man would have been able to make such a sacrifice, or sustain such a passion for me? George loved me, without a doubt, but not to the point of forgetting himself and living through me. He too needed to be loved, recognized, respected.

Luckily, the tour was almost over. All that remained was to finish recording my second American album with Bobby Scott, which would soon appear under the title *Nana Mouskouri Sings*.

George and I spent our last days in New York side by side. George finally spoke to me, and I had been so terrified of losing him that I showered him with questions while doing my best to show the affection he had so sorely missed. He had believed I was betraying him with Irving Green, he admitted to me, and I had been so far from such a possibility that I burst into tears.

'I'll never be unfaithful to you! How could you imagine such a thing?'

'I'm not the only one who thought so. You were always with him, his arms were around you all the time.'

'I love Irving like a father, George. That's as far as it went.'

We wept together. Now we had to let everything out, and I understood at last how humiliating it was for George, deeply imbued as he was with Greek ways, to be the husband of a woman so many men seemed to compete for. Not only was George just a 'little guitar player', as he liked to repeat, while I was applauded wherever I went and my picture had appeared in all the American papers. He wasn't even respected as a husband, as a man.

At some point during those days, when George's plight filled me with remorse and the determination to repair the pain I had caused him, we decided to have a child. What better token of love, mutual need and loyalty could there be than a baby? I suddenly remembered George's joy two years earlier when I found I was pregnant – and our desolation when the pregnancy ended in a miscarriage. Now I told myself that a child would restore equilibrium to our union, that it would bring contentment to George and would anchor me (who had always tended to seek escape in music, to forget my body) more securely in life.

And we arrived at another decision: henceforth we would perform together. George had never forgotten his original group, and now he suggested that we might bring The Athenians back to life. And if we did, why couldn't I become the group's official vocalist? We would remake our world at one stroke, as excited as we had been seven or eight years ago at the Rex cinema when Mimis Plessas told us: 'Not bad at all, what you do together . . . Why don't you make up a quartet?'

George's self-confidence came flowing back. Walking with him along the streets of Manhattan twenty-four hours before we were to leave the city, I wondered what Louis Hazan and André Chapelle would think of our new organization.

15

Tanks Return to the
Streets of Athens

*T*he Hazans invited me to dinner as they did whenever I returned to Paris from abroad. They were extremely concerned by George's distress. I don't know whether they believed in the success of the group we had dreamed up – Nana Mouskouri and the Athenians – but they clearly saw it as the best possible guarantor of our marital harmony. And they trusted me for the musical aspects of the project.

'I think you're stubborn and enough of a perfectionist, Nana, to throw the whole idea over if it doesn't work,' said Louis.

André Chapelle's reaction was more or less the same. Before we left for America, he had given George a lot of support, urging him to work hard there and predicting that he would return with a wealth of experience that would open all doors for him. And in fact George, already a dazzling performer of Greek folk music, was now an accomplished folk, American country and rock musician.

'If your hearts are in it,' André told us, 'you owe it to yourselves to do it! Success always depends on the energy you invest in chasing it.'

It took all George's energy to persuade his friends to join us in Paris. Nine months earlier, thanks to me, he had dropped them. Now he was asking them to drop everything and take the plunge with us. I was aware of the responsibility we were about to shoulder: until now, it had been the two of us seeking to make a living. From now on, there would be five, a much more challenging proposition. André

Chapelle had given it a lot of thought, and he at once advised our new group to make a recording of Greek songs. The last one, *Mes plus belles chansons grecques* (*My Most Beautiful Greek Songs*), made two years earlier with Jacques Denjean's orchestra (to suit the theme, Jacques appeared on the sleeve under the pseudonym of Iakobos Dentjos), had sold very well. Why not follow up on that? Manos and Nikos, who by now had come to know George better, agreed to take a hand, and together we drew up a list of the songs we could perform. We decided to include one or two very lovely songs by Mikis Theodorakis, one written in conjunction with the poet Yannis Ritsos, and even a song written and composed by George, 'Lune sans cœur' ('Fengaro mou', or 'Heartless Moon').

The project appealed to George's fellow-musicians, and soon The Athenians were at full strength: Spyros Livieratos on drums, Kostas Trouptios on base guitar, George both singing and playing the guitar, and Philipos Papatheodorou, equally at home on piano and guitar. Rehearsals could begin.

We were hard at it when we received an invitation to visit Canada for a four-week tour. The offer came from Sam Gesser, a very likable Canadian impresario in love with folk music, who had first approached me when I was singing in Montreal with Belafonte. We spent a whole evening talking music, and for once, George was with us.

Sam had learned that I now had my own group, and was convinced we could manage a tour on our own.

'You know,' I told him, 'that's something I've never done. I've performed in Germany with two other singers and in America with Belafonte, but never as the star with my own group.'

'Well, this time you will be.'

'What if no one comes to hear me?'

'Trust me, we'll fill every seat. You saw what the critics said when you performed with Belafonte?'

'People came for him, Sam. I don't know if they'll bother if it's just for me.'

In spite of my doubts, we decided to accept. We were only just getting off the ground, and it was too big an opportunity for us to let pass. The four boys were enthusiastic – even George, who had been so wary of America a year ago. But this time, it's true, he was returning with his name displayed in big letters.

Our Greek record would have to wait. In early January 1966, we flew to Canada. Our first show was at Montreal's famous venue, the Place des Arts. Throughout the flight, I silently went over the songs I would sing. This was the first time I would have to carry a show on my own from the first curtain to the last, and I teetered from enthusiasm to fear and back again. We had plenty of time to rehearse, with André's demanding support, but it did little to banish a fear that made my head swim if I let it get the upper hand. I would of course be singing the Greek numbers that had made my name – 'White Roses of Athens' and 'Les enfants du Pirée' – but also Michel Legrand's French songs which everyone was now whistling in Paris, including 'The Umbrellas of Cherbourg', and 'L'enfant au tambour', ('Little Drummer Boy') which I recorded before my tour with Belafonte and which had in the meantime become a hit. In the first half of the program, I planned to appear in a pale, very Parisian little silk suit, and then change to red for the Greek second half.

We seemed to have overlooked nothing, and George's presence was a comfort even though I felt his nerves begin to fray as the hour approached.

Nothing but the weather, that is! Meeting us at the airport in trapper gear, Sam Gesser put us in the picture right away. Apparently it had snowed heavily the past few days, but there was no problem, and Montreal's streets were snow-free.

'The only snag,' he concluded, 'is that they're predicting a storm tonight.'

'For the premiere?'

'Exactly. But don't worry. In Montreal, things always turn out all right in the end.'

The hotel welcomed us with bouquets and chocolates, helping us forget the color of the sky, a dirty yellow that bode no good and seemed to weigh down the ice-floes crowding the river.

That afternoon, we rehearsed. Sam Gesser was exultant, certain that success lay ahead. Besides, the media remembered me and announced my arrival as though I were a star. I still remember the following sentence, picked out at random from the press releases which Sam waved under my nose and set my heart thumping: 'Montreal fans can't wait to hear the young Greek artist who sings superbly and with sovereign grace ...' Did I really deserve that kind of praise? And how could the writer be so certain the fans 'couldn't wait'? I wasn't so sure.

And unfortunately I was the one who appeared to have guessed correctly. At seven forty-five, fifteen minutes before curtain time, the auditorium was virtually empty. We were horrified, but Sam Gesser wore a big smile.

'Come outside and see how it's coming down!' he said.

It was a scene beyond imagining. As if hurled angrily from a sky now invaded by night, snow was falling on Montreal with a violence I had never witnessed. It immobilized cars, piled up on sidewalks and around streetlights, its furious flurries harrying the last fleeing pedestrians. The traffic lights continued to switch bravely from red to green and back again, but there was no traffic for them to direct. Montreal's pulse seemed to have stopped beating. Trapped and motionless in this monumental chaos, cars and buses stood in line like the remains of a hastily abandoned caravan, their headlights slowly fading from sight beneath the mantle of snow.

'This is a disaster!' I said. 'Don't all these people need help?'

'Don't you worry. They'll manage without help. We're used to storms here, you know.'

'So the premiere has to be postponed, right?'

'Not on your life! Let's sit back and see what the storm decides to do.'

Half an hour later, the snow stopped. Men and machines appeared and began clearing streets and sidewalks. In a matter of minutes, a city that had seemed on the brink of disappearing was once again teeming with life. Pedestrians hurried to and fro, vehicles roared into life, and people hailed one another cheerfully from sidewalk to sidewalk in that Québecois accent that raises a smile from visiting Frenchmen and at once warms their hearts.

Without hurrying, as though they knew that we would have waited for them, people appeared outside the box office a little before ten p.m., chattering, muffled to the ears and happy. In less than fifteen minutes the auditorium was full. Watching all this from the wings, I was moved to tears.

'Look, George, Sam was right. They waited for the storm to die and then they came – all of them. There's not a single empty seat! I can't believe it.'

After all our fears, and knowing how fervently we had looked forward to this moment, the music could not fail to fuse all hearts together. What did it matter if my voice was a little shaky at the start, for the silent response of the audience reached us from the opening bars, exhilarated and supportive, as if this was exactly how we had arranged to meet.

To close my recital, I decided to revive an old Quebec song I had discovered during my visit with Belafonte. It had utterly overwhelmed me. Written in 1839 by Antoine Gérin-Lajoie, 'Un Canadien errant' ('A Canadian Exile') spoke of the despair of Quebec's French population, hounded into exile after the failure of their uprising against the British in 1837.

I had scarcely sung the first line when the whole auditorium rose to its feet and joined in. It was a moment of such unforgettable intensity, a moment so moving that on each of my future visits there were always people who reminded me of it and who begged me to sing it again. It is a song that still perfectly illustrates the attachment of Canadians to their home:

> *Un Candien errant / Banni de ses foyers*
> *Parcourait en pleurant / Des pays étrangers.*
>
> *Un jour, triste et pensif / Assis au Nord des flots,*
> *Au courant fugitif / Il adressa ces mots :*
>
> *Si tu vois mon pays, / Mon pays malheureux,*
> *Va, dis à mes amis / Que je me souviens d'eux.*
>
> *Ô jours si pleins d'appas / Vous êtes disparus,*
> *Et ma patrie, hélas ! / Je ne la verrai plus!*
>
> *Non, mais en expirant, / Ô mon cher Canada,*

Tanks Return to the Streets of Athens

Mon regard languissant / Vers toi se portera.

[An exiled Canadian, / Banished from his home,
Traveled full of tears / Through countries not his own.

One day, pensive and sad / He saw a passing stream,
And uttered loud these words / As if half-sunk in dream:

If you pass through my land, / My poor tormented home,
Go tell all my old friends / That they are not alone.

Your well-remembered charms / Have all been swept away.
And my homeland, alas, / Yearns for a happier day!

But when I come to die, / Oh sweet homeland of mine,
Let my last expiring gaze / Turn to that land of mine!

We were scheduled to stage only one show next evening, still at the Place des Arts, but the demand for tickets was such that we decided to organize a matinee as well. The same success accompanied us throughout the tour. So Sam Gesser's optimism was amply justified!

'The ovation Nana Mouskouri earned was not due simply to her devotion to the French language and her totally unexpected rendering of "A Canadian Exile",' wrote one critic on our final day. He was right. Something much more significant than that passed between Canada and me – an instant awareness of mutual attraction. Every one of my subsequent visits to Canada would be a joy. One day, Canadian Prime Minister Pierre Trudeau went so far as to open the portals of Canada's House of Commons to me in Ottawa to hear me sing 'A Canadian Exile' for the assembled legislators . . .

Wherever The Athenians went we were a smash hit. We returned to France infinitely more self-confident than a month earlier. We spent the tail end of the winter confined to the Blanqui Studios, recording *Chants de mon pays* (*Songs of My Country*), my first album with George and his group.

George was in much brighter fettle. I had learned to pay him more attention, and I understood now how heavily Paris must have weighed on him. We had spent a totally harmonious month in Quebec, hand-in-hand, and now I was caught up once again in the whirlwind of events. André Chapelle and Louis Hazan kept introducing me to new musicians, while Michel Legrand, Eddy Marnay, Christian Chevalier, Michel Jourdan, and Pierre Delanoë constantly proposed new ideas. And George felt that I was once again drifting away from him. Now, however, he felt able to say so, and I was prepared to make any sacrifice that would make him happy.

'We can leave Paris if you like.'

'Why couldn't we go and live in Geneva?'

His three friends had already settled in Geneva two or three years earlier, initially in order to be closer to Amsterdam and Zurich where they often performed. All three were married and tired of living far from wives left behind in Athens. Close both to Paris and Amsterdam, Switzerland's location made it possible for them to maintain normal family life. Yes, why not leave for Geneva if that suited George better?

With that decided, we moved in mid-spring of 1966. We were preparing for a summer studded with a dozen concerts in cities around France. Nothing very exciting, however. I had the impression I was very much more appreciated – and loved – in Canada, Germany or the United States than in France.

Yet it was during that somewhat uneventful summer that I met a man who (thirty years later) would become the brother I had never known – the actor Jean-Claude Brialy.

The Antibes Festival of Song had invited me to sing a few numbers during the official dinner that preceded the awards ceremony. For some reason, the prospect filled me with tension, and I suddenly realized that my stage-fright was more intense when I sang in France than in other countries. Why? Probably, I thought, because I was still traumatized by the memory of my Paris beginnings, of the anger my accent had triggered in Pierre Delanoë and Louis Hazan. Particularly in Delanoë. So that when faced with a French audience, I still trembled at the possibility that I might roll my r's 'like a Greek peasant' or mangle a difficult word. To add to my anxieties, I had been told that several major performers would be hearing me in Antibes, including Charles Aznavour and Charles Trenet.

So I was tense and deep inside my shell when I arrived. My manager, Roland Ribet, was with me, and although he had a lively sense of humor he was unable to make me relax. 'A woman of the East, and therefore the product of a culture that has treated women as submissive, vulnerable creatures for thousands of years, Nana was terrified by the pitfalls of our world in which every individual has to fight to find himself a place,' he would say a few years later.[13] Terrified – yes, he was right, above all if I felt that I might be ambushed around the next corner.

I accordingly left the dining room midway through the meal (of which I hadn't touched a mouthful) and fled to the wings where I paced nervously in an attempt to master my stage-fright.

That was when I saw Jean-Claude Brialy approaching. He didn't know me, but I had fallen for him three years earlier during a showing of *Cinq colonises à la Une* (*Front-Page News*), the famous French TV broadcast. At that showing, the three Jeans were center-stage: Jean-Paul Belmondo, Jean-Pierre Cassel, and Jean-Claude Brialy. Of those three anchormen, Jean-Claude, that evening's master of ceremonies, struck me as the most poetic, the most generous, and perhaps the most sparkling. But he couldn't have guessed any of that as he came toward me (he was a fellow-guest at the dinner I had fled) in the wings at Antibes. Yet he was smiling at me! That first smile from Jean-Claude! As though he already knew everything without ever having met me. My fear of disappointing, my pride, my determination to make no compromises about my physical appearance, my lunatic hope that I would be loved in spite of everything. Loved for what lay hidden behind my 'awful glasses', as everyone called them.

Yes – as though he already knew. And he did, because his words were right on the mark:

'No reason to be worried, Nana, everyone here loves you. They love you for the truth and beauty you give them. I love you too, you know. I don't know you, yet I *do* know you. "C'est jolie la mer", "Celui que

---

[13] *Pleins feux*, May 1972.

j'aime", "Try to Remember" ... See? So come back and sing. Every-one's dying to hear you.'

He was holding my hand as we went onstage, and from my audience I heard something like the soughing of the wind in tall grass, a soft and benevolent rustling that made me want to offer them my face and abandon myself to song.

I believe it was in the following autumn that a call from Louis Hazan froze the blood in my veins. He called me in Geneva, which was now our home.

'Nana, Claude Dejacques no longer has the time to look after you. I've decided to give you a new artistic director.'

'Oh my God, no!'

Admittedly, I didn't see much of Claude Dejacques, but his assistant André was now such an important factor in my musical choices, so invaluable during recordings, that the prospect of breaking with him at once assumed catastrophic dimensions. I didn't even try to conceal my dismay.

'Why not? You don't agree?'

'Monsieur Hazan, you know how hard it is for me to break away from people I'm used to working with.'

'I know, I know, so let me finish instead of protesting before you know what I'm getting at. I'm stealing Claude Dejacques from you, but your new artistic director will be André Chapelle.'

'André! But that's fantastic!'

'You see? And I think he has the warmest admiration for you.'

'Thank you, what wonderful news ...'

'Well, since you feel that way, here's André.'

André came on the line and we talked for a moment.

'When are you coming to Paris? I have a heap of things to show you.'

'For a new record?'

'No, for an album that will make you the greatest singer of all – and not just in France!'

When we met in his office a week later, André did indeed have treasure in store. First of all, he wanted me to perform a Bob Dylan song,

'Farewell Angelina', which he quickly rechristened 'Adieu Angelina'. Meanwhile, Pierre Delanoë had adapted a Manos Hadjidakis song for me, to be called 'Mon gentil pêcheur' ('My Sweet Sinner'). And Eddie Marnay had done a marvelous adaptation of a traditional Greek song, 'Aide to malono', renaming it 'Robe bleue . . . robe blanche' ('Blue Dress . . . White Dress'). Nor was this all. André himself had unearthed a song I had mentioned to him during a phone call from New York, 'The 59th Street Bridge Song' by Paul Simon.

It was late one evening. Harry Belafonte had driven me to my hotel. As he drove he drummed on the dashboard with his fingers, but I managed to catch the last notes of an absolutely magnificent song.

'What is that, Harry?'

'Don't know,' said Harry. 'Never heard it before . . .'

'It's so beautiful. I'd love to sing it.'

As soon as I was back in my room I called André. I hummed what I had caught of the melody and spoke the only two words I remembered: *'feeling groovy'*.

'OK. I'll try to dig it out for you,' he promised.

And now here he was at the other end of the line – with the song! I recognized it right away.

'"Fifty-Ninth Street Bridge Song", by Simon and Garfunkel,' he told me.

'How I'd love to sing it.'

'Yes, it's made for you. I've already mentioned it to Pierre Delanoë.'

The title we gave it was 'C'est bon la vie'.

We spent the afternoon talking, burning with the excitement that overtakes you when you feel you're on the verge of a major project. Why shouldn't we throw into the mix the song that linked me eternally to Harry Belafonte, 'Try to Remember'? André thought it was a splendid idea, and Eddie Marnay now transformed it into 'Au cœur de Septembre'. And there was more. I had always wanted to record 'Le temps des cerises' ('Cherry Blossom Time'). George and I had discovered it one evening when we went to hear Tino Rossi sing, and ever since we had sung it together from time to time. André had no objections to that, either, and since George loved it as much as I did, we decided that he should do the musical arrangement.

And there (on paper) was the new album. We had to delay recording, however, because Sam Gesser wanted us back in Quebec for three or four concerts at the Place des Arts and the Palais Montcalm.

We left for Canada in the first weeks of 1967. It was a brief and triumphant tour, and the critical reactions were even more gratifying than last time, because for the first time they also had high praise for The Athenians. 'How,' asked Jean Royer in *L'Action*, 'can we mention Nana Mouskouri without praising the virtuosity of her backup group? They are not just talented musicians: their presence defines the evening.'[14]

'Because Nana is someone we love from the word "go"', added *La Semaine Illustrée*, 'we will be forever grateful to her for possessing so much talent as well ... the talent of a child of Piraeus who marries the sunlight of Greece to the snows of Canada, all of it solidly anchored in the classic form of the love song.'[15]

By the time we returned it felt as though the enthusiasm we inspired on the other side of the Atlantic was timidly raising its head in France. For the first time, the monthly magazine *Fantaisie-Variété* gave me two whole pages.

'It has become almost a cliché,' said its critic. 'When you mention Nana Mouskouri the invariable response is "what a singer!" As though people are astonished to find that we have a singer in France – at least one – who can actually sing! Unfortunately for our cherished national pride, Nana is not French: she was born in Athens of unimpeachably Greek parents. But she has decided to stay here with us, so we hereby lay claim to her without allowing ourselves to be inhibited by the charming hint of an accent with which she spices her songs.'[16]

Even the writer-philosopher Maurice Clavel opened his column in *Le Nouvel Observateur* with this superb compliment: 'Sunday 12. Election night. The first joy of the day has been my discovery of Nana Mouskouri, whose singing uplifts me, confirms me in my critical faculties, and

---

[14] *L'Action*, Quebec, 2 February 1967.
[15] *La Semaine Illustrée*, 23-29 January 1967.
[16] *Fantaisie-Variété*, January-February 1967.

confirms that singing is the profoundest of human utterances, complete with contradictions and layered meanings.'[17]

I remember André's delighted smile as he read me those words of Clavel's. Followed by his roar of 'We'll win because we're the strongest!' André had never doubted it for a second. Only the other day he said it to me again, repeating the same defiant wartime slogan with a twinkle in his eye, as I sat retracing the course of my life for the book before your eyes ... 'The strongest!' He firmly believed it because he truly worshipped me – and I believe it because André is forever by my side. In this way we depend on our mutual support to maintain the illusion that the world is our oyster.

And we were off. We began recording the album on which we pinned our hopes of 'winning'. A print was made of 'Feeling Groovy', as well as 'Tous les arbres Sont en fleurs'. But it was already April, and on the twenty-first we decided to leave for Athens and spend Easter with my parents. Our two families would be united for the occasion, joined by Jenny, her husband and my niece Aliki whom I was dying to see. Not long before, I had given George, who loved cars, a gorgeous Mercedes. We planned to drive it all the way to Athens to give him all the time he needed to luxuriate in his new gift. I was touched by George's secret pride at being able to return home in that superb automobile.

We were preparing to leave our Geneva apartment when the phone rang. It was Odile Hazan.

'I've been listening to the radio, Nana. Apparently there's been a military coup in Greece. Athens is surrounded by tanks.'

'Oh, Lord!'

'Well, for heaven's sake don't leave until you know a little more.'

When I managed to reach Mama, her voice was so choked I barely recognized her.

'No one will tell us what's going on,' she said. 'The streets are empty and the shops are closed.'

'They're saying here that Athens is under siege.'

---

[17] *Le Nouvel Observateur*, 22 March 1967.

'Yes, your father says there are soldiers everywhere. Why doesn't the king speak? He isn't dead, is he?'

'I'm sure he'll speak, Mama. You just have to wait.'

We loved the king, as many simple people in Greece did, simply because he was our king – but he did not speak. And everything we heard as the hours went by took us back to the worst days of the civil war. Army officers had apparently seized power and arrested hundreds of people, artists, politicians. It was said that masses of people were attempting to leave the country in panic but that the frontiers were sealed and the airport temporarily closed.

It seemed incredible that Greece could have toppled back into horrors belonging to another age, whereas its Western neighbors – France and the German Federal Republic in particular – had not only achieved reconciliation after the war but had become the foundation stone of a democratic and transparent Europe. The more news came our way, the more ashamed I felt. As if overtaken by its archaic traditions, its hatreds, its ancient demons, my country was turning its back on democracy, culture, and enlightenment to submit to the yoke of a handful of *colonels*! What had we done to deserve such punishment?

The commentators were soon saying that King Constantine II was the chief culprit. Two years earlier, he had dismissed the democratically elected left-wing prime minister, George Papandreou, thus himself flouting the democratic order and opening the door to the colonels. In fact, the king did not immediately condemn the coup d'état. By the time he finally attempted to restore his authority six or seven months later, declaring that the colonels were 'leading the country to disaster', it was too late. Constantine II failed, and was forced to leave the country. He joined the majority of Greece's democratic leaders in exile including the one I respected most, Constantine Karamanlis.

Greece vanished into the night, and George and I suffered agonies. How could we go on singing, laughing, amusing ourselves, when those we held dear were prisoners of 'a bloody buffoonery of a dictatorship', as Jean-Paul Sartre called it? We were grateful on opening our eyes each morning to find ourselves still in a free country, but in the very next second we remembered the sorrow of our loved ones and reproached ourselves for not being closer to them. Every time I called my parents,

Athens, Barcelona…and suddenly Berlin! How did I end up in Berlin in the autumn of 1960, a year decidedly rich in surprises? The Germans had requested that Manos Hadjidakis and his performer (in other words, me) attend the Berlin Festival. Manos didn't hesitate for a second: he would not go! Nevertheless, I decided to accept the invitation and travel to Berlin alone.

The recording studio was set up in the ruins of the former Grand Hotel Esplanade. Before the sessions began, I locked myself away in my hotel room with a tape recorder and the German-language versions of my songs. I was terrified that I might be unable to sing them in a language of which I knew nothing.

How many hours did I spend rehearsing, interrupted only by the visits of my German producer, Herr Fech (above, right)? But at long last we piled into the studio (my whole technical team was there). By midsummer 1961, my sales in Germany brought me a Gold Record, meaning that I had sold one million records there. One million! A million German homes had opened their doors to me. I couldn't believe it!

I was approaching my twenty-sixth birthday. But although I had flown aboard army propeller-planes on my way to sing at military installations, I had never boarded one of those jetliners that seemed reserved for the rich and famous. I was simultaneously curious and horribly anxious…

Above In February 1961 I left an Athens bathed in our balmy winter sunlight, and discovered a somber Paris beneath the lowering sky of a February evening. Athens suddenly seemed part of another century. As we approached the city's center, I was awed by the harmony and regularity of the façades. They were black with soot, admittedly, but I was enchanted by all those balconies and those streetlamps whose light sometimes revealed a kissing couple.

By chance, Charles Aznavour landed from France at Athens Airport just as I was leaving Athens for Paris. I was with Takis Kambas (dark glasses, right), and the press was there in droves to greet Aznavour. The few words we exchanged – in English – were full of warmth and promise.

On my first visit to Paris, I was unknown there. But German reporters had been following me since the Berlin Festival, and they took this shot of me in the middle of Paris as my bus pulled away. The photo appeared in a Berlin newspaper.

Louis Hazan

Greece's musical rebirth was beginning to attract attention in Europe, and France in particular. Louis Hazan, the youthful chief of Fontana, had unshakable confidence in my future, and advised me to come to Paris to make recordings there. 'You'll never become a star if you stay in Athens,' he told me. 'If you want to become a great singer, an international singer, you have to make Paris your base of operations.'

Michel Legrand

Michel Legrand plays 'Umbrellas of Cherbourg' for me. It was his latest creation, for a musical comedy which soon had people speculating about its chances at the next Cannes Film Festival. Here he is at his piano, with me beside him fitting words to notes he had scribbled down only moments before. But I was already in love with his music.

Michel Legrand (lower right) suggested that we put out a record together. The idea attracted composer Eddie Marnay (standing, left-center), who co-wrote four songs with Michel. Behind Michel is my artistic director, Claude Dejaques.

We spent many evenings with Monsieur Hazan in the jazz bars around Saint-Germain-des Prés. I loved their atmosphere from the start. Jazz was so much a part of my being that I often felt I had been transported back to an Athens taverna with George at my side. (The man beside me here, however – on an evening in 1963 – is not George but Manos.)

Jacques Caillard, Louis Hazan's successor, who had faith in me from the very beginning.

As the days went by, my French improved. I no longer rolled my r's, had lost almost everything of my accent, and no longer needed a dictionary to understand lyrics. Here I'm being congratulated by Philips' CEO, M. Meyerstein (right).

In the mid-Sixties, the performers who got all the attention in France were the kind the entertainment magazine *Salut les Copains!* ran on its covers: Johnny Halliday, Sylvie Vartan and Claude François (left) ... I didn't yet belong with the stars.

Quincy Jones

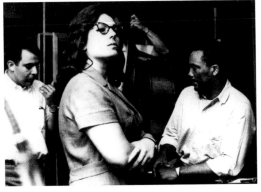

Unexpected good news greeted me on my return from my first German tour. Quincy Jones wanted me to go to New York to make a jazz recording with him. When Louis Hazan told me, I couldn't at first believe it. But it was true, and they intended to distribute it worldwide. The prospect of working face to face with a musician who had played with Duke Ellington, Sarah Vaughan and Ray Charles thrilled me and terrified me. As always with me, I was mortally afraid of disappointing whichever person who had singled me out, and the only redemption came when I heard myself singing alongside the voices of the great.

Theater of Herodus Atticus, Athens 1984

Returning to Greece after twenty years' absence, I sang at the Theater of Herodus Atticus in the capital. I had the strong sense that I had come back from a long journey that began on the little stage at my father's movie theater. I was no longer bothered by my hands, which I used to hide by clasping them behind my back, by my body, by my glasses, by my too-wide-set eyes. I had come back to Greece (dare I say it?) simply as the spirit of music itself!

OLYMPIA, PARIS 1962

My first invitation to the legendary music hall! I performed during the first half of the evening, but the star of the show was Georges Brassens (left). The first verdict on my performance came from Brassens himself, who said after hearing me: 'That little Greek kid, she's going to go far...'

LONDON, THE BBC

Yvonne Littlewood

In 1972, Yvonne Littlewood (director and producer of many BBC broadcasts), invited me to her Saturday night musical program. Yvonne discovered me seven years earlier during my Eurovision appearance. She opened the doors of the whole Commonwealth to me. Singing into the mike on the left is Marinella, a very popular Greek singer.

Harry Belafonte

Am I really with Harry Belafonte in New York? Has he really just asked me to be his singing partner for the next two or three years? It was the most wonderful proposal I ever received. We left to perform for five or six months in Phoenix, Chicago, and Los Angeles (six weeks!). Later, we also performed in Canada – Vancouver, Calgary, Toronto, and Montreal.

THE STREETS OF NEW YORK

Victory! George would play alongside Belafonte's musicians throughout the tour, and we would simply split my check between us. I was happy for him and for us. Once the deal was done, Belafonte said he looked forward to whatever George imparted to his musicians.

BROADWAY THEATRE

'At the Broadway Theatre last night,' wrote one critic, 'Nana Mouskouri made her debut on the Great White Way. Madame Mouskouri always injects something strong and positive into her performances. She sings her French songs with an intensity that recalls Piaf. In English, her songs are softer, more contained, with sometimes a hint of pop to them. As for her Greek songs, everyone sooner or later ends up clapping rhythmically along.' (*The New York Times*, April 27 1977)

Nicolas and Hélène

Nicolas was born on February 13 1968 and Hélène arrived on July 7 1970. To me, that summer of 1970 marked the unhoped-for realization of a family dream. George and I lived through it together, watching for Hélène's first smile, entranced by the strides Nicolas was making as he entered his third year... With my inborn horror of shouts and quarreling, I thanked Heaven every day for leading us so safely into this shared time of tranquility.

© X. D. R./ARCHIVES UNIVERSAL MUSIC FRANCE

At the 1969 Cannes Film Festival the photographers stalked me, followed by a good-natured throng in search of autographs. André Assio (on my left), who handled Philips' press relations, was tickled pink to be part of the unending celebrity minuet.

OLYMPIA 1969

I'll always remember my 1969 Olympia appearance (my third) as the moment when Nicolas realized I am a singer. I tried to keep his adorable face in mind during those terrible moments just before going onstage. What would he think when he saw me?

Jean-Claude Brialy

I was invited to the Antibes Song Festival in the summer of 1966. There I met a man who (thirty years later!) was to become the brother I had never had – Jean-Claude Brialy. He held my hand when we went onstage, and I would hear something like the murmur of the wind in tall grass, a gentle, benevolent stirring, and find myself longing to offer my face, to abandon myself.

I heard that so-and-so had been arrested. The poet Yannis Ritsos, whose words I had sung, was deported to Yaros, and so was the playwright Yannis Negrepontis. Manos Hadjidakis had managed to escape. Nikos Gatsos refused to leave his house, his books, and his country behind, and listening between the lines of our lengthy phone calls I sensed how much poetry shielded him from oppression and stupidity, just as *Amorgos* had shielded him during the German occupation.

> *Seize life's banner and shroud death in its folds*
> *And may your heart stay calm*
> *May your tears not water this pitiless earth*
> *As penguins' tears once watered the ice*
> *To complain is useless*
> *On this planet of ghosts life is everywhere the same.*

And paradoxically, when we should have been losing hope during this first spring under dictatorship, life gave us the gift we had awaited so long: I was finally pregnant! From the bottom-most depths of my faith I saw in this a sign from Heaven, a way for the Lord to let us know that a new light would one day shine on Greece, on this child, and on all those soon to be born.

On the phone that night, I was filled with joy by my parents' happy cries, and it felt as if this still-tiny event was already helping us escape the night. When would we see them again? Would my parents be able to come over for the baby's birth? For my own part, I decided never to return to Greece as long as she lay under the colonels' power.

It was nearly the end of May, and George and I faced a serious and urgent decision. Should we go ahead as planned with our nationwide tour of France, or (given my condition) should we cancel it? This was my first opportunity to sing in the country's major spas and thus encounter audiences that had never seen me onstage and perhaps never even heard me. Until now, I had not been well enough known in France to risk a real tour, limiting myself to occasional concerts. So cancellation would be a great sacrifice, not only for me but also for The Athenians, who badly needed the work.

As so often in such situations, we decided to seek medical advice. We told the doctor everything: the thousands of miles of car travel, the three hours onstage almost every night, the abbreviated nights and days without rest – for eight whole weeks.

'Is there a risk I might lose my baby, doctor?'

Yes, there was. The doctor examined me, shook his head over the various factors involved, pursed his lips in thought.

'It will be very hard on you,' he said at last. 'But I wonder whether it wouldn't be harder still to condemn you to spending the whole summer in bed. I can see you pacing up and down, fretting and impatient, and I don't know whether that wouldn't be worse for your pregnancy ...'

'So what should we do?'

'Go ahead! I think you can safely try it, provided you take a few precautions.' I left his office with his written advice and a prescription for three injections every week. I was at once happy as a lark and terribly worried.

Nevertheless, I soon felt sure the doctor had made the right choice. Buoyed by my own enthusiasm and by the welcome awaiting us at every stop, I was so confident about myself and about this child that I was certain we ran no risk. I spoke to the child constantly, telling it how glad I was to have it there listening to my songs, how I was feeling, and even how tired I was. I felt its constant presence, sensed how *comfortable* it was, and knew that we would never be apart. And there was George, always by my side, ready to help, attentive, floating on his little cloud from morning to night, and it was such a comfort to be able to count on him. He had wanted this child ever since our marriage seven years ago. When we finally got back to our hotel room at night, exhausted but elated, he unfailingly thanked it just for being there, listened to it, chatted to it.

We played to full audiences everywhere. The spectators were warm, moved, grateful, and the press reaction was extraordinary. 'Night of Triumph for a Flawless Nana Mouskouri', ran a headline in *La Marseillaise*, confirming the predictions of André Chapelle, who called every night from Paris for our news. This tour was also a success for him, since I sang all the new songs I had recorded that spring: 'Adieu

Angelina', 'C'est bon la vie', 'Mon gentil pêcheur', 'Cu-cu-rru-cu-cu paloma', 'Guantanamera' as well as a very beautiful song by Eddie Marnay and Nachum Heiman. It would lend its name to my forthcoming album – *Le jour où la colombe* (*The Day When the Dove*) ... To quote from that same article in *La Marseillaise*, 'She sings of love, flowers, children, war. She leaves us spellbound, enchanted by the seductive charms of her singing.'

In the middle of that summer tour, during my appearance on a television program in Cannes, I learned that I had already sold eight million records worldwide. Eight million – but relatively few of them in France compared to the United States, Canada and Germany.

'Didn't you know?' asked the TV host, clearly surprised.

'No, I've never dared ask whether my records sell.'

It was true. I trusted Louis Hazan so completely, and above all was so grateful to him, that I never asked him anything of that kind, as though I didn't want to hurt him by talking finances. George tolerated all my little ways – except on one point: I was not to leave a single blemish on the seats of his beloved Mercedes. He got me all the fruit I asked for, even the most exotic ones, but he insisted that I eat them on the side of the road. I clearly remember inquisitive motorists slowing down, probably intrigued by the similarity between this girl gobbling down a pineapple on the edge of the Cannes-Saint Raphaël highway and Nana Mouskouri, whose posters were plastered even on tree-trunks. It must certainly have been the glasses ...

The tour was almost over when I was called to the phone one evening the moment we reached our hotel.

'For you. André Chapelle.'

'André! Hello!'

'I have something important to tell you. Are you sitting down?'

'Well, now I am. Is it serious?'

'No, but it's very important.'

'Go ahead, I'm listening.'

'Bruno Coquatrix wants you to top the bill at the Olympia!'

'Oh! But ... but when is he thinking of?'

'Right away, in October.'

'October! But by then I'll be five months pregnant, André.'

'I know, I've thought of that.'

'It's impossible!'

'Don't say that, Nana, this is a chance in a million!'

'It's a great chance all right, but I can't appear onstage with a stomach like a balloon. People make fun of my glasses as it is, so just think what they'll say if—'

'Listen, I'm aware of all that. But you have to think before you turn it down. What if I came down to the coast to talk to you? That way the three of us can talk it over calmly, you, me and George.'

'Well, come down if you like, but for me it's No, André. In any case, I don't feel ready yet to take on the Olympia on my own. And pregnant into the bargain!'

I was so upset when we hung up that I fretted for a whole hour before I felt able to tell George the news. At first he seemed delighted, but once he had studied my expression he went off and joined his friends, as though deciding that the decision was mine alone.

In the next three days my manager, Roland Ribet, left me fifteen messages begging me to call him back, which I studiously avoided doing. I knew exactly what he wanted: to persuade me to accept Coquatrix's offer. But I had no wish to listen to his arguments. At least not until I had seen André, who would be spending the weekend with us – André, who never insisted too much, whose unfailing calm did such wonders for my state of mind.

I learned from him that I owed this Olympia proposal not to my talent but to Gilbert Bécaud's sudden cancellation of his singing date, leaving Bruno Coquatrix with a three-week gap in the middle of his autumn season.

'Don't worry about Coquatrix,' André told me. 'Just think about yourself, and we'll call him as soon as you've decided. Give yourself time to think about it, keep in mind that this is a fantastic chance – and that if you accept you'll have nothing to lose.'

'And if everyone laughs at me?'

'Nana, no one is going to laugh at you. If you're worrying about the baby, don't! The media will mention it, but there'll be nothing mean-spirited in what they say. And every French mama will be on your side.'

'The biggest problem is that I'm not yet ready to top the bill.'

'Nana, maybe you lack self-confidence, but I've been following you for several years now and I'm telling you that you've never sung so well. And for the first time you have a complete French repertoire.'

Lying sleepless in bed that night, I admitted to myself that André was right: my voice had never been fuller. And my latest songs, about to be issued as an album, had netted me high praise. 'Buy her next LP,' wrote René Bourdier in *Les Lettres françaises*, 'and you'll be favored with that rarest of pleasures, the kind only the very greatest performers can provide.'

Next morning, I wasn't quite so set on refusing, and decided to give Bruno Coquatrix a tentative call.

'You know,' I told him, 'I'm afraid I'll be leading you to ruin. What will you think of me if the auditorium is half-empty?'

The voice that answered was unflappable:

'Of course I'm aware that you're not going to fill the Olympia all on your own, Nana. I'm not crazy. So I've planned a talent-packed first half. Jacques Martin will warm them up, and Serge Lama will be making his comeback. So don't worry. Just those two are worth an army of seats between them . . . So it's Yes, my sweet?'

'It's Yes, Monsieur Coquatrix.'

16

A Pregnant Women in a Red Velvet Kaftan on the Olympia Stage

I'd like to write for a moment about *agony* – I can find no better word – the moment of *agony* that preceded my appearance onstage on 26 October 1967 for my first night as top of the bill at the Olympia.

I locked myself in my dressing room, my heart beating so hard that at times I thought it would fail me. Then for some reason I forgot about my heart and looked at myself in the mirror: a young brunette wearing glasses and a red velvet kaftan. What were we doing there, the two of us, amid all this disorder in this small harshly-lit room? Was I really alive, or on the point of expiring? And then, like a violent blow to the chest, awareness of the dreadful fate ahead came flooding back. In one hour . . . in forty-five minutes . . . Oh no, I would never have the strength. I thought of condemned men waiting on death row. At any moment now there would be a knock at the door. It would be time, and I would have to say 'I'm ready.' No trembling, sobbing or begging allowed: I would have to be steadfast. A matter of dignity, right? Look your executioner in the eye, give him your hand, let him lead you away.

Sometimes the seconds flashed past. 'My God,' I whispered to myself, 'this can't be, five minutes have just gone by in no time at all: maybe the clock is malfunctioning.' But no, I can hear its malevolent ticking, implacable, terrifying. At other times the opposite happened: every second dragged on interminably, and then every smallest sound from the world outside my dressing room reached me. George in the room next door, so nervous that he had just broken every string on his guitar. The technicians calling out to each other in the corridor. Distant applause from the auditorium, like a sudden hail-storm on a tin roof. Was that for Jacques Martin? For Serge Lama? Was this already the intermission?

A little earlier, Odile and Louis Hazan had briefly dropped in. 'It's fantastic, Nana,' they told me. 'The place is packed and people are still lining up outside.' How they smiled, how their eyes sparkled!

I tried to respond in the same spirit:

'Oh? That's good . . .'

'That's all you can say?' Odile exclaimed. 'Even for Brassens there were fewer spectators!'

Odile kissed me. Louis Hazan said a few words, but my heart was thudding too hard for me to register them. They left, and now their brief visit came back to me. How long ago had it been?

A knock at the door! My legs turned to water. I was about to collapse. 'Come in.'

It was my voice, but how had I managed it?

'You're up next, my sweet. The audience is fantastic. You're going to knock them cold.'

Bruno Coquatrix – red bow tie, silver-flecked suit – offered me his arm. An Olympia tradition. On first nights, the theater owner personally led his star onstage.

A knot of people had formed outside my dressing room door. I caught Odile Hazan's smile, André's grave, encouraging look, Serge Lama's surprised expression. I hadn't a word or even a smile for any of them. I felt empty, numb, perched on the very brink.

'When I saw you go past,' Serge Lama told me later (he became one of my closest friends), 'I had the impression of a lamb going to the slaughter.'

But the second we appeared onstage – Coquatrix's legendary figure, and me in my ample red kaftan encrusted at the wrists and on my breast with scarlet gems (a Per Spook creation) – feverish applause raced through the audience, like a sustained surge of impatience and eager anticipation.

I launched into 'Telalima', and at once the music bore me aloft, high above my fear, obliterating the agonizing hours I had just spent. I was no longer a pitiful, numb body, a fluttering heart. I sang, and it was as if the sky suddenly opened to lend me wings. My fear was no more, as if all that remained of me was my voice and the unborn child who meant everything to me.

I was thinking of that child and of our unhappy country when I launched into 'Le jour où la colombe'. That song (one of the last we had recorded, early last September) expressed all the sorrow we had endured since 21 April 1967, the day when life suddenly turned its back on Greece.

Je ne sais pas où sont partis ces hommes
Que d'autres sont venus chercher.
Ils ont disparu par un matin de Pâques,
Des chaînes à leurs poignets.
Combien d'entre eux vivront encore
Le jour où la colombe reviendra sur l'olivier ?

Who knows where all those men have gone
Led away by other men?
They left us one fine Easter day,
Their wrists festooned with chains.
How many of them will we see again
When the dove returns to the olive tree?

Can I be sure of the moment when I felt certain that the audience was with me, that there were now a thousand of us sharing the emotion I alone had felt just a second before? I thought once more of Judy Garland. I thought of my father's astonishment when I insisted to him that people had been transformed between the opening and the end of the movie, and I silently thanked Heaven for giving me this mysterious ability to move men's hearts and to be moved myself. Back then, Papa didn't understand what I was trying to tell him. But if he were here tonight, I thought, he might understand. Applause takes a hundred different forms, but there was one particular form that I recognized and that struck chords deep within me, for it spoke in unmistakable terms of passion, even if I was singing in Greek.

When it was over, the whole audience rose to its feet. I don't know how many encores we answered, how many curtains. But it was impossible to end it all just like that. Without the orchestra, I sang 'Paper

Moon', standing all alone on center stage. It was like a kiss from afar for Nikos Gatsos, locked away in his home for the curfew.

In next day's *Le Monde*, Claude Sarraute had this to say: 'With Nana Mouskouri, the Olympia took on the atmosphere of Carnegie Hall. Her voice is a crystal, a gushing spring, a river of velvet. Her songs are beautiful, simple, and passionate. And she herself resembles them, innocently and serenely accepting her myopia and the imminent birth of her child, sure of the quality of her singing and sure of her public. Trained at the Athens Conservatory but in love with jazz, she preferred the tavernas of Piraeus to La Scala.

'She is a concert singer, masterfully accompanied by her husband and three of his fellow-musicians: she is a patriot favored by events which have elevated the folk refrains of her country far above the chintzy charms of tourist brochures, charging them with a passion that transforms their range and their accents.'

'She is music,' wrote Paul Carrière that same day in *Le Figaro*. 'She gives a superior meaning to the words she sings.'

'She sings the way Rudolph Nureyev dances,' wrote Jacqueline Cartier in *France-Soir*, 'because that's what she was born to do.'

And *Paris-Match*: 'Go and applaud her. She weaves a spell for eyes and ears. And for hearts. Thank you, Nana.'

There can be no doubt. That first night at the Olympia marked a revolution in my artistic life. Forty-eight hours later, every seat in the house was booked for the whole of the run, which ended on 13 November. Exultant, somewhat bewildered by our success, Bruno Coquatrix predicted 'an immense career' for me. Louis Hazan admitted that right up to the last minute he had his doubts about my ability to pack the Olympia – even though he was the one who had promised me that one day my name would blaze across its façade in giant red letters, just like Edith Piaf's. Only Andre was unsurprised. 'We won because we were the strongest,' he wrote on the little card that came with the flowers he sent.

In fact, France had suddenly discovered me. Juliette Boisriveaud explained it in *Candide* in words I cannot match:

'It would be too easy,' she wrote, 'to turn up one evening at the

Olympia, to be swept off our feet by a pregnant woman in red velvet, to realize that she is one of the greatest singers of her time, and to imagine as well that we were the ones who discovered her.

'Because she sings in French. Because she has lived in Paris since 1962. Because we have stuck an anthropometric label on her – "the Greek singer in glasses." And since we're more alive to "hits" than to genuine presence, we have in fact been the last people in the world to recognize Nana Mouskouri, to find out who she is.

'America, Russia, Germany, Japan, the whole world (and even our own despised provinces) knew before Paris did. We have only now reached the point of registering our amazement at seeing this young woman top the bill at the Olympia – a woman we know as just one face among many, and one voice a little more impressive than the run-of-the-mill.

'But in America, she performs before large crowds: 16,00 fans, for example, in Lawrence, Kansas, 15,000 students at the University of California in Los Angeles, and a forty-day run at the Greek Theater in Los Angeles. In Germany, she has sold more records than any other singer since 1962.

'Her "Roses blanches de Corfou" has set a European record, with sales of 1,200,000.

'So much for those of us who measure success in figures, who need such yardsticks before we can be sure that this is what we're supposed to like. Perhaps that's why Nana Mouskouri's presence in our midst has so long gone unnoticed.

'A voice. A presence. And moments when time stands still. The description fits only the truly great, Ella Fitzgerald, Marian Anderson, Edith Piaf, Amalia Rodriguez, Judy Garland and a handful of others. Including Nana Mouskouri.'

Another long article about me in *Rock and Folk* ended with these words: 'Today, when at long last the French have begun to listen to Nana Mouskouri, I have just three words: Welcome Nana and . . . our humblest apologies for recognizing you so late!'

Recognition at last! Yet as soon as the curtain came down on the last act, George and I sneaked away like thieves. We couldn't wait to get back to Geneva and home. The baby's arrival was three months away. We longed to arrest the passage of time and luxuriate in the steady growth of this child inside me, this child we hadn't caressed and conversed with enough. And of course we had to prepare the baby's room, think about finding a nanny for the three months immediately following its birth, and quietly prepare for this event we knew would change our lives.

How does one learn to be a parent? By revisiting one's own childhood, obviously, and by remembering one's own parents. I had recently spent more and more time on the phone with my mother. And although his own daughter's birth had slipped his mind, my father was now counting the days until his grandchild's arrival. So excitedly, indeed, that my parents decided to come to Switzerland! They planned to spend Christmas with us and stay until the baby was born, and perhaps even longer. Then George's parents announced that they too would be coming. The birth began to look like a gesture of defiance directed at the barbed wire encircling Greece. In spite of everything, it would be a festive event, a precursor of the day when the dove . . .

I had the same nightmare almost every night: I wandered about in an empty house, terrified at the thought of the impending birth, wondering where I might find the tiny bed we would need, how we could round up the necessary after-care, the baby's clothes and shoes. It was a nightmare that wrenched me from my bed in a state of panic.

'Did you have that kind of dream, Mama?'

She smiled, but her smile was wry.

'With us, you know, it wasn't a nightmare, we *really* had nothing.'

So why was I – so much more spoiled by life than my parents – flagellating myself in this way? I asked Nikos the same question:

'Do you know why, Nikos?'

He let me go on. My call was interrupting him in his work, even though he pretended I never disturbed him and never would disturb him.

'Tell me some more about that empty house.'

'How I wish it was smaller, Nikos ! But it's much bigger than our apartment. That's what gives me these nightmares.'

He thought for a moment before answering in grave, measured tones:

'That house is your new life as a mother. It's big and empty, but it's offering itself to you ... Maybe you're afraid you'll get lost in it, who knows? Or afraid you won't know how to furnish it ... But in the end, you've always managed to do things right. Think: it's ten years since we first met, and in that time you've ventured far across the seas. If you couldn't tame sea monsters, don't you think the sea would already have swallowed you?'

It was the media that threatened to swallow me when I went to the maternity clinic. If popularity can be measured by the number of photographers and TV cameramen who besiege celebrity births, then I was popular indeed, for the clinic was soon on battle alert. The Olympia concert had vaulted me on to the covers of large-circulation magazines which were now sniffing avidly into my private life. The success of my last album, *Le jour où la colombe* (which quickly became a French Gold Record), only whetted this newborn curiosity. We had to learn how to manage it, and I was certainly not best placed to do so. Still grateful for the praise that greeted my last singing tour, I felt unable to do anything but be cordial with representatives of the media.

Nicolas was born on 13 February 1968, and I think his picture as he lay in my arms went right around the world. But it didn't bother me, because it had no effect on the tenderness that submerged the three of us whenever we could be alone together, with George and me taking care of the baby's needs – and shortly thereafter the seven of us, with his grandparents' fond, radiant faces bent for the first time over his sleeping form.

And now Fernande Schweitzer entered our lives. She was to become all-important to Nicolas, to his little sister Hélène, and of course to me.

It was the midwife who first mentioned Fernande to me.

'Now you need a nanny you can rely on,' she said.

'I know, but I can't leave my baby to just anyone.'

'You're not going to stop singing?'

'No, but I prefer not to think of the day I'll have to entrust Nicolas to a stranger ...'

'That's a mistake. You should start thinking about it right now.'

'Well, can you think of anyone?'

'Only one. She's truly a wonder, but she's already committed elsewhere.'

'Could you call her anyway? You never know . . .'

That's how Fernande turned up at the clinic to meet me. Just out of politeness, she told me, for she had decided not to look after children any more.

'I see. But why?'

'Because I get too attached, Madame Mouskouri. After six months or a year, it's very hard to abandon these children and begin all over again in a new household.'

'But for me it wouldn't be just six months. If we get along, you could stay . . .'

'No, sooner or later a day would come when I'd have to leave. I'm sorry, but I can't do it any more.'

With that, we said goodbye, and I returned home. The two grandmothers were vying for Nicolas' attention, which left me ample time for resting.

A few days went by, and I was still thinking about hiring a girl when Fernande called me.

'The other day,' she said, 'I took a good look at the little one. He stole my heart away, he looked so sweet . . .'

'Does this mean you'd agree to take him on?'

'I believe it means I wouldn't want anyone else to take care of him, Madame.' And that's how Fernande (Nicolas would learn to call her Féfé) became one of the family. Nicolas was three weeks old when she joined us. When Fernande passed away, he was twenty-five . . .

My vacation ended in early May 1968. For almost six months we had lived like hermits, first waiting impatiently and then going into ecstasy over our child. Now André wanted us back in Paris to make a new recording which had been on his mind since the Olympia. Roland Ribet had signed me on for various dates, both on television and onstage, in Paris, Brussels, and Amsterdam. It was time for us to dive back into the whirlpool and for our parents to return to the gloom of daily life in Athens.

But I didn't want to abandon Nicolas. We flew to Paris with him and Fernande and all the needed accessories, feeding bottles, Guigoz powdered milk, baby clothes, disposable diapers, medicine. We hoped the Boulogne apartment would be big enough to house the four of us.

Fernande was extraordinary: tactful but ever-present, attentive, careful, and above all so fond of Nicolas that I felt jealous at having to leave him for a few hours each day.

The Athenians were raring to play again after these months of inaction, and between May and June we recorded my next album, *Summer Dresses*. It included several songs that went around the world, such as 'Puisque tu m'aimes' ('Because You love Me') by Pierre Delanoë and Manos Hadjidakis, and 'Over and Over', a traditional song George arranged himself, and 'Little Drummer Boy'.

Meanwhile, protesting students were running wild in the streets of Paris, and I spontaneously sympathized with their cause. Every morning I listened to reports of what had gone on the day before, and I couldn't help being pleased when I heard them chanting 'Forbidding is Forbidden' or delivering fiery speeches outside the Latin Quarter's Théâtre de l'Odéon about freedom, solidarity, and the redistribution of wealth. But Odile Hazan was furious, and listening to her protests suggested to me that my infatuation with this uprising, and even with the general strike that was beginning to paralyze France, was misplaced, out of touch with reality. It was obviously Greece I unconsciously had in mind, displacing the situation from one country to another, as if the French students here were giving voice to aspirations their Athenian counterparts dared not utter aloud.

Ever since it was published to commemorate the first anniversary of the colonels' coup d'état, I have kept on my person, like a wound that refuses to close, an article by the law professor Maurice Duverger, entitled 'Greece and Our Shame'. In it, he said: 'Sixteen thousand arrests in the country as a whole, summary executions in concentration camps (including that of the Resistance hero Panayotis Ellis, according to *The Times* of London – we can never forget this day.' I felt beyond personal shame. I lived in sorrow and disbelief, and I believe the living and exultant anger of the Paris students saved me from drowning.

What is more (and as if they had already sensed it), I found myself ambushed by these same students one day in an incident which still makes me want to laugh nearly forty years later.

That day, Odile insisted that I go with her to do some shopping and then head somewhere for tea.

'Good idea,' I said, 'but let's go on foot.'

But her husband was now entitled to a chauffeur-driven limousine, and Odile was determined to take advantage of it.

'There are barricades on every street, Odile.'

'It doesn't matter, we'll manage.'

But we didn't manage. Near the Luxembourg Gardens we were surrounded by a gang of students. They weren't threatening; in fact I think they couldn't get over the sight of a limousine, complete with chauffeur, smack in the middle of their barricade-strewn Latin Quarter playground. We were immobilized, unable to advance or retreat.

'Let's get out,' I said, and opened the door.

I have no idea whether the students recognized me. At all events, they pulled me back from the car (possibly to keep me out of harm's way), closed the door and started pouring bags of flour over the vehicle. Within seconds, it was unrecognizable. Its fenders disappeared from sight. I couldn't help bursting out laughing.

And then they wandered off, leaving us alone. When I opened the door again, Odile was white with fury. And, unwilling to add insult to injury, she refused to leave the car. But the chauffeur had no choice. Amid the mocking cackle of bystanders, he set to work all alone on the task of removing the snow from our lovely limousine.

Then came summer, and a tour of France unlike any I had yet experienced. News of the Olympia concert had spread, and I was in demand more or less everywhere. The Athenians were delighted, but I saw things a little differently. I was torn between my private distress at having to leave Nicolas and the promise I'd made to my musicians to accept as many engagements as possible. Because of Nicolas' arrival, they had done nothing this past winter, so I already felt guilty. We finally reached a compromise: every week I would fly to Geneva for two days. When I returned we would perform every evening.

It was during this protracted tour that Yvonne Littlewood called.

Ever since the Eurovision contest, she had occasionally invited me to sing in the BBC's London studios. But this time, she had something quite different to propose: one broadcast a week for six weeks.

'Six weeks, just for me? That's a mighty tall order! I'll never have enough songs to fill so many broadcasts.'

'Don't let that worry you, I've been thinking about it, and you have a wonderful repertoire. And you'll have a guest performer for each broadcast. How would October suit you?'

André was all for it. I was still obsessed with my tally of song titles, but I believe that the second I told him, he foresaw the worldwide impact those broadcasts would have. And it was a wonderful opportunity for The Athenians as well.

So from mid September on we found ourselves in London, rehearsing and then performing for two solid months. We rented one of those charming little two-floor London houses called Mews houses with a garden in the back. Nicolas and Féfé had adjoining bedrooms on the first floor. George and I were downstairs, with a little room where we played music most of the time.

Fortunately the broadcasts, each lasting fifty minutes, were recorded, not live, so that being onstage was a relaxed affair. As my guest for the first broadcast, Yvonne and I decided to invite Amalia Rodriguez, whom I worshipped as fervently as I did Maria Callas. And we had so many things in common. Like me, she was born in a poor neighborhood, but in Lisbon. She too started out singing here and there, in nightclubs and soon in what used to be called *fado* joints. There she at once developed a deep affinity with fado, of which she became – and remained – the figurehead. Fado is the intimate heart of Portugal, age-old songs drenched in poetry and nostalgia. Neglected for years, Amalia Rodriguez was revealed to the world thanks to her appearance at the Olympia in 1956. It led to an international career which made her a world-famous star.

We sang turn by turn, mingling the sorrows and legends of our small countries clinging precariously to Western Europe's two extremities – and both of them cut off from the light by military dictators. The Athenians even played fado-style to mark the occasion.

*

As we flew back to Paris, those broadcasts winged their way to every country in the Commonwealth, all the way to Australia and New Zealand. They were also beamed to Canada, Scandinavia, the Netherlands, to various countries in Asia, and even to certain states in Communist Eastern Europe, behind the barrier then known as the Iron Curtain.

Via the BBC, Yvonne Littlewood was spreading our fame worldwide.

The first hint of this came when a young British promoter, Robert Paterson, asked me to return to London to give a major recital . . . at the Royal Albert Hall.

'The Albert Hall! But that's a huge place!'

'Eight thousand seats.'

'And you really think . . .'

'I've seen all your BBC broadcasts, Nana. People really loved them. Now they know who you are. Trust me. If you agree, I guarantee the place will be packed.'

If I agreed! How could I refuse? What performer could refuse to appear at the legendary Albert Hall?

But first I had to take it all in. I decided to spend a day in London and look the auditorium over.

What I found was astonishing. In those days (the Albert Hall's capacity has since been somewhat reduced), the stalls alone boasted 4,000 seats, four times the Olympia's. But there was room for just as many in the terraced seats above, from the dome right down to the red velvet boxes looking straight down on the stage. It was staggering, dizzying, and I stood alone in the middle of that eerily silent cathedral, trying to project myself fearlessly forward to the night I would come onstage. Was it possible that so many people would crowd in here one night just to hear me? Was it possible that for two or three hours one night my voice would ring out all alone in this space, occupied before me by the very greatest performers? Then my mother's face appeared before me. Because there was something religious in this silence, in this petrified solemnity. I wanted her to be there (she had never seen me onstage) on the big night. Wasn't that her dream for us, for Jenny and me, when she accompanied us to the Conservatory? I felt a secret pride that I had been able to give life to that dream, and at the same time the possibility that she might be there made my heart miss a beat – as though I suddenly feared her gaze more than that of all the other thousands of spectators. No, I whispered to myself, I'd prefer her not to be here. Another time, maybe another time, if I can pluck up the courage.

Robert Paterson was beaming when I returned four months later and entered the Albert Hall.

'Congratulations! We're sold out.'

So eight thousand people would be there tonight. Every seat was booked, and the concert would be broadcast live on Europe 1 by Pierre Bouteiller, who was here for the opening.

I didn't know it, but selling out the Albert Hall confers instant prestige, crowning you with an aura reflected in the eyes of everyone who helped put the evening together, from the director to the technicians and usherettes. I had never felt such support, such affection, such encouragement as I did in that hall during the final rehearsal.

And in that vast intimidating building, so reminiscent of a Roman arena where victims were thrown to the lions, I felt that the audience was mine from the very first. As though we were old acquaintances. Had they all heard me already on the radio? From the imperceptible stir that occasionally rustled through the auditorium, like an inadvertent sigh, I had the feeling that some of my songs were old friends of theirs.

The finest moment came at the end. We were called back ten times, and ten times we came back to the footlights. And then – since we really did have to say goodbye – I came back alone, lit by a solitary spotlight and without my musicians. The theater was in deep darkness. Not a breath could be heard. In that silence, so complete you could swear time itself stood still, I sang 'Amazing Grace'. One of the most moving of all English hymns, it was apparently written around 1760 by John Newton, skipper of a slave-ship, who was converted by divine grace during a storm and became a parson and a fervent abolitionist. They also say that the poignant melody was derived in its turn from old songs brought over by the slaves:

> Amazing grace,
> How sweet the sound
> That sav'd a wretch like me!
> I once was lost, but now am found,
> Was blind, but now I see . . .

As the last note faded, the hall seemed transfixed for a split second, and then the audience exploded into applause as though the heavens were suddenly rent asunder. The whole audience, the whole theater rose to its feet. I was heaped with flowers, submerged by ovations, and I believe I stood there in tears for twenty minutes, too overcome to say anything at all, accepting the unending cheers for what they were – the most unbelievable homage I had ever been paid.

'Tonight you made the Albert Hall your own,' Robert Paterson told me later. 'From now on, it's your home.'

That was in April 1969. In the months leading up to the Albert Hall concert, I had already sensed that events were gathering speed.

I had just returned to Paris after my six BBC broadcasts when Philips' new London manager, Olaf Wiper, called Louis Hazan.

'I'd like to cut an album of international songs for the UK with Nana Mouskouri,' he told Louis.

I imagine that behind his glasses, Louis' eyes betrayed discreet mirth. For it was Wiper's predecessor at Philips who called Hazan five years earlier to tell him he was wasting his money on me. 'She sings well enough,' were his words, 'but she has no chance of making it in this country.'

Now, it appeared, London did believe I had a future, and André and I began to ponder the contents of the proposed album. We decided on 'Try to Remember', 'Over and Over' (originally 'Roule s'enroule') and 'Coucouroucoucou Paloma'. The album, which we recorded in London in 1969, was so successful that it netted me a second series of BBC broadcasts, followed by my first tour of the United Kingdom in the winter of 1970.

*

This wasn't the end of it. Sam Gesser (this was still pre-Albert Hall) wanted us back in Canada. So as 1969 began, we took off once again for Montreal. Since we were planning a six-week tour, Nicolas and Féfé came along as well. Neither George nor I could bear the thought of such a long separation from our little boy. And it was on his first birthday, 13 February, that I fully appreciated the kindness and generosity of Canadians for the first time.

We had performed at Baie-Comeau on the Saint Lawrence in northern Quebec, and I wasn't scheduled to sing on the day after. I set the day aside to be with Nicolas in Montreal to celebrate his birthday.

It was a joyful birthday, thanks in particular to Sam Gesser's wife, who arrived with their children, flowers, and an armful of presents.

With the birthday party behind us, I was scheduled to take a light plane next morning to Rimouski for my next performance. Rimouski lay across the Saint Lawrence from Baie-Comeau. George and The Athenians, who had only to cross the river on an ice-breaker ferry, were already there.

I was preparing to leave for the airport when Air Quebec called. A snowstorm was expected, and my flight was canceled. I at once called Sam Gesser in a panic.

'No problem,' he said. 'I'll drive you from Montreal to Quebec and put you in a taxi for Rimouski. You'll be there in time to sing.'

We set out. The road was of course snowed under at that time of year, but there was a brilliant sun and we talked lightheartedly about this unexpected storm. The taxi driver who took charge of me in Quebec was no less optimistic.

'Don't worry. Rimouski's just a little hop, you'll be there in time.'

The first miles were splendid. We drove beneath the pale winter sun whose slanting rays picked out the ice-floes on the river in gold. Then clouds filled the sky, and gradually it began to snow.

'Isn't this a bit worrying?' I asked the driver.

'Not on your life! And if it gets worse we'll fit the chains.'

The rich Quebec accent only made his optimism more convincing.

But suddenly the tiny flakes seemed to go crazy, an unpredictable wind started to blow, and I witnessed a phenomenon I had never encountered: instead of settling on the road surface the snow danced in our headlight beams as though we were driving into waves of sea-spray.

'Oh no,' said the driver, 'I think it's turning ugly.'

He stopped, buckled the chains over the tires, and – encased from head to foot in ice – got back in the car.

'The way things look,' he said, 'I don't see us getting past Rivière-du-Loup. But I can put you on the train there.'

Rivière-du-Loup was exactly halfway between Quebec and Rimouski. I was scheduled to sing there the following night, on the heels of tonight's performance in Rimouski.

I began to pray that I could put my trust in the train. Meanwhile, we struggled to reach Rivière-du-Loup. I asked my driver, clearly nearing the end of his tether, if he would mind dropping by the hotel where I had reserved a room for the morrow. I was hoping to call George in order to put his mind at rest, then travel on to the railroad station.

It was an amazing hotel made entirely of wood, a relic of the Gold Rush. The moment I pushed my way in, I heard a surprised voice:

'Ah, Nana! We've been expecting you. People are calling from everywhere to find out whether you'd arrived.'

'You were expecting me? But I'm not singing here tonight!'

'Of course, that's for tomorrow, but with this weather people are starting to get anxious about you.'

They were already helping me off with my coat. Piping-hot tea arrived.

'I promised to get her to Rimouski,' my driver broke in. 'The highway is a disaster and she needs our help. We have to get her to the train.'

'The train! It's not going anywhere,' said the hotel owner. 'Madame Mouskouri, they called from Rimouski to say your show's been canceled. Nobody there can put his nose outdoors . . . Come and get warm by the fire!'

It was unbelievable to encounter such warmth on coming in from the storm. All evening, people came in for news. They were so afraid I would never reach Rivière-du-Loup, they told me, and now they didn't know how to express their relief. I couldn't make them understand that I was the grateful one. I felt that I had never before been so treasured, so valued, as I was in that little town cut off for the night from the rest of the world.

*

A few days later, we were in Ottawa. There I was the supper guest of the new prime minister, Pierre Elliott Trudeau, at the House of Commons. Many of his colleagues, cabinet ministers and members of parliament, sat around the table with us. Toward the end, Trudeau rose and offered me his arm:

'Come with me, I have something to show you.'

He took me into the chamber and led me to the Speaker's podium.

'Would you do me a great pleasure?' he asked.

'Of course.'

'Would you sing "Un Canadien errant" for me? And then "Le temps des cerises"? Of all your songs, those are my favorites.'

Everything seemed so simple and natural that night that I didn't hesitate for a second. As Prime Minister Trudeau sat alone on the government's benches, I sang a cappella for him in the deserted chamber.

Our Canadian tour was over, but now I was scheduled to appear in New York's legendary Carnegie Hall. I owed that invitation to Sam Gesser. One evening he had mentioned the greatest of all classical music managers, Sol Hurok. Elegant, civilized, Sol Hurok represented mythic stars around the world, people like Callas, von Karajan, and Bernstein. One evening when he came to listen to me he invited me to breakfast next day – on condition, he immediately added, that my husband would not take it amiss. At that breakfast, he told me he would like to take care of me in the United States.

So it was really Sol Hurok who was behind that invitation to a one-night concert at Carnegie Hall. I had planned my program unaided. I would sing 'Try to Remember', Fifty-Ninth Street Bridge Song', 'The White Roses of Athens', 'Lily of the West', 'Over and Over', 'My Coloring Book', 'Prelude', and a few of my Greek and French hits.

From that first public appearance in New York I still have the article that appeared a few days later in *Cash Box*. It was couched in the form of an invitation to go out and conquer America: 'Nana Mouskouri is already an international star, but her full impact has not yet been felt in this country. Judging by the reaction to her first solo concert here, a sell-out show at Carnegie Hall, her time won't be long in coming.

'A native of Greece, and popular in that country, Nana enjoys her greatest fame in France, and the reason for her probable success here is that Nana not only sings foreign languages, she feels them, and chooses her material with care. Her voice carries the same angelic properties as that of Joan Baez, but her stylings are her own, very personal.'[18]

---

[18] *Cash Box*, 29 March 1969.

17

'My Nightingale!'

*T*here was much talk of Greece in 1969. Melina Mercouri toured the European capitals and sang songs by Mikis Theodorakis, now interned in Oropos concentration camp. The colonels' regime was a blot on the conscience of Western Europe, unanimously excoriated by all democrats, whether politicians, artists, or intellectuals. In France, the magazine *Les Temps Modernes* published a special report on Greece in which exiled poets and writers spoke of those whose voices had been temporarily silenced, men I loved and admired from the bottom of my heart: Yannis Ritsos, Odysseas Elytis, and Nikos Gastos. The Greek film-maker Costa-Gavras had just finished his film *Z*, with Jean-Louis Trintignant and Yves Montand. The movie dissected the circumstances surrounding the murder of parliamentarian and physician Grigoris Lambrakis on 23 May 1963. It made it clear that his killers, members of an extreme right-wing group, forewarned the whole world of the imminence of a military coup.

That same year, *Z* was in contention at the Cannes Festival (where it received the Jury Prize), and since Greece was now, alas, on everyone's mind, people turned to me. They asked whether I would agree to represent my country's soul on the Festival stage. Moved and proud that they had thought of me, I naturally accepted. While the jury deliberated during the closing ceremonies, I would sing some of the songs that inflamed the hearts of all who shared our own sorrow.

I was delighted to be returning to Cannes, whose Festival brought back happy memories. The year 1960 had seen the triumph of Jules Dassin's film *Never on Sunday* and the overnight success of 'Children of

Piraeus'. In 1964, Jacques Demy's 'Umbrellas of Cherbourg' won first prize, and I sang in accompaniment to Michel Legrand's score. And now I had been invited to sing for Greece.

Five years earlier I had gone pretty well unnoticed. This time I was the quarry of photographers and of a rapturous crowd in search of autographs. The difficulties began at the very bottom of the famous stairway, where there was no one to offer me a gallant arm. George, who loathed pomp and circumstance, opted out. André Chapelle was equally publicity-shy. The only volunteer was André Asseo. I first met him at an earlier Cannes Festival. He now ran Philips' advertising department, and was delighted to be a part of this ritual minuet surrounding the stars.

Yet that promise-filled evening turned sour on me.

I had of course taken care to let the festival's organizers know what songs I proposed to sing. The first was by Manos Hadjidakis, the next two by Mikis Theodorakis, followed by 'Try to Remember'. I intended to round out this mini-recital with a third Theodorakis song whose lyrics were sublime but very difficult to translate, something on the lines of *'The rain outside falls as heavily as in my heart . . .'*

There was utter silence as I appeared onstage. It was the moment in which all the crowned heads of world cinema hoped to celebrate a kind of high Mass in homage to Greece. Their emotion was palpable, and my heart was overflowing.

Sustained applause greeted the first song, and I was about launch into Theodorakis when the great tragic actress Irene Papas, who had appeared in *Z* and whom I could clearly see in the third row, just in front of Costa-Gavras, jumped to her feet and screamed:

'Please! Sing Theodorakis for us!'

Costa-Gavras at once stood up and joined in, followed by a dozen others, including Simone Signoret and Yves Montand.

'Theodorakis! Theodorakis!' they chanted at the top of their voices.

I cannot describe the humiliation and distress that overcame me. There they stood with raised fists, as if they were the living symbols of justice, the heroes of Greek resistance, and there I stood onstage, paralyzed, offered up as a public sacrifice, implicitly accused in everyone's eyes of not doing enough for our lofty cause. It was a horrible feeling, deeply wounding, deeply insulting, and I had to muster all my courage to fight back my tears as I calmly announced:

'I was about to sing Theodorakis. I am sorry you lack the good manners to let me go on with this concert in the spirit we all shared only moments ago.'

I believe the audience understood, and a brief burst of applause brought the incident to an end. But the grace that attended the start had evaporated, and I doubt whether I sang Theodorakis that night the way I would have liked.

As I left the stage, I burst into tears. It took all of André's tact and powers of persuasion to prevent me leaving immediately for Paris and missing the closing ceremonies.

Irene Papas must have been lying in wait for me. The moment I entered the reception room, she burst into tears and embraced me. It was an appalling scene, naturally immortalized by the photographers present. It embodied everything that horrifies me – hypocrisy, fanaticism, manipulation. For while Irene was being emotional with me, I was telling her what I thought:

'If you'd wanted to kill me, Irene, you couldn't have done a better job.'

To which she replied:

'Forgive me, but I had to do it. For the cause, don't you see? For the cause!'

'No, I don't see. As far as I'm concerned, no cause in the world justifies humiliating anyone.'

That incident left me with a lifelong distaste and distrust for public piety. Is political struggle more effective if you raise clenched fists and drape yourself in moral outrage and the somber hues of tragedy? Perhaps: I don't know. But I have remained faithful to my own nature, which impels me to discretion. I hadn't forgotten my country during the dark days of the colonels, but I had never been able to associate myself with those who proclaimed themselves her standard-bearers. No doubt certain people found me much too quiet in comparison to Irene Papas or Mikis Theodorakis, set free in April 1970 and welcomed in Paris as the living symbol of resistance. Yes, it's true my voice was not often heard, but I think that in life everyone fights in his own way, following the dictates of his heart and intelligence.

The papers gave full coverage to the Cannes incident, and a few days later I received a dinner invitation from Constantine Karamanlis, now in exile in Paris. We had known each other for ten years, and in those years my love for this man – in whose intelligence and intentions I glimpsed a future for Greece – had steadily increased. I was sure it would one day be his task to restore democracy to our country, and it was of course this hope that dominated our conversation. He was the leader of a methodically-organized political resistance movement, regularly meeting with the leaders of all the Western democracies as well as their political adversaries. A seasoned diplomat, Karamanlis campaigned with extreme discretion. But that night, I believe his chief aim was to comfort me.

'I've read the newspapers,' he told me, 'and I think you were right not to succumb to the temptations of rabble-rousing. You know, politics is dangerous territory for neophytes. There's the constant risk of being recruited by this or that faction against your will, and then of regretting it. Just go on acting the way you do.'

Four months after that dinner, I had the honor of meeting Karamanlis again at the dress rehearsal of my next appearance at the Olympia, as though he sought by his presence to assure me of his support and wipe out forever the memory of Cannes.

Bruno Coquatrix was so sure I would triumph at this third Olympia concert that he decided to dispense with a supporting cast of singers. This time there was to be no Jacques Martin to warm up the crowd. I would be alone onstage for three hours with The Athenians, every night for six weeks. The experiment had not been attempted since Edith Piaf, and it would be up to me to pull it off.

Louis Hazan saw a certain irony in the challenge. He reminded me of what I said after Piaf's concert in 1971 (I had wept throughout it): 'After hearing that I don't think I'll ever again have the nerve to go onstage ...' Well, not only did I muster the nerve, but my name stood out on the Olympia's façade in huge red letters, just like Piaf's name on that unforgettable night.

'What did I tell you!' Louis crowed as he took my arm on opening night. 'It's taken us ten years to make you famous, but tonight you're the winner!'

I prepared for that concert with André and George. I planned to sing 'Dans le soleil et dans le vent', 'Love Minus Zero', a Bob Dylan song, and 'Both Sides Now', by Joni Mitchell. But we would open with a magnificent song by Manos Hadjidakis, 'Den Itan Nissi', and a call to continue living and loving in those tragic days: 'Let's Go For a Walk to the Moon' ('Pame mia volta sto fengari'):

> *Il n'est jamais trop tard pour vivre,*
> *Jamais trop tard pour être libre.*
> *Raison de plus, raison de plus pour vivre ensemble:*
> *De ce désert, de cet hiver naîtra la joie*
> *Car le bonheur par-dessus la mer des étoiles*
> *Tisse son fil jusqu' à cette île où tu m'attends*
> *Et notre bateau claque au vent de toutes ses voiles*
> *J'aurai enfin un cœur tout neuf pour le printemps.*

> It's never too late to live,
> Never too late to be free.
> All the more reason for living together:
> From this desert, this winter, joy will rise again,
> For happiness high above the sea of stars
> Spins its web over that island where you wait,
> And our ship's sails flap in the urgent breeze,
> And I will at last have a new heart for the spring.

For the second half of the show, I planned to repeat all the old hits audiences now demanded whenever I appeared – 'Little Drummer Boy', 'Le jour où la colombe' and 'Try to Remember'.

For Nicolas, that Olympia represented the discovery that I was a singer. Two years earlier, in October 1967, he still slumbered inside me on that same stage, and I felt his tiny kicks of protest as the applause disturbed him. This time, he sat in his box on Féfé's lap. I had picked his seat, slightly right of center so that he could see me clearly, and his sweet little-boy face was in my mind's eye during the awful moments before going onstage. What would he think when he saw me?

At first, despite Féfé's repeated whispers of 'Look, Nicolas, that's Mama down there!' he didn't understand. He was probably more intent on the play of the spotlights than on the lady approaching the microphone.

Then I began to sing, and suddenly all the neighboring spectators were treated to his delighted amazement:

'That's Mama! It's Mama! Look, Féfé, that's Mama!'

Some understood and laughed. Others said 'Shhh!', and poor Féfé had to hurry out of the auditorium with Nicolas in her arms.

For me, in addition to the general media reaction (as warm and full of praise as on the previous occasion), that Olympia also brought a handsome compliment from the writer Alphonse Boudard:

'That voice, reaching us from sky, wind, sea and the stars . . .

'A voice that gushes like a mountain spring . . .

'A voice that restores the meaning of forgotten words: purity, beauty, harmony . . .

'Nana Mouskouri sings, and we are at once borne beyond time.

'Fashion ceases to exist, the trendy melts away. This same voice sang a hundred years ago, two centuries ago, and men listened in the same way, caught in the spell of this most beautiful of musical instruments.

'When Nana Mouskouri finishes a song, I recall what Sacha Guitry once said about Mozart . . . that the silence which followed him was still Mozart . . .'

In the meantime, my first British album, *Over and Over*, had joined the ranks of top sellers from the day it appeared. This brought me another invitation from Yvonne Littlewood for a series of broadcasts for the BBC, as well as urgent requests for a tour of the biggest British cities. When should we leave? As soon as possible, said André, eager to strike while the iron was still hot. He added that I had given a lot of myself to France in recent months, and could leave with a clear conscience for the conquest of another country. (And other continents, I might add, since the BBC's broadcasts would once again fan out to the rest of the Commonwealth.)

I decided to tackle Yvonne Littlewood's project first, and the tour – planned to take place in the depths of winter – would follow. But after our experiences in Canada, neither snow nor ice held any fears for us, and as 1970 began we flew to London.

I felt that George and I had never been happier together. Nicolas' arrival had bound us forever. (At all events, that is what we deeply believed.) And thanks to The Athenians we had found our modus operandi. George no longer feared that people were trying to take me from him, we no longer played except as a group, almost as intimately as a family, and we never separated any more. The days when George drowned in silence while I launched out alone on my singing tours with Harry Belafonte and my recordings with Quincy Jones and Bobby Scott were behind us. What's more, we left France bearing a secret we kept to ourselves: I was pregnant again!

By now, London welcomed me as a star: cameras and reporters at the airport, flowers, small platoons of fans, and I had to smile when I thought back to those tears on the cross-Channel ferry during my first trip to the United Kingdom. Back then, I was afraid that no one wanted me. But now people recognized me in the street, and it was strange on my first morning to hear a newspaper seller in his kiosk say:

'Oh, Miss Mouskouri! How's the little boy?'

Indeed, my private life seemed to hold no secrets from anyone, as though we were all part of a big family. It was at once reassuring and a little disturbing. Was this what celebrity meant?

Within three or four weeks my tummy was visibly rounder, and for the last BBC broadcast I had to have my dress altered in order to hide the evidence of this new pregnancy.

A wonderful thing happened during that series of recordings. Every day, Yvonne Littlewood was sweet enough to send me one of those majestic London taxis complete with chauffeur in peaked cap. One morning, I was struck by the chauffeur's smile.

'You look like a happy man,' I told him.

'I certainly am, Miss Mouskouri. Today's my birthday, and my mates all know how much I love your songs. So they put their heads together and arranged for me to drive you to the studio. A birthday present, like . . .'

'Well, if that's the case,' I said to him, 'come back to the studio and pick me up tonight. I'll have a birthday present of my latest recordings ready for you. And I wish you a very happy birthday!'

'Thank you, thank you so much! Everyone at home loves you, you know . . .'

We went on talking, and this man began to tell me about the famous people he had chauffeured. It was a lovely conversation, with much laughter, and suddenly I thought I heard him mention the name of Stewart Granger.

'What was that you said? Do you know Stewart Granger?'

'Do I know him! He likes me better than the other drivers, if you see what I mean. I often drive him to see his grandchildren at tea-time.'

Stewart Granger, hero of my childhood movies . . . In Asquith's *Fanny by Gaslight* he seemed to my young eyes a much more romantic hero than Humphrey Bogart or Robert Taylor. Stewart Granger, beyond a doubt my first calf-love.

'If we had time, I'd tell you how much that man meant to me,' I said to the driver. 'Stewart was my favorite actor.'

But we had reached the studio and my confessions had to end there.

That evening, the same driver was waiting for me. I gave him his birthday present.

'Just a moment,' he said, 'I've got a present for you too.'

I opened his package and found a book signed by Stewart Granger. It was his autobiography.

'Go to the first page,' he told me.

I did so, and read: 'Dear Nana, thank you for all the wonderful hours of pleasure that you give us with your music. Stewart Granger.'

'Good Lord! How did you manage this?'

'I phoned him to tell him how important he was in your life, and right away he said, "And I like Miss Mouskouri very much myself. Come round and I'll give you a little something for her".'

Then it was time to go touring. The Athenians traveled in a minibus, while I was given a big, comfortable Austin whose deep seats and luxurious interior allowed me to travel as if in a small living room. We told the driver our secret, and he was careful to avoid bumpy surfaces. I remember some good moments in that car, dividing my time between rehearsing new songs and writing long letters to Nikos Gatsos. The years had rolled by, but Nikos was still my bosom-friend, the one with whom I needed to share my triumphs and fears. Was it right for me to get drunk on music every night, for example? Was I on the right path? What would our children's future be?

We played in Glasgow, Birmingham, and Manchester, always to sell-out audiences, and everywhere the media rolled out the red carpet. I can still see the titles of a handful of articles George cut out and handed to me in my car as we set out for a new city: 'Mouskouri, More Please!', 'A Storming Reception for Nana', and 'Nana Supreme!'

I needed that enthusiastic response to help me survive the terrible British damp, something I had never so far encountered. Canadian cold was nothing compared to UK smog, to that damp mist that seemed to rise from below and bite through to your bones. I spent that tour terrified that I might fall ill and have to cancel the next recital. And in those days, British hotels weren't very comfortable – often badly heated and drafty, so that I occasionally woke with a sore throat.

Yet I was back in Great Britain a year later, recalled by a listening public that in the meantime had given me a Gold Record. I mention that second tour here because I have it confused in my memory with the first: the same welcome, the same enthusiasm wherever we played, aptly summed up by this headline in the Bristol *Evening Post:* 'Come Back Soon, Nana, You Were Superb!'.[19]

An unnoticed event, but one that meant everything to me, occurred during that second tour: Marlene Dietrich dropped by! For the gorgeous Marlene – the woman who haunted my childhood, the unforgettable Lola in Josef von Sternberg's *Blue Angel* – was herself on a tour whose itinerary crisscrossed mine. She made the first move, leaving me an encouraging little word in the city she had just left and where I was to sing that very evening: 'You're like a bird! Marlene.'

I at once wrote a return message describing the impact she had had on me – her face, her voice. I mentioned *Shanghai Express* and *The Scarlet Empress*, which did so much to lift me out of myself when I was

---

[19] *Evening Post*, Bristol, 20 April, 1971.

a little girl with absolutely no idea of the future. On the mirror in my dressing room a few days later, I found these four words written in crimson lipstick: 'Nana, I love you! Marlene.' After that we never stopped leaving each other little notes of this kind. If I was singing first, I would leave her a bouquet of flowers and a little note in the theater. And if she preceded me, I looked out for her messages, always romantic and unexpected.

We never once met, but when the tour was over I felt as though I had been living in her aura. Had she guessed the depth of my love for her? Did I now possess a small place in her life?

Many years later, I was asking myself those same questions as I went to hear her sing in the small Cardin auditorium on the Champs-Elysées. It was one of her last performances. André went with me, and it was he who insisted that I wait outside her dressing room at the end of the show, just for the pleasure of seeing her up close. I was dying to do just that, but as usual, I couldn't pluck up the courage. I was afraid of appearing ridiculous, fearful that my intrusion would be taken the wrong way.

At last I steeled myself. I stood outside her dressing-room door with a small cluster of her close friends, who included Zsa-Zsa Gabor. I recognized her at once, as she stood arm in arm with her eighth husband, as the star of John Huston's *Moulin Rouge*. Then a male voice announced, 'Miss Dietrich will come out now,' and there at last she was, looking absolutely ethereal. Keeping in the background, I watched her greet everyone, smiling, as if floating on the little cloud that seemed always to lift her above the commonplace. But suddenly our eyes met. She stood still, and I saw her face light up. 'My nightingale!' she exclaimed, and the next second I was in her arms.

'What a delight,' she said. 'I'm so happy to meet you at last.'

Except that I burst into tears. It was as if Marlene Dietrich had briefly stepped out of the screen in one of my childhood dreams and taken me by the hand, whispering into my ear: 'Come on, let's get back into the movie, your place is up there beside me.' It was more like an apparition than an emotion-charged moment.

And my only response was tears. Seeing us embrace, and perhaps suspecting hidden drama, Zsa-Zsa also started to weep. And while Marlene uttered sweet words to me, I heard Zsa-Zsa singing out to me though her tears, 'Dahling, dahling! Stop crying, my eyelashes are falling out!'

Between those two British tours, Hélène came into the world via Caesarean on 7 July 1970. We were expecting her on 13 July, and George and I were already chuckling at this little joke on the part of destiny, since my sister Jenny was also born on 13 June, Nicolas on 13 February, and I on 13 October. But the doctor decided to intervene six days before time.

With the little girl's arrival, we felt that our cup was full. After all our difficulties, after so many obstacles, we had finally stepped on to the path of blissful happiness in this city of Geneva, a place far removed from the turmoil of the outside world. We had been forced to invent everything from scratch. I had learned how to express tenderness to a man while defending my right to be an artist. George was forced to break the stereotypical (and often selfish and overbearing) Greek male mold to find himself a special place alongside me. And we learned how to be parents against an exceptional background, with both of us in perpetual motion, spending most of our nights onstage and our days on the road or in the air. Meanwhile, Geneva became our secret retreat, the place where we jettisoned our baggage and returned to silence and intimacy. Until our next departure ...

We spent that fine summer of 1970 watching for Hélène's first smiles, absorbed in the strides Nicolas was making as he entered his third year. For me it marked the unhoped-for realization of my dreams of a family. Both of us had learned to make compromises to allow our union to flourish and bear fruit, and with Fernande's invaluable support we were now raising the two children born of our love in peace and harmony. Haunted by my horror of yelling and quarrel, I now remembered to thank Heaven every day for leading us so caringly to peace and equilibrium. George and I never quarreled, never raised our voices to one another. It explains why we felt so strong, so sure of ourselves.

But life is full of pitfalls, infinitely more complex and patient than we can imagine. When George and I separated four years later I spent long, sorrowing months wondering whether this hard-won harmony I've described didn't help mask deeper conflicts we were never able to resolve.

The United Kingdom tour of late 1971 yanked us unceremoniously away from our rapt contemplation of our two children. Then came a Netherlands tour, new recording projects in England, Holland and France (with 'I Have a Dream', 'A Place in My Heart', 'Coucouroucoucou Paloma', and 'Turn on the Sun'), and then yet another Olympia date in October.

The day after the dress rehearsal, Claude Sarraute wrote the following appraisal in *Le Monde*: 'From season to season and triumph to triumph, the beautiful black-eyed Greek child has made great strides and very little noise. Without ballyhoo and drum-beating, she has piled up awards, medals, and trophies, and her presence, whether onstage or record, has the comforting weightlessness of a well-loved companion.'[20]

True enough: by the end of 1971 I had garnered six Gold Records: one in England, two in Holland (one of them Platinum), one in France, and one in Australia, where I had never yet set foot. And to complete this roll of honors, I was elected Number One Singer for the year in every English-speaking country.

---

[20] *Le Monde*, 8 October 1971.

18

'A Hard Rain's a-Gonna Fall'

I'm still not sure why I chose to sing in Belfast at the height of Northern Ireland's troubles. During my 1971 UK tour, a crippling bout of flu had forced me to drop plans to perform in Ireland. At the last moment, we had to cancel two concerts scheduled for Cork and Dublin in the Irish Republic. Genuinely frustrated, and concerned at disappointing the fans awaiting me, I went on television to apologize to them, despite a high temperature that left me with wobbly legs.

'Will you come back to Ireland?' asked my producer, Jim Aiken, during that interview.

'Yes,' I promised, 'and when I return I'll go to Belfast as well.'

He registered brief surprise. For the last year or two, entertainers had stopped visiting Northern Ireland because of the extremely violent street-fighting there between Protestants and Catholics.

'Belfast?' he said. 'Be careful what you say, Nana. A lot of people are watching this broadcast, and they'll hold you to your word.'

'And I'll keep my word,' I replied.

I went on to tell him how much I sympathized with the people of Belfast, trapped as they were in a vicious civil conflict, and how unjust it would be for me to leave them out of the picture while fans were applauding me in Dublin.

And then of course we discussed my influenza. I explained that I was used to Greece's dry, sunny climate, and that I suffered badly in Ireland, as I did in England, from the awful damp that seeped in everywhere, including, I said, though doors and windows.

I wished I could swallow those words when I returned to my hotel! I was amazed. The window in my room had been tightly padded, two small space-heaters installed, and a hot-water bottle slipped between my sheets ... And sitting on the bedside table was a steaming pot of tea complete with honey and lemon slices – exactly as I had just prescribed on TV when asked what I did to take care of my throat. All that kindness and loving care only strengthened my determination to come back.

And so, in early spring 1972, The Athenians and I were back in Ireland. I was happy to see Jim Aiken again: he was a man in a million, infatuated with artists and performers, and quite capable of spending the night gluing posters to walls if he felt the publicity people hadn't done their job. Jim insisted on being my driver, and while I was there he practically gave up smoking and drinking whiskey to avoid offending me. With Jim beside me, invariably enthusiastic and helpful, I believe I could tour the whole world in an Austin.

As planned, we performed at Dublin's National Stadium on April 27, and at the Savoy Cinema in Cork next day. I remember the headline in the Dublin *Sunday Press*, which summed up Irish attitudes to my keeping that promise: 'Nana Asked To Come Here'.[21] Both shows were sell-outs, and the audiences especially exuberant, as though the burden of a war next door enhanced the value of the present moment.

Then we headed for Belfast. There, tensions were rapidly escalating. The night before, the Irish Republican Army had reportedly interrupted a show and kidnapped the group scheduled to perform. There were even rumors of murders. Jim, who was one of the first to congratulate me on my earlier decision to sing in Belfast, was no longer so sure. Might it not be wiser to cancel? What if we went ahead and there was an incident? I could see he was worried as he weighed the disappointment of the five or six thousand fans expecting us against his own responsibility for encouraging me in this act of folly.

The highway into Ulster was winding, wearying, and sewn with checkpoints manned by soldiers whose tension was obvious and worrying. Yet we pushed on. As though each extra mile progressively relieved us of the burden of a decision we would have preferred not to face.

---

[21] *The Sunday Press*, Dublin, 23 April 1972.

When we reached the barn-like structure where the concert was to be held, we found utter disorder. It was agreed that we would rehearse that afternoon, since the show was to take place that very evening. But the police had warned that identity checks would be stiffer than usual, and many spectators, deciding to beat the crowd, were already in the auditorium. A path was cleared for us, and as we quickly installed our gear we realized that the hall was full of drafts and the acoustics terrible. Rehearsal had barely begun when the police controls went into action: the authorities planned a thorough body search of every spectator – an operation that might easily last four or five hours.

It was all simultaneously strange and wonderful – the dazzled faces of the first spectators to take their seats, the technicians' heroic efforts to salvage that impossible sound system, the cold (I had to pull on a thick sweater and abandon all thought of my traditional stage attire), and finally our strange sense that we were braving fortune. No doubt about it, we would be playing in the middle of a war, trying to show people who were killing each other that love of life can sometimes be stronger than hatred.

Dare I say that the wave of emotion triggered by the very first notes made up for all our anxiety and difficulties? The sound was bad, the lighting pitiful, we were cold, yet I had never felt such warmth of feeling and such reverence as in that hall. Writing with the benefit of hindsight, even the momentary panic (it brought a cry of alarm from us) when the electricity went dead in the middle of the concert merely reinforced our sense of happiness at being gathered there. For a second we believed that it was a terrorist act, that it was the signal for the kind of atrocity we had dreaded all day. But it wasn't. It was just that everything in that martyred city was run-down, decaying. When the power came back on, we all sighed with relief to find ourselves still alive and still together.

We thought it too risky to spend the night in Belfast. It was only when we began the return drive to Dublin in the middle of the night that I understood why I was so determined to give that concert. By representing the soul of music in a city torn by civil unrest, I had just paid tribute to the ideal I had ascribed to art since my very earliest years. During the period when Greeks too were slaughtering one another, I had seen the profound changes wrought in human beings by film. They took their seats tense and anxious, and they left a little drunk, as though Heaven had given them a small sign. They were no longer quite the same. And later on, listening to Ella Fitzgerald or Maria Callas, I realized that music possessed the same mysterious power of lifting us out of our everyday selves. I saw that art could tell us secrets about ourselves and the world that we wouldn't otherwise have discovered. Wasn't it truly thanks to music that I was born and that people loved me? And there we were in Belfast, communing in music, no matter where we came from, no matter our religion or our language, no matter whether friend or foe. What better hope could you offer people at war than gathering them together in a single space to share an evening of song? They believed they hated each other, they thought the world was their enemy, and yet they applauded in unison, swept up by a shared emotion.

Recalling that night in Belfast, I was suddenly reminded of my bewilderment when I myself was the target of racism on my tour with Harry Belafonte. It was during the Los Angeles race riots of summer 1965, which resulted in thirty-four deaths and hundreds of injuries. The black community could not forgive Harry for singing with a white woman, and he was receiving death threats. As a result, I too became a target and we both had to hire bodyguards. I don't like mentioning that episode, and I know why: it spells out for me the limitations of music. What was the point of singing if you were ringed by bodyguards? Artistic creation and guns seemed to me to be at opposite ends of the spectrum. But on the other hand, how sad to surrender, to abandon the terrain to those who no longer believed in anything but war!

Where did I get it from, that deep yearning for harmony which had me running headlong to Belfast, yet allowed the smallest of conflicts to drive me to the depths of despair? At this stage of my life, I can at last explain its origin. I was a child as the Second World War began, and grew up against a background of civil war in which Royalists and Communists butchered one another. In a way, it also had its origin in the domestic warfare between a father who was an irresponsible, compulsive gambler and a mother whose heart was full of bitter sorrows she would one day make him pay for. I believe that ever since my teens I have had the word 'harmony' perpetually on my lips.

Musical harmony, day-to-day harmony. In high school, I believe, just knowing that the word existed pulled me through those terrifying fights between our parents. If someone had invented the word, it meant harmony must really exist somewhere. I clung to that dream, the kind of dream that music sustains (and I listened to music every day – that was something I already knew). I built for myself a life based on a horror of hatred, of vengefulness and malice. When George came into my life, I believe that I unconsciously turned a blind eye to everything that might spark conflict between us. I saw in him only those characteristics I loved. And so, for far too long, I refused to acknowledge his fear of losing me, his *jealousy* (I was careful not to put a name to it), right up the day he tried to kill himself. That attempt shattered at one stroke the illusion of happiness I nurtured, and I then set about saving our marriage with the desperation of a drowning woman. In a few short months, I managed to restore the harmony vital to my own survival and to the coming of our children. First Nicolas, then Hélène, convinced me that I had discovered the secret music of our lives.

All too soon, however, there were small hints that things weren't going so well. The first signs of tension among The Athenians emerged on our return from Belfast. One of the group was thinking of returning to Greece with his wife. This triggered animated arguments among the group's members. George was my only source of information on these developments, but the more we discussed it the clearer it seemed that the crisis would gradually spread to include the two of us.

'Spyros is leaving us,' George told me one day. 'This time it's for sure.'

'What a nuisance. Who do you think could replace him?'

'I don't know yet . . . it depends on the other two.'

'Well, what do they think?'

'I get the feeling that they wouldn't mind following Spyros.'

'You don't say so! What's going on with you guys, George?'

'They've had enough of traveling. They want to live with their wives, like everyone else.'

'That I understand. But still, I thought they were glad to be playing.'

'You know, we've played together for nearly twenty years now.'

'Do you mean they're thinking of giving up music?'

'Why not? They've made enough money now to think about doing something else.'

At that point in our conversation I remembered an exchange I overheard between George and his friends while we were touring the United States. One of them had examined a car-wash machine, and they were wondering whether it would be a good idea to set up a business in Greece to import that kind of equipment. I didn't understand how one could be concerned with such matters and be a musician as well, and the conversation left me wondering. I asked myself if I had ever thought of turning to some other way of life than a musician's. The answer was No: the thought had never entered my mind for a second. What kind of performers could they be if they preferred business to music? I quickly forgot the episode, but now I was worrying about it again.

'What about you, George, could you give up music?'

'Well, I'm starting to get homesick myself, you know. And what would I do if they left me alone?'

Meanwhile, however, we were rehearsing for a commitment which dwarfed anything we had ever done. For the first time, I was to sing at the Théâtre des Champs-Elysées!

For an exile like me, the Champs-Elysées represented both a challenge and a kind of consecration. Here I was, a 'little Greek peasant girl', preparing to take by storm the world's most beautiful thoroughfare! The idea originated with André, who wanted to break the Olympia habit for a while. It took me several days to make my mind up, but once I agreed I was raring to go – and simultaneously scared stiff. What if I flopped? What if I wasn't up to it? Should that happen, my whole love affair with France would be sadly tarnished. That's how high the stakes seemed – high enough in any case to get The Athenians up and running again and forget the worry George's words had caused me.

What is more, my parents and Jenny would be there to see me perform – for the very first time. That was another challenge. I knew I would have to put them out of my mind – particularly Mama, whose opinion meant more to me than that of all the other two thousand spectators.

I had a number of new French songs in my arsenal, some traditional, such as 'Aux marches du palais' and 'Plaisir d'amour', (some written and composed by young authors, such as 'Attic Toys' by Jean Vallée and Herbie Kretzmer, Serge Lama's 'Que je sois un ange' ('Some Say I am an Angel'), or, 'I Have a Dream' by Michel Fugain. I had new Greek songs, including 'Milisse mou' by Nikos Gatsos and Manos Hadjidakis, or 'My Love is Somewhere' ('Kapou iparhi i agapi mou'), by Manos alone. But far and away the biggest knockout of them all was one I would be performing for the first time, 'Le ciel est noir', a dark, splendid work by Bob Dylan ('A Hard Rain's a-Gonna Fall'), adapted for me by Pierre Delanoë. The song was a deeply disturbing portrait of our world, the melody so powerful that it became at times oppressive, the more so because the song lasts almost ten minutes:

> Oh, where have you been, my blue-eyed son?
> Oh, where have you been, my darling young one?
>
> And what did you hear, my blue-eyed son?
> And what did you hear, my darling young one?
> I heard the sound of a thunder, it roared out a warnin',
> Heard the sound of a wave that could drown the whole world,
> Heard one hundred drummers whose hands were a-blazin',
> Heard ten thousand whisperin' and nobody listenin'.
> Heard one person starve, I heard many people laughin',
> Heard the song of a poet who died in the gutter,
> Heard the sound of a clown who cried in the alley,
> And it's a hard, it's a hard, it's a hard, it's a hard,
> And it's a hard rain's a-gonna fall.

My parents were bowled over when they saw my name up there in big letters on the marquee. It was about two in the afternoon. They were there to take it all in, to get the full impact of the place in tranquility, before the scrimmage that would attend tonight's dress rehearsal. Now they stood frozen on the sidewalk, as if stunned. They couldn't read the

Latin-alphabet wording, but they saw my photo and couldn't believe their eyes. It was obvious from their astonished expressions and from the way each suddenly put an arm around the other (and this was a couple I had never in my life seen holding hands!). Then Mama began to cry softly, and Papa guided her into the theater. I was watching them from the vestibule where I was waiting for them. I believe that when my father caught sight of me, his first reflex was that they shouldn't take up too much of my time now that I was Someone. Yet I would really have liked to go on studying them forever. They had come a long way, Mama from Corfu, Papa from the Peloponnese. How many wars had they survived to come and see their baby daughter sing?

Then came Mama's first glimpse of the stage from the front seat of her box. She was silent, perhaps retracing in her mind the long road traveled since the days when she herself sang as she hung out the laundry for the Kapodistria household. I couldn't help thinking that she was picturing herself behind the mic that hung just over the footlights. Herself, not me. Perhaps that thought simply reflected my guilt at having become what she had dreamed of being. At robbing her of her destiny. If she hadn't cherished that dream I might never have fulfilled it, I finally decided – and both of us should be up there on the stage tonight.

During the concert I tried not to think too hard about her, about them, but I couldn't help it. I knew exactly where they were sitting: I had chosen their seats myself, a little off-center, and every now and then I felt that it was Mama's voice singing through mine. Her voice was graver, as though rusted by her sorrows. But my singing drew strength from that secret presence. The music did not take umbrage, it had always been our ally, and that evening I felt it was on our side, benevolent, as if seeking to serve those who had served it so well. The whole audience was with us as well, as I could tell from the expectant silence that followed each round of applause, as though the spectators awaited the emotion the next song aroused in me – an emotion I burned to share with them.

Oh, the power of music! It reconciled me with my childhood, it brought reconciliation to my parents – to Mama who was singing through me, and to Papa who could finally forget he had wanted a boy. And the music magically endowed the spectators with a single shared soul. Through the final fifteen minutes they showered the stage with flowers and at the end stood as one man to applaud me.

In my dressing room just a few seconds later, Papa and Mama were hugging me, tears running down their faces. Henceforth, the Théâtre des Champs-Elysées would represent a before-and-after watershed for them. It was on that night, I believe, that they finally discovered me.

'Modest, too-modest Nana,' Jean Macabies wrote in *France-Soir* next day. 'Listening to her, I've often imagined some untoward event breaking brutally into the serene procession of her songs. If the microphone were suddenly transformed into a naked man, for example, if a wind ripped her dress off, or if the musicians launched into the *Internationale* as she prepared to warble her "Coucouroucoucou Paloma". In other words, if a big stone suddenly splashed into her placid stream, finally provoking that graceful form into losing her sangfroid, protesting, cursing, yelling, swooning, sobbing, or doing all those things simultaneously. Anything – so long as she embraced even for a moment that over-the-top, passionate, torrential life the stage requires!

'Well, last night we saw that unknown Nana come to life on the stage for the very first time.'[22]

Re-reading those remarks by Jean Macabies, I decided that the Champs-Elysées show, which bore the heavy stamp of Bob Dylan's 'A Hard Rain's a-Gonna Fall', must indeed have contained the seeds of the storm whose first signs I had already seen and which I would soon have to confront.

I didn't admit it to myself, but George's confused state of mind filled me with pain. It took me back to the worst moments of that night in New York when, right after reading his last word, I found him unconscious: 'Make sure you don't bury me alive.' We had decided then to reactivate The Athenians and turn them into my permanent accompanists. That decision restored George to his place in the world and saved our marriage. But now The Athenians were breaking up, and

---

[22] *France-Soir*, 15 December 1973.

all the problems we thought we had solved were looming again, in particular the problem of George's jealousy.

Over the years, two men had assumed an overriding importance in my life: my artistic director André Chapelle, who guided me step by step and whom I trusted implicitly, and Serge Lama. Serge was a ladies' man. He had just written the lyrics of 'Que je sois un ange' ('Some Say I am an Angel'), set to Melanie Safka's music, but in fact he preferred to see me as a devil. Serge made no attempt to hide his somewhat ambiguously amorous approach to me. He was probably surprised that I would not yield to his advances, as most women did, but I loved him simply for what he was, I admired him, and his presence both warmed and illuminated me. George slowly realized that he was jealous of the place these two men held in my life. He might have been less thin-skinned about it if his group had held together, but the threatened defections left him feeling naked. He probably imagined himself back in the same position that had tortured him so in the United States, when he was sure I was betraying him with Quincy Jones and Irving Green.

Now, with his friends admitting they wanted to return to their homes in Greece, he too began to suggest the same possibility for us: 'Why not go back now that we have enough money to live comfortably with our two children?'

The first time he said this, I was astounded:

'But George, I haven't been singing all these years just to make money! I sing the way others have to paint or write, don't you understand? I sing to feel alive, to have my place in the world, to be loved.'

'We could buy a house, watch the children grow, enjoy the sun.'

'Don't ask that of me, George. You know how much I love singing, how much I need it . . . What would happen to me, shut away in a house?'

'And what will become of me, living in your shadow?'

'You're not in my shadow, we've built up our repertoire together, and without The Athenians I don't know what I'll do.'

'The Athenians! Pretty soon I'll be the only one left.'

'Well then, you can rebuild the group!'

'I'm not at all sure I want to.'

*

For the first time, we began to argue, not specifically over whether we should return to Greece, but over the choice of my songs. And of course it was the songs suggested by Serge Lama that George was against. I made the mistake of telling him one day that I saw a little of myself in 'Some Say I am an Angel' and ever since, George had turned down everything that came to me from Serge. But he did it in his way (although I should really say *our way*, since I was the one who established the rule that we would never raise our voices or indulge in direct confrontation). He would tell me he didn't like such-and-such a song, and since I did like it and ignored his remark, he would play it with the utmost ill-will.

'Why are you playing so softly?' I asked him. 'I can't hear your guitar.'

Whereupon he played too loudly, and I had to break off again.

'George, you're drowning me out.'

'I don't understand what you want.'

'I want you to play as you usually do.'

'You said just now that I was playing too softly.'

The ill-will soon spread through our life like gangrene. It was daily inflamed by the crisis facing The Athenians and its painful effect on George. One of them had already left for Greece with his wife, and the others longed to do the same. As they made their plans, George felt he was the only one whose wife was not enthralled by the idea of a house and swimming pool in a fashionable Athens neighborhood or (as George would have preferred) on the island of Corfu. It only reinforced his suspicions about the men around me, particularly André – André Chapelle, who was no more enthusiastic than I was about a return to Greece, and who was still working with me on the creation of new songs.

The gap between my artistic and emotional lives was clearly widening. Until now, George, by my side both onstage and at home, had provided the essential close link between the two. His tacit withdrawal, colored by anger and resentment, meant that he no longer took part in my discussions with André about my next recording or my next shows. This of course fueled the bitterness he felt toward André, locking him into a mood of despair I was powerless to counteract. At bottom, I knew exactly what George wanted of me – to abandon my artistic career and become the housewife he had always dreamed of – but I also knew that making that sacrifice would spell the end of us as a couple. Nothing beautiful or lasting is built on a renunciation of oneself. Yes – but meanwhile, wasn't it George who was sacrificing himself?

I felt trapped in a dilemma with no solution, and gradually George's despair infected me as well. What was to become of us? What gloomy future were we preparing for our children? They were the ones I worried about most.

Between 1973 and 1974, my health underwent a series of crises – tonsillitis, tracheitis, bronchitis – and at first I made no connection with the illness that was undermining our love. Recalling the old saying that bad luck always comes in threes, I put it down to coincidence. Unable to sing, I had to cancel engagement after engagement despite my horror of failing to honor commitments. At the last moment, I had to pull out of a London variety show presided over by Queen Elizabeth II, the famous Royal Command Performance. 'Nana Quits Royal Show', trumpeted the *Sun*, while a French weekly blew up the event in an enormous banner headline: 'Nana Mouskouri Charged With Insulting the Queen'.[23] I also canceled at Rennes and Arras ... 'Overcome by fatigue after an extraordinary tour,' was *Nord Matin*'s somewhat kinder comment, 'Nana Mouskouri has promised to return and sing free of charge for Arras fans.'[24] Whereupon the tabloids launched into laborious speculations about what they called the fragility of my vocal cords, even discussing the possibility that I might actually lose my voice altogether. 'That golden voice, so pure, so perfectly modulated,' said one such daily, 'is as fragile as crystal. Her vocal cords could at any moment be irreparably damaged.'

My vocal cords stood the strain, but one night when I was Philippe Bouvard's guest on a live RTL broadcast, my voice suddenly died. Thousands of viewers thus witnessed, live, the disaster the tabloids had been predicting. André, George and Serge Lama were there to support me in the control room that night, and André signaled to Philippe from behind the glass partition to call a total halt. By then, I was practically inaudible. Serge at once offered to salvage the broadcast

---

[23] *France Dimanche*, 9 December 1973.
[24] *Nord Matin*, 23 February 1974.

by taking my place, and Philippe Bouvard needed no urging.

Meanwhile, Odile Hazan rushed to meet us outside the studio. She listened to me in the tranquility of her home, and realized that something was seriously wrong. She grasped the whole picture, in fact, for she drove all three of us, André, George, and me, to a doctor recommended by friends, an allergy specialist and ... psychotherapist. An allergy specialist, since for months I had put my throat problems down to allergies.

The doctor saw me alone, leaving the other three in the waiting room. He carried out some tests in an effort to understand why my voice had fallen silent. When the tests were over with, he began to question me as if he had all the time in the world:

'Who is the gentleman sitting beside your husband in the waiting room?'

'André Chapelle, my artistic director.'

'I see ... And does your husband think it's right for André to wait with him while his wife is seeing the doctor?'

'We've all worked together for years. We're constantly together.'

'I understand. But what does your husband think about it?'

'My husband wants me for himself alone.'

'And you don't agree.'

'Yes, I do. I belong only to George and my children, but I share my passion for music with André and others.'

'Well, what's wrong, then?'

'My throat, or perhaps my lungs, I don't know. In any case, I've been sick more and more often of late, and I've had to cancel several concerts. I've just left a radio broadcast because my voice failed me.'

'I've examined you and I can't find anything specific. Your throat may be slightly irritated, of course.'

'Then what's happened to my voice?'

'You really want me to tell you?'

'Please!'

'*You no longer want to sing.*'

'How can you say such a thing? Perhaps George would like me to stop singing, but I can't even think about it without fearing that I'm dying.'

'Precisely. And since it's impossible for you to choose between family life and your love of music, you have temporarily decided to lose your voice. Perhaps to punish yourself for not choosing George – in a sense for preferring music to him.'

I realized at least one thing when I left the doctor. It wasn't my body that was sick: it was my life that had come to a halt at the intersection of two conflicting paths – and I was unable to choose either one, for that would automatically mean giving up the other option.

Luckily, Australia offered us an extraordinary escape from all this. André, George and I (ceaselessly snapped up by other countries more insistent than Australia) had for too long put off our first visit there. But this time, it was the Australians making the demands, through the mouth of a producer, Pat Condon, who promised us a triumphant tour.

'Do you realize,' he asked me, 'that nineteen of your albums are Gold Records in Australia?'

Well, no: I didn't know that. I had no idea the Australians liked me so much.

19

'Nana *Who?*' Asks Sinatra

On 24 June 1974, after a twenty-five-hour flight and a stopover in Bombay, our plane was finally flying over the West Australian coast. We had decided to begin our tour in the big western city of Perth, followed by three weeks that took us to Brisbane on the East coast via Adelaide, Melbourne, and of course Sydney. Then New Zealand and Japan, where I was scheduled to give five concerts.

For such a major exodus, we mobilized the whole team. Hélène and Nicolas were with us, chaperoned by Fernande, and so were George and his Athenians. The group was not quite its old self (there was a new guitarist and a new drummer), but the enthusiasm of its remaining members counteracted that. Yet it was to be our last major tour together. Shortly after we returned to France, George and I separated and The Athenians vanished from the world of music.

Oh, that Australian welcome! We had never yet been given red-carpet treatment, but Perth literally rolled it out for us! So sumptuously, indeed, that when I saw below us the small flower-laden crowd waiting in a semi-circle on the tarmac, I discreetly asked the flight attendant who they could be waiting for.

'Why, they're here for you, Miss Mouskouri! The papers have been talking about your arrival for weeks.'

It's an extraordinary feeling to be received like a queen in a country you don't know, a country you've never visited. These people must have liked me in secret for years, I thought, but what had I done to deserve their affection? For me – always prone to guilt trips – it was at once grounds for remorse. Why hadn't I come earlier? How could I have left them waiting without at least letting them know how well-disposed I was? How I hoped they wouldn't think I had been ignoring them deliberately!

Those were the thoughts going through my mind as they read the welcoming speech, as they embraced me and heaped the children, George, and me with flowers, and as the photographers prowled around us, not missing a single moment of the scene.

A press conference was scheduled for the Perth Sheraton, where representatives of all the Australian papers were apparently expecting us, and I at once saw a chance of redeeming myself. In the motorcade ferrying us across the city, I was already mulling over the right way of expressing my friendship for this country, which had discovered me through the BBC and had been snapping up my latest records ever since.

My encounter with the reporters that afternoon lasted a long time. They spoke of the melancholy and nostalgia of my songs, and were eager (as many would write in the next day's papers) to know what lay hidden 'behind the Mouskouri smile'. Then we talked about Greece, the war, my childhood, and the residue of melancholy I had certainly inherited.

And while we were taking our time at the Sheraton press conference, the airport was witnessing a curious event.

About two hours after we landed, Frank Sinatra landed in his turn at Perth. Sinatra too was beginning an Australian tour. The media had certainly given ample notice of his arrival, yet there was not a single photographer waiting on the tarmac. Sinatra's amazement was reported to us by his manager, a friend of my own manager.

'Where are the reporters?' asked Sinatra. 'Weren't they told I was coming?'

'Of course they were, but they're at another press conference now. They'll welcome you later.'

'What do you mean, another press conference? Who with?'

'Nana Mouskouri.'

'Nana *who?*'

'Mouskouri, Frank. A European singer, Greek origin . . .'

'Never heard of her.'

Doubtless somewhat put out, Sinatra too headed for the Sheraton. He often visited Australia, and knew the hotel well. It was his habit to rent the entire top floor so that he could house his whole entourage on the same level as his own suite.

'Mister Sinatra!' said the hotel manager. 'What a pleasure to have you under our roof again!'

'Have you reserved my usual suite for me?'

'No, I'm very sorry.'

'How's that? No? Listen, there's something going on here today that I don't understand. There were no photographers at the airport and there are no rooms here! Can you tell me what's up?'

'Well, we had to give your floor to Nana Mouskouri, Mister Sinatra. It's the first time she's come to Australia with her whole team and—'

'Her again! But who the heck is this Nana?'

The manager made no attempt to explain. He took refuge in a flood of apologies, and settled Frank Sinatra and his staff on the floor below mine. But next morning the manager hurried up to Sinatra brandishing Perth's leading newspaper, *The West Australian*.

'You asked me yesterday who Nana Mouskouri was. Well, here's her picture.'

Sinatra took the paper, in which he shared the front-page story with me. His picture was on the left, mine on the right. They were exactly the same size.

'OK. Would you tell this girl I'd like to meet her?'

Next evening, he sang in the hotel's club, and invited me for a drink. He was a little cold, as if still irritated that I had stolen his thunder. Then I told him our paths had already crossed in Athens during the early Sixties. I had attended one of his shows and then, since I was beginning to be recognized, I was invited to the reception held in his honor by the United States embassy. We had been introduced.

'I don't remember that,' he grumbled.

'But I do!'

And just from memory, I listed all the films I had seen him in: Fred Zinnemann's *From Here to Eternity*, Vincente Minnelli's *Some Came Running*, and Frank Capra's *A Hole In the Head* and some of his records as well, like 'New York, New York'. I tried to convey all the admiration I had for him, but it didn't do much to break the ice.

What astonished Sinatra was that I could be so well known in Australia but unknown in the United States. I did talk to him about my tours with Belafonte, but he listened with only half an ear. In that moment, I realized I would never count for anything in his eyes, that he was now the prisoner of his own image, forever condemned to be interested only in himself. For I had already discussed Sinatra's tours with Mia Farrow, his wife at the time, when she came to listen to us. We got on well together: Mia Farrow was invariably curious about others, whereas he was so ice-cold, so indifferent. Was that what it meant to be an international star? When we parted, I made a silent vow never to forget who I am or where I come from.

Who I am . . . But while I was leaving Frank Sinatra (our paths would cross during the tour, but he was never curious enough to come and hear me sing), another Frank, his exact opposite, was seeking me high and low. This one's name was Hardy, Frank Hardy. An Australian and a writer, he made his name in his own country and then abroad with a dark, pessimistic novel about the social scourings of Melbourne's suburbs, *Power Without Glory*.[25]

Frank Hardy happened upon a report of my press conference at the Sheraton. Ever since, he had been angry with me. He was in the middle of a novel, he had not a moment to lose, but every evening when he finished writing, his anger returned and he grabbed the phone. He tried to contact me in Perth, then in Brisbane, then in Sydney. He called all our hotels but was never connected with me, because whenever he called I was either in my dressing room or already onstage. All the while his rage steadily mounted, because this man (who was soon to become a kind of Australian Nikos Gatsos for me) was a passionate crusader, a rebel, a man of febrile energies who might put the world to fire and the sword if he was denied justice.

One night, the phone rang in my hotel bedroom in Sydney.

'Nana Mouskouri?'

---

[25] Frank J. Hardy, *Power Without Glory*, 1950.

'Yes, speaking.'

'You don't know me, my name's Frank Hardy. I read an interview you gave the *Sydney Morning Herald*. You said a lot about poverty and sorrow, but what do you know about such things? You're very well known, everyone admires you, you always sing to sell-out crowds. I've been told that you're married and have two young kids, so how could you have the ghost of an idea about destitution and injustice?'

'Well, I'm forty, you know, and I wasn't always the woman you describe. But why are you telling me all this?'

'Because you told that reporter that unless you've really suffered you can't really appreciate the beauty of life. Well, I *have* suffered, and life has become unbearable to me.'

'Oh, I understand. Forgive me, I wasn't trying to preach to anyone. All suffering isn't alike: some sorrow is certainly too devastating to leave even the slightest chance for hope. I really meant the fleeting joy of living, the kind of joy that can sometimes sweep you away in spite of yourself, in spite of all you've gone through ...'

It was very late, around the middle of the night, and we knew nothing about one another, yet here we were talking together of serious, weighty matters one rarely mentions in daily life. But everything about this man – his voice, his despair, his sincerity, his insatiable urge to explain the inexplicable – moved me deeply.

'I must see you,' he said at length. 'I absolutely must.'

'Where are you calling from?'

'From Adelaide.'

'Then it's impossible. I leave tomorrow morning for Japan.'

'I'll come to Europe. Will you remember me?'

'By the time we meet, I'll have read all your books.'

Our first meeting took place at the Café Flore in Paris perhaps two years later. But in the interim, and reading between his lines, I had a clear understanding of what his inconsolable sorrow was based on. He had lived through a whole gamut of tragic incidents: a brother sentenced for crimes he apparently did not commit and who hanged himself in prison, impossible – or extraordinarily painful – love affairs. And now I understood the dark and tortured universe of his books.

*

But to go back to Perth and the first days of that Australian tour on which (without wanting to) I shadowed the great Sinatra. Everything was happening as if we had left our troubles behind in Europe, and with the help of that Australian welcome, the mood of our team was cheerful. Then I suggested throwing a thirtieth birthday party for our company manager, Andrew Miller, who would later become my promoter. Everyone agreed, and we reserved one of the Sheraton's guest suites for the occasion. It was an unforgettable party, and it nearly turned me into the heroine of a soap-opera drama which, on top of everything, could have relegated Frank Sinatra to the back pages.

The party began as I left the guests to tuck the children in.

'Fifteen minutes for a quick hug and I'll be right back,' I told them.

I took the elevator to the twenty-fifth floor. To move from our suite to the children's quarters, I had gotten into the habit of turning off the corridor into the emergency exit, which spared me going the whole length of the floor's endless carpeted corridors. That was what I did that night, finding the fire doors wide open as they always were during the day.

Fernande had just finished feeding them. I brushed Hélène's teeth, told her a story, made sure that Nicolas had enjoyed the afternoon ... and returned by the same route. In the meantime, the fire doors had been closed, but I ignored this and mechanically opened the first, which immediately shut behind me. However, when I pushed on the door giving me access to the other end of the corridor, I realized that those doors could not be opened from the inside.

A small moment of panic. I was locked in on the top floor of the emergency stairway. It wasn't heated, although it was mid-winter here, and the lighting was as dim as a cellar's. Very well, I said to myself, the doors below are probably open, and I began to descend, holding on to the steel handrail in order not to stumble on one of the dimly-lit steps.

But the doors on the next floor down were also locked.

'Oh, Lord!'

For a few seconds I stood there in disbelief on that icy landing, in a silk dress and high heels, thinking about my crew twenty-four floors below. By now, they must be wondering what I was doing. Then anger took over from disbelief, and I began to batter desperately with my fists on those steel doors, as solid as armor and not designed to communicate the slightest sound.

What should I do? I had no way of contacting anybody, and if I stayed where I was I would probably freeze to death before help arrived. So I decided to move down another flight, hoping this time to find a door that had failed to lock properly. It was an ordeal in high heels, but I hadn't yet considered taking off my shoes, as though they represented stages in one's acceptance of distress.

A prisoner! A prisoner in that gloomy cage of a stairwell, sentenced to walking down every floor before finding whether I'd be able to get out. What would happen if even the bottom doors were locked? Was there actually a chance that I might spend the night here?

'My God, if you can hear me, if you can see me, please do something!'

Feeling the onset of panic, I steeled myself to making the long descent, my breathing uncontrollable, my legs wobbling beneath me.

How long did it take me to walk back down the whole height of that hotel, acutely aware of the need to avoid injury at all costs, if only for the sake of Hélène and Nicolas, who needed me and would be calling for me tomorrow morning? How long? An hour and a half, perhaps, the whole while fighting my urge to flop down helplessly and weep?

Every one of the floors beneath me, on which I initially based my hopes, proved to be sealed tight. That was why I thought I was going mad when I found that the ground-floor fire doors were also locked. I was numb with cold, exhausted, and I don't know what inspired me to carry on my descent. Where could that stairway be leading? I was afraid I wouldn't have the strength to climb back up again. I was afraid I would find myself in a labyrinth of basement corridors, but as long as there was the smallest chance I would take it.

And suddenly I came to an open door – but open to the night outside! I went through. Beneath me I heard voices, and then I saw flashlight beams and cars. I was in an underground parking lot. But what were all these people doing? Parking lots had always scared me, and I hesitated before approaching the people wielding flashlights. I stepped forward, my breath failing, and suddenly I was caught in the beam of a flashlight.

'Who goes there?' exclaimed a voice.

Police! They're going to arrest me, I immediately thought, I must have done something illegal, I shouldn't be down here. And in my panic I began to stammer:

'Excuse me . . . I am a resident of this hotel . . .'

'Miss Mouskouri!'

The man at once lowered his flashlight and came toward me.

'Crikey, where did you come from? What happened to you?' he said when he saw that I was barefoot and shivering.

'The stairway . . . Locked . . .'

Ten policemen quickly encircled me. One of them slipped a pea jacket over my shoulders.

'The hotel sounded the alarm. We thought you'd been kidnapped. We've just shut down the whole perimeter.'

Much later, back in France and recalling how quickly I had tumbled from the red carpet to extreme distress, I decided that Heaven had doubtless used that strange experience to show me how alone and vulnerable we are on this earth, despite every success and all the gratitude of our fellow beings.

Luckily, news of my adventure never reached the reporters, and on the following evening many of them were in the auditorium for my first recital. It began with the presentation of an award marking my twentieth Australian Gold Record, and the *Daily Telegraph* (well aware that all this activity around me annoyed Frank Sinatra) ran this nice little headline over a picture of me: 'While Frankie Sulks, Nana Has the Last Laugh'.

I have toured the world many times, but I have rarely met a people as genial and warmhearted as the Australians. During those few days in Perth, I tried to make the most of the children's presence. We enjoyed many family excursions, shopping on the city's broad avenues, visiting the zoo and the theme parks. Everywhere, people smiled at us, called out to me by my first name, asked if we were enjoying Australia. And we rarely emerged from visits to stores and restaurants without gifts for the children and flowers for me.

'While Frank Sinatra stayed aloof in his twenty-third-floor hotel suite yesterday,' commented the *Daily Telegraph*, 'Greek charmer Nana Mouskouri was out meeting the people.

'Nana and The Athenians are on their first visit, and she cannot hide the fact that she is enjoying every minute of the tour. With her husband Georgiou and their two children, they have been seeing as much of Australia as possible in between concerts.'

The big moment of this Australian tour, as on those that followed, was of course my appearance on the stage of the prestigious Sydney Opera House for the last two concerts. As in the Albert Hall, or Carnegie Hall, I was aware of the honor paid me by offering me those legendary stages which had heard the world's greatest voices long before me. And how could I fail to be swept in delirium when, after multiple encores, the whole audience rose to its feet for a standing ovation?

'Vibrant Greek warmth' was the headline in next day's *Sydney Morning Herald*. 'Quietly and surely,' wrote the music critic Jill Sykes, 'Nana Mouskouri gets to the guts of a song and to the hearts of her listeners.

'The audience for her first concert in Sydney were with her all the way. There were many nationalities and ages, from grannies all in black to toddlers in dressing gowns. And Nana Mouskouri had something to please all of them.

'I particularly enjoyed her Greek songs – she captures the typical, vibrant warmth without becoming strident – and the thoughtful phrasing and sensitive musicianship which brought out so much meaning in songs like "Try to Remember" "Seasons in the Sun" and "The First Time Ever I Saw Your Face".

'The Athenians, technically her backing group, play a front-line role in her success, both as musicians and entertainers.'[26]

In New Zealand, I sang in Auckland, Wellington, and Christchurch, the capital of South Island. For the Christchurch concert, knowing that the island has a considerable Maori population, I had taken care to learn a Maori song which speaks for that people's soul, much as 'Un Canadien

---

[26] *Sydney Morning Herald*, 10 July 1974.

errant' did for the Québécois. I could think of no better way of returning some of the affection lavished on me by the people who came to hear me. And it was a unique chance of creating a shared enjoyment, both for them and for me, for the whole audience sang along with me from the first notes.

Slap in the middle of the concert that night in Christchurch, I was given a telegram from a group of scientists doing research at the South Pole. 'Dear Nana,' it ran, 'we're sad not to be in the auditorium with you tonight, but so happy to know that you're not far away, just two hours by air. We're listening to you live, you're singing for us! Please don't forget to sing "Plaisir d'amour," Gounod's *Ave Maria*, and "Four and Twenty Hours".' I read the message out loud, the audience clapped its head off, and to please that research group we immediately changed the program to include 'Plaisir d'amour'. I pictured the notes rising for the first time over the icy Antarctic wastes.

Then it was back to Sydney, en route to Japan. That country intimidated me because I hadn't yet had time to learn its language. Until now, I had been careful to speak all the languages of the countries that welcomed me: English, French, German, Spanish, and a little Italian. But Japan, where they had discovered me long ago with 'Les enfants du Pirée', and fallen in love with 'Umbrellas of Cherbourg' and 'Plaisir d'amour', Japan was asking for me, and I did not have the heart to postpone the trip.

But I was quite right to be intimidated, and I paid for my ignorance as soon as I landed in Tokyo.

With the help of the Greek embassy and my record company, our producer had set up a press conference as soon as our feet touched terra firma. I was told that most of the media would be there – written press, radio and television – which pleased me because I would be able to tell them (and through them, the Japanese public) a little bit about myself, to form a preliminary bond with these people who listened to me without knowing me. I was introduced to my interpreter, a young man, cultivated, and well-dressed in typical Japanese style, and the conference began.

From the very first words, I was astonished by how long the

interpretation took, as though each one of my sentences needed three or four in Japanese. For the first fifteen minutes I went along with this, then I suddenly had doubts.

'Excuse me,' I said to the young man, 'but would you repeat for me what you've just said?'

I saw that he was embarrassed, but he remained mute, as if determined not to answer me. Beginning to feel angry, I repeated myself in firmer tones:

'I would like you to tell me what you just told these reporters in my name.'

At that juncture, I saw the Greek ambassador moving in my direction, as if fearing a diplomatic incident, and my producer had turned purple. But my tone was enough for the interpreter.

'I conveyed to the journalists the honorable Madame Mouskouri's greetings to the Japanese people, but I phrased your greetings as we traditionally present them in our country.'

'Wouldn't it be better to translate *exactly* what I say? Perhaps it is different, but it is my way of saying things, and I believe the Japanese are quite able to understand that our traditions are different.'

Further confusion. The ambassador was clearly embarrassed, and my producer took it upon himself to explain things to the interpreter. Meanwhile, our listeners sat perfectly silent. Did they understand what was going on?

'He will try to translate as you wish him to,' my producer finally told me.

Was I wrong to be upset? I learned new customs from Japan, and I finally determined to accept them. In the middle of a concert, for example, an interpreter would intervene every two or three songs to explain what they said and perhaps suggest how to judge them. From my standpoint, this broke the continuity of my performance and arrested the rising tide of shared emotion, breaking in like a brutal recall to reality. But the Japanese were used to this way of proceeding.

Just as they were used to their own very Japanese way of applauding, holding their palms very flat as they clapped. It produced a rhythmic effect, untouched by overt enthusiasm of any kind.

'I don't think they liked it,' I said to my producer on my first return to the wings.

'How can you say such a thing? I have seldom heard a more enthusiastic audience!'

He was right, as it turned out. By the time of my second concert I had learned to interpret Japanese levels of enthusiasm. It was a moving experience, as though, little by little, we were learning to know one another.

I was still in Tokyo, on 23 July 1974, when every radio station blared the news. General Ghizikis, leader of the military junta in power in Greece for the past seven years, had just tendered his resignation to the civilian authorities. Humiliated by the recent Turkish invasion of Cyprus, unanimously rejected by the country, the colonels' regime collapsed under the weight of its own failure. People were already talking of Constantine Karamanlis' return to Athens.

Our group went crazy. We at once hurried to the Greek embassy, where laughter and tears saluted the event. The ambassador and I fell into one another's arms, and after that I called my parents and then Jenny. In Greece, too, people were torn between euphoria and tears. The army had left the streets, abandoning them to incredulous people who were said to be strolling about with transistor radios glued to their ears. My parents confirmed that Karamanlis might very soon return from exile.

I tried to reach him in order to let him know how much I was thinking of him on this historic day, and I finally spoke to his brother. The former prime minister was indeed expected in Athens next day, he said, to form a government whose first task would be to restore democracy.

20

My Life is Shattered

In my heart of hearts, I had been hoping that this world tour would revive our enthusiasm for playing together, but once we returned from Australia all George's inner demons regained the upper hand. As I launched into preparations for a new album, still with André's support, I saw George, somber and mute, gradually retreating into himself again. Were we now condemned to reliving those dreadful months that preceded our tour? That period at least taught me that I couldn't go on singing in the climate of tension George had created between us. I was sick again, I seemed to be shrinking away, and finally things became so bad that I totally lost my voice. At that point, I remembered how hopeless I felt when I visited that doctor after fleeing Philippe Bouvard's studio in mid-broadcast, and I began to feel that heady rage which overtakes you when you feel you are the object of undeserved suspicion. What had I done, after all, to merit George's reproaches? We had lived together for fifteen years, we had two children, we had fled Paris to calm his nerves, and I loved him too much to give any other man a second glance. What more could he want of me?

It was that rage which finally pushed me, in spite of my horror of quarrels, into provoking him.

'I can see we're no longer happy together, George, but I no longer know what to do. I don't know how much is my fault.'

'I've told you, I don't like our life any more.'

'I can't imagine not singing any more. Do you understand that?'

'I'm not asking you to stop singing.'

'You're asking me to return to Greece, like your friends.'

'Yes, and become a Greek singer again. They all love you there, and now that democracy is back you can sing as much as you please.'

'Like a caged bird ... We've traveled all over the world, so why do you want to put me behind bars now?'

'What bars? We'd be living in a big house, much closer to each other and to the children.'

'But so far from the outside world.'

'Who cares about the world? We're rich enough now to do without traveling.'

'I don't give a damn about how rich we are, I've already told you that, but I could never do without those amazing moments music gives me. When a whole auditorium shares your feelings ... Remember the Royal Albert Hall, the Place des Arts in Montreal, the Théâtre des Champs-Elysées ... When you love music as I do, George, the whole world seems too small to contain all your dreams.'

Perhaps it was during this long exchange that I first concluded that if George truly loved me, he would urge me to set my goals higher and higher instead of seeking to push me into isolation. What kind of love was it when one of the two parties insisted that the other sacrifice herself?

I believe that this idea gained on me through that fall of 1974, raising fresh problems as it progressed. It contributed to my growing distance from George despite the deep sorrow that sometimes overwhelmed me. We decided provisionally that he would stay in Geneva and I would return to Paris. A year earlier, the resentment he harbored against me would probably have made me ill, but now I was able to bear it. Very gradually, I had lost respect for this man, whose selfishness and possessive attitudes were now glaringly obvious. It helped me protect myself.

In any case, I no longer lost my voice. So now, with the disbanded Athenians no longer in the picture, I had to decide which musicians I would record with. I discussed the problem with Louis Hazan and André, who decided to introduce me to Alain Goraguer. Alain already worked with Serge Gainsbourg, Isabelle Aubret, and Jean Ferrat. He was a sensitive and talented musician, and I came away from our very first meeting full of confidence in him.

That fall, we recorded the album *Ave Maria* together. It included several songs destined to become classics, such as 'Romance de maître Pathelin', 'Nous ne serons jamais plus seuls' ('We'll Never Be Alone Again'), and 'Il est passé' ('He Dropped By'), all arranged by Alain Goraguer and accompanied by his orchestra.

Right after that, I sank back into depression. For six or seven months, I vanished from recording studios and theaters. How did it all come about? Even today, I have trouble returning to that period, which remains one of the saddest in my life.

Meanwhile, George had become ever more determined. During one of my visits to Geneva, he again brought up our return to Greece.

'I've told you what I think about that,' I told him.

'Well, if that's how it's going to be, let's separate. I've decided to leave.'

'George, we have two children. We can't separate just like that, almost overnight . . .'

'Do what you like, it's your business. But I'm leaving – and taking the children with me.'

Two years before, we had bought a plot of land on the island of Corfu, where George now planned to build a house as quickly as possible and make it his home. How could we transplant our children from Geneva to Corfu in such haste? Hélène was only five, and Nicolas had just started elementary school. How would they react to such an abrupt change of scenery? And above all, how would they take my disappearance from their lives?

George's parents weighed in with their advice, and we finally settled on a compromise. The children would go on living in Geneva with Fernande and me, and would spend their school vacations, still under Fernande's wing, with their father in Greece.

At first, even though he was in Greece and I was in Geneva, I believe each of us still hoped that we would eventually reconcile. I spent my days in a state of stunned astonishment, quite unable to understand how things had reached this pass. I was obsessed by the memory of my mother, saying over and over again to Jenny and me, 'I'm waiting until you're grown-up enough for me to leave your father. While you're still small you need him, and I have no right to deprive you of him.' And what about me? What had I done to be able to afford myself that right? There were days when I felt overcome by guilt. It was my fault, I told myself. All I had to do was give up my artistic career – and the four of us would be living together under Corfu's bountiful sun. On such days I felt sure I was making my children unhappy and adding to the despair of a man who, after all, asked nothing more than permission to live with his wife . . . But there were other days when I choked with anger at his unhealthy jealousy, at his narrow-mindedness, at the money fixation which had finally (or so it seemed to me) stifled his artistic impulse. Then regret for the past would suddenly drive anger away, and I missed his guitar so sorely that I often caught myself on the verge of tears. His guitar notes reached with infinite delicacy into my heart! So at a given moment I was silently reproaching him for selling his soul, and at the very next moment I was ready to shout from the rooftops that I had never felt such emotion at the sound of a guitar. Well, yes, but I also had to admit that I missed the guitar more than the man. As though I was growing indifferent to this man who so consistently disappointed me, who so stubbornly shut himself off.

And on the day when Odile Hazan came to tell me that George had met *someone*, I found to my surprise that I didn't care, and even that I was relieved. As though this news unburdened me at one stroke of the guilt I had been feeling on his behalf.

'Oh?' I said to Odile. 'That's fine.'

'Is that all it means to you?'

'No, I'm happy for him. I can't stand the thought of George all alone and depressed.'

'I've been talking to him, you know. If you don't want a divorce, there's still time.'

'How do you mean?'

'I believe he'd like to be sure there's no hope with you before he marries this woman.'

'I don't understand. If you truly love someone, you can choose to wait – but then you don't commit yourself to someone else.'

'I think you should be flattered.'

No, I wasn't flattered. And far from changing my mind, that conversation simply made my withdrawal from George absolute.

Now the divorce was official, and the word itself made me feel like a traitor. It afflicted my conscience and my long-held notions of commitment and loyalty. It decreed the end of my romantic life as well as family life. In the early, lacerating phase of the process, I found myself casting doubt upon our whole shared history. Had I ever loved George? At times it struck me that I was losing a friend more than a husband. But then what did people mean when they spoke about love? Before meeting George, I had not had the faintest idea, and our early years suddenly seemed surprisingly empty of that flame attributed to love – that *loving passion* Flaubert and Stendhal invoked. Perhaps, raised by parents who no longer loved one another, and knowing nothing of attraction, of desire, I had somewhere along the line confused love and friendship? But the bottom line, I decided, was that we had not done any better than our parents – and we had dragged our two children down with us as we sank.

It was my determination not to lose my footing, not to allow us to be buried under the ruins, which made me decide on building a chalet. It could have been a windmill, a waterside villa, anything at all, but I was obsessed with the need to build something in order to prove to myself that we were well and truly alive, still capable of inventing tomorrows despite the horror we were living through. A chalet because we lived in the homeland of the chalet, and because someone had mentioned a plot for sale near Villars-sur-Ollon. I bought the land and threw myself heart and soul into the project. At least, I told myself, our children would never want for a roof over their heads, since George was already supervising the construction of his house in Corfu when we began digging the foundations of my Swiss chalet.

And then I flew to Greece. Alone. I needed to put my parents in the picture, to speak to Nikos, and I was possessed by the vague idea of rediscovering memories that pre-dated George, as if I had to rebuild old connections, to relive my earliest desires, find the strength to begin all over again.

My parents were not very helpful.

'How dare you do this to me?' exclaimed my mother.

At first I didn't understand her, and thought only of calming her fears.

'It won't change anything for you. I'll always be here and you'll lack for nothing.'

'But I'll never dare leave the house again!'

'You'll be afraid to be seen in public just because I'm getting a divorce?'

'Nana, I implore you, just think . . .'

'It was you who said George wasn't the man for me, Mama. And now you'd like me to go on living with a man I no longer love and who no longer loves me?'

'You can't just break up a marriage. Think of the children.'

'You yourself wanted to leave Papa.'

'That was different, and in any case I didn't want a divorce. And what's more, we still live together.'

'I've thought about it hard, you know, and I'm not going to turn back.'

'Then you're condemning us to live in shame.'

My father was equally indifferent to my own distress, as though 'what-will-the-neighbors-say' was a consideration that outweighed everything else in life. With him, too, I found myself defending the divorce which already caused me so much pain.

'People will ask questions, and what am I supposed to say?'

'Say that I'm forty, that I'm raising my children all alone, and that I earn my living.'

How wonderful it was to see Nikos again ! He had acquired a stoop and his face was hollower, but he had endured the pain of recent years on his two feet. He was still the same man, thoughtful, impatient of compromise and posturing but always eager to listen, always benevolent. Nikos had followed my progress since my first steps in France, and I rediscovered in him the same exacting standards I so appreciated in André.

'You're an artist, Nana, don't let yourself be weighed down by petty everyday things. Work, never stop, and you'll see that a whole life isn't enough to express the feelings we experience.'

We chatted, we strolled together in the Athens streets, and I took him to the Floka. I needed to be in his company as we remembered those first years when he and Manos admitted me into their circle and opened my eyes to the world. What would have I become if our paths had not crossed? Who would have taught me passion and beauty?

Nikos reawakened my earliest enthusiasms, the times when, after my own performances were over, I raced from one nightclub to another for the simple pleasure of unearthing the best musicians. I found myself doing it again. I missed bouzouki. I missed George's guitar, and I returned with a handful of old friends to make a tour of the tavernas. I wondered why I shouldn't take three or four of these musicians back to France with me. Why shouldn't I form a new group as good as The Athenians but much more dedicated to playing? I discovered several performers, we talked, exchanged phone numbers, and I dreamed in private of a new beginning.

What was André's opinion? That was the question that preoccupied me now. I knew he was worried about me, and for good reason. In the space of a few months I had lost all my musicians and then my husband. And I had requested that phone calls to me should be blocked. André respected my silence, but knowing him as I did, I knew full well that he thought every day about my next album, the next Olympia, and the tours awaiting me in Canada, the United Kingdom, and Germany.

André liked my idea of forming a new group. But he would probably have approved any idea provided that it raised my spirits. That possibility certainly occurred to me, but it didn't discourage me, and I began to sound out Greek musicians more directly. The ones who showed interest tended to be old friends, much more deeply committed to music than The Athenians, and by mid fall of 1975 I was poised to launch out with a new group.

Then I called Yvonne Littlewood. I planned to start out with televised shows before tackling the stage or the recording studios. I told Yvonne (by now a close friend) some of the things that had happened to me on tour before asking whether she would consider inviting us back to her own studio.

'Whenever you like,' she said. 'Here in England, everyone wants to have you back, and I'm very curious to meet your new musicians.'

We were in the midst of preparations for Yvonne's broadcasts, scheduled for the BBC's end-of-the-year festivities, when Louis Hazan and I quarreled for the first time.

The episode would have been of little importance, except that it preceded an event which was to upset the Hazans' lives and result in the permanent loss of the friendship and trust we had enjoyed for the past fifteen years. During a stopover in London, I learned from Philips' director that they were considering issuing all my hits under one label.

'I'm against it,' I told him. 'I don't like compilations in principle. First of all, they prolong the life of certain songs which no longer interest me, and second, they can overshadow recent creations.'

As it happened, I was dining that night with the Hazans. I therefore repeated my opposition to this idea of a British compilation.

'Whether you like it or not,' Monsieur Hazan returned dryly, 'we're going to do it.'

'I beg your pardon? I don't understand.'

He had never used that tone with me.

'Your fans are asking for this compilation, Nana. Sales will be sky-high, so I've decided to do it, and I have that right.'

'Even if I'm against it, is that what you mean?'

'That's exactly what I mean. And I don't even need your approval. It's right there in your contract. All you had to do was read it.'

Stunned, all I could manage was a feeble rejoinder:

'It's true that until now I've never read my contracts, Monsieur Hazan, but only because I placed blind trust in you. I never dreamed of suspecting that you might insert anything likely to damage me.'

He did not respond, and the evening ended in icy silence.

What had happened? What had I done to deserve this humiliation? I recalled that after two seven-year contracts with Philips, I had recently suggested the idea of operating as my own producer from Switzerland, while remaining with Philips as my distributor. Could Louis Hazan have interpreted this as an unfriendly act after everything he had done for me? I saw no other reason for such a turnaround, and promised myself I would dispel this misunderstanding when we next met. It was now that the drama I have mentioned took place, an event that would permanently estrange us.

We were deep into rehearsals on 31 December 1975 when someone came into the studio with a message – an urgent call from Paris. I at once recognized the voice of Simone, Louis Hazan's secretary.

'Nana, Odile needs you. It's urgent. Could you return to Paris right away?'

'Lord, what's going on, Simone? Has something happened?'

'I can't tell you over the phone, but it's very serious. Odile is asking for you.'

'Tell her I'll be there. I'll take the next plane.'

I abandoned my musicians. They were not yet used to working with me, and they looked at me as though I had lost my wits. I had myself driven to the airport without even dropping by my hotel. If Odile had asked Simone to contact me, it meant that something unexpected had happened to her husband. If it was a question of Louis' health, Odile would never have sworn Simone to secrecy. So what could the problem be? What could be serious enough to justify disrupting the labors of a whole crew and endangering an important broadcast? I made that flight like a sleepwalker, crazed with anxiety.

I knew that André, the only person who could tell me everything, would not be at Orly. It was the Christmas vacation, and he was with his family in Burgundy. However, they had sent a car for me. Its driver was a man I didn't know, cold and taciturn, who hauled me at top speed through the big lounge, opened the car door for me, and set off as if the devil was on his heels.

'Where are we going?'

'To the Hazans, Madame. They are expecting you.'

I walked alone across the threshold of that building I knew so well and climbed to the seventh floor. The door opened, and I saw the entire Philips management team, about a dozen men, arranged around the room as if they were indeed waiting only for me.

'My God, don't tell me . . .'

Seeing their expressions, I at once feared the worst: Louis Hazan was dead. Then his right-hand man, Jacques Caillard, came over to me.

'Come in and sit down, Nana. Here's what's happened: Monsieur Hazan has been kidnapped.'

'Kidnapped!'

'Yes, in the middle of a management meeting. Armed, masked men. We could do nothing.'

'Oh, Lord! How could this be? Where is Odile?'

'She's waiting for you.'

I found her in tears, distraught, unable to believe that this could be true. Generous, considerate Louis in the hands of killers. Who could wish him harm? I spent a long time trying to comfort her, but in reality I was as lost as Odile.

A moment later the managers joined us, and I overheard this remark from M. Caillard's mouth: 'This will teach us to work with untrustworthy people.' Who could he be talking about? What did he mean? I recalled his words when it appeared that the manager of the company responsible for the cleaning and maintenance of our offices was implicated in the kidnapping. But in that tense atmosphere, Caillard's words merely added to my confusion, and Odile's distress was what most concerned me.

Next morning I had to fly back to London, feeling guilty at leaving Odile sunk deep in horror.

A week went by. I called Odile several times a day. Every police force in France was involved, but so far we had heard nothing definite.

Finally, André called me:

'We're approaching crisis point. Things may turn out very badly. I think it might be better if you came back.'

'I'll try to get the next flight.'

This time André was waiting. There were reports that the police were about to arrest the kidnappers. Meanwhile, though, there were rumors that Louis Hazan had already been killed. The police team investigating the deed could neither confirm nor deny these terrifying rumors – which left Odile racked with anguish. But the climax was near.

Arriving on Rue de Montalembert in the gathering dusk, we were greeted by an unbelievable sight. A dense crowd blocked the whole street. I sensed clusters of photographers on the rooftops, onlookers at every window; the police seemed unable to contain the swelling tide of people. Two motorbike policemen had to open a way through for us, and the police stationed in front of the building practically had to carry me into the vestibule. But reporters blocked off the elevators, and I had to walk up those seven flights of stairs surrounded by a forest of microphones and the popping of flashbulbs.

'Nana, Nana, what do you think? They're saying that Louis Hazan is dead. Have you heard from him? What are you going to tell his wife?'

I had never experienced anything like this. I was jostled as though caught up in a crowd animated by the fever and excitement at a racetrack gathering – while the man they were asking about, whose agony I was being asked to describe, was as precious to me as a father. Obviously, I was much too upset to say anything at all, and I could no longer hold back my tears when the Hazans' door finally shut out my hysterical escort.

Many friends were gathered there, wordless, tense. I was taken to Odile, who was unrecognizable, much thinner, her face ravaged, her eyelids swollen.

'Oh, Nana! We don't know anything, I think I'm going crazy. There may no longer be any hope.'

We fell into one another's arms. Odile sobbed, and I was so choked with anguish that I couldn't find the words to tell her we should at least keep on hoping.

At that point, the phone rang.

Odile picked up.

I saw her face relax and light up almost miraculously.

'He's alive! He's alive!' she cried out through her tears. 'Quick, they're waiting for us at police headquarters on Quai des Orfèvres.'

In the meantime, a police car had succeeded in parking at the foot of the building. We piled in, and since there wasn't enough room I found myself on an inspector's knees. What did it matter? Now all we wanted to do was laugh.

'When I tell my wife that I rode with Nana Mouskouri on my lap, she'll never believe me!' said the inspector.

In a few minutes we reached Quai des Orfèvres. A staircase with worn steps, a maze of corridors under dirty yellow light, and suddenly we were asked to step into an office. Louis Hazan was sitting on a chair, his face pale, his features so ravaged he seemed to have aged ten years. He didn't have the strength to smile. All he could manage was to rise and embrace Odile.

That night, I spent no more than ten minutes with them. But since I had to return to London the following afternoon, we agreed that I would come and say my farewells next morning on Rue de Montalambert.

I picked up some croissants on my way, and found them, as I hoped, eating breakfast. He was in an armchair, still very pale and clearly still shocked. Odile, who opened the door for me, sat down again cross-legged in front of the low table, and I did the same. Louis Hazan described his ordeal. For a week, they had kept him crammed into a closet. They gave him just enough food to keep him alive, and never once allowed him to stretch out full-length. He spoke of his physical suffering, and went on to tell us of everything that crossed his mind during those days and nights when he was unable to sleep.

'I didn't know what those guys wanted, why they were torturing me, and I finally decided that I wasn't going to survive. That I'd never see the light again, that I'd never see you again, Odile.'

It was deeply disturbing to listen to him. He had just escaped death, in fact, after all that time looking it in the face.

When it was over, he turned to me.

'It wasn't easy to survive, doubled over in the closet, but I thought a lot about what you said to me last time, Nana — that you would never have suspected me of inserting anything that might damage you in one of your contracts. Your words deeply wounded me, and I want you to know it.'

Should I have apologized even though from my point of view it was I, not Louis, who had been betrayed? I couldn't muster the words that might have dispelled the misunderstanding, let him know how much I still trusted him despite that strange clause authorizing him to make a compilation of my songs against my will. I couldn't muster the right words, and in any case this was not the right time to return to that stupid quarrel. So we parted with that wound still in our hearts, permanently, I should say, because we never mentioned it again.

21

Mama will Never Sing Again

I do not know exactly when André entered my life in earnest. Indeed, when I look back over all those years, it seems to me that André had *always* been in my life.

Both demanding and affectionate, he was self-effacing but sure about his artistic choices. But there came a day when I started to look at him with different eyes, no longer seeing him just as a precious friend, generous, a spirit filled with light, but as a man quite capable of making my heart beat faster. Yes, that's probably right, but that 'day' lasted more like a year or ten years, until my love for him became obvious to me, like the sudden blossoming of spring after winter.

I should say here what kind of man André is and how he stands out among all the men who have followed my artistic career since the beginning. They all meant a great deal to me, from Manos Hadjidakis to Louis Hazan, Quincy Jones to Michel Legrand, and including of course Nikos Gatsos, Harry Belafonte, George, Pierre Delanoë, Claude Lemesle, and Alain Goraguer. But none of them gave me the same sense of shared emotion I so often saw in André's eyes while I was singing. I believe that before he became my artistic director, André must have been very deeply touched by something mysterious he sensed in me, something he alone could see, or perhaps I should write *hear*. I think that from the start our relations were a hundred miles removed from traditional professional norms, in a hidden corner of his soul where my voice happened to strike a chord, distant but so obvious to him that he at once accorded me a place apart. I say this without pride but with bottomless gratitude. And henceforth, with so much love! 'I'll be in the

274

studio all day with the singer,' he used to say. Not 'Nana', but *the singer*. And now, after thirty years of living together, after we were finally married, he still calls me 'the singer', with that blend of good manners and love he has never stopped showing me.

It was during a concert at the Brussels Palace of Fine Arts, at the very beginning of the Seventies, that I first realized there was no one else like André. He was there for the dress rehearsal, and had discreetly seated himself dead-center in the front row so that he was the only person I saw from the stage. As I sang I was at first very surprised, and then moved, to see how he reacted: he even discreetly dabbed his eyes while the audience applauded. He left for Paris next morning, and I found a little note from him slipped beneath my bedroom door. It said that he would never forget the previous night, adding that my interpretation of the songs had knocked him off his feet. In those early years of rock, when scoring a hit at any cost seemed to be a determining factor in the minds of music publishers, he preferred to give his own feelings priority. 'You're a great artist,' he often told me, 'you can sing whatever you want. So let's be ambitious. You'll achieve success without having to go looking for it.'

In the early years, when I still wrestled with the pronunciation of certain words, bursting into tears or throwing the mic on the floor, André never lost faith, never once raised his voice. The crew would leave the studio, with musicians and technicians exchanging jokes in the corridors. André never left. It seems to me that he didn't see himself as being *at work*, like the majority of Philips executives, but as the spectator of a work I had to create, with him there to accompany me. A child violinist and a music-lover, he left his native Burgundy at twenty to serve the cause of music – and there he found himself and his life's work. 'If you like, we can just start over again tomorrow. I'll be there, and we have all the time in the world.' I could lose my foothold, but not André. He always knew exactly what stage the preparations for a given song had reached. He knew exactly how far I was from mastering it, and I knew I could count on him to carry me right to the end of the road. Nobody had ever had such faith in me. Our eyes met, and I read: 'You'll get there! Of course you will! Don't forget, we're the strongest.' His faith in me was like an act of grace.

He embodied patience and respect. When I abruptly broke off during a rehearsal because nothing seemed to be going right, and immediately afterward felt embarrassed because I had wasted the time of all these people who were there only for me, he was always the one to say: 'That's OK, don't be angry with yourself, you have the right, we aren't the ones who have to go onstage in a few hours.'

When George and I separated, with George returning to Greece and with me abandoning singing for several months, André said not a word. I think he guessed that any move on his part would be seen as impatience – the natural impatience of an artistic director with his sights set on the next recording – and he said nothing. But when I announced my return to Paris, he met me at Charles de Gaulle airport with a white rose in his hand.

I was back just for two or three days, time for him to show me the songs he had unearthed for me.

'Here, I thought of this one.'

We listened to it in its English or German version.

'I like it a lot.'

'So do I. I think you'll sing it superbly. I'd like to ask Pierre Delanoë and Claude Lemesle to do the adaptation.'

Once again, I was without musicians. The ones who came with me to London for the BBC series were returning to Greece. So we decided that I would record my next album with Alain Goraguer and his orchestra.

'What if we do it this summer?' he asked me.

'Right after Australia, then.'

'It won't keep you away from the children too long?'

'No, they'll be with me in Australia, and then in Corfu with George.'

I let myself be drawn gently back into music. In July 1976, I left for my second Australian tour. And as soon as I got back, I recorded the new album: *Vielles Chansons de France.*

Our life in Geneva underwent a change after George left. Little by little, Fernande assumed control, and I was relieved to be able to lean on her. I knew that I could disappear for several days without the whole house collapsing. She scrupulously watched over the children's schedules and made sure they were always spotless. Her loving care of them relieved me of all anxiety.

I sometimes felt she was not altogether unhappy about the absence of the man of the house, as though George had somehow prevented her from exerting full authority. She needed that authority more than ever, since Hélène too now went to school. The days when we left on tour as a family were long past. Except during vacation time, I departed alone, leaving all responsibility for the children to Fernande.

Very soon, I had the impression that I was upsetting the order and peace of the household when I returned from my long travels. Hélène and Nicolas, who had sometimes not seen me for three weeks or a month, plied me with questions, breakfast would go on and on, and Féfé would be annoyed.

'It's always this way, children,' she told them as she drove them to school. 'Whenever Mama comes back we're always late!'

Which the children repeated.

And to the teachers they would say:

'Forgive me, but my mother was home this morning.'

There was no ill-will in her attitude. Even though it secretly hurt me, as though I had become the interloper in my own house, I never reproached her. But today, with hindsight, I'm sorry I kept my silence, for such innocent remarks were the precursors of painful conflicts that later set me against Fernande. Without her (or me, for that matter) being aware of it, she was gradually distancing me from my children, digging a ditch between us it would take years to fill in.

I was in the rehearsal stages for my Australian tour when Frank Hardy called to say he was coming to Paris. Since our first midnight phone conversation in Sydney, I had read several of his books and we had kept in constant touch. Many of his calls were about the pain his wife's departure had caused him. It was a new and disturbing development in his life, and by a coincidence that troubled us both, it happened at the precise moment George and I separated.

I arranged to meet him at the Flore, and I got there first. For months now, without ever meeting, we had been exchanging deeply confidential secrets, and I was so anxious that my throat was dry. At last he appeared, tall, looking like a lumberjack in his plaid shirt, his face tanned and deeply lined. He too must have been intimidated, because for the first few minutes he didn't sit down. He stood as he spoke, towering broad-shouldered over me, very agitated, a little out of breath, constantly fiddling with his pipe.

'I don't like pipe smoke,' I said to him. 'Would it bother you to put it away?'

He sat down, and from close up all the violence inside him struck me with terrible force. It leapt from his eyes, his forehead, his gestures.

But it was his sorrow that chiefly concerned us that day. He wanted to know what went through a woman's heart when she broke with a man, and he questioned me feverishly, passionately. Without intending to, I spoke of my relationship with George, of my present attitude to love following that failure, and soon, inevitably, we began to speak of ourselves. Was I slipping into an indefinable attraction for him? This man touched me, and at the same time I was scared by the vehemence with which he approached everything. Now he told me he wanted to see me again, very soon. He said that perhaps I embodied the woman he sought, because I was able to respond sensitively to all the questions tormenting him. His words were uncompromising and overwrought. It frightened me, and I told him so. I said I didn't like being rushed, that I craved harmony. Did he understand? I sensed at that point that he was a little lost, and perhaps very sorry to have alarmed me. He would write to me, he said, but would I answer?

'Yes, of course!'

As I watched him melt away into the crowd on Boulevard Saint-Germain, I felt suddenly overcome by all the feelings I had withheld during our talk. Had I done the right thing by acting so rationally in the face of all his dreams, all his desires? Lord, where did life have its being? In reason or in madness? To George, I was the embodiment of madness, but with this man, most probably crazier than I was, I was afraid and I shrank back.

But we decided to meet just over a month later in Adelaide, and I was content with the idea that time would perhaps decide things for me and for him.

*

When the Australians discovered me I was with George and The Athenians. Now I was back without a husband and with Greek musicians they didn't know (this was the group put together for London, and it was their last trip with me). Inevitably, the papers speculated about my private life. 'Nana Plays It Cool', said the headline in the Perth *West Australian*. The article that followed began this way: '"Get married again?" said Nana Mouskouri with a charming lift of her strong black eyebrows. "Why, I'm still married," she added mysteriously.' And it was true that I wasn't yet officially a divorcee. As for *The Australian*, it proclaimed that 'Nana Mouskouri Prefers the Voice of Freedom'.

I had totally reconstructed my program since our first Australian tour. Two years earlier, the Athenians opened the show, playing alone onstage before I appeared. This time I began all alone with an a cappella rendering of 'Amazing Grace'. In a way I was challenging myself, for it is truly terrifying to confront an audience sitting in palpable silence with your lone, unsupported voice. But I also did it to *cover* my musicians, who were unaccustomed to a foreign audience and wanted to remain farther in the background than The Athenians. For me, it seemed to be one more step into solitude, and that tour, in which everything rested on my shoulders, gave me a self-confidence I never knew when George and his group were there.

And of course I saw Frank Hardy again. We had supper together after my concert and spent the rest of the night talking. He told me he was overwhelmed by the way I sang 'Waltzing Matilda', one of the most famous of Australian folk songs. Many people wanted it to replace 'Advance Australia Fair' as the country's national anthem. 'Waltzing Matilda' tells the story of a vagabond (a 'swagman') who steals a sheep to avoid starvation and chooses to drown rather than be captured by the 'troopers'.

'What did you do to make me blubber over a song I heard a thousand times when I was a child?' asked Frank.

'I know what it is to be poor and leave home with all your things slung over your back in a bundle.'

'Yes, this evening I realized that you did.'

Naturally, we spoke of his brother, who died in prison, and of the inextinguishable rage he had nurtured against the world ever since. We talked about his childhood and mine, speaking very seriously, both of us seeking to understand where destiny lay hidden and why so many men and women go through life without ever finding why they were brought into the world. Frank was intelligent and sensitive, and I experienced occasional echoes of my conversations with Nikos.

Yet something about him continued to frighten me. Perhaps it was precisely the vehemence of his love for me, which he now openly declared. I thought that if I yielded now to the passionate fires banked up in this man I might easily destroy myself, that I would no longer hear amid the tumult the small inner voice which had guided me through my childhood and which might be swept away for good by his anger.

He asked if I would at least agree to let him write songs for me. To go on reading his still-unfinished novel to me over the phone? Oh, yes! But how could I tell him how much I loved his voice – yet felt the need to protect myself from him?

As daylight approached he left me, once again a little frustrated.

When I got back to France, I found his first poem, 'Where Has the Pilgrim Gone?'

> Where has the pilgrim gone,
> Tossing her raven head, arching her brow?
> Will the winds of the West
> Waken her now?

From then on, he called me 'pilgrim'. Perhaps he hoped the west winds would bring me back to him some day? At least, that was what I sensed, and we kept up a regular correspondence without being really sure of what fate held in store for us.

As so often in life, it took a great tragedy to explain why I was so attached to André. I wound up 1976 with a series of appearances at the Olympia, and 1977 promised to be extraordinary: tours of Belgium and Holland in January, of France in February, of Germany in March, of the United States (where I was scheduled to appear on Broadway) in April, of Canada in May, and so on . . .

By now I was traveling with an entourage of about fifteen people – musicians, lighting technicians, sound engineers, my dresser, and my producer. Having them around me waiting for my next decision put considerable pressure on me. Although I was close to each of the musicians, we didn't enjoy the close relationship which had bound me to The Athenians. It was all a bit too much for me to bear alone, and André, who was aware of this, had gotten into the habit of being with me for the first two or three days of each tour. He had directed me for fifteen years now, and could speak for me and make most decisions in my absence.

As usual, Belgium and Holland gave me a warm welcome. 'Whether evoking the bloody tears of an exile at his last sight of his country's flag, or gently deploring the murderous excesses of our world, or lingering over the wounds inflicted by an unhappy love, Nana Mouskouri instinctively hits on the appropriate tone and gestures,' wrote the critic of Brussels' *Le Soir*.[27]

Then I meandered across France, where the welcome was equally warm.

The greatest challenge ahead was the German tour, the first since my earliest days. A whole month in which I would sing in all the country's major cities.

On the morning of my departure for Frankfurt, where I was giving my first concert that very evening, Jenny called me from Athens:

'Nana, I don't want to worry you about something that may turn out to be unimportant, but Mama's in hospital. She's had a mild stroke.'

'Oh my God! I'll try to get a seat on the first flight out . . . tell her I'm on the way.'

'No, don't rush things, the doctors aren't worried.'

'I was about to head out to the airport for my German tour, and you might have trouble getting hold of me if anything happens.'

'I know. That's why I'm calling so early. But don't cancel anything for the moment. Call me tonight and I'll give you the latest news.'

I hung up, and briefly hesitated over whether to cancel everything

---

[27] *Le Soir*, 26 January 1977.

and fly to Athens at once. But Jenny had not seemed really worried, and with a heavy heart I decided to leave for Frankfurt.

André and some of my crew were on the same flight. As soon as we reached Frankfurt we went straight to the theater, located beside the autobahn far from the city center. Rehearsals at once got under way. When I asked where I could find a telephone, they told me I would have to go to the cafeteria at the other end of the building. Not wanting to leave the musicians and technicians, who could make no progress without me, in enforced idleness, I decided to postpone my call.

But I was able to escape briefly at the end of the afternoon.

My father picked up. He had left my mother at the hospital in Jenny's care. He seemed completely lost at finding himself alone in the house, and I spoke to him for a long time, unwilling to leave him in that state. When I hung up, he seemed a little less careworn, and I at once called the hospital to try to speak with my mother.

When they connected me, the first thing I heard was sobbing.

'Oh, Nana, it's over! It's all over!'

'Jenny!'

I gathered through her sobbing that Mama died alone while Jenny was driving Papa back to the house. The pain was so great that we remained weeping silently, each at our own end of the line, for long moments, neither of us able to say anything at all.

Stunned, I walked back to the concert hall. André understood the instant he saw me. We made up our minds in a matter of moments: he postponed the two shows scheduled for Frankfurt, including the one due to start in two hours' time, called for information on the next flight to Athens. Unfortunately, I had to wait until the morrow.

Unable to sleep that night, I told André how sad I felt to have missed that last talk with my mother. It might have set us both free, liberating her from the sorrow of having sacrificed her life to a man who did not deserve her, and me from my guilt at having 'stolen' her destiny. The two-way confession every child must dream of once he is grown, but which death always manages to snatch away, leaving ineradicable regrets in its wake.

I would have liked to tell her that without the dream she had kept alive despite all the horrors that broke into her life, I could never have become the artist Manos Hadjidakis adopted. I would have liked to tell her that she was the flame that kept our family alive. That without her stubborn battle to conquer despair, to outwit fate, neither Jenny nor I would have had the strength to build lives for ourselves. After our respective marriages, Mama had begun to smoke and play cards, almost as if she were surrendering to melancholia, and we had never come to pay her homage, never showed up simply to thank her. Would she have aged more happily if we had done so?

I would have liked to hear her tell me once – just once – that she was proud of how I had turned out. Then I would have been able to whisper softly into her ear: 'But it was all your doing, Mama,' and it struck me that those seven little words might miraculously have brought peace to us both. Her sacrifices would have acquired meaning, and I would have settled my debt to her.

That night, I confided all this to André. I had never spoken to him so seriously about the realities of my childhood, and now I realized that the devotion he had always brought to my artistic life was equal to this new, utterly overwhelming sorrow. Maybe it's in such moments that we discover the best of the material that makes a human soul. André's soul was full of light, and boundlessly generous. With infinite delicacy, this man who rarely spoke and never asserted himself found exactly the right words to comfort me. And the longer we spoke, the stronger the hidden bonds that linked us became – the bonds that make it possible to recognize yourself in what the other is saying and free you from the sense of being all alone on the brink of the abyss. I believe that André truly entered my heart that night. And that, blinded by tears though I was, I saw him for the first time as a companion sent to me from Heaven.

Next morning I left for Athens. Burials in Greece take place very soon after death, and Mama's was scheduled for that very morning. When I reached the house, Jenny told me that her body was already lying in the church. And with that concern we Greeks always have for what the neighbors might say, even at times of greatest sorrow, we at once began discussing what I should wear. I was dressed in black, but was wearing trousers.

'You can't go to church in trousers.'

'Yes I can, it'll be just fine.'

'Nana, it's out of the question! Don't you realize how shocked people will be?'

We finally sent my niece Aliki hurrying out to buy me a black skirt.

Papa took it all very badly. As always when faced with an event that tortured him, an event he couldn't cope with, he sought refuge in silence, as if paralyzed. I watched as he shut himself in the bathroom, then emerged deathly pale and choked by sobs.

At the last moment, as we prepared to leave for the church, he suddenly turned to us.

'It's so hard to see her leave like this,' he murmured, 'so hard, without having a chance to speak after all she suffered ... the war ... the war ...' he said over and over.

And then he said no more, as though he lacked the strength to go on, and Jenny and I guessed that what he regretted most of all was the chance to ask her forgiveness. Not for the war, of course, but for the cruel life he had forced on her.

Poor Papa! How often Jenny and I had dinned it into him that you should never settle down for a night's sleep without first making peace with those you love. 'Whatever your age, you can never know for sure whether you will wake up next morning. Imagine your own remorse and the sorrow of those you leave behind if you depart without atoning for words or deeds you regret ...' And as things had turned out, it was Mama who was the first of us to depart this world, leaving him no time to pour out his soul to her. Could she see us from on high? Would she find some way of communicating her forgiveness to him? Those were the questions I silently put to her throughout that long valedictory mass.

For two days, the three of us stayed close together, prisoners of our insatiable need to talk about her, to hold on to one another, as though our words, our tears and our love would help keep her with us yet awhile. After this I was supposed to leave for Germany, but Papa's distress seemed so unbearable that on the point of departure I suddenly decided to take him with me.

'Papa, why don't you come along too? With Mama gone, it's going to be a strange kind of tour, so having you there would be a real gift to me, and perhaps being with me will help you as well.'

My proposal appeared to offer hope, however small, to my drowning parent.

Yes, he told me, he did want to go with me, but only after the ninth day of mourning. Without wasting a moment, I bought him a ticket to Berlin, where I was due to sing on the day he had chosen for leaving Greece.

My Frankfurt shows had been postponed until the scheduled end of the tour, so I rejoined André and my whole crew in Berlin.

For once, I didn't have any heart for singing, but I was much too conscientious to permit myself to disappear. I thought of the musicians and technicians who would not be working if I were not there, and that thought alone filled me with shame. I thought of the people who had bought their tickets long since and were looking forward to the concert ahead. I had no right to bask in their affection or glory in their pleasure when things went well if I turned my back on them the moment things went badly.

Oh, that Hamburg concert! Never in my whole life as a performer, I believe, had I been swept along on such crests of emotion. After the Frankfurt cancellation, the German media naturally discussed my personal tragedy, so when I came onstage I said a few words about it as a kind of overture, but otherwise I made no changes in my scheduled program. I wanted tonight's show to be as happy as all my preceding concerts.

The whole crew was more considerate toward me than usual, and André was in charge up to the very last second, his unflappability keeping me afloat. When I reached Hamburg I was a mess, but by the time the curtain went up their faith in me had worked wonders.

What greeted me as I came onstage was something I had never before experienced. Rising as one man, the audience broke into thunderous applause. Audiences have a language of their own for expressing their feelings, a language that dispenses with words but draws on spontaneity, on the stirrings of the heart, on the very act of breathing – and my Hamburg audience chose that opening ovation to tell me that it knew, that in its own way it shared my heartache.

The applause went on and on, and inevitably I began to cry despite my promises to myself ... But how could I not weep? With tears of emotion, of gratitude for this gesture that told me these people shared my distress. Standing stock still in center stage, I let the tears flow, and they went on applauding. Seen from Heaven, our mutual confrontation must have seemed strange indeed, with me weeping and unable to say a word and the audience standing and applauding. I don't know how long it went on. Ten minutes perhaps, and by the end I realized that they too were weeping, that we were weeping together.

Then I found the strength to ask them to stop, and soon an impressive silence fell over the vast auditorium.

'My mother was very proud that I became a singer,' I said. 'Tonight I'll be singing for her, and I thank you for being here with me.'

More applause, and halfway between tears and joy I immediately launched into Schubert's *Lindenbaum*. Could Mama hear me or see us? I could have sworn she could, so inspired and windborne did I feel. I had never before sung in this intoxicated state. It was as if I had assumed the physical shape of the music, as if the notes were bearing me toward that elsewhere in which pain is dissolved in a luminous awareness of eternity. If there is a life after death – as I believe – that is how I would like it to be.

It was an evening I will never forget. In fact, that whole German tour, begun in such anguish, remains engraved in my memory as though imbued with a special grace.

My father joined us in Berlin. This time, I sang heavy metal and rock'n'roll in a five-thousand-seat theater, on a stage so big that it dwarfed the enormous amplifiers. Papa couldn't believe his eyes. He had seen the Champs-Elysées, and had never imagined that anything could be more impressive. I still had three Greek musicians in my group. They took him on a tour of the city and he came back mesmerized by everything he saw – majestic avenues, glass buildings, lights that set the sky on fire. As well as my posters! He had carefully counted them, unable to grasp that his baby daughter, the one who sang 'The Wizard of Oz' for him thirty years before, was now looking down on him from every wall in Berlin.

Then we left for Munich, where I sang at the Philharmonic. After that came Vienna's Concert Hall, one of the world's most beautiful theaters – and there Papa burst into tears.

Once again, the audience's response reached unheard-of levels of intensity. They wouldn't let me leave the stage. Encore followed encore, and I finished by singing Mozart. I returned to my dressing room and was already in my bathrobe when someone came and begged me to return to the stage. The applause had reached a new crescendo, and it was impossible not to respond. But I had no time to get dressed again, so taking my cue from Jacques Brel at the Olympia in 1963, I reappeared onstage in that same bathrobe. There was a sudden moment of silence, as though the spectators were holding their breath, stunned by this moment stolen out of time, this final moment we were to spend together in full awareness that there would be no more such moments.

And I sang 'Paper Moon', a cappella and even without the microphone, which had already been disconnected. When it was over, the audience rose and there was a second of silence before the roars of applause rang out.

Perspiring and in tears, I left the stage, and in the gallery leading to my dressing room I ran into my father. His face too was wet with tears.

'Look at yourself, look at yourself,' he stammered. 'You're dead on your feet. You shouldn't have gone back, it was too much, too much.'

Still shaken by sobs, he took me in his arms.

'Almighty God, how I wish she could have seen this! How I wish she had! All evening long I was thinking of her. I kept saying to myself, "If only she could hear this, if only she could see this!"'

Two weeks later, I was in New York City's Broadway Theatre.

'When Nana Mouskouri, the Greek singer, first appeared in the United States a dozen years ago,' commented John S. Wilson of the *New York Times*, 'Harry Belafonte introduced her to American audiences on one of his concert tours. Since then Miss Mouskouri has made several American concert tours of her own. Last night, when she made her Broadway debut in "Nana Mouskouri on Broadway" at the Broadway Theater, where she will continue through Sunday, Mr Belafonte was again on hand, this time in the audience. And, appropriately, one of her most effective songs was a hauntingly appealing melody with a lazy, rolling rhythm, "Coucouroucoucou Paloma" which she got from Mr Belafonte on that initial visit.

'In any language, and in any mood, Miss Mouskouri has a strong, positive projection. Her French songs had an intensity that one associates with Piaf. Her English songs were gentler, more subdued, often with a touch of folksong. And her Greek songs, by one means or another, erupted into lively handclapping dances.'[28]

---

[28] The *New York Times*, 27 April 1977.

22

André Brings Spring Again

I had long felt welcome in Canada and the United States, but a new album, *Roses and Sunshine*, now offered me a kind of beatification.

The album had an unusual history. It was suggested to us by a young Canadian company, Cachet Records, which specialized in country folk music. André was enthusiastic, and so – as a card-carrying fan of Bob Dylan and Joan Baez – was I. Alain Goraguer, now a good friend and my favorite orchestra leader, at once leapt on board. In a few short weeks we came up with a list of the songs we could adapt for the album, 'Even Now', 'Down by the Greenwood Side', 'Roses Love Sunshine', and 'Autumn Leaves'.

Eager to forge ahead with the project, Cachet Records urged speed: they insisted on bringing out the album in the fall of 1978, and we rose to the challenge. In just two lunatic days, we recorded the whole thing. We worked so closely together that only two or three takes proved necessary for each song. It was one of those occasions which proved that friendship and mutual confidence can move mountains.

With the energetic support of Cachet Records, the album came out on schedule, and I was made aware for the first time of the importance of popularity. Invited to attend a signing in a big Toronto department store, I was astounded by the spectacle awaiting me. The building was literally besieged on every floor by a crowd that blocked the escalators and spilled out into the street. In the space of a few hours, I must have signed three thousand copies. 'The fastest pen in the West!' – that was what the store manager (amazed that I should have satisfied most of his customers) later called me.

Borne on the album's tide, I naturally left on a tour of the whole North American continent. First I sang in Toronto, Winnipeg, Calgary, Vancouver, and Edmonton. 'Mouskouri is pure magic,' wrote the daily *Winnipeg Free Press*[29], while *The Edmonton Sun* wondered, 'Is Nana too perfect?'[30] Then I was off on my United States campaign. And it was in Los Angeles' Greek Theater, where I had appeared fifteen years earlier with Harry Belafonte, that I finally met the man whose poetry had haunted me for so long – Bob Dylan!

Leonard Cohen introduced us. Cohen lived in Montreal, and we met every time I passed through. He came to my concerts, and I went to his. We had the same respect for music, we were fond of each other, and we would often spend the whole night after a performance discussing the best angle from which to attack a given song. One evening before I went onstage, he knocked on my dressing room door and came in with Bob Dylan and a friend we all had in common, Malka.

'Bob, this is Nana.'

And turning to me:

'I've told him about your voice and your music. He'd really like to attend your show, but unfortunately he isn't free tonight.'

I like to be alone when I'm due to go onstage, but meeting Bob Dylan was such happiness, such joy, that I stood there for a moment, dazzled but paralyzed.

'How come I don't know you?' Dylan exclaimed. 'Show me what you sing.'

I gave him my latest album, and then told him how much he meant to me, how many of his songs I had lifted from him. I mentioned 'A Hard Rain's a-Gonna Fall', of course, which I had sung at the Théâtre des Champs-Elysées and which people still remembered. Was he listening to me? I can't say for sure. He seemed to be elsewhere, sunk in his dreams.

'I have to give an interview during your concert,' he broke in. 'If you like, we can meet after the show at Alice's. It's a small place and we'll be able to talk there.'

---

[29] *Winnipeg Free Press*, 8 September 1978.
[30] *The Edmonton Sun*, 21 September 1978.

They left, and I tried to stop thinking about Dylan and get back into concert mood.

I was decidedly happy the way this tour was going, and I sang the first part with passion. But when I left the stage at intermission, I ran into Bob Dylan in the wings.

'You're still here! I thought you had an interview ...'

'Oh, yeah ... Yeah ... I asked them to give me a little time.'

And Bob followed me to my dressing room. In somewhat feverish and hurried tones, he began to inquire about the people who influenced me, about the importance of Greek music in my melodies, on the way I sang this or that one of his own songs. I responded as best I could, given the circumstances, before I saw that my dresser was getting impatient, and I was practically forced to show him the door.

'I have to get ready now – change my dress and so forth,' I told him. 'I'm due back onstage in ten minutes.'

'Right. So we'll meet again later.'

As it happened, I opened the second half of the concert with 'The Sky is Black'. But I felt certain he was no longer there this time, and I privately regretted it. Yet when I left the stage after umpteen encores, Bob Dylan was waiting for me at exactly the same spot in the wings. He hadn't moved, but he did not look very happy.

'I heard you sing "The Sky is Black".'

'And you didn't like it.'

'No, I don't sing it that way at all.'

'I know, but it's my way of loving it, and it got to a whole lot of French fans.'

And off we went again, back to my dressing room. Did we have enough night ahead of us to reach agreement?

He finally got his interview out of the way and joined us at Alice's. Now he wanted to hear about my favorite songs, and I sensed that he was trying to get an idea of the influences that had shaped me. I talked at some length about Ella Fitzgerald, Billie Holiday, Quincy Jones, Harry Belafonte, and Mahalia Jackson, and then of course about Maria Callas. Maria Callas, who had died one year before, the same year as my mother, and who was often on my mind during that tour.

'Who is that one?'

'You don't know La Callas?'

'Nope, never heard of her.'

'Well, then, let me introduce you to her. She was the greatest singer in the world, the most talented, the kindest-hearted. She was Greek too, and I like to think that part of her soul has lived on inside me.'

'Who else do you like?'

'Oum Kalsoum.'

'Aha, now that's different. Oum Kalsoum is my favorite singer. I love her! She's the greatest!'

About a week later, I came across a long interview with Bob Dylan in *Rolling Stone*. The interviewer asked him to name his favorite female singers, and I was surprised to read 'Nana Mouskouri and Oum Kalsoum'!

Soon after that, Bob Dylan called me:

'Nana, I've written a song for you, "Every Grain of Sand".' I think it's you.'

I would later record that song with Alain Goraguer, not only in English but in German too.

My friendship with Bob Dylan thus developed by fits and starts. It continued until time and minor misunderstanding drove us apart.

When he came to Bercy in Paris in the Eighties, André and I made the trip from Geneva to listen to him. At the intermission, I tried to get to his dressing room to say hello. A big crowd jostled outside the door, and when I asked his manager I was rather summarily dismissed.

'Bob doesn't want to see anyone. He wants everyone to go away. There's no point insisting.'

'Fine, I understand. Would you just tell him I'm in the audience and thinking of him?'

I was on the point of taking my seat again when the same manager came down, hot on my heels.

'I'm sorry, Bob would like to speak to you as soon as possible.'

We hurried back to the dressing room. Bob was in the same excited state as when we were at Alice's in Los Angeles.

'What are you doing after the show?' he asked me.

'A million people want to talk to you, Bob. I imagine they've laid on some kind of reception. It would be best if I left you alone, I'm a bit tired anyway ...'

'No, nothing's been laid on. Have dinner with me, I need to talk to you.'

'OK, we'll see, but don't put yourself out.'

He finished his concert, and since I was truly feeling a little off-color I didn't return to his dressing room. André and I just went home to bed.

Around four in the morning, the phone woke me. It was his manager again.

'Nana? Bob's expecting you. He's mad as hell. Could you come over right away?'

'No, I'm very sorry but I don't feel well. Tell him I'll call tomorrow.'

'Tomorrow he goes back to the United States, you won't be able to reach him.'

'Well then, tell him I'll talk to him in the States.'

But without knowing it, I had hurt Bob's feelings, and when our paths crossed in Australia in 2001 he didn't answer the short message I left him.

The respectable welcome that greeted *Roses and Sunshine* opened the doors of country music for me in North America, and I returned to Europe to celebrate my twentieth year as a singer at the Olympia. The papers noted that during those years I had notched up a total of sixty-seven Gold Records across the world. This, they pointed out, made me 'the most international of all French-speaking singers.'

I might have been an acclaimed international performer, but was I a happy woman? After three years of utter loneliness, André was now a discreet part of my life. Why had it taken us so long to come together? I've already said how deeply the intelligence and subtlety of this man affected me, but he was married, which made it impossible for me to think of him other than as a friend. Frank Hardy, on the other hand, was all too free, and so very insistent! Passionate letters, poems, and small-hours phone calls ... He too affected me, but I had not the slightest amorous inclination toward him, doubtless because I felt unable to give him everything he expected of me. His despair was immense, unfathomable. Where could I (who so badly needed to be loved and comforted) ever have found the strength to reconcile him to the possibility of happiness? His despair frightened me. I could imagine getting lost in it, drowning in it, and I found myself gradually erecting defenses against this great rebel whose furious energy was beginning to wear me down. I was very willing to fight, but in my own way, for example by giving flowers to soldiers. I was no revolutionary. I had been hurt quite enough by hatred, I had been too close to death during the war, for me to start hurling threats at the world.

André had never been insistent. Not once had he spoken about himself throughout those three years. I would arrive and find him at Orly or Charles de Gaulle, holding flowers, smiling and reserved. He knew how sad I was to leave my children, and the flowers were his way of telling me. One day, he told me he was divorced, nothing more, but it took me some time to realize that henceforth he was a free man. Little by little, I began to look on him with new eyes. He was handsome and romantic, and we shared our passion for music. Then came my mother's death, and André's comforting words – and I suddenly realized that he brought the same open-heartedness to life in general as he brought to artistic creation.

I believe I let myself sink into love, exactly as one wonders anew at the arrival of spring. How long had he been in love with me? We never spoke of it. We simply accepted this unhoped-for happiness without question. For once, I felt guilty about nothing, unless it was because I was happy. Neither of us imagined that anyone would reproach us for this love. But we were wrong.

Since our separation, George had been hatching a sullen hatred for André. I knew it without knowing it. When I went to Athens soon after our separation to tell my parents that we intended to divorce, I heard from all my friends that George was openly criticizing André, telling everyone that he was the cause of our separation. It was ridiculous. But George had nursed the same suspicions about Quincy Jones, Irving Green, and Serge Lama, and I had put his scandal-mongering down to his disoriented state. Then I had dismissed it from my mind. Three years went by. André and I were now in the opening phase of a love affair that seemed likely to last, and naturally I wanted to put my children and Fernande in the picture. My dream was to rebuild our family around

André. I couldn't imagine this man – sensitive, discreet, devoted to art – failing to appeal to Nicolas and Hélène.

With infinite care but, despite everything, a little flustered at having to speak to them of my life as a grownup woman (they were only nine and seven respectively), I told them that André and I were thinking of marriage. The second I did so, I sensed their negative reaction to the mere mention of his name. Could George have been talking to them about André? Only then did I think back to George's earlier remarks, and I turned to Fernande. If anything of the kind had taken place, Féfé (who spent every school vacation at George's home in Corfu with the children and George's second wife) would know.

But as soon as I mentioned André, I saw Fernande's expression close down. It was not difficult to imagine the hostile light in which she saw him. What could George have been saying? Fernande greeted everything I told her in icy silence, as though she knew a lot more than I did.

I had approached my loved ones overflowing with illusions. When I left them, I was absolutely shattered. I was certain that they had been deliberately lied to. It was cruel and unjust to André, to me, and to my children, who were now primed to turn their backs on a man far out of the ordinary. What I didn't understand was how and why such harm had been done. Neither André nor I had ever betrayed George's secrets, so why was he pursuing us with such hatred?

I thrashed around in this silent nightmare, desperate to find out what had been said so that I could set things right and to find the words to present André in his real light.

But the facts were much more complicated than I at first realized. Shortly before her death in 1992, Fernande told me that many letters were exchanged after it became known that André and I intended to live together. A hefty correspondence between André's first wife and Odile Hazan, between Odile Hazan and Fernande ... On top of George's malicious innuendo, it amounted to portraying André as a man who had wrecked two families and made several children unhappy.

Although ignorant at the time of these busy exchanges, I sensed something like a conspiracy in the air, and soon gave up trying to battle against Fernande's mute veto. What surprises me today, as I unravel the long strands of my life for this book, is my memory of passivity, my *own* passivity. Why didn't I just fight Fernande and force her to accept André's presence in my life? Why did I let myself be terrorized by that woman? Was it fear of losing her? Was it my lifelong horror of quarrels? Everything happened as though, having relinquished authority to Fernande for so many years, I now felt obliged to comply with her opinions. Looking back, I believe this was my way of assuaging my ever-present guilt at having abandoned my children to her. While I sang my way across the world, she had supplanted me, she had lavished on them the affection I was unable to give. Deep within me, I must certainly have thought that she had the right to punish me.

Whatever the reason, we all suffered in consequence. André never came to the house until after Fernande was dead, and then only rarely, as if both of us felt we were violating a taboo. Only then, when they were both in their twenties, did Hélène and Nicolas get to know the man of my life – and give me the delectable surprise of hearing them say: 'Why didn't you introduce us to him earlier? We're all interested in the same things, you must have seen that, it's such a pleasure talking to him.'

So we were secret lovers for all those years. We met only when I was passing through Paris, in the feverish days that preceded every tour. But it was enough to teach me how different and how fulfilling love can be when it's guided by the wish to make the other happy, and not just by the need for personal reassurance. It was André who revealed this new horizon to me. André, whose critical eye constantly urged me to surpass myself. And the more I succeeded, the more André himself grew in his turn. As a teenage girl I thought my parents *did not know* how to love, simply because they had never been taught how, and I believe now that I already had an inkling of the love I felt for André. Yet George and I had never been able to find the necessary key.

André sought always to bring me out into the light. And in that spirit, he gave me a song that was to circumnavigate the planet in the early Eighties: 'Je chante avec toi liberté' ('I Sing with You, Freedom').

For many years, André had itched to open the doors to classical music for me. In 1972, he had me record both the Gounod and the Schubert versions of *Ave Maria*. He also persuaded me to sing Mozart and certain

In New York, I was a guest on Johnny Carson's very popular talk show. First he asked me where I came from, who I was, what I thought about my tours with Harry Belafonte. Then he asked me for a live rendering of *Prelude*.

WHERE HAS THE PILGRIM GONE?

Where has the pilgrim gone
Tossing her raven head
Arching her brow
Will the winds of the west
Waken her now?

Frank Hardy

Frank Hardy is an Australian writer, sensitive and intelligent, with whom I had a close, affectionate and platonic relationship for several years. On returning from my first Australian tour I found a poem he had sent me: 'Where Has the Pilgrim Gone?' Did he want the west winds to bring me back to him? Over the years, we kept up an intense correspondence without knowing too clearly where fate was leading us.

Leonard Cohen

At the Greek Theater in Los Angeles, I finally met the man whose poetry had haunted me for years: Bob Dylan! It was Leonard Cohen (left) who introduced us. Leonard and I got on very well, and could spend the whole night following a concert talking about how to approach this or that song. He brought Dylan (below) into my dressing room for the first time only seconds before I was due onstage.

In Auckland with King Constantine II, then in exile. I met the King many years before, when he was about to marry Princess Anne-Marie of Denmark. The royal family invited me to sing at a farewell reception to mark Anne-Marie's imminent departure for Athens.

At the Royal Variety Performance in London, meeting HRH the Queen Mother.

Greece tugged at my heartstrings. I was about to turn fifty, and had sung on all the world's stages, but the colonels' dictatorial regime had turned me away from my own country. Then, with the restoration of democracy, I thought the Greeks had forgotten me. So I almost stopped breathing when I was invited to give a major concert in Athens to salute ten years of the reestablishment of democracy. For the occasion, I was given the extraordinary, ancient Theater of Herodus Atticus, hugging the slopes of the Acropolis.

Melina Mercouri

During the military dictatorship, Melina Mercouri had toured European capitals to alert their governments to Greece's sorrows. When I last saw her she was an actress and singer. Now she was Minister of Culture in a restored democracy, and one of Greece's outstanding personalities. Over the years, she became a very close personal friend.

Constantine Karamanlis

In Athens, I was reunited with Greek President Constantine Karamanlis, whom I had met several times during his exile. I told him how ecstatic I was to be there that night, in that wonderful theatre and under a Greek sky after so many years of war and suffering. I had bottomless admiration for this man, who had engineered the return of democracy without shedding a drop of blood.

I met Miltos Evert (above right) through Constantine Karamanlis, a close friend of his. Miltos was responsible for urging me (or perhaps I should say forcing me) to become a member of the European Parliament (below) in 1994.

The United Nations Children's Emergency Fund (UNICEF) asked me to campaign on behalf of children's rights across the world. I threw myself into the effort with all the passion I could muster, and in 1993 was officially selected as a Goodwill Ambassador (far left). One year earlier, I had already undertaken a mission to the street children of Mexico (below). Four years later, UNICEF sent me to Viet Nam to celebrate the country's fiftieth birthday (near left).

After repeated campaigns in the European Parliament for a coming together of the world's religions, I met the Greek Patriarch Bartholomeos (center) in Turkey. The Patriarch introduced me to Pope John Paul II in the course of our discussions.

On September 7 1997 I received the Legion of Honor from Jacques Chirac, President of France.

The commander of French forces in Berlin asked if I would be willing to perform 'Song for Liberty' at the Berlin Wall for Bastille Day celebrations in 1982. Naturally I agreed to extol Liberty in front of the wall that imprisoned East Berliners. Just for the occasion, I was given the rank of a French army officer.

André entered my life little by little. I met him at the very beginning of the Sixties when he was a sound engineer (photo above, when André was twenty-two) at the Blanqui Studios in Paris. I believe I let myself fall in love the way one marvels at the return of spring. By autumn of 1988 we had plucked up the courage to say we wanted to get married. For ten years we had been virtually secret lovers, and now we had finally dared to come out with our story. I at once started dreaming of a party for all our friends – but in fact we didn't take the step until 2003!

JEAN-CLAUDE, BROTHER AND FRIEND

Jean-Claude Brialy and I had known one another for years, but we had always been too busy to get acquainted. It was thanks to Jean-Claude's partner Bruno that we learned to know one another, and then to become inseparable friends.

With my children in Denmark in the Nineties. They had come to be with me for a show in Copenhagen. Lénou is pointing at the Little Mermaid, who gave up her voice in order to acquire legs and win over Prince Charming.

Jean-Claude Brialy died on May 30 2007, just as I was finishing this book about my life. In Cuba, Cairo, Moscow and New York, I learned as I listened to him that behind everything, every happening, even the most harrowing or the ugliest, beauty lies hidden. He taught me how to see, to live for each moment, and simply to love.

Schubert *Lieder*. Now he wanted me to sing the Chorus of the Hebrew Slaves from Verdi's *Nabucco* (*Nebuchadnezzar*). That seemed to be carrying things too far, yet at the same time I was privately struck by a coincidence. *Nebuchadnezzar* was my father's favorite opera, and now here was André proposing that I sing its best-known song.

'But we'd need a chorus. Do you have anyone in mind?'

'You'll have the chorus of the Paris Opera.'

'You think so?'

'I'm sure of it.'

But before thinking about a chorus, we had to arrange the words of Verdi's dazzling composition in the form of a hymn.

It had become our habit to hold work sessions in my little Boulogne apartment. André called in Pierre Delanoë, Claude Lemesle and Alain Goraguer to discuss this adaptation, which struck me as terribly risk-fraught. We worked at it together, then the meeting broke up, and I could see how worried Delanoë and Lemesle looked. Was it possible – a whole century after the composition of a work of this stature – to find contemporary words worthy of it? Words that would not cheapen it? They could never before have faced such a challenge, I thought: certainly, neither they nor I could afford a single slip.

A second session a few days later. They told us they had come up with a beginning. They seemed very excited, and we met again that same afternoon in Boulogne – André, Alain, Claude, and me. Only Pierre Delanoë was missing. At last, he rang the doorbell. When he came in he seemed somewhat breathless, and perhaps more exultant than he wanted to appear.

Alain Goraguer at once sat down at the piano, and Pierre Delanoë sang us the first couplet:

> *Quand tu chantes, je chante avec toi Liberté,*
> *Quand tu pleures, je pleure aussi to peine,*
> *Quand tu trembles, je prie pour toi liberté*
> *Dans la joie ou les larmes, je t'aime . . .*

> When you sing, I sing freedom with you,
> When you weep, I also share your tears,

When you tremble, I pray for your freedom
In joy or in tears, I love you . . .

And there he stopped. They hadn't yet found the rest, but what did it matter? As soon as he sang 'When you sing, I sing freedom with you,' I felt my heart leap, and we were all caught up in such intense emotion that we had tears in our eyes when Pierre fell silent.

'That's magnificent, that's exactly right,' breathed André.

We all embraced before giving free rein to our joy.

With such a beginning, we knew failure was no longer a possibility.

As André predicted, the Opera chorus readily agreed to accompany me, and in mid 1981 we recorded 'Je chante avec toi liberté'. It seemed clear to us that this should be the title of the new album, but Louis Hazan wasn't so sure, and on his advice we named the album after a song by Claude Lemesle and Alain Goraguer, 'Qu'il est loin l'amour'.

A few days after the album came out, I was asked to take part in one of those mammoth TV music broadcasts organized by Maritie and Gilbert Carpentier. Joan Baez was also there, and we decided to sing a duet together, 'Plaisir d'amour', the song which had established my French identity. Two days earlier, the Carpentiers asked me which of the songs from my new album I would like to perform. I briefly hesitated, doubtless influenced by Louis Hazan's reservations, but then, despite everything, I plumped for 'Je chante avec toi liberté'. That night, I sang it for the first time from a television stage.

Then something astonishing happened: in the next few minutes, the switchboard of the television station was flooded by calls. Hundreds, even thousands, of people wanted to know the title of that song.

Next morning, the first print of my album sold out in a few hours. Overwhelmed, the recording company raced to reissue it. But the demand was so great that it was impossible to satisfy it without asking several other producers to come to our rescue. It reached a point where we were selling more than seventy thousand albums a day! An overnight Gold Record, my nineteenth French album became a Triple Platinum in the space of a few weeks.

I then recorded 'Liberté' in German ('Land der Freiheit'), in English

('Song for Liberty'), in Spanish ('Libertad'), and in Portuguese ('Liberdade'), and everywhere the song received the same welcome. It marked my return to Spain and opened up Latin America for me. It introduced me to both Portugal and Brazil. My French sales amounted to two million, plus those in the United Kingdom and the Commonwealth, and I was ahead in all the German bestseller charts.

I like to imagine that Giuseppe Verdi would not have been unhappy with the special destiny awaiting 'Liberté' in Berlin. In the middle of the nineteenth century, Verdi fought for Italian unity alongside the patriots of the *Risorgimento*. Now the commander-in-chief of French forces in Berlin solemnly requested me to sing 'Liberté' in front of the Berlin Wall to celebrate Bastille Day. Seven years before the Wall's demolition and the reunification of the two Germanies, General Jean-Pierre Liron seemed to be trying to force destiny's hand with the help of the great Verdi and with the words we had been bold enough to lend to his music.

Of course I agreed. In fact, it was the only way of protesting, of *making war*, that I could allow myself. To sing freedom in front of the wall holding East Berliners captive, the wall where so many Germans bent on freedom had been killed – I was all for it! For the occasion, I was the guest of the general and his wife, and enjoyed the services of an aide-de-camp. I also sang 'La Marseillaise', which I found intimidating. The effort reminded me in timely fashion that I was not French despite this honor paid to me.

The day after the event, the general gave me a copy of the page-long coverage in the daily *Bild-Zeitung*. The paper showed me standing to attention in French uniform, singing into a mic with eyes closed, which conveys better than I can my feelings as I sang the French national anthem for the first time.

'The secret of the three cue cards,' said the paper. 'Or why singing star Nana Mouskouri kept her eyes lowered as she sang the French national anthem during yesterday's Berlin celebrations.

'The forty-five-year-old Greek singing star Nana Mouskouri ('Wiesse Rosen aus Athen') had a little trick up her sleeve to help her find her way through an error-filled text she sang during the parade of France's defense forces in Berlin:

'Three gigantic handwritten cue cards at her feet allowed her to read off the exact words of the French national anthem which she sang to the assembled guests.

'Nana (wearing a French uniform for the singing of "La Marseillaise") had to keep shifting her gaze lower and lower. Many guests of honor on the viewing platform believed it was emotion that impelled her to close her eyes.

'Although Nana Mouskouri lives in Paris, she was nevertheless somewhat concerned that she might trip up over the exact wording of the anthem.

'Nana's trepidations were laid to rest only when the 300-man choir of the Gendarmerie came to her support.

'The guests of honor and the three thousand Berlin spectators greeted the singer's efforts with thunderous applause.

'The parade, in honor of the French national holiday (the storming of the Bastille in 1789), was organized by French Ambassador Henri Froment-Meurice and French commander-in-chief General Jean-Pierre Liron.

'More than 1,100 soldiers took part in the parade in front of the Reinickendorf City Hall, along with 171 military vehicles (including thirty-five tanks). Three paratroops landed right in front of the viewing stand, although one of them had to disentangle his chute from a nearby tree.'[31]

---

[31] *Bild-Zeitung*, 15 July 1982 (English translation).

23

A Homecoming Concert

*A*nd suddenly Greece was calling me. I would soon turn fifty and had sung on every stage in the world, but it was twenty years since I had performed in my homeland. The dictators' regime had turned me away from Greece and now, with democracy restored, I felt that I was forgotten there, no longer known. So that when I was told that Constantine Karamanlis, now first president of the young Greek Republic, had sent for me, I went briefly into shock. My admiration for Karamanlis, whom I had known in exile and who had restored our dignity to us without spilling a single drop of blood, was boundless. How could I best serve him? I believe I decided to accept his invitation, to comply with his wishes even before I knew what he expected of me.

What he expected was a major concert in Athens on 24 July 1984 to celebrate the ten years since the restoration of democracy. It was such an honor and at the same time such a responsibility that I spent several days privately oscillating between exhilaration and terror. I wondered whether I would rise to the occasion, whether people would attend, and whether – because of my own long absence – the Greek people would be willing to accept me back.

For the occasion, I was offered the extraordinarily beautiful Theater of Herodus Atticus at the foot of the Acropolis, a venerable site normally reserved for lyrical spectacles and tragedy. It was as if Greece, which had only known me in my earliest days as a minor singer in the nightclubs of Athens, had decided to eliminate the intervening stages of my career in order to make up for all the lost years.

I couldn't have dreamed of a more wonderful gift. Once I cast my doubts aside I threw myself into this great enterprise with the youthful enthusiasm of a child prodigy. It could not have been otherwise, for I would be returning to my first songs, to those poems by Nikos Gatsos, Yannis Ritsos, and Elytis, beautifully set to music by Manos Hadjidakis or Mikis Theodorakis: 'Paper Moon', 'The Young Cypress', 'Somewhere in the World', 'Enos mythos' . . . How long had it been since I devoted a concert to the music on which I was raised? To the poetry so intimately familiar to me before I discovered Paris and the rest of the world? Naturally, I would also sing 'Song for Liberty', which might itself have been written for this great day, a day it illustrated with such power, as well as 'Amazing Grace' and Schubert's 'Ave Maria'.

My dress designer since the late 1970s was Mine Barrat-Vergez, who would soon become an intimate friend. She had an extraordinary talent for dressing her artists on the basis of what she saw as their innermost souls. She was dressmaker for such theater artists and opera singers as Juliette Gréco, Dalida and Barbara. I knew that in her hands I (still almost incapable of loving myself) would be at peace with myself, weightless, sublimated.

We finished with rehearsals, and were about to fly to Athens when one of my Greek guitar players came to see me. He was embarrassed, almost in despair. He had left Greece several years earlier to avoid military service, and was now considered a deserter. He was afraid he would be arrested as soon as we reached Greece.

'You're telling me this now, a week before the concert?'

'Nana, I'm sorry, I was afraid to tell you earlier.'

I tried to think calmly. It was too late to replace him, but I couldn't take the risk of sending him to prison and endangering my concert. The only solution that occurred to me was to appeal to Melina Mercouri, who was now Greece's minister of culture. I still remembered her turning up in a bathrobe with Jules Dassin on that distant night when Manos Hadjidakis composed 'Never on Sunday' . . . We had kept in touch ever since.

'Melina, I'm facing a disaster. I've just learned that one of my musicians is a deserter!'

'Don't you worry, my darling, let me handle everything. Just tell him to send me his papers.'

Two days later I called her again.

'Your guitar player can stop worrying. Someone will meet him at the airport and put him back on the plane three days later. He'll have a safe-conduct.'

But I continued to worry. What if things went wrong? What if the army (which couldn't be all that fond of Melina Mercouri after her international campaigns against the colonels) were looking for a chance to score off her? Racked (as usual) by worry, I spent that night imagining the worst.

Next morning, I decided to call the Greek military authorities myself. I had to be sure of what lay ahead, otherwise I would spend the whole flight in a frenzy of worry. Then another fear swept over me. What if they refused to accept my call, or hung up on me? At once I pictured myself giving my name to the switchboard operator, being obliged to spell it out three times, then being passed from person to person in the icy labyrinth of a barracks, before being told that the commandant was in a meeting and that it would be better to call back tomorrow.

But the exact opposite occurred. I had scarcely mentioned my name before there was a gasp at the other end:

'Madame Mouskouri! Is that really you?'

'Yes, it's me. I have a little problem with one of my musicians ...'

'I'll connect you with the colonel right away, Madame Mouskouri.'

The colonel was equally cordial:

'Madame Mouskouri! What an honor to hear your voice.'

'Thank you, thank you so much. Forgive me for disturbing you, but one of my Greek guitar players ...'

'We know all about it, Madame. We've done the necessary and you'll have no problems. But let me pass you to the general. He'll be so flattered to hear your voice.'

I had a sudden vision, straight out of old-time comic movies, of the colonel clicking his heels to the phone as he called the general.

And the general in his turn assured me that they would not touch a hair on my guitar player's head.

'Oh, thank you, general!'

So much for my fears that people had forgotten me. In fact, the five thousand seats at the Herodus Atticus Theater had been sold out in a few hours (the proceeds going to Greek cultural affairs) and I was thankful that I had bought a few seats in advance for close friends. I was told that many people were seeking feverishly to get their hands on tickets.

My father would of course be there, my sister Jenny and my niece Aliki, as well as Nikos Gatsos and André, the two men in my life. But the guests I most wanted to see were Hélène and Nicolas. They were then on vacation with their father in Corfu, accompanied as usual by Fernande. Nicolas was sixteen, Hélène fourteen, quite old enough to grasp the importance to me of this exceptional occasion, a concert in my own country, at the foot of the Acropolis. I couldn't imagine that they wouldn't be there.

Was it André's presence that put George's back up? Whatever the reason, he seemed to be seeking every possible excuse for not sending the children to me.

'Every Athens flight is full,' he told me. 'There's not a ticket available before July 25.'

I knew this was untrue. 'Then leave it to me,' I said. 'I'll get hold of tickets for them.'

'There's no point. I've tried everything.'

I quickly found three seats and had the tickets delivered to Corfu. Would George let them leave now? Until the very last moment, I hoped so with all my strength. Yet their seats remained empty. Today, more than twenty years later, I can honestly say that their failure to be there remains one of the deepest sorrows of my life – and perhaps the only sin I can never forgive George. I would have given anything for Hélène and Nicolas to be present in Athens on the day Greece finally recognized me. I had triumphed all over the world and sung in most of its great capitals, but I had never been acknowledged by my own people. Now it suddenly seemed to me that I had taken that long journey with only one goal in mind – to attract the attention of this small country which brought me into the world and then seemed to have forgotten me. To me, the concert should have represented our reconciliation with Greece, should have told Hélène and Nicolas that they hadn't emerged from nowhere, but from here, from this sun-baked, arid land where I was celebrated and loved.

*

President Karamanlis sat in the front row. Most of his cabinet, including of course Melina Mercouri, sat with him. I wanted to tell them all how moved I was to be there, in that theater, under that sky, after so much fighting and so much suffering. But when I came onstage and the first ripple of applause ran down from top to bottom of that ancient amphitheater, I was suddenly afraid I would burst into tears. I immediately sought refuge in the music. One day Manos Hadjidakis had confided to Nikos that when he watched me sing he had the impression he was seeing a woman getting undressed. It wasn't Nikos who told me this, but a sound engineer who heard them chatting. Well, as I stood there that evening in a spotless dress, I felt more strongly than ever that I was naked, that my soul was stripped bare.

I felt I was reaching the end of the long journey begun forty years before on the stage of Papa's small theater. My hands no longer bothered me the way they did in the days when I kept them hidden behind my back. I was no longer aware of my figure, my glasses, my too wide-spaced eyes, of everything people criticized in me and that I criticized in myself. I had become – can I really be writing this? – music itself. That was exactly what I had yearned for at twelve, at fourteen – that people would one day forget my appearance and hear only my voice. And now that wish had come true. If I had possessed the courage, I could have left the stage forever after that night.

Moreover, I was publicly repaying my emotional debt to Constantine Karamanlis, as though we were never to see one another again. Toward the end, I came down from the stage to stand in front of him as I sang 'Kapou ipari agapi mou' ('My Love is Somewhere'), his favorite. It was the song that earned me the top award at the first Festival of Greek Song in 1959. After the contest Karamanlis told me: 'No song moves me so deeply. Manos Hadjidakis is a musician of immense talent, but he's lucky to have you.'

The morning after that concert in the Theater of Herodus Atticus, the president called to thank me. 'I've known you forever,' he said, 'but last night you knocked me off my feet. Thank you, Nana! Thank you! Go on casting your spell over us, over the whole world, and never forget Greece. You are the living embodiment of our country.

When you sing, you allow the face and soul of our country to be seen.'

I had dreamed of introducing my two children to Karamanlis, and they arrived the day after the concert. After the wound deliberately inflicted by George, their visit was obviously destined to go badly. And it went horribly badly. They were frigid, sulky, closed, and Fernande didn't utter a word. The hotel I reserved was not to their taste, nor was the beach we went to. I finally exploded:

'Fernande, you might at least make an effort to be friendly. I've tried to organize things to please all three of you, but nothing seems good enough. It's as if your only wish is to leave as soon as possible.'

'Well, yes, Madame. If you want the truth, I have absolutely no desire to be here. And I believe the children feel the same way as I do.'

That was the straw that broke the camel's back. What gave Fernande the right to speak in my children's name? How dare she treat me this way – criticizing everything, sulking, encouraging the children's hateful attitude? For the very first time, I told her everything that was bottled up inside me. And, with my anger fanned by their absence from the concert, I undoubtedly went too far. What happened next staggered me, stunned me: Hélène and Nicolas at once leapt to Fernande's defense! All three were ganged up against me, and the children in their turn told me what was in their hearts: yes, it was true, they had not wanted to come.

'But why? If there were only one concert you should ever have attended it was this one!'

'It was your fault we didn't come.'

'Why? What in heaven's name did I do to deserve this?'

'We don't want to see André, Mama. He's not our father, and it's because of him that Papa is unhappy and we're all unhappy today.'

I recognized George's words, his resentment of André, the hatred he felt for him. It was easy to guess the things George had said about him to the children – and to Fernande, who had never accepted our divorce even though it left her free to rule our home on her own.

'The children don't wish to know this man who has separated you from their father,' added George's ever-loyal Fernande.

It was all untrue. Andre hadn't separated me from George. We sep-

arated because George was on the point of stifling me, because I would
have died slowly in the world he planned for us. But how could I explain
all this to the children in this climate of hysteria? All at once, I realized
how wrong I had been to let Fernande dig this deep ditch between them
and me. I should have been able to find the right words to explain the
profound reasons behind our divorce. I should have found the courage
to make them accept my love for André. That would have given them
an accurate perception of the rights and wrongs on both sides. Instead,
I let myself be intimidated by Fernande's mute opposition to the arrival
of another man. And I left the field clear for George who (obsessed by
his old demon, jealousy) was now rewriting our family history.

'Fernande, stop interfering in what doesn't concern you! You're stupidly repeating every word George says and instead of helping the
children see things clearly you're leading them astray.'

I had never spoken so sharply to her, and she burst into tears.

'If that's the case, Madame,' she sobbed, 'I'll go straight back to
Geneva and take the children with me.'

And that was all it took for me to lay down my weapons! Any other
woman would of course have said: 'Go back if you want to, Fernande,
but you'll go alone. These children are mine, and their future is none of
your business.' But I couldn't grant myself such freedom. I felt far too
guilty myself. Guilty for giving precedence to my life as an artist, to my
passion for music and the stage. And so, pitiful though it must seem, I
stepped back from my anger and tried to persuade her to remain, to
convince her that everything could be set to rights with a little good
will.

And it was Fernande who returned to the driver's seat (if indeed she
ever left it!). Next day, she flew back to Geneva with Hélène and Nicolas,
leaving me feeling utterly lost.

A few months before my return to Greece, I sang for four weeks, and
for the first time, at Paris' Palais des Congrès. And right after Greece I
left again for a third Pacific tour, opening in New Zealand.

We landed in Auckland in the middle of the night, worn out by our
twenty-four-hour flight. Around six in the morning the phone dragged
me out of a deep sleep. Where was I? My surroundings were completely

unfamiliar. Dazed by fatigue and jetlagged, I struggled for a moment to reconstruct the immediate past. Oh yes! New Zealand, my hotel, good Lord, how tired I am! And that shrill telephone! Who besides André and the children knew where I was? The children! Immediately beside myself with worry, I picked up. But it was a man's voice at the other end, and this man spoke to me in Greek.

'Madame Mouskouri?'

'Yes, speaking. Who is calling?'

'The king.'

'The king? What king? Are you making fun of me?'

'Not at all. May I speak to you for a moment?'

'Listen, I have no idea who you are, but we got here from Europe in the middle of the night and I'd like to be allowed to sleep.'

'I'm truly sorry to insist, but I myself am leaving for Los Angeles this afternoon and I absolutely have to meet you before then.'

'But who on earth are you?'

'I already told you, I'm the king, Constantine. Don't you recognize my voice?'

'Oh, your majesty! Is it really you?'

'Of course it's me. I'm so sorry for interrupting your sleep.'

'No, no, I'm the one who's sorry, I spoke so unpleasantly . . .'

'It's of no importance, it's my fault. May I count on meeting you at noon?'

'Of course. Tell me where and I'll be there.'

And a few hours later I met Constantine and his aide-de-camp on the hotel terrace. He was quite unfazed by way I had addressed him. Indeed, he replayed our conversation to me, roaring with laughter as he recalled my amazement. He had a favor to ask of me before he left. He had established a Greek school in London, and wondered if I would agree to give a benefit concert for it. I was happy to do so, and we arranged to meet in London. I didn't suspect that my renewed contact with our exiled monarch would lead by roundabout ways to dinner at the table of the queen of England . . .

After New Zealand, I flew to Australia. Once again, I sang at the Sydney Opera House. Then I moved on to Melbourne, Canberra, Hobart, Adelaide, and Perth. As always, the welcome I encountered in Australia was overwhelming. Full houses, flowers, encores, and on every street a devastating warm-heartedness. 'Mouskouri Superb', ran the headline in the *Canberra Times*, echoed by the Perth *West Australian*'s 'Hard to Forget Nana'.

The media had gotten wind of my friendship with Frank Hardy, with whom I had corresponded regularly for ten years. ('The Best of Friends – Frank and Nana' was the title of an article in a Sydney weekly.) And I was touched to read the compliment below, penned by Helen Trikilis, a reporter who interviewed my writer friend:

'Frank attributes his development as a writer during the past ten years largely to Nana.

'"She has been a positive influence on my character. I am a better writer now than I was – and that has been partly because I have known Nana," he said.

'"She has a certain wisdom because of her sadness," he said. One of Nana's favourite lines is one that Frank wrote for her – "sadness is close to loving."

'Frank said: "Sadness is a very clean emotion, not like jealousy or even love. It comes from a person with a kind heart – like Nana."'

Some time later, the benefit gala at St James's Palace for King Constantine's London school turned out to be a success. As we were about to say goodbye, the exiled sovereign took me to one side. He hoped to organize a big party for the fortieth birthday of his wife, Queen Anna-Maria, and he wondered if I would consent to sing for the occasion.

'With great pleasure!'

'You know,' Constantine told me, 'she's never forgotten that evening when you came to sing in Copenhagen for all her childhood friends before she left for Athens.'

'I haven't forgotten either. It was a very moving experience. And next day, I sang at the *Humanité* party! I didn't dare tell you at the time!'

Constantine burst out laughing.

'Well, this time there'll be a lot more crowned heads to cheer you on. My sister will be there – Queen Sophia of Spain – my step-sister Queen Margaret II of Denmark, Queen Noor of Jordan, and the Empress of

Iran, Farah Diba ... But don't be anxious, I won't abandon you, we'll both be at my aunt's table.'

'Very good! Wonderful!'

I had no idea who his aunt was, but I pictured a kindly, witty old lady who would put herself out to make me feel at home.

The great day came around. That evening I wore a dress created for me by Per Spook for the TV broadcast at which I first sang 'Song for Liberty'. It was magnificent, glistening with pearls, the only snag being that I had put on a little weight since then. Since it was now a little tight-fitting, I promised myself I would eat nothing beforehand in order to avoid making things worse. In any case, I never ate anything before singing.

The reception took place at Claridge's, drawing a small patient knot of bystanders attracted by the busy to-and-fro of limousines outside the Palace. Did they realize how distinguished the guest-list was? Once inside, you had to stand in the line of guests waiting to be officially introduced to the Greek sovereigns. Queen Anna-Maria kissed me, saying she was happy to see me again, while King Constantine had a few encouraging words for me, and suddenly I was swimming among faces so well-known I felt dizzy. Prince Charles and Lady Di were there, while Juan Carlos of Spain chatted with the Swedish monarchs. Fortunately, Farah Diba recognized me, and it was with great relief that I sought protection under her wing. She perfectly remembered my performance at the Palais de Chaillot twenty years before, during her first official visit to General de Gaulle's France in the company of her young husband, the Shah of Iran. And I hadn't forgotten her flowers on the evening of my first singing assignment at the Olympia. Since then, Farah had tried several times to invite me to Iran, but I had never been free. Now I had the chance to tell her how sorry I was.

Then they announced that dinner was served, and King Constantine came to interrupt us.

'Come, Nana,' he said, 'you're with me at my aunt's table. You too, Farah.'

I followed him, curious to know who this *aunt* might be. On our way we greeted a number of crowned heads introduced by Constantine as the guests looked about for their seats. There were many tables, and our progress was slow. But at length we reached our table, which was round and prominently situated. That was all I took in amidst the general confusion. By now I had looked into so many faces that I no longer really saw anyone. When Constantine turned solemnly toward me and said, 'Nana, allow me to introduce you to my aunt,' I assumed a polite, almost absentminded smile.

I took the elegant hand extended to me, and looking up I saw a smile it took me a split second to recognize ... My God, it was the Queen of England! I think I actually staggered. Was I dreaming, or was it really Elizabeth II, her smile deepening as she held my hand in hers?

'My dear, I'm so happy to meet you. Whenever Constantine mentions you he smiles most charmingly. I know that you sang at the Royal Palace in Copenhagen and in Greece too, I believe, for Sophia's engagement.'

I heard her, but I was so awed that words failed me. I believe all I could say was a few pitiful 'Thank yous' before Constantine came to my rescue.

So the Queen of England sat at the head of our table, presiding over Queen Noor, Farah Diba, King Constantine, the United States ambassador, Prince Michael of Greece ... and me. And Constantine had assumed that mention of his 'aunt' would put me at my ease! I would have given anything to be seated at another table in the farthest corner of the room.

They served the first dish. It was a Greek hors d'oeuvres, a few olives and some meatballs. I adore meatballs, so I said to myself, 'This is all I'm going to eat,' planning to give the other dishes a discreet miss so that I wouldn't be full when time came to sing. But then I saw how the American ambassador was struggling to spear his meatballs. They seemed very hard, and his fork wouldn't pierce them; indeed, there were two or three occasions when they almost flew off his plate. I at once imagined the worst: I too would bungle my fork-handling and send a meatball flying onto the plate of Elizabeth II, seated right across the table from me. What a humiliation that would be! I would be forced to flee the gathering. All right, I said to myself, meatballs are out, definitely out, and I set down my knife and fork without attempting another dish.

But our waiter was discreetly insistent.

'Miss Mouskouri, you haven't touched a thing. You must eat some-thing if you want to have the strength to sing.'

Clearly, the staff had passed the word around, and I sensed.that they were impatient to hear that part of the program.

'Thank you,' I told the waiter, 'but I mustn't eat before singing.'

At that, the whole table turned toward me, and half-dead with shame I was forced to explain myself. To placate the Queen of England, who was now looking fondly at me as though I were a vulnerable little thing, I managed to swallow a few mouthfuls of spinach, but my stage-fright was so acute that they sat heavily on my stomach. It occurred to me that the Sydney Opera or the Palais des Congrès were nothing in comparison to this floorful of monarchs. 'Lord,' I said to myself, 'how I hope they call on me soon. Every minute is sheer torture.'

The call finally came. I sang first in Greek, then in English, and I finished in French with 'Plaisir d'amour'. This mini-concert wasn't supposed to last more than forty-five minutes, but to my great surprise the applause reached a crescendo at the end, and I came back on to the little stage for a last song, 'Amazing Grace'. Then King Constantine presented me with an enormous bouquet, and the guests rose to dance.

It was at this point that the Duke of Edinburgh arrived, wearing a tuxedo but also, and most curiously, sporting training shoes.

'There you are, Philip!' cried the Queen of England. 'You're too late for Miss Mouskouri. She was wonderful.'

The Duke greeted me, and then asked me to excuse his footwear. He had just come in on his all-terrain vehicle, he said, which he liked to drive himself.

As I left the scene, I took away with me my last glimpse of that extraordinary evening – King Constantine giving his arm to Lady Di, Juan Carlos executing an elegant waltz with Farah Diba, Caroline of Monaco in the arms of the Grand Duke of Luxembourg, and Queen Sophia dancing with Prince Michael of Greece . . .

That year, 1986, I returned to the Olympia. The comedian Thierry Le Luron had been ill for some time, and I took advantage of my long stay in Paris to spend time with him between rehearsals. We had been friends for only five or six years, but I felt that this little man, whose humor could be lethal, had always shown me his gentlest side. We had funny conversations about love, about the celebrity life, about wisdom, about music.

Thierry – aping Gilbert Bécaud – was the man who had all France singing 'L'emmerdant, c'est la rose' ('The Rose is the Problem'), halfway through the long presidency of François Mitterrand, who had chosen the rose as his symbol. Dalida, Mireille Mathieu, Brigitte Bardot and François Mitterrand had all been been victims of his genius for imitation.

'And why have you never imitated me?' I asked him one day.

'Because I can't.'

'I don't believe you.'

I guessed that he imitated me very well, in fact – all alone in front of his mirror, donning my square glasses and closing his eyes – but that since we were friends he was afraid of hurting me.

Some days, he was exhausted, and on others, he said, he felt revived. So he promised to be at the Olympia on opening night. It had become a kind of joke between us.

'Get a lot of rest so you'll be on form that night, Thierry,' I told him.

'I'll be there, I promise.'

But one day before opening night, he withdrew his promise.

'I'm afraid I can't be there, Nana. I'm worn out.'

'Then take good care of yourself and come some other night.'

I was in my dressing room an hour before the dress rehearsal when there was a knock at my door. It was André. With him was Thierry's manager, Roland Hubert. Both men were pale as death.

'Nana, Thierry . . . Thierry has passed away.'

'Oh, no!'

In such moments you feel as if you have plunged into the nothingness a death inevitably brings with it, and you scrabble for a hold on what you and the departed last said to one another, what you promised one another. As though words could still have meaning. You say stupid things. You say 'No, it can't be, only yesterday he . . .' I felt the same stupefaction I experienced when Jenny announced Mama's death to me as I stood in that vast concert hall in Frankfurt overlooking the autobahn. And once again, I kept saying, 'It can't be ... it can't be ...' And then, very slowly, you begin to comprehend the void inside you, the absolute powerlessness, and you begin to weep because the only sanctuary left to you is tears.

'André, I don't want to sing tonight ... Go and tell the audience I don't have the strength. Please! Please!'

'The house is full, Nana, you can't do that.'

'But I won't be able to ... You can see that, can't you? How can I sing in this state?'

'Do it for Thierry. The audience will hear the news when they leave, so it would be much better if you told them yourself, right away. Most of them loved him or knew him personally. They'll understand. It will be a special evening, all about Thierry.'

Patricia Coquatrix burst in during this exchange. She heartily agreed with André. It was too late to postpone: I had to sing. So I decided to dedicate this opening night to Thierry as André had just suggested.

I no longer recall the words I said when I came onstage. My chief concern was not to weep, to announce Thierry's death in a dignified manner, and to tell them I would be singing for him, whose front-row seat remained empty (although many of his friends, including Line Renaud and Jean-Claude Brialy, were there).

And then I sang, and once again music came to my rescue, as though it were the only language capable of transcending death, of speaking to us of another world where time was no longer counted off.

When it was over, I didn't respond to the encores, but I came back onstage to sing Schubert's 'Ave Maria' a cappella. It was not on the program, of course, but I felt the need to sing it the way you feel the urge to enter a church in order to weep in silence.

In *France-Soir* next day, Jacqueline Cartier wrote that 'standing face to face with Nana Mouskouri, who sang without her musicians, the audience wept and applauded simultaneously.'[32]

*

---

[32] *France-Soir*, 15 November 1986.

I'm not sure why I agreed to sing 'Ave Maria' again at the church of La Madeleine for Thierry's funeral service. When I left the stage, they all rushed into my Olympia dressing room to request it of me: André, Jean-Claude Brialy, Roland Hubert, the Coquatrix family.

'No, I couldn't. I nearly broke down just now, you're asking the impossible.'

'Do it for Thierry,' Jean-Claude insisted. 'He was very fond of you. You owe it to him.'

And naturally I agreed.

But when the day came I was so choked with feelings that I lost my voice, and the 'Ave Maria' I gave Thierry's friends was drowned in tears.

A few days later, a remorseful Jean-Claude Brialy whispered kindly into my ear: 'Um, I want you to know that I've just added to my will my absolute refusal to have you sing "Ave Maria" at my funeral.'

24

My Last Journey with Manos and Nikos

So Greece had not forgotten me, and my recital at the Theater of Herodus Atticus suddenly restored links severed by the dark years of dictatorship. The live album of that show very quickly achieved Gold Record status in my country, and was shortly afterward elevated to a Platinum Disk. Throughout those years, Nikos Gatsos had never abandoned me for a second. We never stopped talking to one another, sometimes spending whole nights on the phone. Now Nikos wanted to make a new recording with me. Perhaps he had been nursing the idea for years without finding the courage to propose it, knowing as he did that I would be in Sydney one day, in Montreal the next, and in London on the morrow. But now that I was willingly retracing the meanderings of my earliest years, why wouldn't I also want to reconnect with the poetry of Nikos, who had initiated me to the world's solemnity and splendor?

I jumped at the idea, of course. André, who had come to know Nikos, encouraged us to follow the project through. The only problem was finding someone to put Nikos' lines to music, since Manos Hadjidakis claimed, for reasons I failed to understand, that we had quarreled. Perhaps he simply refused to forgive me for *betraying* him by working with other composers. But Nikos was sure that we would sooner or later make friends again, and meanwhile, he introduced me to a most talented young composer, Yorgos Hadjinassios, whose musical sense he greatly admired.

They both worked in the same inspired frenzy, and by the time I returned to Greece again, their songs were ready. One in particular had an overwhelming effect on me. Nikos had entitled it 'The Eleventh Commandment'. Its power and the despair it evoked recalled Bob Dylan's 'A Hard Rain's a-Gonna Fall'. Nikos had spent his whole life in the shadow of wars and tyranny, and in his song he seeks reasons for the tragedies which continue to darken the world, wondering aloud which commandment we have flouted to deserve so much suffering. What was this eleventh commandment which we have chosen to ignore – or which Heaven has deliberately kept hidden from us?

I recorded that album on the kind of emotional wave that swept me through my singing of 'Never on Sunday', standing beside and watching his fingers flow over the piano keys. And all three of us agreed to entitle the album *Endekati endoli* (*The Eleventh Commandment*).

The record came out while the live recording of my Athens concert was still in people's minds. As a result, it was an immediate hit. For the concert, I had dusted off my very first Greek songs. This time I was coming back with new musical compositions and the luminous verses of Nikos Gatsos, now finally acknowledged as one of our great contemporary poets.

It was the record's popularity among young people that inspired the Mayor of Athens, Miltos Evert, to organize a major event: a concert on the grand scale in Athens' Kalimarmaro stadium, which could seat more than a hundred thousand spectators.

I met Miltos Evert through Constantine Karamanlis, a close friend of his and one of his young talented ministers. Miltos was extremely enterprising, bubbling with imagination, and ferociously stubborn when he had a goal in mind. It was he who encouraged me (it would be more accurate to write *forced* me) to stand as a member of the European Parliament in 1994. But in the summer of 1986 his only ambition was to have me sing for the young people of Athens. We had dinner on a restaurant terrace. André and Nikos were also there, and suddenly Miltos Evert burst out: 'And what if we brought together our three greatest composers, Manos Hadjidakis, Mikis Theodorakis and Stavros Xarkakos, and you sang songs by all three of them right in the middle of Kalimarmaro Stadium? What do you say to that?'

At first you could have knocked me down with a feather. I had already sung in a sports arena, but that was with Harry Belafonte, and for just twenty thousand spectators. Not one hundred thousand! And Manos and I were no longer speaking to each other. Would he agree to appear onstage with me?

'That sounds fantastic,' I said, 'but I don't believe it's possible.'

'Let's start by asking each of them what he thinks,' said Miltos, fired as always by the smallest hint of an obstacle.

Mikis Theodorakis turned the invitation down flat. A legendary figure of the political left, he was probably unwilling to be associated with a proposal from Miltos Evert – a right-of-center figure, like Hadjidakis. Manos and Xarkakos didn't say no, but they agreed to the idea only on condition that they appeared with their own musicians, whereas Miltos and I had planned to have a single orchestra and a single singer (who happened to be me).

'Since that's how it is,' Miltos said to me, 'you bring your own musicians as well. Instead of performing together you'll perform separately, one after the other. It won't be as good, but it'll still be extraordinary.'

I agreed. After all, our aim was to celebrate Greek music, to put on an outstanding show, not to squabble over how to share the limelight. It would be enormously important for the audience to see Manos and I on stage together. We would all be giving our services free, with the evening's proceeds going to the city of Athens.

Speaking of the limelight, I learned that Manos Hadjidakis had made another stipulation. He wanted to perform first with his musicians, then dismantle his equipment and leave before I arrived. I thought this was stupid – hard on the spectators, who would have to wait while each group installed its own sound system – and I thought it a real pity that we wouldn't be seen onstage together. That was what the public was eager to witness. As the papers pointed out, Manos and I had not appeared together for twenty-five years.

So I suggested that I set up the equipment for everyone (I was working at the time with a German assistant, Elke, and a team of technicians who were arguably one of the best in the world), and that Manos and I perform at least one song together. I asked Miltos to exert all his influence to get Manos to agree to the compromise.

The great day dawned. Not only was every seat filled, but they allowed the people still outside the gates to come in and sit on the turf surrounding the stage so that nobody should be left out. I was in my dressing room, still uncertain whether Manos had agreed. Would he go on first, or would I? Would we sing together, or would he avoid me? There was a knock at my door, and a breathless Miltos came in.

'You're on first, Nana!' he said. 'Manos is next, and he's agreed to have you join him at the end of his segment.'

'Fantastic! How did you manage it?'

'Well, he wasn't too happy. He said that men these days let women manipulate them. But he accepted anyway.'

My technical crew had timed my arrival in the stadium to the second, and I was delighted to find that it coincided exactly with the opening notes of the show. The plan they came up with was perfect. I made my appearance at one end of the stadium, picked out by a spotlight, and at once launched into 'To kiparissaki' ('The Young Cypress') as I walked through the crowd to the stage set up in the middle. It was September, the moon was full, the sky was of unearthly beauty, and as if to intoxicate us all an unbelievably violent wind suddenly swooped down and bore aloft the notes that swirled above our heads like a snowstorm.

'The young Cypress', which had earned me another first prize at the second Festival of Greek Song in 1960, was a tribute to Manos Hadjidakis who had written that song for me. I guessed from the ovation which followed me through the crowd that all hundred thousand spectators immediately understood this. I wondered whether Manos (who was following the concert on the radio in his nearby apartment) was moved. I sincerely hoped so. I longed to regain the trust and the friendship that had bound us in those far-off days.

Then I began a medley of old and contemporary songs, finishing with the song so eagerly awaited by our youthful audience, 'The Eleventh Commandment'.

We planned a brief intermission between me and Manos, just long enough to allow for installation of the extra instruments his musicians needed and the time it took him to walk from his home to the stadium. I slipped into the wings to watch him come onstage. Inflexible, rigid, he received the crowd's applause as if it were his by right, then directed his players with the peremptory authority I knew so well. It had been arranged that when his turn was over I would emerge from the wings and he would come over to get me. How would he greet me? I knew he was capable of anything – even refusing to approach me.

In other words, my mind was in a whirl as I tentatively emerged from the wings. But Manos didn't pretend to forget me. No. He approached me with a decided air, his sulky-child's face suddenly alight with excitement. What would he do? He simply took me by the hand and led me to the mic, but before we even reached it the stadium exploded. A tidal wave of applause, far surpassing what we had received when we appeared on our own. Once again, I thought how curious it was that crowds always knew what they wanted.

'You see,' I whispered to him, 'I knew this was what they were waiting for.'

Perhaps he smiled inwardly. In any case, he paused briefly in front of the microphone, then left me and sat down at his piano.

And then, in the deep silence that suddenly followed the storm, I heard the first notes of 'Paper Moon' as though we were back in his music room a quarter-century earlier, just the two of us. Trembling a little, I launched into that song which had forever sealed our friendship – or so I thought back then.

And I sang it for Manos alone, leaving the spectators – who seemed to be holding their breath – to witness the reconciliation I hoped for.

The last note faded, and the whole stadium rose to its feet. It was sheer madness. The applause went on and on, and I couldn't see how we could wave goodbye and leave the audience in this state of wild exhilaration.

'Let's sing something else, Manos. We owe them at least that . . .'

'No. It's fine this way.'

'Please. Anything you want . . . I don't need to rehearse, I know all your songs.'

But it was no, a definite no, and we abandoned the stage to Stavros Xarkakos.

But it didn't matter. Manos had buried his grudge. That night, as my musicians and I kept the evening going in an Athens taverna with Miltos Evert, I was astonished to see Manos appear. He was no longer the same man but the Manos I had always known, at once playful and impassioned.

He sat down beside me and subjected me to friendly teasing. Then Nikos turned up. There was no more room for doubt: that great concert had wrought the miracle of reconciling us all.

It may have been that same night that we discussed the possibility of recording an album jointly signed by the three of us. It was either that night or next day, for we remained together during the days that followed as though aware that for us time was now running short.

It was Nikos who threw the idea out, and Manos' face at once lit up. Manos had not recovered from the death of his mother, whom he revered, and the prospect of this recording, of renewed artistic creation, seemed to restore him to life. The two friends set to work as I flew off to resume traveling the planet.

When I met them again a few months later, they were changed men. Nikos had written quite outstanding verses, possibly the most beautiful he had ever achieved. And Manos was spending his nights at the piano composing. It was just like the good old days, when his mother would whisper to me as she opened their door: 'Quick! Come in, he's expecting you, I think he's going crazy . . .'

Yes. Manos was back in his old creative frenzy, and I sent up private thanks to life. Once again, he started to call me at all hours of the day and night, and as though I were twenty-five again I stood by his piano and wrestled through his melodies with him.

'No,' he would say, his eternal cigarette between his fingers, 'that bit you have to sing like this: listen carefully.'

I listened and began again, sometimes filling in with *la-la-las*, since we didn't yet have Nikos' definitive words.

'Bravo! That was exactly right!'

I know he told Nikos (who passed his words along to me) how astonished he was that I was still the same despite fame and success.

'You know,' he told Nikos, 'I thought she would be offended, but she listens as attentively as she used to, and what's extraordinary is that she still seems as happy as ever to be singing.'

They too were happy, as if unexpectedly visited by grace. They had hit on the album's title, *I mythi mias gynaikas* (*Legends of a Woman*). Their twelve songs amounted to a hymn to love, to the world's beauty, to nostalgia, to the loss of those we have loved. One of them evoked Federico Garcia Lorca, the Andalusian poet executed by one of Franco's firing squads in 1936. Nikos had treasured Lorca ever since childhood. Another song, perhaps my favorite, was a deeply moving tribute to the singer Oum Kalsoum, who died in 1975.

But during our recording sessions, the orchestra disappointed me. Manos was no longer the inspired, risk-taking, wildly imaginative musician he had once been. His melodies now struck me as a little rigid, a little pompous.

'Manos,' I said to him, 'I no longer get a sense of the poetry this song possessed when we were rehearsing it.'

'It's a bit different now, but trust me, I know you'll like it.'

I only half-liked it. Nikos too was somewhat disappointed, but this seemed trivial alongside our satisfaction at seeing our three names linked once more.

And it was again Miltos Evert who found a way of prolonging our renewed cooperation. Miltos was no longer Mayor of Athens. He was now Greece's attorney general, and on each of my visits he arranged a reception to which he would invite several artists. Like Constantine Karamanlis, Miltos was a devotee of artistic expression, believing it his duty to introduce artists into every Greek household, including the poorest, including those living in the remotest corners of the country.

One evening, Manos and I were at one of those receptions. Among the guests was a guitar player who drifted from one small performing group to another, as often happened in Greece. Manos and I began to sing old tunes, followed by one or two songs from the just-published *Legends of a Woman*. I saw Miltos approach discreetly and sit down next to us. When we finished our singing, he exclaimed:

'How enchanting! Why don't you make a tour of Greece? Not in big cities, if you take my meaning, but across the islands, where people don't ever get a chance to see you in the flesh.'

'And who's going to go island-hopping with all our equipment?' asked Manos. 'Do you think we go on tour with a backpack?'

'What if I made people available to you?' Miltos persisted.

'If you find anyone crazy enough to go with us I'm certainly prepared to consider it.'

That night, the defense minister Ioannis Varvitsiotis was a fellow guest, and Miltos at once called him over. The man in question approached, smiling and holding a glass of wine in his hand.

'I'm trying to persuade them to tour the islands,' Miltos told him. 'The problem is how to transport them with all their musicians and their equipment. Do you think you could help us?'

'I can certainly lend you a couple of naval vessels. Or even a plane. Why not?'

Manos burst out laughing.

'Well, if the army is taking a hand, you can count me in!'

Which was how that idea – thrown out by Miltos more or less as a challenge – became flesh. Over the next few days, he confirmed that the defense minister hadn't spoken lightly. Two naval craft were indeed called into service to ferry us. Whereupon, still with Miltos Evert's support, we began to plan our itinerary. We would sing in all those far-flung islands strung out along the Turkish coast, Kasteloriso, Chios, Rhodes. But we would also journey northward to the borders of Bulgaria and Macedonia before coming back down to the Peloponnese.

What with my recording sessions, my concerts, and our preparations for that tour, I spent much of the late Eighties in Greece, as if I felt an imperious need to take my place once more among my own people, to bask in their affection, to return to the language of my childhood. And I recall too that this was the time when my father's health began to decline. Perhaps it was also the unconscious urge to hold on to him that kept me returning to Greece. Who knows what impulses drive us? I like to think that the Lord discreetly guides our footsteps as long as we know how to listen and let ourselves be led.

Whenever I returned, I spent as much time as I could with Papa. His heart was failing and his face was hollower, but he wasn't unhappy. He struck me as a man finally at peace after a life tortured by guilt.

One day he said to me:

'When I'm gone, Nana, take good care of your sister. You'll be all she has left.'

I realized then how responsible he had become since Mama's death. This man, who had been unable to help his wife, now had the strength to comfort Jenny, whose husband had died prematurely. And Jenny in her turn consoled him.

I had never forgiven myself for being away from my mother when she died, and now I lived in terror of being far from my father when the moment came. Jenny no longer left his side, and as the end approached she kept me informed of his condition. When he fell and lost his appetite I came back. Then he recovered, and I was off again.

And on the day in June 1989 when Papa left us forever I was once again far from him, in an aircraft somewhere over the Atlantic. I wondered then whether the Lord wanted to punish me for giving too much of myself to music and not enough to my loved ones. But perhaps I was wrong. Perhaps it was merely chance.

At all events, I wanted to be in Greece to help ease my grief, and I saw that long tour around the outskirts of my country as a gift of grace. An air force plane took us to Rhodes, where we were welcomed by the navy. The defense minister had played his part well – a cruiser just for Manos and his musicians and a destroyer for me and mine (plus André)! The admiral who met us on Rhodes told us we would be considered as regular officers for the three or four weeks the tour lasted. As a result, we would each have the services of an aide-de-camp and would partake of shipboard life.

In the event, the whole thing quickly turned into a game. Since I was an officer, whistling shrilled out and every man on deck snapped to attention whenever I left the ship or came back on board. It is a Greek custom to whistle, but it always reminded me of 'My Love is Somewhere', in which I sang that with the arrival of spring 'every night I hear the boys whistle and it makes my head turn'.

'I love it when they whistle at me,' I said to Manos.

He was delighted:

'I didn't think it would still thrill you at your age!'

Sometimes we sang on tiny islands for a few hundred spectators, amazed by what was being done on their behalf. And what a pleasure it was after the show to have all the time in the world to talk, to meet everyone!

We often had to make do with what we found on the spot – benches, chairs belonging to the islanders – and many spectators sat on the grass in front of the little stage the sailors had hammered together for us.

One night it was so windy in the little port of Symi where we were to sing that we decided to moor the two ships in such a way that they shielded us. I imagine that the officers had a hard time believing their eyes when they saw two warships deployed to shelter a concert from the wind!

It was certainly the nicest tour I had ever made – affectionate, somewhat melancholy, yet at the same time filled with joy. I sensed that I might be participating in one of Manos' last public appearances, for as he aged he was increasingly shrinking back inside himself. He spent more and more time at home, ruminating, writing, and traveling in his dreams.

While I was giving new life to my Greek roots, another of my songs ('Only Love') had become a worldwide hit, rivaling 'Song for Liberty' five years earlier. The history of 'Only Love' can be told in a few words. American TV was planning an eight-hour series, *Mistral's Daughter*, and since the series was intended for a worldwide audience they were looking for someone capable of singing the score (written by Vladimir Cosma) in every imaginable language. It was my friends Monique Le Marcis and Roger Kreicher of Radio Television Luxembourg who thought of me. Pierre Delanoë wrote the lyrics, while André supervised the French-language recording. For every other language I was monitored by a different artistic director, so that there should not be the slightest flaw in my accent. When the series was broadcast, my album escorted it into every country in the world, borne on the phenomenal success of the televised saga whose events unfolded between America and France in the 1930s.

But the song would not have enjoyed such international success unless Alain Lévy, the new chief of Phonogram, had not shepherded its fortunes. Louis Hazan had retired and was replaced by Jacques Caillard, and it was while I was performing at the Olympia (when Thierry Le Luron died) that Alain Lévy took over from Caillard. The company was not doing well, and Alain Lévy didn't even bother to attend my concert. My feelings were hurt, and I sent him this little note: 'I have the feeling that the ship is sinking, the rats are leaving, and I'm all alone.' Next morning I was surprised to receive the following message, which immediately set my mind at rest. 'Contrary to what you may think, the ship isn't sinking. She has a new skipper, and I invite you to come aboard.' Indeed, the helm was in firm hands, and from that day on my artistic career acquired a second wind, particularly in the direction of the United States. And in 1988, while I was recording *Legends of a Woman* in Greece with Manos and Nikos, André was cooking up a new project for me in Paris. Ever since the runaway success of 'Song for Liberty', he had secretly dreamed of having me record a classical album. If I had mastered the Slave Chorus from Verdi's *Nebuchadnezzar*, he thought, what was to prevent me from singing Handel, Bellini or Brahms? He made several veiled allusions to it, and must certainly have sensed that I was torn between the wish to try and fear of failure. I hadn't forgotten my years at the Athens Conservatory and the disapproval (as though I had let people down) that accompanied my transition to pop singing. Now that I had chosen the easy route – as my Conservatory teachers claimed – would I be able to make the return trip? That was what I asked André when he first openly referred to this intimidating prospect. As the months (and perhaps the years) went by, he had quietly unearthed and noted down a number of extracts from classical works – works he believed I would be able to manage and my pop-oriented fans might welcome. The list included Albinoni's 'Adagio', 'Habanera' from Bizet's *Carmen*, and 'Casta Diva', from Bellini's *Norma*.

'You know how much faith I have in you,' he told me. 'If I didn't think you were up to these arias I would never have suggested them.'

André had been such an enormous help to me throughout my performing career precisely because he never deceived or flattered me. In spite of our mutual love, he never hesitated to ask me to tackle a recording a second time if he didn't consider it perfect. It meant that he was a man in whom I had absolute confidence, the only man in the whole world whose suggestions I was ready to follow blindly. I say this now because I believe I would never have dared attempt this return to the classical mode unless I had been borne up by his trust, and buoyed by the conviction that he would never publish an album that failed to meet his expectations.

With that said, however, no recording ever demanded more discipline and hard work than this one. Between the spring and summer of 1988, I devoted four months to it. But hard work kept me on an even keel, whereas I was always plagued by doubts and guilt whenever a recording hit the right note too effortlessly. For this album I worked with another wonderful conductor, Roger Berthier.

The album came out in the fall to a respectful and positive reception by the French media. 'The diva of popular song records twenty great classical arias,' said *France-Soir*, which insisted on posing me in front of the legendary Opera Garnier (where I had never sung!). 'Taking Mozart By Storm', ran the headline in *Ouest-France*. 'Capping a thirty-year career, an enviable tally of two hundred and fifty Gold Records, and concerts on all the world's stages, Nana Mouskouri has now embarked on a flight back to her teens. In a sense, she has given a taste of their own medicine to opera's great stars – Berganza, Hendricks, Norman, Pavarotti, Domingo, Carreras – who have invaded the terrain of traditional song and pop singing.'[33]

But it was my father's pride, much more than acclaim from the critics, that went to my heart. He was in the last months of his life when I gave him this album. The first notes of Schubert's *Adagio Notturno* had scarcely rung out when I saw his eyes mist over. And when he heard me sing *Le Nozze di Figaro* he was trembling as he folded me in his arms, and I sensed that he was weeping. Poor Papa! I believe that for the first time in his long life I had given him what he had secretly expected of me since I entered the Conservatory forty years earlier.

'Thank you, my sweet girl,' he whispered. 'How beautiful it is!'

It was my last gift to him.

During that autumn of 1988, André and I said publicly that we wished to marry. For ten years we had been more or less secretly in love, and now that the children were grown up we finally asserted our right to declare ourselves. I pictured a big party for all the people we loved, and

---

[33] *Ouest-France*, 24 December 1988.

of course I thought of my father's happiness. The news inevitably spread, a number of tabloids swiftly announced the event with blaring headlines over photos in which André and I, finally 'outed', appeared for the first time hand in hand. 'It took her two years to tell him "Yes, forever",' said one, which had no idea that I had long since told André 'Yes'. Another paper, catching me between airplanes, quoted me as saying 'I'm determined not to rush this wedding.'

Not rush our wedding? Well, not exactly ... since we didn't finally tie the knot until 2003!

My father's death, followed by the deaths of André's parents, forced the postponement of our first attempt. A wedding should be a happy affair, and after those losses we no longer felt like dancing and celebrating. And we couldn't ignore the fact that our personal horizon was growing terribly dark. Nikos was diagnosed with cancer, Manos was slipping into the melancholia of old age, and now Fernande in her turn fell ill. She had given us twenty years of her life, and I loved her in spite of our confrontations.

So I put aside our wedding and went off on a second world tour. Following 'Only Love', my classical recording was on sale worldwide. I flew first to Canada and the United States. Then came Latin America. I sang in Mexico, Chile, Argentina, and Brazil. I revisited Asia, singing in Hong Kong, Tokyo, and South Korea.

And I finished that world tour in Paris, performing at the Zenith with more than a hundred musicians onstage.

'Somewhere between angel and high priestess, draped all in white in antique style, and accompanied by the orchestra and choirs of the Concerts Colonne,' wrote *France-Soir*'s critic Nicole Duault, 'Nana Mouskouri has spent the last three nights transforming the Zenith, that temple of rock and variety, into a sanctuary. Sublime, divine moments, in which the fans' enthusiasm (not a single empty seat) on the one hand and panache, elegance and beauty on the other, combined to create a miracle.'[34]

---

[34] *France-Soir*, 11 December 1989.

25

One By One They Leave...

*T*he knowledge that Nikos was sick and that he too would soon leave us was unbearable to me, and I made repeated visits to Greece in the early Nineties. I needed to drink deeply of his presence, to listen to his voice. André came with me, and we would spend the day at his home. Nikos was very serene, still curious to hear what I had to tell him, to learn of the things that worried me, to hear about my latest shows.

'And what did you sing that night?' he would ask.

I brought him my songs and saw him nod approvingly, his expression lively despite his weariness.

'Oh,' he would say, 'I see you sang "Aspri mera" ("Les jours meilleurs") . . . A wonderful song, isn't it? Would you mind . . .'

'Not at all. I'll sing it just for you.'

Sometimes Manos was there, so depressed that I would ask him to sing along with me.

And then I would leave them. But next day I'd call from Geneva. Not a day went by without a call from me.

In April 1992 I spent a whole week in Athens. Nikos had just come out of hospital and seemed to be doing better. For two or three days we talked endlessly. He read poems to me and I sang my first songs.

Then it was time to go back to Geneva.

'You have to leave, don't you?' he said.

'Yes, I have to leave.'

'That's good.'

Usually, he at once added, 'No problem then, we'll see each other again soon.' This time, he didn't say it.

'I have to leave too, you know,' he said with a smile. 'I have to go home.'

Why didn't I hear what he was trying to tell me? I understood him to say that he was going back to the village of Acea, his birthplace. I knew he wanted to be taken there, and I left him on that misunderstanding.

Next morning I was in Paris, and next day on a plane to the United States where I was scheduled to give several concerts.

During the tour I called two or three times a day. One morning, I learned from Manos that Nikos was in hospital.

I called him in his room.

'Ah, Nana! Where are you? Tell me the name of the city you're calling from.'

'Atlanta, Nikos.'

'Atlanta! Well then, you're not so far from me.'

'Yes I am, Nikos, I'm a long way away. Atlanta is in the United States.'

'I know that, I understand. But look at the map. Atlanta is next door to Athens, in Georgia.'

All his life Nikos had traveled without once leaving Greece. I believe that distances didn't matter to him: he operated according to a different geography from ours. And he was right: barely sixty-five miles separated Atlanta, Georgia, from Athens in the same state. Oddly enough, I felt relieved that he should feel we were so close to one another.

'Of course!' I said. 'You're right, I am there, almost next door. So I'll talk to you tomorrow.'

But next day, Nikos was no longer there, and I had to restrain myself from screaming my anguish into the phone. All of a sudden I no longer had the strength to imagine the world without him, and I looked stupidly around me in search of Manos' face, as though he might appear before me so far from Greece. I yearned for us to wrap our arms around each other. It was as though only Manos could share my sorrow. I managed to dial his number. The phone rang and rang, and at last he picked up.

'Oh, Manos!'

But he was voiceless. I could hear him sob, and I was powerless to console him.

Two months later I was in Acea. Our mutual friend of many years' standing, Giorgios, and my friend Manuela drove me. Nikos rests there, in the little cemetery adjacent to the chapel. It stood on the crest of a hill planted with cypresses, standing upright and absolutely still that morning under a crystalline summer sky. From that height, the plain below seemed frozen in a gilded light, and the men working the fields looked tiny.

How much I have loved you only I can know,
I who sometimes brushed you with the eyes of the stars
Locked in the moon's embrace and dancing with you
In summer fields amid crumbling houses of stone ...

Nikos wrote that poem in 1943, and I believe that he was speaking about life.

In those early years of the Nineties, death was a deeply disruptive presence in my life. First it took my father, and now Nikos. Where would it pounce next? Manos was so stricken by his friend's death that he couldn't find the strength to attend his funeral. I had never seen him so desolate, so downcast, and I prayed that he would rediscover his will to live. Fernande too had cancer. Her distress was profound, and every time I passed through Geneva I found her a little bit sadder, more diminished. And now Melina Mercouri too had to confront the same disease. Melina, for so long the personal goddess of Manos, and for many years now a precious friend of mine.

It was yet another death, Audrey Hepburn's, on 20 January 1993, which marked a turning point in my life. Several months earlier, UNICEF (the United Nations Children's Fund) had been pressing me to act as a goodwill ambassador for the defense of children's rights around the world. Audrey, for whom I had bottomless respect, had proposed me as her replacement. She had devoted herself to the struggle for years, and now she needed to rest. I accepted at once, and even before stepping into her shoes I launched into the job with all the passion I possessed. From my earliest years I had been convinced that children are always the first victims – of wars, of poverty, of family conflict – and I believe I had forever been obsessed with their struggle. I never went to sing in an impoverished country without learning beforehand what I might be able to do for its children, and without visiting hospitals and schools while I was there. Being entrusted with this mission gave a new direction to my artistic career. The recognition music had brought me could now be put to the service of a noble cause – to the greatest of causes, I should perhaps say. I wasn't smooth enough to succeed as a politician, and this UNICEF mission would satisfy my need to help improve our world.

But first I must tell how I met Audrey Hepburn. It was in the early Eighties, during an AIDS benefit gala organized by Line Renaud at the Paradis Latin in Paris. President Jacques Chirac, who was then Mayor of Paris, was the guest of honor. I found myself seated between him and Audrey Hepburn, and she and I spent most of the dinner chatting. My two close friends, Jean-Claude Brialy and Serge Lama, also sat at our table, and so did the dazzling Elizabeth Taylor. That dinner also marked the beginning of my friendship with Jacques Chirac, following an incident that still makes us laugh whenever we meet.

I had discreetly set my handbag under the table, between his feet and mine. Suddenly it was no longer there. I stooped a little lower in an effort to see it, but no, nothing. My bag and its precious contents had vanished into thin air.

Then Jacques Chirac, who had certainly noticed my movements and sensed my anxiety, asked me politely:

'Have you lost something?'

'Well, yes, my handbag. It was on the floor but it's no longer there.'

He too looked under the table.

'How very odd. Where was it exactly?'

'Down there, on the floor!'

'We may have moved it accidentally with our feet. Let's see if it's across the table from us.'

By now the whole table knew what was up, and everyone looked around under his seat. But there was no sign of my bag.

'I take it we can exclude the possibility of a thief in our midst?' the Mayor of Paris whispered to me.

'That we can take for granted,' I replied.

'Well, since none of us believes in magic, we must try to work out what's happened.'

Meanwhile, Elizabeth Taylor had left the table to move about among the other guests. She had told us at the start of dinner that she was suffering agonies in her back, and would have to leave the table at regular intervals to relieve the pressure on her spine. That evening she was wearing a gorgeous long gown with a train: watching her walk up and down was a spectacle all by itself. In fact, that was exactly what Jacques Chirac and I were doing as we puzzled, ever more bewildered, over the fate of my handbag.

When suddenly I heard him say:

'Hold on, Nana, I think I know what's happened.'

'I'm sorry?'

'I think I know where your bag may be.'

'Really?'

'Does anything strike you about Elizabeth Taylor?'

'Well, I wish I were as beautiful ... And I love that gown ...'

'Exactly, her gown!'

The future President of the French Republic rose, said a few quiet words to the British actress, and then, blushing like a choirboy ... stooped and lifted her gown!

What a nerve, I thought, half-amused, half-astounded. It lasted only a split second, for I at once recognized my bag rising from among the voluminous folds of Elizabeth Taylor's long regal train.

The star was most embarrassed. Unknown to her, her train had swept up my handbag. Jacques Chirac was full of glee, and finally we all roared with laughter.

At that dinner, I told Audrey Hepburn how eager I was to follow in her footsteps, and she encouraged me to get in touch with the United Nations. It was following this conversation that I gave a benefit recital in the UN's General Assembly Hall in 1987 for the earthquake-stricken city of Kalamata in the southern Peloponnese.

In March 1994, I had been an official goodwill ambassador for a year. I had already visited Bolivia, Colombia, and Mexico when Miltos Evert suddenly reentered my life. The former mayor of Athens and Greece's attorney general was now head of the New Democracy Party, a center-right formation. I was touring Denmark when I received a call from him in my hotel room.

'There you are, Nana! Would you mind listening to me for a moment? Are you sitting down?'

'No, I wasn't, but now I am.'

'Good. What would you say if I nominated you for election to the European Parliament?'

'Are you making fun of me, Miltos?'

'No, I'm very serious.'

'I don't think so, no. If you were serious, you'd know I've never attended a university and know nothing about politics. I'm just a singer, and I don't think Europe needs a singer to plan its future.'

'Forgive me, but what you're saying is plain stupid. Europe has quite enough professional politicians as it is. I'm calling on you because of your fame in society at large. You're known in every European country, in the whole world, you speak pretty well every language, and you can be a fantastic ambassador for Greece and Greek ideas.'

'I speak a few languages, true enough. But I don't know how the world works, Miltos, and apart from holding benefit concerts, I have no ideas of my own for bettering the lot of the poor.'

'We have plenty of ideas, and you'll have helpers who will show you how Europe works. Listen, Nana, you must do it. I need you and Greece needs you, that's all I have to say. I'll give you twenty-four hours to think it over and I'll call you tomorrow. But you'd better not refuse. OK?'

He hung up, and I sat there for some time unable to react, wondering if all this could be true. Then, little by little, the pieces came together. There was no denying that Miltos called me, and knowing him as I did I knew I had to think fast. What I needed most was the right reason for turning him down. My first idea was of course to call Constantine Karamanlis, whose words during his Parisian exile now came back to me: 'Nana, never get mixed up in politics. If you're a political novice you run the risk of being manipulated and losing your soul.' Karamanlis was still our president, and I promised myself I would call him next day.

Except that Miltos didn't give me the time. Just as I was about to call the presidential palace, my phone rang.

'Nana! Yorgos Levendarios speaking. How are you?'

Yorgos was an old friend, and a friend as well of Manos and Nikos. He had often taken care of my relations with the media.

'It's a pleasure to hear your voice again,' I said.

'And that goes for me too. You know we're going to be working together again?'

'Oh yes? What's the occasion?'

'Well, you're on the New Democracy list, and I'm handling the press follow-up.'

'I beg your pardon? I'm on the New Democracy list?'

'You bet! In fact, you're number three on the list.'

'What! Miltos is crazy, we were supposed to discuss it today. I told him yesterday that it was out of the question.'

'Nana, you know Miltos. He's a bulldozer. Whatever he wants, he gets. You can't turn him down. But don't you worry, we'll all be there with you, we'll give you a hand.'

As soon as we hung up, I called Miltos Evert.

'Miltos, this isn't funny at all. You didn't even give me time to speak to André or ask Karamanlis' advice. I haven't decided to give up singing.'

'Calling Karamanlis wouldn't have helped. In any case, he'd have told you not to stand. And who's asking you to quit your profession? On the contrary, you have to go on singing – it's your best way of serving Greece. You won't have to show up in Parliament all that often.'

'Don't tell me that! You know very well that if I accept a responsibility I don't go in for half-measures. If I become a member of the European parliament as a result of your maneuverings, I know I'll be in my office every day. Not to mention that I'd have to learn from scratch. You've made a fool of me, Miltos, you're no friend of mine.'

'Nana, you should be thanking me instead of insulting me. If you were just a little bit patriotic ...'

'I'm not insulting you, Miltos. I'm just saying how disrespectful it is of you to make a decision on my behalf that involves my whole future. Which is why I consider that what you've done is none of my business. So listen carefully: right now, I'm not a candidate!'

'How dare you wriggle out of this when the country needs you? How dare you? Greece is just emerging from decades of suffering, and now she needs to be able to call on all her people. You are one of her best ambassadors, but you prefer your comfort to your country's service. Nana, you know we've lost Melina. You know, and I saw you crying at her funeral. So today I'm telling you in all seriousness: we desperately need you.'

Melina! Melina Mercouri had died a few days earlier, on 6 March 1994, and thousands of us mourned. Melina was unique, larger than life, yet I didn't resent Miltos' use of her name in this context. For it was true that in losing Melina, Greece lost a part of her soul and one of her most universally respected voices.

On the eve of her departure for New York and the operation she wouldn't survive, she came to watch one of my rehearsals. I was preparing a benefit show on behalf of children for Mariana Vardinoyannis' Elpida Foundation, a show we had dreamed up together. Although seriously ill, Melina was still our minister of culture. Her voice was heard everywhere, she was seen everywhere, vibrant and passionate. She would not be attending our festival, since she was leaving for the United States, so she came unannounced to the theater, accompanied only by Jules Dassin, her husband, and her assistant Manuela, who over the years had become one of my closest friends.

The three of them sat in the second row in the empty theater. Melina sat with her arms folded on the back of the seat in front of her, her chin resting on her arms. She listened attentively until the end.

And then, looking sad all of a sudden, she asked me:

'Now sing me this one, please.'

And of course I sang everything she asked for. I would have sung all night for her if she wanted. I knew she didn't want to go to the United States. A few weeks earlier she had broken her arm, and Jules felt that this was her way of rebelling against the journey. As I said, I would have sung all that night if it made her happy. It was so sad to see her suddenly assailed by doubts – Melina, who had never stopped fighting: against the colonels, against stupidity, against every kind of injustice.

Manos, who also needed medical care, joined her in the United States.

He had therefore been able to spend time with her in the days leading up to her surgery. (This was the Manos who once told me he loved her so deeply in his youth that after losing her he opted in favor of young men, convinced that he would never find another Melina.)

I was told that when the nurses came into her room, Melina would tell them, pointing at Manos:

'Do you see this man? He's the one who wrote the score for *Never on Sunday*!'

And Manos replied:

'Be quiet, Melina. You know I don't like that song any more.'

He arrived every day with a small pot of flowers, Manuela told me, blushing as he gave them to her.

'How handsome you are,' she told him. 'You've lost weight.'

Then the two of them would spend the afternoon singing Manos' old songs. The nurses flocked in to listen, and Melina hid her tears.

When her body was brought back, I believe the whole of Greece wept as her flag-draped coffin appeared at the aircraft's door. People flooded into the streets, massed the whole length of the funeral cortege's itinerary, all of them weeping. I had never seen a whole nation immersed in such grief.

So I didn't resent Miltos Evert's reference to Melina's death. Deep inside me, fully conscious as I was of all she had done for Greece, I was beginning to feel ashamed of my reluctance to heed the call I had received.

After that memorable exchange with Miltos, when we hung up on each other in mutual acrimony, I turned to André. I was surprised to hear him say: 'Why not? Europe is a noble endeavor, and you've reached a point in your career when you can afford to spread your energy a little. You're already doing it for UNICEF.'

I had forgotten UNICEF! Could membership in the European parliament – becoming a 'Euro-MP' – be reconciled with my goodwill mission? Now that I thought about it, it seemed clear to me that I would never abandon the world's children for parliamentary duties. I was committed to my ambassadorial role: I felt useful and effective performing it, and I had no intention of betraying that commitment for

European affairs that seemed far beyond my capabilities. With that in mind, I called Miltos Evert back.

'Things sound better,' he observed. 'You don't seem quite so angry.'

He assured me that I wouldn't have to leave UNICEF, and UNICEF for its part encouraged me to stand for the European parliament, pointing out that membership could strengthen my authority on certain missions.

'It's Yes,' I told Miltos at last.

'Thank you. I was sure you'd accept.'

As a condition of my agreement I stipulated that I should not take part in the election campaign which had just begun. I felt far too much of a novice to climb on to platforms and improvise speeches. However, I returned to Athens at the end of May 1994 to meet members of the New Democracy Party and discuss our program with Miltos. I took advantage of the occasion to see Manos. He had not recovered from Melina's death. He remained at home, prostrate, and it was terribly sad to be unable to offer him any hope.

On 12 June I went back to Geneva, and this time my sister came with me. I had decided to move into a new house on the heights of Lake Geneva, and Jenny accompanied me to lend a hand and so that we could spend a little time together after all these deaths. It was her birthday on 13 June, and for once we were able to celebrate it together.

We had barely arrived when Yorgos Levendarios called.

'Nana,' he said, 'you have to come back right away. Miltos has called a meeting of all the candidates and Party leaders.'

'That's impossible. I've just got home. In fact it was you who drove me to the airport.'

'I know. But that's politics for you! The Party chairman expects you tomorrow, no ifs or buts.'

The meeting was scheduled for 15 June, so I was back in Athens late in the afternoon of 14 June.

The first thing I did was call on Manos. I found him much weaker, very depressed, but I did manage to make him smile a little at my new venture into politics.

By chance, the morrow's meeting would be held not fifty yards from his apartment, so I could promise I would be back.

'As soon as it's over,' I said as I kissed him goodbye, 'I'll be back and we'll spend the evening together.'

'Good, and you'll bring me up to date on your meeting, right?'

It was a strange meeting. It was my first opportunity of meeting all my colleagues in the same room, and I had the curious sense that I was entering a nest of vipers. The only one who seemed sincerely glad to see me was Miltos Evert, our chairman. The others looked at me with the forced smile you usually put on at the dentist's. I gradually learned the reason for this: the fact that I had been brought in from outside the regular political circuit soured and angered every other candidate. But once the photographers spotted me, I noticed how eagerly those who had ostracized me struggled to get themselves into the photos. Well, I thought, at least I'm of some use to them ...

The speeches began, and I was surprised to see people get up here and there in order to chat unconcernedly in distant corners, with no regard for the speaker of the moment. If people behaved that way during my recitals, I thought, I believe I would consider a change of profession. But everybody seemed to think it quite acceptable to listen with only half an ear. In fact, I seemed to be the only one who was bothered by it. Despite the confusion, I tried to register what was being said, and the more I heard the more terrified I became. Not only did the meaning of every second sentence elude me, but everything seemed to be in code, and even those who weren't listening guessed when it was time to applaud ... I wondered whether I would ever be able to deliver such speeches.

I was still thinking about that when someone came over unobtrusively and whispered in my ear:

'Madame Mouskouri, the chairman wants to see you right away.'

I looked over toward Miltos, who was seated on the platform, and our eyes met. How long had he been staring at me? He looked shattered, on the verge of tears.

I rose and made my way to the platform as discreetly as I could. Miltos leaned over to me.

'Manos is dying, Nana! Get over there as quick as you can. Hurry!'

I crossed the room like an automaton, intending to race to Manos' flat. But I had hardly crossed the threshold when Miltos' bodyguards and driver, already alerted, took me in hand, running me straight through the pack of reporters outside. In a few seconds I was in front of Manos' building.

'You're too late, an ambulance has just taken him away,' said a policeman.

Without stopping to breathe, we raced for the hospital.

Meanwhile, the news had spread and all the reporters were also speeding to the hospital.

We went inside, but as I entered the building I saw Yorgos Levendarios emerge in tears, followed by a doctor in a white tunic.

'Madame Mouskouri, I'm so sorry . . . so sorry . . . it's all over.'

'No!'

'He died in the ambulance. They did everything they could to revive him . . . I'm so very sorry.'

By now the reporters were on the scene. They wanted me to say something, to tell them how I felt, what Manos had meant to me. But how ridiculous to say in a few short words how much I had loved him! I tried to speak a little, but I couldn't. I was ashamed. I couldn't bear the thought that I wasn't in the ambulance when he died. I wished I could have held his hand, that he hadn't left this life alone. I wished he had known he would live on in my heart until the end of my own life.

That night we didn't sleep. First we all met at Manos' place to talk about him. His closest friends were there: Jules Dassin, Manuela, his sister Miranda, Yorgos and I . . . In the middle of the night, we went together to the hospital to sit in silent wake over Manos' mortal remains. Then we went to Yorgos' house. It was an old, typically Greek building, its whitewashed walls covered with icons, illuminated as always on such occasions by flickering candles. Inside, photos of Manos and Nikos sat on every piece of furniture.

Manos had requested that he be buried in the little mountain village where Yorgos had a house, an hour's drive from Athens. At dawn we went to prepare for the service. We brought flowers and candles and made everything ready for the ceremony, and going to all this trouble for him together on this young summer morning made us want to laugh.

The mass was moving, tender, pregnant with reflection, and I tried to imagine three of them together again, reunited for eternity – Nikos, Melina and Manos. Were they walking in light? Did they see us – orphaned, bereaved – from above? I wanted to think they had found peace and rest after their long struggle against the world's wickedness.

> *Through the course of his hidden life the man bequeathed*
> *To those he left behind a thousand tokens*
> *Of his immortal nature*
> *Just as he left in the heavens the tracks of evening landslides*
> *Of serpents of adamantine kites*
> *And the gaze of hyacinths*
> *Amid sighs and tears of hunger of lamentation*
> *Of ash from subterranean depths.*

Nikos Gatsos

26

An Ambassadorial Role

*I*n June 1994 I was elected, and a month later was in Strasbourg, seat of the European parliament, to take on my new functions. It was a little bit like back-to-school season, with dozens of forms to fill out and a list of committees on which I might prefer to serve. I was of course thinking of those connected with culture, youth and women's rights. But the discussions that followed made me feel even more of a novice than I had feared. When I said I could be useful in this or that area, they told me it was not quite that simple, that there were other factors involved. What factors? No one really took the time to explain it to me. And all this went on against a background of utter chaos. The bureau of newly-elected Greek deputies was under permanent siege by the international media, all focused on me alone – even though I certainly had less to say than any other of the novice politicians present. They wanted to interview me, sketch the outlines of my life, film me, record my words, follow my every footstep, learn why I had decided to enter parliament, hear my ideas on Europe's future, find out whether I was going to give up singing … All of this made my Greek colleagues – who already looked on me askance – green with jealousy. I was made aware of this by the hostility that became palpable as the days went by, as though my celebrity (which I had assumed would be of service to our group) made me its black sheep. Very soon, I was unable to find anyone ready to give me advice or lift my spirits. So I turned to the representatives of other countries, such as Michel Rocard, Nicole Fontaine, Doris Pack, and Daniel Cohn-Bendit (the German-born

'Red Danny' of Paris' 1968 student uprising), whose independent spirit appealed to me. All would become good friends of mine.

In other words, my introduction to politics left me with a somewhat unpleasant aftertaste. But I hung on stubbornly and conscientiously, and managed despite all obstacles to land a place on committees that interested me, the cultural committee in particular. One of my goals was to carry on Melina Mercouri's struggle to recover the marble friezes from the Parthenon, carried off two centuries earlier by the British and exhibited ever since in the British Museum.

The other committees were more obviously humanitarian, more rooted in issues that were close to my heart: education, access to schooling for all children, violence against women, cultural exchanges, supported foreign-language translations, the arts in general, aid to developing countries and to refugees in conflict zones, particularly in the countries of the former Yugoslavia.

I went there full of ideals. I thought that after singing of peace and poetry for twenty-five years I had now been offered the chance of making a concrete impact. But I must admit that I was constantly frustrated by the lack of means to support effective action. So much energy poured into such tiny results! But no doubt that such is politics – a hard schooling in patience – and when all is said and done I don't regret those difficult years.

But I did underestimate the impact of my political commitment on my singing career. The truth is, I was not really given time to think about that, and the problem only became clear to me – to my growing dismay – over the first two years of my parliamentary term. For me, the job meant being at my office early each morning to sort through my files, attending committee meetings as well as plenary sessions of parliament, traveling constantly into the field in order to know what I was talking about. I went to Bulgaria, Romania, and Sarajevo. In practical terms, all this meant short nights, mounting fatigue, skipped meals or meals swallowed on the run, dawn meetings at mist-shrouded airports, forays into distant neighborhoods in freezing winds, snow or rain.

Lack of sleep and the overall disruptions of daily life have an irreparable effect on the human voice. When the body is tired the voice fades and gradually vanishes altogether. Since I was determined to continue to sing, I got into the habit of chartering private planes which picked me up at the last moment and ferried me to Germany, Canada, Finland or Vietnam, where I generally gave a concert that same evening. These trips came on top of the journeys that took me all over the world on UNICEF's behalf. At last I began to realize as I went onstage that my voice was no longer the same.

At first this was very disturbing, even frightening. Then I was swept back into my parliamentary functions and I tried not to think about it. Was it serious? No, I thought, it must surely be a passing phase. But the problem returned, and little by little the failure of my voice left me in a state of apprehension that froze my blood when it was time to go onstage. Good Lord, what was I doing to myself? Music was my whole life, and now, having entered politics almost on a whim, I was perhaps betraying both music and myself. What was my place in this world if I was no longer a singer? Sometimes I felt I was sinking out of my depth, as though my childhood terrors had returned. And to make it all worse, I saw that I no longer had time to rehearse as I needed to. And so little time even to work! I was someone who always tried to do everything perfectly, and now I was desperately aware that everything I did was hurried, rushed.

When a singer loses self-confidence, it's her voice that first betrays her doubts. For the first time in my life, it seems to me, I lost faith in my voice, and it felt as though an earthquake was rumbling through my whole being. As the months went by, I sensed that within myself I was beginning to fragment. Did Andre see it? Was he aware of it? He had his work and I had mine, and when we were able to spend a few hours together we both wanted those hours to be joyful. I reasoned that it was more important to protect the life we shared than to involve him in my private distress. In truth, the only one in whom I could confide without shame, without breaking down in tears, was of course Nikos. He would listen to me, guide me, and help me find the right words for this unnamable evil which might well be destroying me. I had never missed Nikos so badly.

I was utterly alone in Geneva too. Fernande had died, the children were far away – Hélène was studying in London and Nicolas, now a cameraman, was filming somewhere else. The house was empty, echoing with the memory of happy times that would never return.

In the summer of 1996, two years after my election, it became clear to me that my determination to handle my multiple commitments was sapping my soul. And then, as so often happens, life itself decided to sound the alarm.

Manuela was with me in Geneva, where I was resting for a few days. It was August, it was very hot, and we stayed close to the swimming-pool. For some time I had been drinking a little bit too much, probably to take the edge off my fears and give me the strength to go on leading this insane life which had brought me so close to the edge. Yet I should have felt some pride. A few weeks earlier Miltos Evert called me to say: 'I absolutely must meet President Chirac. Can you help me? I've tried everything, but without success.' With Line Renaud's invaluable help, I was able to get Miltos an interview with the French president. Jacques Chirac let me know that he would be glad to see me at the same time, so it was arranged for me to accompany my party chairman to the Elysée Palace.

I was thinking about that meeting, and the pile of political assignments that awaited me when the European parliament reconvened, as I emerged from the pool to shower and get dressed. It was late. The light was fading, we had certainly drunk a bit too much, and I was rash enough to run across the wet floor . . . My punishment was swift: I slipped, fell . . . and broke my arm.

Accidents rarely happen by chance. You bottle up a growing sense of disappointment, feeling that you're on the wrong track, losing faith in your star, and since you're doing nothing to save yourself, fate takes over. It tells us in its own way that we're in danger. Now of course I couldn't go on hiding the truth from myself. All the pain I strove to ignore, the doubts I struggled to suppress and even to drown in drink (I had only recently begun to drink) I now wore on my sleeve – there for the whole world to see.

For several weeks, that broken arm forced me to take a clear look at things. I realized at last that I wasn't meant for politics. I had been elected to a five-year term, and I had no intention of resigning, but I finally accepted those five years as a once-only parenthesis in my life as an artist. And I convinced myself that my voice, which I was treating so badly, would come back to me intact once I closed that parenthesis.

UNICEF, on the other hand, had brought a kind of fulfillment to my life. It seemed in fact the ideal way of repaying my debt to a world which had unstintingly given me recognition and love. Of returning those gifts by helping the least favored of its children.

I had visited, or planned to visit, most of Latin America's countries on UNICEF's behalf, including Chile, Brazil, Colombia, and Honduras, as well as Kenya, Burkina Faso, Sudan, and South Africa. I had worked in almost every East European country, Poland, Bulgaria, Serbia, and of course many countries in Asia, especially Vietnam.

In December 1996, after I had served as a goodwill ambassador for three years, UNICEF invited all its representatives to United Nations headquarters in New York to celebrate the world body's fiftieth birthday. Among them was Harry Belafonte, in his tenth year as an ambassador, along with Roger Moore, Liv Ullmann, Jeanne Moreau, and Peter Ustinov. Child delegations from many countries were there with us. Each ambassador was asked to talk of his work, and they were followed by a series of performances (I sang with a choir of New York's inner-city children). The event gave me a breath of renewed hope at a difficult time (although they had finally removed the plaster from my arm), for it offered me a concrete vision of what our work had achieved – here a hospital which had launched a vaccination campaign, there a functioning educational system, or else irrigation projects slaking baked soil and feeding networks of villages . . .

The evening it ended, I flew off to Vietnam at the invitation of that country's UNICEF committee, which wanted me on the spot to help celebrate the same anniversary. I was also expected to evaluate the effectiveness of what we had accomplished there in health and education, and canvas the government's views on the country's most pressing needs.

I have the happiest memory of that mission, despite the exhausting New York-Singapore-Hanoi flight and my frantic round of visits and meetings – an object lesson in the irrelevance of fatigue when you feel you're being useful.

We landed mid morning, and I just had time to change before calling on the deputy prime minister of the Socialist Republic of Vietnam, Nguyen Khanh, who invited me to lunch. Both a welcoming and a working lunch. That afternoon I visited several projects. At one location I opened the faucets that brought running water to an elementary school, at another I inaugurated a polio-vaccination campaign. Elsewhere I gave my personal promise to raise funds via public performances to build seven wells in villages dying for lack of water. Whereas I had to labor to deliver fine-sounding speeches in the chamber of the European parliament, I had no trouble at all finding words here as I addressed the villagers who came running to meet us. Their looks and smiles were immediately familiar: they recalled our own expressions, Jenny's, Mama's and mine, at the end of the war as we glimpsed the first signs of recovery. I talked about water, a rare commodity to us Greeks as well, and was utterly overwhelmed by the challenges these people faced.

As a guest of the government, I was lodged in a house reserved for official visitors, just behind the national government buildings. With me was Christa Roth, my UNICEF assistant, who formerly worked with Audrey Hepburn. My pianist Luciano, and Azita, my parliamentary assistant, were put up at the Intercontinental Hotel in resplendent Western-style luxury, whereas I experienced what had represented comfort to us at the end of the Fifties – a narrow metal bed, a table, a closet, and in the steel-and-plastic kitchen an enormous refrigerator with chrome handles of the kind that sent us into ecstasies of awe when we were kids. I opened it: inside were just two bottles of soda water.

I also opened the windows to let in the cool of the evening, for the house was set in a little garden whose delicate fragrance delighted me.

Christa knew Vietnam well.

'I advise you not to open the windows, Nana,' she said.

'Why not? I can't stand air-conditioned air . . .'

'I know, but if you leave them open rats will come in.'

'Rats!'

'There are lots of them here.'

'Don't tell me that, Christa, I won't be able to sleep a wink.'

And indeed, I slept badly.

The fiftieth-birthday celebrations were scheduled for the morrow.

Since I was to sing, I arrived a little ahead of time to reconnoiter the location. I found my pianist chatting with members of the Vietnamese orchestra.

'Nana,' he said to me, 'I believe you have to learn this Vietnamese song.'

'Here, right now? But I don't have time!'

'The vice president of Vietnam will be here, and these guys say it's her favorite song. It's an old Vietnamese lullaby.'

I immediately recalled the surge of emotion that greeted: 'A Canadian Exile' in Montreal, and the cherished place of 'Waltzing Matilda' in Australian hearts, and I decided to learn this cradle-song in the few short minutes left to me. The orchestra and Luciano threw themselves into it, and so long as I kept my eyes riveted on the small page I held in my hand, I more or less managed to master it.

The vice president, Madame Nguyen Thi Binh, arrived. I was seated on her right for our meal. We very quickly made friends. Then it was time for the speeches, each of us taking our turn at the mic. I spoke of what we were trying to do in Vietnam, and she spoke of UNICEF's close collaboration with her country.

'And now,' she said to me as she sat down again, 'I would love you to sing us something.'

'With pleasure, Madame.'

I sang two Greek songs, a few English titles, and then, in French, 'Only Love'.

I returned to the table, and the vice president embraced and congratulated me. And then, perhaps trying to hide her eagerness, she whispered:

'I scarcely have the courage to ask this, but I would love it if you would sing "Plaisir d'amour" for me.'

'Of course.'

'No,' she said, holding me back as I rose to leave the table, 'Stay here beside me.'

Then I sang 'Plaisir d'amour', a cappella, with the audience suddenly frozen in a reverent silence. And soon I was surprised to hear my neighbor's voice blending with mine – the vice president of Vietnam singing 'Plaisir d'amour' for the members of her government, for the UN representatives, for a handful of ambassadors, the whole performance recorded by the silently turning camera of Vietnamese television. Everyone there knew that this was a gesture straight from the heart, unpremeditated, unplanned, and it lent a note of extraordinary grace to a moment stolen from an otherwise meticulously programmed evening.

'Why "Plaisir d'amour"? I asked her when conversation resumed.

She told me that she worked for many exhausting weeks in Paris in the Seventies during the negotiations to end the Vietnam War.

'When I returned to my hotel in the evenings,' she said, 'I would relax by listening to you singing "Plaisir d'amour". It was the only record I had, and I played and replayed that song. It had the mysterious power of giving me hope.'

She stopped. I could tell she was still moved, and I left her with her memories for a moment.

'Now,' she suddenly said, 'I'm going to sing something for you.'

As the first notes rose, I recognized the lullaby Luciano made me learn just before dinner. And this time, it was I who accompanied Mme Nguyen Thi Binh, my little piece of paper before my eyes.

When the song ended, I saw tears well in her eyes.

'Thank you,' she said. 'I had no idea . . . I had no idea you knew that song. It's extraordinarily moving, don't you think?'

She smiled before reverting to her role as my hostess:

'Aren't you going to feel cold with this air-conditioning? Here, please take my shawl – you have to take care of that voice.'

One of my first initiatives on entering the European Parliament was to stress the role of religions in the workings of the world. I said in substance that while Church and State were officially separated in most countries, religion often lay at the heart of conflicts it was the task of States to resolve. I proposed that parliament should bring together the leaders of the various religions to promote a dialogue that might one day lead to better understanding between Catholics and Protestants, Muslims and Christians, Jews and Muslims. My proposal was accepted, and when a parliamentary delegation went to Turkey to meet the Patriarch Bartholomeos of Constantinople, head of the Orthodox Church, I was invited to join them.

As a Greek Orthodox Christian, I knew the patriarch from one of his visits to Rome, where he introduced me to Pope John Paul II. For this reason, the American Orthodox community thought of me when the Patriarch Bartholomeos made an official visit to the United States. They wondered if I would give a concert in his honor in New York. I liked the patriarch, I believe in the benefits of religion, and I at once replied that I would be proud and happy to sing for him and our Church.

The visit took place in October 1997, and I was invited to go with the Patriarch to Washington DC, where he was the guest at the White House of Hillary Clinton. The passing years had not quite conquered my shyness, and when I can avoid appearing in public in such gatherings I do so. But this time, I didn't dare refuse, and I privately prayed that my presence wouldn't attract too much attention.

For once, my wishes were met beyond all my expectations! As I drew closer to Mrs Clinton, who was greeting each guest in person, I was surprised to see only polite interest in her eyes. Well, well, I thought, it's been ages since anyone looked at me as though I were a *normal* person, in other words in the way people had looked at me thirty years before. But the explanation was not long in coming.

'I'm delighted to meet you,' said the first lady of the United States. 'They tell me you're a very famous Greek singer, am I right?'

It was astounding how swiftly these few frank and friendly words lifted a burden from my shoulders. Neither my name nor my face meant anything at all to Mrs Clinton, and at one stroke it seemed there was at least somewhere in the world where I could enjoy the extraordinary freedom of anonymity. The fact that this 'somewhere' was the White House, one of the world's most celebrated places, must certainly be a good-humored nudge from one of my friends in Heaven. Nikos perhaps, who never lost his love of life's ironies. Or perhaps Thierry Le Luron, who would have loved to make up this story.

The Patriarch's visit ended at the Cathedral of Saint John the Divine in New York, where I gave my recital. More than two thousand people piled into the enormous church, where Jessye Norman and Luciano Pavarotti had sung in the past. 'A concert for peace in the world, which was certainly one of the high points of the Patriarch's visit to America,' wrote *The Orthodox Observer*.[35] It had been decided that the proceeds for the evening would go toward the work of our Church throughout the world.

Six weeks later, I made my comeback at the Olympia. It was two years since I last sang in Paris, and I had contracted for just three evenings. The days were long gone when I could take command of a stage for a whole month. Besides, the French media were now portraying me in hyperbolic colors – deploring the deployment of antipersonnel land-mines from the platform of the European parliament, condemning child labor in India, giving a one-night recital at Carnegie Hall in New York, or else reporting my presence in Los Angeles, Sarajevo or Oua-gagoudou, and the next week in Chicago receiving the World of Chil-dren Award from the hands of my friend Harry Belafonte for my work on UNICEF's behalf ... 'Super-Nana' was what many papers were calling me, and the truth is such treatment was beginning to make my head spin. Had my life really become such a whirlwind? Critics who knew me wondered in benevolent vein how I still found time to sing. I was careful to conceal from them how painful my voice's deterioration was to me – but now, on the eve of the Olympia dress rehearsal, I fell ill.

Once again, life was sounding the alarm. After my arm, which had only recently healed, it was my voice itself which let me down. A case of laryngitis, contracted on the plane bringing me back from the United States, condemned me to silence. This had already happened before, particularly in Ireland, but this time I saw it as a form of divine ret-ribution. My voice was protesting at its cavalier treatment, and through my voice, it seemed to me, my soul was abandoning me. A few days earlier, I had told *Le Figaro*'s music critic: 'I'm no longer a singer involved in politics, nor a politician who sings. I'm an artist trying to dedicate my popularity to the service of life.' Maybe. But how could I serve life if I could no longer sing?

I had to cancel two of my Olympia evenings. I spent those forty-eight

---

[35] *The Orthodox Observer*, December 1997.

hours in Geneva looking after myself and trying to set my priorities straight.

Fate chose this interlude to bring me closer to a man who was to become the brother I never had: Jean-Claude Brialy. It was many years since Jean-Claude and I first met, and both of us had been too busy with our own lives to get to know one another. But now Jean-Claude's companion Bruno Finck took over my relations with the media, and it was through him that Jean-Claude and I learned to know each other and eventually to become inseparable.

Indeed, I might almost write that Jean-Claude replaced Nikos Gatsos in my heart. But that would be a lie, for Nikos still lives in me. Not a day goes by without my thoughts turning to him. Yet Jean-Claude is the very same kind of friend, intelligent, kindhearted, the only one to whom I can speak without blushing about my uncertainties because I know for an absolute fact that he'll never judge me – and that he will invariably find the words that allow me to resume living at peace with myself. I was right when I singled him out in the Sixties from among the triumvirate of 'Jeans' (Belmondo, Cassel, and Brialy): Jean-Claude possesses the generosity of truly great artists, of poets like Nikos, people who seek the light behind darkness and find grace amid chaos. For ten years now, he has been the mirror from which I draw the strength and the will to go on singing.

Despite all my problems, that same year, 1997, saw me still in the running with three albums. *Return to Love*, issued in North America and every English-speaking country. *Nana Latina*, in which I sang in Spanish, and recorded for the first time a duet with Julio Iglesias. I'm very fond of Julio, who rose like me from obscurity with only his talent to offer. We had known each other for twenty years, and for twenty years we had promised that we would sing together. And finally, I reappeared on the French scene with *Hommages*, an album in which I sang Jacques Brel, 'Le plat pays' ('The Flat Land') and 'If You Go Away', Prévert and Kosma, 'Les feuilles mortes' ('Autumn Leaves'), Mouloudji, 'Un jour tu verras' ('One Day You'll See'), Serge Lama, 'Une île' ('An Island'), and even Lucio Dalla, 'Caruso'.

It was Pascal Nègre, Louis Hazan's latest successor as the head of Universal, who gave me the idea for that album when he saw me with my arm in a plaster-cast. Pascal, born in 1961, the year of my first German Gold Record, which reminded me that I had now been singing for forty years ... I was sixty-three, it was the right time for me to sing my praises of some of my favorite poets, and those weeks of recording filled me with love and wistful memories of the France of my early years.

This trouble-fraught period ended with another accident. As though – walking as I was on the lip of the precipice – I actually had to fall into it before I could recover my faith in life and in my voice.

My parliamentary term had ended, and I was preparing to return to the wider world. My first tour was to be in Asia – Taipei, Hong Kong, and Tokyo – followed by Australia. After that came Germany – a long-deferred return.

Geneva lay under snow, and I was in the thick of rehearsing. It was a radiant winter morning. That afternoon I was to join André in Paris, and in the morning I went into town to do some shopping and handle a few business matters. The accident happened after I left the taxi that brought me back home. Failing to see the sheet of ice on my driveway, I felt my legs sliding out from under me. Why do we never remember how vulnerable we are? In a fraction of a second, all my travel plans were shattered. When my head cleared, I was on the ground, immobilized by a pain that seemed to radiate up into my hip. Luckily, Odette (who had replaced Fernande) heard my calls for help. I couldn't get up, and poor Odette had to drag me to the porch before calling for an ambulance.

The X-ray showed an ankle fracture. A very nasty fracture requiring surgery. Immediate surgery, so as to avoid complications caused by the rapid swelling of my leg. There was no point in self-recrimination. In my mind I was already airborne and en route to Paris, and instead here I was condemned to several weeks of total immobility. What's more, I knew how dangerous anesthesia can be for the voice ... I could have sworn that all the world's most malignant trolls were conspiring to destroy me!

'André, it's a disaster! I've broken my ankle!'

There was a silence, followed by André's calm voice:

'Where are you? Don't worry about anything. I'll be there on the next flight out.'

27

On Stage with Lénou

W as my voice permanently compromised? What if my ankle didn't recover? Had any singer ever hobbled on to a stage? But as I lay there wallowing in my personal doldrums, I suddenly recalled a story about Marlene Dietrich. It was in the Sixties, while she was on a tour of Germany. One night, as she took her final curtain, Marlene was overcome by vertigo and pitched head first into the orchestra pit. Her manager, Fritz Rau (who was also my manager for Germany), leapt to the rescue.

Marlene had a broken arm and multiple bruises. An ambulance was called, and of course Fritz, who worshipped her, accompanied her to the hospital.

'I am so sorry,' he said. 'But you must rest, and we'll carry on with the tour later.'

'Why later?' she asked. 'Let's see how I am tomorrow before talking about canceling.'

'Tomorrow! But you won't be able to sing tomorrow!'

'That's just what you think, Fritz my sweet.'

Out of respect for Marlene, Fritz didn't cancel the next show. He would wait until the last moment before deciding.

Three hours before the curtain went up, Fritz saw the same ambulance return. Out came a wheelchair and Marlene was deposited in it, her arm slung in a scarf. Then she was wheeled into the theater.

'You see? I'm not dead yet. We shall overcome.'

'Marlene! You're not going to sing in this state!'

'Then why do you think I got out of bed?'

The second she appeared onstage, with Fritz pushing her wheelchair, there was a kind of gasp of surprise from the audience. Then the spectators grasped the situation. Their applause rang out as though it would never end. Marlene's tour, which had apparently got off to a shaky start, turned into an unbelievable success.

What would Marlene have done in my place? The doctor advised against any movement at all for three months, but long before that period was over we had parted company. We had to postpone my Asian and Australian tours, but I was determined not to postpone a recording session scheduled for Oslo. The Norwegian orchestra leader came in person to see me in Geneva, we arranged everything, and I decided to go, escorted by André and Pierre Satgé, the man in charge of Universal's international operations.

At Geneva airport, by now almost a second home where everybody knew me, my arrival in a wheelchair took on a gala air. So many people ran over to say hello, smiling and wishing me a speedy recovery, that I almost grew fond of that awful wheelchair.

But it came as a shock in Oslo when I saw it emerging from the plane. It made me feel that the years had suddenly caught up with me. Was I really so old, so diminished, that I had to go everywhere with a wheelchair for company?

'André, I think I'd rather die right here than live this way,' I said to him once we were in the car sent to pick us up.

'Now come on, it's not a question of "living this way"! You'll get better, and in a couple of months you'll be walking the way you've always done.'

I didn't know how to tell him of this new fear torturing me – that I might never be the same again. Until now, I hadn't given a thought to encroaching old age, but now the prospect weighed on me. Did my body possess the vitality needed for full recovery? Did this fracture mark the beginning of my decline? Of my inability to stand or move about onstage for three hours at a stretch?

Luckily, and certainly thanks to the confidence I saw in Pierre's and André's eyes, my collaboration with the Oslo musicians went off very well. After a few initial signs of weakness, my voice seemed to take wing with all its former power.

So by the time we left, I had privately decided to do without the wheelchair, in large part because André gave me a new stick that could almost have passed for a fashion item.

Except that the company had thought of everything. The first thing I saw on arriving at the airport counter was my wheelchair.

'Thanks so much,' I said, 'but I can manage on my own.'

André, ever tactful, said nothing, and we went to the waiting room on foot. Perhaps he realized that I absolutely had to win this tiny battle? That it was a matter of survival? In any case, I noticed his discreet smile as I collapsed, breathless but proud, into one of the couches there.

But Scandinavians are stubborn people, and when we were asked to board the bus to switch planes in Stockholm, there was that hateful wheelchair again.

And once again, I insisted on walking in as dignified a manner as I could to the waiting flight attendants.

When I reached them, I saw the man with the wheelchair stationed discreetly behind the counter. Was he waiting for me to collapse? Was there another test ahead? And who would be the first to yield?

In the event, I was! Our next task was to walk to the plane, about a hundred yards away, and I accepted his help with relief. But I had won two games out of three!

That Norwegian trip marked the beginning of my resurrection, and as soon as I was back in Geneva I dived into preparations for my German tour.

Germany held a special place in my heart. She was herself the land of resurrection. The land whose barbarity and inhumanity my generation cannot forget, and the land which showed the world that after committing the worst of crimes a people is capable of the best of actions. Germany, which hurt me so cruelly when I was a child, was also the first country after Greece to recognize and love me. The first to heap me with laurels after 'Weisse Rosen aus Athen' appeared, selling one and a half million disks in just eight months. The first time I landed in Berlin I was trembling with fear, yet now Berlin was one of my favorite destinations. As though my friendship with the Germans had evolved despite myself and despite the nightmares that still occasionally haunted my sleep. Perhaps such friendships, so hard to build, are the deepest kind.

In any case, when my daughter Hélène agreed to go with me on that tour I immediately saw it as a happy omen. Hélène was now thirty. After five years at London's Royal Academy of Dramatic Arts, where she studied drama, song, and dance, she had decided to be a singer. In 1995 she married. Since then, like all young performers, she appeared wherever she was invited, doing so under the stage-name Lénou.

She may well have been walking in my footsteps, but she didn't want to owe her success to my fame. She agreed to accompany me on that long German tour only on condition that our relationship remained undisclosed. With other members of the chorus, Lénou accompanied me in some of my songs, but it was understood that she would sing alone in the overture to my performance, just as I had done for Brassens in 1962 when I was practically her present age.

Perhaps it was her presence, perhaps it was the pleasure of rediscovering Germany, but that tour began in great high spirits. Very quickly, my confidence returned. The first few nights I was shaking as I came onstage. I still wore screws in my ankle, and they had designed a special heel to avoid the kind of little side-step which might prove fatal, but I couldn't help fearing the worst. What if I fell? What if my still-fragile ankle broke again? And the specter of that wheelchair returned. Then, so delighted to see that I could once again hold up for three hours onstage without pain or fatigue, I forgot about all that. At every intermission I immersed my swollen foot in an ice bucket, which worked wonders.

And at last, with a sudden burst of emotion, I had the leisure to listen to Lénou. Her voice was so warm, so different from mine . . . I knew she didn't want to resemble me. She wanted to exist in her own right, far from me, for what she herself created, for what she herself offered. At times, I had to stifle feelings of resentment, for it would have been so easy for me to help her. I felt that it was much harder for her than it had been for me. What courage to become a singer when you are a singer's daughter! I was proud that she possessed that strength, proud of the solitary role she demanded. And as I listened to her that first evening I wanted to tell her: 'You're nothing like me, Lénou. If only you knew how different we are! But you can't know: you weren't born when I started out. I hid my hands behind my back, I sang with my eyes closed, I was ashamed of my body and concealed it under shapeless dresses. Whereas you have your very own way of taking over the stage. You give free rein to your body, with a charm and a confidence I didn't possess at your age. It's obvious anyway, isn't it? No one has guessed that you're my daughter.' Inwardly, I was praying: please love her, please applaud her. And the audience did applaud her, and then I so desperately wanted to tell them: 'This is my daughter! Can you imagine? This is my daughter!'

One night as we approached the end of the tour, we were at Innsbruck in Austria. When I entered the hall, I found Lénou rehearsing as photographers and reporters looked on. I noticed that she was chatting with a number of them. When she came over, I asked softly:

'Have you told them you're my daughter?'

'No, but I'm wondering if they haven't guessed.'

'What if we announced it tonight, since the tour is over?'

'You only have to say it once and then everyone will know!'

'Yes, but now you've proved that you don't need me to win over an audience.'

'All right . . . if you like.'

'You won't hold it against me?'

'No, I don't think so.'

That night I made no change in the program, except that at the end Lénou came back onstage and I said:

'I would like to introduce my daughter, Lénou!'

There was a moment's surprise, and the audience went wild. As though the spectators, who might already have asked themselves the question, were relieved to be in on the secret! They called Lénou back and she had to sing again. After that, it was over. She was quite willing to let me tell everyone she was my daughter.

A few months later, she came with me to Asia. And she wasn't the only one. André too decided to come along – not just for the first two or three days, as he had done so far, but for the whole tour. So we asked Jean-Claude and Bruno to come with us as well, and they accepted. André,

Jean-Claude, and Bruno – my closest circle, my family. We had often dreamed of going off together, but it never seemed feasible. Now the horizon suddenly cleared, as though each of us realized that time was going by and we urgently needed to declare our mutual love, to share moments that might never again occur.

We had postponed this tour after I broke my ankle. At that time I feared I would never be able to climb onstage again, and I believe each of us was inwardly grateful for the extension granted to me. It was a gift from Heaven, a gift to be grasped and experienced intensely.

Every concert seemed an exceptional event. I don't think I have ever sung so well or so passionately, my whole being dedicated all over again to music. We spent our days together, exchanging fond memories, profiting from the major and minor pleasures offered by everyday life to those who are ready to accept them.

And now, inevitably, the subject of marriage came up again. I think it was Jean-Claude who revived the idea.

'You two seem so happy together,' he said. 'Why don't you tie the knot?'

André smiled under the broad hat-rim that cast deep shadows over his blue eyes. But he said nothing. He was waiting for me to say it.

'He's right, André,' I said. 'Why don't we get married?'

We had been on the brink of marrying twelve years earlier, but that sequence of deaths had made havoc of our plans. In a few short years we lost my father, André's parents, then Nikos, Melina, Manos, and Fernande. A tragic interlude! Then Miltos Evert had frog-marched me into the European parliament, and after that André and I met only rarely. Then I lost my voice, broke a couple of bones, and so it went . . .

But now the skies had miraculously cleared and the sun was shining down on André and me. Suddenly, the long-deferred prospect of marriage seemed like life's revenge over all those reversals.

'André, why don't we get married?'

He put his mouth close to my ear.

'Can I tell you a secret? I no longer had the courage to ask.'

That year, 2002, the year before our marriage, was one of the sweetest of my life. I recorded another French-language disk, *Fille du soleil* (*The*

Sun's Daughter), but that record was a completely new departure. For the first time, Jean-Claude Brialy wrote two songs for me, 'Où es-tu passé? ('Where Have You Gone My Past?') and 'Fille du soleil' both of them pregnant with nostalgia:

> *Le voyage de ma vie fut joyeux, parfois douloureux,*
> *Je garde en moi cet océan qui fut mon rêve,*
> *Je suis fille du soleil et de la mer . . .*

> My life's journey has brought me joy and pain,
> But within me I hold the ocean of my dreams,
> I'm a daughter of the sun, an offspring of the sea . . .

In addition, Charles Aznavour gave me 'On cueille la rose' ('Plucking the rose'), Jean-Loup Dabadie 'Petite valse pour un enfant' ('Little Waltz for a Child') and 'Le plaisir d'aimer' ('The Joy of Loving'), written in conjunction with Alain Goraguer. Daniel Lavoie contributed 'Cette chance-là' ('That Kind of Luck'), while in tribute to Nikos and Manos I resurrected 'Paper Moon'.

The record came out on the eve of my return to the Olympia and a series of recitals in Belgium. Journalists wondered about my future. I told some of them I was thinking of retiring. 'I'd like to leave before people get tired of me,' I said. But I told others: 'To me, quitting the stage would mean dying.' And I didn't want to die. I'd never been so happy to be alive, so close to André, and in a sense . . . so free, as though with the passage of the years my terror of rejection had gradually faded away, leaving me face to face with music and with everyone who shared that passion with me.

Twenty years earlier, no doubt, I wouldn't have agreed so casually to take part in that Stuttgart jazz festival. I would probably have feared disappointing people, failing to come up to the mark. But now, at sixty-eight, I could give free rein to my desires, to my sudden wish to reacquaint myself with the jazz which had seduced me away from the Conservatory half a century earlier.

It all began with the reissue of the recording I made with Quincy

Jones in 1962. The idea came from my company, Universal. It was a good idea, since the album was an immediate hit in every English-speaking country, above all Australia, the United States, and Canada. It was soon a Gold Record in Great Britain, then in Scandinavia, and finally in Germany.

It was in Germany that my friend Elke heard about it. Elke was introduced to me twenty years before by Fritz Rau, my German manager. At that time I urgently needed a private assistant in Germany, a country I often visited. What's more, she was a girl with whom I could practice my German. Elke was then only twenty-five, and free as a bird. We soon got on so well that she agreed to come with me on my world-wide tours. For fifteen years we were inseparable, then she found true love, we said our tearful farewells, and she settled down in Stuttgart.

There she came up with the idea of creating a jazz festival, and since she is intelligent, aware, very enterprising, and knows everyone everywhere, her festival was an overnight success. It had already been running for several years when I received a call from Elke. I was in Paris in the midst of rehearsing.

'Nana, did you know that your recording with Quincy Jones is selling like crazy here?'

'Really? That's terrific!'

'Why did you never mention that album to me?'

'I don't know ... We always had so much to do, didn't we? How are you? Tell me what you're doing.'

'Give me a second, I'll tell you about all that later. Right now I have a proposal for you: would you be willing to put on an evening of jazz for my festival?'

'An evening of jazz! You must be kidding, Elke. Jazz is very tough ... it's like asking me to switch overnight to classical arias!'

'Nana, the Lord knows I've heard you sing, and I know the feeling you put into everything you sing. I'm sure that after a couple of rehearsals you could get back into it.'

'But what jazz musician in his right mind would agree to accompany me?'

'That's why I'm calling. I have one for you. A wonderful pianist, Ralf Smith. He's heard your record and I think he'd really like to accompany you. We could put together a whole evening with Berlin's Big Band.'

'Really?'

'Listen, do me a favor, come and see me in Stuttgart. I'll fix up a meeting with this pianist and we'll see.'

Knowing that it was an act of madness, I heard myself acquiesce. But at heart I was delighted, as if a magic wand had given me permission to revisit my earliest years.

It was late when I reached Stuttgart, where Elke had already set up a first meeting with Ralf at the bar of my hotel. With its dark blue lighting, it seemed a place designed to recreate the mood of jazz. Couples sat talking behind clouds of cigarette smoke, lone men were drinking at the bar, and a piano was playing in the background.

With Elke looking on, both amused and curious, Ralf Smith and I began to talk. Ralf was only thirty-four, half my age. Gradually, its occupants drifted from the bar. Soon the piano fell silent, and as though it was the natural thing to do, Ralf slid on to its seat. He began to play ... and I to sing. The miraculous power of music! Like all great friendships, it remains unwithered by the years. A few notes and it all came back to me, the emotion unchanged. How long did I sing that night? I was elsewhere, raised high on that headiness which jazz instills, giving you the sense that you're touching life's innermost soul, its most distant extremes of feeling. It was the kind of moment you want to prolong forever, never letting it go, acutely aware of your helplessness and ineptitude when music ceases to inspire you.

From time to time, my eyes met Elke's. She stood motionless, riveted by what we improvised that night in the bar – now deserted, with the small hours approaching – of my big hotel.

And when I finally collapsed she said:

'That settles it, Nana. I expect you to be at my festival!'

What a delight that festival was! I rediscovered the delirium Quincy Jones introduced me to when we spent our days recording and our nights in Harlem listening to Sarah Vaughan, Chet Baker and Dizzy Gillespie. With jazz, you always give everything you have and at the same time listen to everyone else – perhaps that's what is so magnificent about jazz, as though when all is said and done everyone involved exists only to serve the music. My family was there, of course: André, Jean-Claude and Bruno, as well as Pierre Satgé and Yves Billet, Universal's former artistic director who had now attached himself to me. That one evening in Stuttgart generated yet another jazz album, *Nana Swings*, a live recording of the eighteen great classics I sang there.

During that wonderful year of 2002, the four of us – André, Jean-Claude, Bruno and I – took another trip together. And this time Russia was our goal.

I had circumnavigated the planet several times and sung in most major capitals, but one of my great regrets was that I had never been to Russia.

How on earth could that be? In truth, it was partly my fault. During the Eighties, before the Wall came down, I sang several times in East Berlin. It was never very easy. I had to agree to sing for no financial return, because Communist countries had no money for performers, but all the same they had to find the money to pay the musicians, and this meant prolonged bargaining sessions. Yet we never regretted it. In those days, people on the other side of the Wall led joyless lives. They lacked everything, particularly freedom, and they greeted us with such warmth that it made up for all our enforced belt-tightening.

While I was in East Germany, the Soviet authorities let me know that I would be welcome in Russia (then still the USSR) if I happened to wish to perform there. I accepted the invitation at once. André and I began to dream of concerts in Moscow and in Leningrad, on the banks of the Neva in the beautiful depths of the northern winter. Our dreams swiftly took concrete shape. We had reached the point of setting dates when I received an unusual request. The Soviet authorities wanted to know which songs I intended to sing. I replied that I never decided ahead of time what the program of a concert would be, preferring to make my choice according to the audience I performed for. It was the first time I had ever received such a request. Was it just a bureaucratic formality, or were they planning to censor me? I had been warned that Bob Dylan, for example, was outlawed in the Soviet Union, and André suggested that the Kremlin might not appreciate me singing 'Song for Liberty' on Red Square after performing it at the foot of the Berlin Wall. But it was no mere formality. I was asked by return mail to provide a list of my songs for each of my concerts – on the understanding, I was told, that if that list was acceptable, I would have to follow it to the letter. I gave way to anger. I replied that no country in the world had ever dictated the content of my concerts to me, and that therefore I would not be singing in the USSR.

Deeply depressed, we canceled the whole thing. Depressed for our own sake, but perhaps even more so for the great many people who had already sought to acquire tickets. Five hundred of them now did something that broke my heart. On my birthday they placed a flower bouquet outside the railings of the French embassy in Moscow, as a mark of regret and of protest against the authorities.

But now I could make Moscow's acquaintance, as well as that of Leningrad (which had meanwhile adopted its old name, St. Petersburg), on André's arm, just like any tourist. While there we celebrated Jean-Claude's birthday – a wonderful moment. And, just as I did whenever I traveled, I led a mission on UNICEF's behalf to evaluate an educational complex which had just seen the light of day.

Yes, but what about this marriage?

Jean-Claude returned to the attack:

'You've been talking about it forever, so . . .'

And André:

'So we should set a date for the show – is that what you're driving at?'

'Yes, I was about to suggest that very thing.'

And the matter had indeed become pressing, because my son Nicolas was also thinking of getting married. August 2003 was the date he had in mind.

'Let's try to beat them to it,' I said. 'That way, André and I won't be in a state of mortal sin when Nicolas' big day comes up.'

The only trouble was, my eternal round was getting under way again. I would be touring Canada in the spring of 2003, and Jean-Claude himself would be involved in his own show. We compared our schedules, and finally only one date seemed possible – 13 January 2003. For me, born as I was on a thirteenth, it seemed a sign from Heaven.

'Let's get married on January thirteenth, then!'

*

All our closest friends gathered in Geneva for the great day. André made lunch. If he had not been a musician at heart, he would certainly have made a famous chef. He liked to forage for what he needed as soon as the market opened and then settle down quietly to monitor the course of his operations. He cooked with the subtlety he strove to attain in music.

Jean-Claude and Bruno were naturally at the feast, as well as Nicolas and Lénou, André's brother Paul and Paul's wife Lilette, and finally my three true friends, Manuela, Yvonne Littlewood, and Mine Barrat-Vergez. I hadn't asked Mine to make me a dress for the ceremony, and in my heart I knew very well why. It had been the same before Nicolas' birth: I waited until he was born before making his room ready, sending for his crib and doing all the other things needed to welcome him, as though some dark superstition were quietly warning me not to rejoice too soon. So now I waited until the very moment we were due to go to Geneva's city hall, acting as though nothing special was afoot even though I was secretly tense and full of apprehension. Just as long as no catastrophe occurred to prevent our marriage! André too pretended to be completely relaxed, but I guessed he reacted as nervously as I did when the phone rang.

'Forgive me, Madame Mouskouri, but when exactly is this wedding taking place?'

'We were planning to leave in twenty minutes.'

'The problem is that your flowers are still here in the store. Monsieur Chapelle was supposed to drop by and . . .'

'Oh! André! André! You forgot about the flowers!'

No problem. The flowers would be waiting at city hall. We piled into the cars.

By chance, Jean-Claude (who, along with Manuela, was to be our witness) got in with us.

'This time,' he said, 'I hope you've forgotten nothing, André.'

'Stop worrying. I'm not a child.'

'Then at least you have the rings?'

'Oh, hell! I forgot them.'

Poor André: we had to make a hasty U-turn to get the rings.

But the mayor was waiting for us, smiling, very friendly, and that night André and I sealed our union for the rest of our lives.

A few weeks later, André organized a lavish nuptial dinner in his native Burgundy to celebrate my entry into his family. And so, more than twenty-five years after privately declaring our love, our right to that love finally received the stamp of official approval.

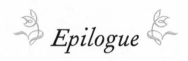

Epilogue

One Last Song to Say Thank You and Goodbye

For a long time, waiting for the year 2000 had been like a child's dream. Would the good Lord grant me the gift of witnessing the third millennium? Yes, He did, but André and I had barely welcomed it when I broke my ankle.

I told myself that things might have been much worse. I might have fractured my skull when I fell, or been run over by a car and pointlessly died on the eve of a tour. That ankle fracture, I concluded, had perhaps been a warning, a sign from Heaven. I was sixty-five. How many more years did I have? Was the Lord trying to tell me that my days were now numbered?

The media unconsciously took over from the Lord. I had never received so many calls from the press as during those weeks in hospital. And oddly enough, they all asked me the same question: 'Do you think you'll be able to go back onstage after this accident?' I could have sworn they were much more conscious of my age, and of all the dangers now looming ahead, than I was.

The fear that I might no longer be able to perform onstage did indeed occur to me. But I rejected it. It was unthinkable, and the doctors assured me every day that I would walk again. So we were all fairly confident. Yet there it was – a warning –and I was obliged to heed it. Next time, I told myself, I wanted to be ready to depart.

To depart, to leave this world. I had long since repressed that idea, but I had never yet found myself so close to the waning of the day, so close to what Nikos appropriately called 'the avalanche of evening'. It was then that I felt the sudden desire to bid you all farewell. Why hadn't

I thought of it earlier? Yet on the other hand, how could I have thought of it as I rushed from one stage to the next, drunk on the affection you were lavishing on me?

'André, if I ever walk again, I'd like to make a last world tour to say goodbye.'

'What does that mean – goodbye?'

Anger flared from his eyes. I believe that at first he took my words as a sign of despair. Yet the more intent I became on the idea, the better André understood it.

If I was indeed succumbing to any hint of despair, it was despair at having to leave you without telling you how much I owe you. Or rather, without ever *thanking* you. But all of a sudden those words strike me as so feeble, so inadequate, so wooden in comparison with everything you have given me in the course of my fifty years on the stage.

Yes, everything you've given me. That's something which has become clear to me in the course of writing this book. The decision to write it came to me in my hospital bed, as though that broken ankle at last gave me permission to look inside myself. What would have become of me if you hadn't loved me? Today, half a century after the event, I can say that everything my future held was revealed to me on 4 July 1957 on the flight deck of the American carrier *Forrestal*. On that day, you remember, Takis Kambas was hoping for a starlet, a budding star. And when he saw my rotund body and my glasses he couldn't help wailing, from the bottom of his heart, 'What a disaster!'

I was twenty-two, and for him I was a *disaster*. Doubtless any other girl would immediately have fled in tears. Why didn't I? It has taken me years to find the answer – that fleeing and weeping would have been a luxury I couldn't afford. If I had gone back home that day, I believe I would never have gotten over it. In a sense, it would have killed me.

We all have a treasure inside us, but mine (unlike that of the dazzling Marilyn Monroe Takis Kambas was hoping for) was hidden deep within me, buried far out of sight. No, you're wrong, I'm not a disaster, I wanted to tell Mr Kambas as I watched him dissolve. Give me a chance and you'll see. But I was shy, I had trouble finding the right words, and instead I simply told him: 'I'm not a bad singer, you know. You shouldn't allow yourself to get into this state.'

It was my good fortune that there was no one more presentable than me to offer the four thousand crewmen of the *Forrestal* and the senior staff of the Sixth Fleet. So he let me sing, rather in the spirit of one who throws himself off a cliff – and something extraordinary, something utterly unexpected happened. After a half-dozen a cappella notes the seamen cheered me!

They were the first to acknowledge me, to give me my place in this world. Then came Greek, Spanish, German and soon French and English and the whole world's audiences, people I was initially too scared to look in the eye. I didn't want to know what you thought of me as I first came onstage in my black lace dress and my butterfly glasses. So I shut my eyes tight, in exactly the way I turned away from the mirror in the privacy of my home. I didn't appeal to myself, so why should I appeal to you? I would wait for the applause before I dared open my eyes, and what I then sensed from your expressions was like a miracle for me every time, like an apparition. You seemed moved, touched, sometimes even dazzled. Never mind my glasses, my figure – now it was as though you no longer noticed them. You loved me for what my voice said about the woman I am, you quite simply loved me, and little by little (I can say it to you today) it was through your eyes that I learned to love myself. You gave me the desire to live. You rescued me!

For that is what I owe you: being alive. And loving life with passion. Do you understand? It isn't a small thing. It's an enormous debt, a debt that made this book (which I've finally finished) worth writing, and justified that final world tour to tell you farewell – and thank you.

The tour began in Germany, the country of my first major success, in October 2004. It was a month of symbolic importance to me, for my seventieth birthday was looming. On 4 October I sang at the Berlin Philharmonic, where I had performed twenty years earlier at the invitation of Herbert von Karajan. On 11 and 12 October I was at the Palace of Music in Athens, and on the night of 12–13 October I celebrated my actual birth date at the King George Hotel. It was in that same hotel that

I won those two first prizes at the Festival of Greek Song on 3 September 1959.

Then I visited every country in Europe, leaving out only France, the United Kingdom (where I gave my farewell concert at the Albert Hall on 29 October 2007) and Greece, three countries that hold a special place in my heart. I wanted to end my farewell tour in Greece in the summer of 2008, with a major concert in the Theater of Herodus Atticus in Athens. As for France, my second homeland, I planned to say goodbye in the ornate setting of the old Opera Garnier where I would sing for the very first time – and probably the last – on 24 November 2007.

After Europe, I flew off to Asia. I went to Singapore, Hong Kong, Taiwan, and South Korea. I had no idea I was known in Korea, yet every night we performed before five or six thousand fans. I gave two concerts in Seoul, one in Taegu, a mere speck on the map, and one at Pusan on the extreme southern tip of the country. When I arrived there on 13 October 2006, seven thousand people sang 'Happy Birthday' for me in English.

Keeping China and Japan for later, I then left for Australia and New Zealand. It was in the latter country, in Christchurch, that extraordinary emotion flooded me. Since this was a farewell tour I observed a kind of ritual. A white rose was attached to the microphone in memory of 'White Roses of Athens', which I have sung on every stage in the world. I opened my concert with Bob Dylan's 'I'll Remember You', and I closed by offering the little rose to my listeners.

> I'll remember you
> At the end of the trail,
> I had so much left to do,
> I had so little time to fail.
> There's some people that
> You don't forget,
> Even though you've only seen'm
> One time or two.
> When the roses fade

And I'm in the shade,
I'll remember you.

That night in Christchurch I responded to as many encores as I could.
It was obvious that the audience was in a mood of extraordinary fervor.
The spectators had been on their feet since the very first encore, and
there was such intense feeling in the air that I was choking back a sob.
But I had to make an end, I had to say goodbye, and the sign that I
would not be back was that little white rose which I plucked from the
mic at the very end, after singing 'My Way', and tossed into the
audience.

When I threw them that flower the auditorium was almost in
darkness. The musicians had left the stage and I was alone, tracked
by just one spotlight. But the audience was still on its feet, still
cheering. To avoid turning my back on them, I retreated from
the stage walking backward, waving and feeling the tears begin to
flow.

I was just backing into the wings when the applause abruptly died.
'That's very strange,' I thought, 'that's never happened before.' And I
stopped, half hidden by the curtain.

Then I heard a kind of murmur rising from the auditorium. My
God, what could that be? I listened, the murmur rose, grew louder,
and only then did I realize that the audience was singing. But with
one voice, as if a message had been passed around. 'They're singing
for me,' I said to myself, 'they're singing for me!' And suddenly,
the feelings that swept over me were so intense that I went back
onstage.

It was something I had never dreamed of in fifty years of singing:
several thousand spectators on their feet, singing for a performer standing alone and weeping on the stage. Because of course I was absolutely
incapable of holding back my tears.

And this is what they sang:

Now is the hour
When we must say goodbye
Soon you'll be sailing, far across the sea.

One Last Song to Say Thank You and Goodbye

When you return
You'll find me waiting here
While you're away, oh please remember me.

And I cried and I cried . . .
Farewell, and thank you.

Acknowledgements

To the friends that fate has set along my path, friends who have let me sing my black notes as well as my white, filling my life with the light, freedom and hope I hungered for.

My encounters with them have become landmarks in my journey through music.

My thanks to Bernard Fixot and his brilliant, enthusiastic, youthful staff.

Dear Bernard, thank you for having faith in me and for bringing me together with Lionel Duroy who helped me write my story.

Life is a journey, not a goal.

Thanks for encouraging me to retrace a wonderful journey which has taught me to accept my defeats and my wounds, leaving me better equipped to savor the end of the trail and to prize those who showed me the way.

Thanks to Jean-Claude Brialy and Bruno Finck, my dear friends, for introducing me to Bernard Fixot.

All my gratitude to Monsieur Hazan and Odile for believing in me, for guiding my first steps in the recording world, for becoming my second family. I hope I have given you all the satisfaction that you deserve.

Thanks also to Jacques Caillard, Georges Meyerstein, and Gérard Davoust.

And to my great friends Quincy Jones, Irving Green, Bobby Scott, Harry Belafonte, Charles Aznavour, Michel Legrand, Eddy Marnay, Serge Lama, Serge Gainsbourg, Gilbert Bécaud, Jacques Brel, Mick Michelle and Line Renaud.

Thanks to The Athenians – George, Spiros, Philipos, Kostas and my faithful Youssie.

I would also like to thank Monique Lemarcis, Roger Kreichers, Philippe Bouvard, Michel Drucker, Françoise Coquet, Maritie and Gilbert Carpentier, Jacques Médjès, Robert Toutan, Patrick Sabatier, Patrick Sébastien, Jean-Pierre Foucault, and Gérard Louvin.

In Britain, I would like to give very special thanks to my dear friend Yvonne Littlewood, producer and director for the BBC, as well as to Peter Knight and Jack Baverstock, Tony Visconti, Robert Paterson, Andrew Miller, John Coast, Jim Aiken, Olaff Wiper, Steve Gottlieb, Fred Marks, Danny Bittensh.

For Germany, my thanks to Ernst Verch, Heinz Allisch, Fred Weirich, Wolfgang Kretschmar, Ossie Drechsler, Jürgen Sauerman, Roland Komerell, Louis Schpielmann, Koch, Franz Selbe and his team, Alfred Biolek, Friedrich Krammer and Gritt Wisse.

More thanks to Alain Levy, Jan Timmer, David Fine, Jörgen Larsen, Doug Morris, but also to Fritz-Rau, Hermjio Klein, Elke Balzer, Sam Gesser, Harold Leventhal, Sol Hurok, Arne Warsaw, Roland Ribet, Horst Stammler, Freddy Burger, and Gilbert Coullier.

To my friends Bob Dylan, Leonard Cohen, Joan Baez, Julio Iglesias, José Luis Moreno, Manolo Diaz, Roberto Livi, Amalia Megapanou and Constantine Karamanlis, Dean and Marianne Metropoulos, Anne-Marie and Constantine, former King of Greece.

To all the singers who have made me dream: the divine Maria Callas, Ella Fitzgerald, Billie Holiday, Judy Garland, Nat King Cole, Annie Lennox.

Thanks to Per Spook and Mine Barral-Vergez, creators and friends.

I mustn't leave out Pierre Delanoé, Claude Lemesle, Jean-Loup Dabadie, Alain Goraguer, Roger Loubet, Graeme Allwright, Michel Jourdan, Luciano Di Napoli, André Asséo, Louis Nucera, Micheline Brunnel, Georges Rovere, and Dominique Segall.

Thank you, Rolland Guillotel, my favorite sound wizard, for all the wonderful songs recorded.

Thanks to Azita, my adored assistant in the European Parliament.

Manos Hadjidakis and Nikos Gatsos, thank you for tracing my path for me, for teaching me to seek truth, freedom and justice through your songs. You were my spiritual parents.

To my parents and my sister, who bequeathed love and simple values to me, sincerity, good behavior, kindness, pride and tenacity.

Fernande, thank you for protecting my children, Lénou and Nicolas. Their love is my strength. I would like them to be proud of their mama.

Andriko, thank you for your unflagging faith in my work and for allowing me to focus all my energies on my artistic career.

And thanks again to our friends the Güggenbühls, always close to us and to our children in the days when I trotted the globe. Thanks to Juliette.

Finally, my thanks to Pascal Nègre, the youngest and most recent Chairman of my recording company (the same company since my very earliest beginnings), and to his whole team and in particular to Jean-Yves Billet and Pierre Satgé.

And Lionel, thanks yet again.

Index